CULTURAL DIVERSITY AND FAMILIES

CULTURAL DIVERSITY AND FAMILIES

Karen G. Arms
University of Connecticut at Stamford

J. Kenneth Davidson, Sr.
University of Wisconsin - Eau Claire

Nelwyn B. Moore
Southwest Texas State University

Brown & Benchmark

Book Team

Editor *Paul L. Tavenner*
Developmental Editor *Sue Pulvermacher-Alt*
Production Coordinator *Jayne Klein*

Brown & Benchmark
A Division of Wm. C. Brown Communications, Inc.

Vice President and General Manager *Thomas E. Doran*
Executive Managing Editor *Ed Bartell*
Executive Editor *Edgar J. Laube*
Director of Marketing *Kathy Law Laube*
National Sales Manager *Eric Ziegler*
Marketing Manager *Pamela S. Cooper*
Advertising Manager *Jodi Rymer*
Managing Editor, Production *Colleen A. Yonda*
Manager of Visuals and Design *Faye M. Schilling*

Production Editorial Manager *Vickie Caughron*
Publishing Services Manager *Karen J. Slaght*
Permissions/Records Manager *Connie Allendorf*

Wm. C. Brown Communications, Inc.

Chairman Emeritus *Wm. C. Brown*
Chairman and Chief Executive Officer *Mark C. Falb*
President and Chief Operating Officer *G. Franklin Lewis*
Corporate Vice President, Operations *Beverly Kolz*
Corporate Vice President, President of WCB Manufacturing *Roger Meyer*

Copyright © 1992 by Wm. C. Brown Communications, Inc. All rights reserved

Library of Congress Catalog Card Number: 91-77235

ISBN 0-697-16410-1

No part of this publication may be reproduced, stored in a retrieval system, or transmitted, in any form or by any means, electronic, mechanical, photocopying, recording, or otherwise, without the prior written permission of the publisher.

Printed in the United States of America by Wm. C. Brown Communications, Inc., 2460 Kerper Boulevard, Dubuque, IA 52001

10 9 8 7 6 5 4 3 2 1

Contents

About the Editors vii

Introduction viii

Chapter 1 Multicultural Perspective of Families 1

Article 1. The American Melting Pot Has Lent Itself to Diversity
  Itabari Njeri 2
Article 2. Gender and Family Issues in Minority Groups
  Barbara W. K. Yee 5
Article 3. Developments in Research on Black Families: A Decade Review
  Robert Joseph Taylor, Linda M. Chatters, M. Belinda Tucker, and Edith Lewis 11
Article 4. Hispanic Families in the 1980s: A Decade of Research
  William A. Vega 33
Article 5. Diversity and Community: Right Objectives & Wrong Arguments
  Frank F. Wong 43
Article 6. The Study of Ethnic Minority Families: Implications for Practitioners and Policymakers
  Peggye Dilworth-Anderson and Harriette Pipes McAdoo 49

Chapter 2 Multicultural Vignettes: Variations on a Theme 53

Article 7. Hmong Customs on Marriage, Divorce, and the Rights of Married Women
  T. Christopher Thao 54
Article 8. Tribal Governments
  Sharon O'Brien 67
Article 9. Cohesion and Adaptability in Mexican-American and Anglo Families
  William A. Vega, Thomas Patterson, James Sallis, Philip Nader, Catherine Atkins, and Ian Abramson 71
Article 10. Sexuality Attitudes of Black Adults
  Constance A. Timberlake and Wayne D. Carpenter 83
Article 11. After Intermarriage: Ethnic Identity among Mixed-Heritage Japanese-Americans and Hispanics
  Cookie White Stephan and Walter G. Stephan 89
Article 12. Minority Status and Childlessness
  Robert L. Boyd 103

Chapter 3 Families Over the Life Cycle 115

Article 13. The Last Link
  Sharline Chiang 116
Article 14. Family Ecologies of Ethnic Minority Children
  Algea O. Harrison, Melvin N. Wilson, Charles J. Pine, Samuel Q. Chan, and Raymond Buriel 119
Article 15. Cultural Differences in the Meaning of Adolescent Pregnancy
  Martha M. Dore and Ana O. Dumois 135
Article 16. The Intergenerational Flow of Income: Family Structure and the Status of Black Americans
  Frances K. Goldscheider and Calvin Goldscheider 145
Article 17. Activities, Family Relationships, and Feelings about Aging in a Multicultural Elderly Sample
  Mary B. Harris, Cynthia Begay, and Polly Page 155

Chapter 4 Prevention and Intervention: Problems Reframed as Challenges 171

Article 18. Layers of Understanding: Counseling Ethnic Minority Families
　　　　　　　Harlan London and Wynetta Devore   172
Article 19. Cross-Ethnic Family Differences: Interactional Assessment of White, Black, and Mexican-American Families
　　　　　　　Robert B. Hampson, W. Robert Beavers, and Yosaf Hulgus   177
Article 20. Income Level, Gender, Ethnicity, and Household Composition as Predictors of Children's School-Based Competence
　　　　　　　Charlotte J. Patterson, Janis B. Kupersmidt, and Nancy A. Vaden   191
Article 21. Cultural Differences—Be Aware!
　　　　　　　Robert D. Morrow   201
Article 22. The Emerging Majority: Resources for Nonwhite Families in the United States
　　　　　　　Robert Staples   205

References   213

About the Editors

Karen G. Arms, is Campus Director of the University of Connecticut at Stamford. Professor Arms holds a Ph.D. in Education from Kent State University where she served as a member of the faculty and as Director of the School of Family and Consumer Studies. Her professional publications are in the areas of leadership, curriculum, gender roles, and work and family. Dr. Arms is a member of the Groves Conference on Marriage and Family and the National Council on Family Relations as well as a member of several scholastic and leadership honor societies including Omicron Delta Kappa, Pi Omega Pi, Pi Lambda Theta, and Kappa Omicron Phi. In addition, she was a consultant for the development of Family Life Education Certification Standards by the National Council on Family Relations. Her honors include being cited in *World Who's Who*, being named a Fellow of the American Council on Education, and receiving a Citizen Salutation by the Ohio House of Representatives.

J. Kenneth Davidson, Sr., Professor of Sociology at the University of Wisconsin-Eau Claire, teaches courses in Marital Relations, Sociology of the Family, Comparative Family Systems, and Human Sexuality. He received his Ph.D. in Sociology/Marriage and Family from the University of Florida and is a Certified Family Life Educator. A member of the American Sociological Association, the National Council on Family Relations, the Society for the Scientific Study of Sex, and the Groves Conference on Marriage and Family, Professor Davidson is also a member and past officer in numerous other professional organizations. He has published widely in professional journals on sexual attitudes and behaviors of college students and adult female sexuality, including the Grafenberg Spot, and has appeared on "CBS News This Morning" to discuss his findings.

Nelwyn B. Moore, who received her Ph.D. from the University of Texas, has taught courses in Marriage and Family, Child Development and Guidance, Cultural Foundations of Families, and Consumer Economics at Southwest Texas State University, where she is Professor of Home Economics. She has authored numerous articles in professional journals on professional issues, family life education, parenting, and interpersonal relationships. Professor Moore is a Certified Family Life Educator, a Clinical Marriage and Family Therapist (AAMFT), and a licensed Professional Counselor. She is a member of the American Association for Marriage and Family Therapy, the American Home Economics Association, the National Council on Family Relations, and the Groves Conference on Marriage and Family, as well as many other professional organizations. Among her leadership roles, she has served as National President of Phi Upsilon Omicron, a Home Economics Honor Society.

Introduction

Within recent years, the "melting pot" metaphor for assimilation has been challenged as archaic. Where salient differences were once silenced to create harmonious social relationships between minorities and the dominant culture, today's cultural differences are celebrated in an effort to maintain distinct cultural identities (Olneck 1990). Even the terminology has changed with the times. "Intercultural education" of the 1950s and 1960s has been replaced with education for "cultural diversity" or for "multicultural perspectives."

As indicated by the beginning article in this collection, "The American Melting Pot Has Lent Itself to Diversity," a multicultural perspective is neither easily defined nor easily attained (Njeri 1991). However, Locke (1986) has identified a series of awareness levels through which an individual moves on such a pilgrimage: awareness of one's own culture; awareness of racism, sexism, and poverty; awareness of individual differences; awareness of other cultures; and awareness of diversity. This book was designed to facilitate, especially, the last two challenges of this journey: awareness of other cultures and awareness of diversity. The intent was to choose articles from research literature that address myriad facets of cultural diversity and families. Such a task is compounded by a scarcity of research on minority families in the family science field. However, we believe that we have succeeded in gathering an impressive collection of current articles with salient information that will promote an understanding of family systems and family dynamics representative of diverse cultures.

The book's purposes are to counter a vast amount of misinformation based on fallacious thinking with facts garnered from the research literature and to educate regarding cultural differences of families by informing people what those cultural differences are. Different is neither better nor worse; neither is different intended to imply a minority measured against a majority standard. Because of our personal/professional backgrounds and philosophies, we have chosen to accentuate the human development and family life-span perspectives. Our belief is that this approach is most useful to students both professionally and personally, and we hope that you will agree.

Table 1: Changes in United States Population by Racial and Ethnic Group, 1970–1990

	Population in Thousands			Percent Change	
	1970	1980	1990	1970–1980	1980–1990
All races	203,212	226,546	248,710	+11.5	+9.8
Black	22,580	26,495	29,986	+17.3	+13.2
White	177,749	188,372	199,686	+6.0	+6.0
Other races[a]	2,883	11,679	19,038	+305.1	+63.0
Hispanic	9,073	14,609	22,354	+61.0	+53.0

[a]Includes Native Americans, Asians, and Pacific Islanders, and persons listing their race as "Other."
Adapted from William P. O'Hare, Kelvin M. Pollard, Taynia L. Mann, and Mary M. Kent, "African Americans in the 1990s," *Population Bulletin,* Vol. 46(1): 6, 1991. Copyright © 1991 Population Reference Bureau. Reprinted with permission.

The four most prominent minority groups in the literature are Blacks, Hispanics, Native Americans, and Asians (table 1). These are also the four minorities predicted to experience burgeoning population growth by the year 2030. Articles were chosen to provide an overview of each of these four groups and, in some cases, to provide cross-comparisons. We acknowledge that there are many other ethnic subgroupings, and some attention has been given to them in articles that were selected for other purposes. However, the four groups, as stated, are conspicuous in their dominance. Further, although considerable research exists on isolated topics considered to be "social problems" by society, some of which focus on select racial/ethnic groups, we have attempted to avoid that which negatively portrays any specific group. Instead, we have focused on family function, not family dysfunction, on differences, not deficiencies. We have listened for the voice of ethnic and racial minorities speaking for themselves. Future editions of this book will take a second step in a positive approach to education regarding cultural diversity and families by exploring issue-oriented, culture-specific, family concerns. Even then, however, we shall remain true to our purpose, and resist the voice of white, middle-class education professionals speaking about "problem groups" (Carby 1980).

In 1955, the famous photographer Edward Steichen defied the challenges in portraying the *Family of Man* in what was billed as the greatest photographic exhibition of all times. Paradoxically, Steichen succeeded because he portrayed "the religious, not religions; basic human consciousness rather than social consciousness." He laid bare "the dreams, aspirations, and the flaming creative forces of love and truth; and the corrosive evils inherent in the lie" (Steichen 1955, 5). Our project is less lofty, but our ultimate goal is no less idealistic. In search of the basic human consciousness, we offer this initial attempt to realistically portray diverse families. Should we succeed, not only can we shatter provincialism and prejudices of the past, but if we listen, really listen, we may hear their voices. With such hope, we continue our own journey of awareness.

Chapter 1   Multicultural Perspective of Families

There is only one man in the world and his name is All Men. There is only one woman in the world and her name is All Women. There is only one child in the world and the child's name is All Children (Carl Sandburg in Steichen 1955, 3).

Belying our common humanity, families, like individuals, come in all shapes, sizes, and appearances. And they reinvent themselves! The particular family into which we are born or adopted emphasizes what is considered important and unimportant. Through the process of enculturation, our family teaches us the rules of society and we are socialized to behave or feel a certain way. We view the world and its inhabitants through the eyes of our families. In fact, anyone or anything different from our family is often considered suspect. It is obviously a lifetime journey from such a context to an awareness of how persons outside our own culture view society. Not only does such understanding benefit others, but it also expands our personal dimensions, enabling us to live more fully.

Chapter 1 of this book spotlights a cosmopolitan society with its cultural differences and similarities. The view is broad; it is as if we are on a hilltop overlooking our nation's people. From this vantage point we see a patchwork that blends and folds into the fabric of our common humanity. The uniquenesses and differences add flavor, spice, and excitement to the richness of our collective lives. However, when the view is obstructed with misunderstanding and superimposed middle-class values, these same uniquenesses and differences can be the basis of prejudice, alienation, and pain.

The melting pot approach to assimilation of foreign-born persons into American society has come under increasing challenge in recent years. Njeri describes the growing trend in our society toward multiculturalism/cultural pluralism, (i.e., viewing the world from the perspective of more than one culture). Despite considerable research, no one is sure of the degree to which the growing emphasis on cultural diversity instead of oneness will affect the fundamental character of American society.

According to Yee, the current research literature on minority families fails to adequately address the influence of culture, social class, historical circumstances, and racism as variables in the adaptability of elderly minority family members in today's society. Sources of unique strengths which aid in adaptability are identified for Asian and Pacific Island, Black, Hispanic, Native Alaskan Eskimo, and Native American families. Since considerable cultural diversity exists among these minority family groups, both social service programs and delivery systems must reflect this heterogeneity.

Taylor and his colleagues reviewed the family science literature on black families from the 1980s. Three broad areas are considered in this decade review: *life course issues* including children, adolescents, married couples, and gender roles of women and men; *substantive issues* such as extended-family households, informal social networks, and psychological well-being; and *demographic trends* including fertility, adolescent motherhood, female-headed households, marriage constraints, and interracial marriage. The authors caution that conducting research only on black family problems often leads to ignoring research opportunities for studying the basic issues of family function, structure, and relationships.

Research in the 1980s on Mexican, Puerto Rican, and Cuban families in the continental United States has led to a re-evaluation of many traditionally-held views about Hispanic families. Vega reviews family structure and socioeconomic conditions, cultural maintenance and family functioning, familism and social support systems, gender roles, and family process. He concludes that conjecture and old references abound in the existing research literature about Hispanic families.

Beginning with a fictional account of several diverse populations who need to climb a mountain to escape rising floodwaters, Wong illustrates how ethnocentric-based arguments can lead to frustration or failure in the attempt to accomplish a common goal. This prologue provides a backdrop to the main thesis of the article: advocates of cultural diversity in colleges and universities who promote separatism and/or exclude the viewpoints of their adversaries erode the true sense of community among academics. And, conversely, academic conservatives who view Western tradition as synonymous with universalism also challenge fundamental tenets of the academic community.

Finally, this chapter concludes with an article by Dilworth-Anderson and McAdoo in which they discuss several conceptual, theoretical, and methodological issues related to the study of ethnic minority families. Problematic issues cited are the use of value-laden perspectives and failure to take into account the unique and distinctive characteristics of Blacks. Among the methodological problems are sample selection, definition of concepts, and the unit of analysis.

1 The American Melting Pot Has Lent Itself to Diversity

Itabari Njeri
Los Angeles Times

Back in what some think were the good old days, Henry Ford ran his company's English Melting Pot School. Graduation was a public spectacle in which the auto maker's foreign-born employees, dressed in Old World costumes and carrying signs noting their birthplace, marched into a large, kettle-shaped prop labeled "Melting Pot." Moments later, they would emerge dressed in neat business suits and waving small American flags.

America, circa 1916.

America, circa 1991.

Jerry Yoshitomi, director of the Japanese-American Community Center, Stanford-educated and married to an Irish-Catholic American, recalls a recent New Year's Day in Los Angeles with their children.

"We woke up in the morning and went to Mass at St. Brigid's (in Los Angeles), which has a black gospel choir. . . . Before or after, we had coffee and doughnuts somewhere. Then we came (to the center) for the Japanese Oshogatsu New Year's program and saw Buddhist archers shoot arrows to ward off evil spirits for the year. Then we ate traditional Japanese rice cakes as part of the New Year's service and listened to a young Japanese-American storyteller. . . . On the way home, we stopped in Chinatown for a lunch at King Taco."

If you think what Yoshitomi describes is another example of the melting pot, think again. Many Americans are.

Blending in was once considered the ideal. But as the racial and ethnic nature of the nation has changed, so has that ideal.

Throughout the nation, multiculturalism—the concept of looking at the world through the eyes of more than one culture—is the new end-of-the-millennium buzzword.

The notion of the melting pot has seen "an astonishing repudiation," said historian Arthur Schlesinger, Jr. in the *Wall Street Journal* last year. "The contemporary ideal is not assimilation but ethnicity. We used to say *e pluribus unum*. Now we glorify *pluribus* and belittle *unum*. The melting pot yields to the Tower of Babel."

We have heard about the demographic future—seen it in Los Angeles where 90 foreign languages are spoken in the public schools—but no one is sure how to define it.

Some say we should call it multiculturalism, or cultural pluralism—the politically correct term on many college campuses. Or is it a salad? A mosaic? A patchwork quilt? Or is it possible to hold onto the beloved melting pot and just admit there are new ingredients in the stew?

The questions over how we define ourselves are triggered by population shifts that will lead us to what demographers say will be the new majority in 21st-Century America: people of color.

A *Time* magazine article last year proclaimed: "By 2056, when someone born today will be 66 years old, the 'average' U.S. resident will trace his or her descent to Africa, Asia, the Hispanic world, the Pacific Islands, Arabia—almost anywhere but white Europe."

What must yield, says literary critic and historian Henry Louis Gates, is the "antebellum aesthetic position, where men were men, and men were white, when scholar-critics were white men, and when women and persons of color were voiceless, faceless servants and laborers, pouring tea and filling brandy snifters in the boardrooms of old boys' clubs."

The melting pot has its defenders.

"I subscribe to the notion of the melting pot," says Karen Klein, a professor of English literature at Brandeis University and the director of a Ford Foundation-funded project to diversify the university's curriculum. It is one of 19 such projects nationwide funded by the foundation.

"There is a certain homogenous culture in the U.S. that is best exemplified by something like motels"—the notion that if you've seen one Howard Johnson's, you've seen them all. "But the melting pot concept has never meant that we give up our sense of pluralistic identity," she says.

From Itabari Njeri, "The American Melting Pot Has Lent Itself to Diversity," *Austin American-Statesman* (February 1991), D1, D4. Copyright © 1991, by *Los Angeles Times*. Reprinted with permission.

But isn't that exactly what the concept represents?

"Yes," she says, "but I am trying to redefine it."

Pot salvagers seek to minimize what Harvard University professor Werner Sollors acknowledged is "sinister dominance." But there is a flip side to the smelting notion, says Sollors, an expert on Afro-American literature and ethnic images in American literature as well as the author of *Beyond Ethnicity*—which provided the Ford Motor Co. Melting Pot School anecdote.

"What I like about the melting pot better than those other terms is the process that is implicit in it"—a culture constantly in change:

"Japanese technology is sold by Hasidic Jews on 47th Street to imaginative artists who . . . living in Harlem or Brooklyn use this technology to create rap," which becomes a national music that is exported.

So far, most of the national debate about multiculturalism has occurred on college campuses.

How will the race or ethnicity of the new majority influence the fundamental character of American society?

Who will hold political, social as well as cultural power in an ethnically transformed America?

Do we need a new social lexicon to define the changed and changing social landscape?

What does the state's growing multiracial population, and its demands for official recognition on the U.S. Census, suggest about the nature of ethnic and racial identity in America?

What will be the nature of relations among people of color, the emerging majority?

What are the hopes and fears of the Anglo population in this changing environment?

These questions are new, but the fundamental issues have been central to American life for more than 200 years. Independence, freedom, conformity, success, community, optimism, cynicism, idealism, materialism, technology, nature and work have been the pivotal issues in the nation's cultural dialogue, the Stanford University's George Spindler and his wife Louise conclude in their book, *The American Cultural Dialogue and Its Transmission*.

"The balancing of assimilation and preservation of identity is constant and full of conflict," they write.

Those arguing against pluralism have to recognize the need to expand America's political, economic and social base with new ideas, new cultural styles.

However, no nation can survive if it is truly pluralistic.

"Large groups of people with really separate identities and languages . . . wouldn't be a nation," Spindler says. "The fact that the Soviet Union is breaking up right now is a case in point."

Says Spindler: "I have real questions as to whether we are going to survive as a society, because it is not just a matter of ethnic combat. It is combat between pro-lifers and pro-choicers, between environmentalists and exploiters and developers and so on. There isn't an area of American life where there isn't a polarized opposition."

That's why the term multiculturalism does not accurately describe the complex dynamics of current American society, sociologist Andersen says.

In trying to get a better understanding of what multiculturalism means and how the term evolved, Linda Wong, executive director of a California research and advocacy group, says she looked at affirmative action, diversity and cultural pluralism by turning to the civil rights movement.

"Clearly, that was the most coherent social movement to bring issues of race, ethnicity and cultural pluralism to the forefront of American life," she says. Laws were enacted "requiring equal opportunity and equal access for disenfranchised peoples in terms of gender, race, ethnicity, age and religion."

"We (tried to) eliminate differences based on gender, race or ethnicity," says Wong, a former practicing attorney. The philosophy then was "colorblindness."

But did colorblindness lead to equal opportunity, equal access? It seldom did, she says. Consequently, affirmative-action policies were developed and goals and timetables were created.

"And what we found," says Wong—even in cases where benchmarks were reached—"was that we could not keep the women, we could not keep the blacks or the Latinos hired under those affirmative-action programs."

Why? Because whether it was in the private or public sector "they had to accommodate themselves to a dominant culture"—Euro-Americans in general and Anglo, middle-class males in particular—"with its own set of values and conduct deemed to be acceptable for success."

Women, blacks, Latinos and Asians couldn't accommodate themselves to this environment and found they were hitting the proverbial glass ceiling.

"Many times, they found that their values, their conduct, their behavior was misinterpreted by those belonging to the dominant culture in those organizational settings. So they left (the organization)," she says.

Increasingly, "as we move into this third generation of understanding, people prefer to use the term diversity," Wong says. It doesn't automatically conjure associations with affirmative action, she pointed out.

Education equals participation and success, says George Spindler. "It's a simple equation. And if whites continue to have the best, the longest . . . the most professional kinds of educational experience," they are going to stay in control.

Potentially the most significant phenomenon in the next decades will be the emergence of the multiracial population. In the United States, interracial marriages tripled from 310,000 in 1970 to 956,000 in 1988. An estimated 1 to 2 million children have been born to interracial couples since about 1970, according to an expert on multiracial children. And early reports show an increase in the number of people who called themselves "multiracial" or "biracial" on the 1990 census, according to the U.S. Census Bureau.

The discussion generated by this new multiethnic generation is going to stimulate a decades-long debate—one that may force Americans to confront the myths that surround race and ethnicity in the United States.

What the coming multicultural, polyethnic, pluralistic—unarguably diverse—America will be no one knows for certain. There are no models anywhere for what is happening here.

2 Gender and Family Issues in Minority Groups

Barbara W. K. Yee, Ph.D.

The current empirical work on minority families raises more questions than it answers. Explaining these gaps in the literature revolves around the complexity of untangling the influence of culture, social class, patterns of individual and group histories, as well as racism (see Markides and Mindel, 1987; Gelfand and Barresi, 1987; Yee, 1989).

The following remarks will highlight some of the critical gender and family issues that impinge upon adaptation of elderly minority in today's society, and will focus on the sources of strength in minority families.

NATIVE AMERICANS & NATIVE ALASKAN ESKIMOS

Diversity among Native American families is reflected in linguistic and cultural features (see Markides and Mindel, 1987; Gelfand and Barresi, 1987; Yee, 1989). The extended family model, as loosely defined, has been identified as one common thread found across a diversity of tribes. The exact form of the extended family takes many shapes, influenced as it is by urban or reservation residence, socioeconomic issues, acculturation factors, and family circumstances (see John, 1988).

Native American families are more interdependent than Anglo-American families. The elderly Native American has been portrayed as a family leader whose advice and social acceptance are sought by younger family members (Red Horse et al., 1978). Elders are an integral resource and play a central role in family life by providing guidance to younger family members for discipline (appropriate interpersonal behavioral training), spiritual guidance, and maintenance of cultural heritage. In ordinary times or during times of crisis, grandmothers will often provide needed childcare and perform household duties (Red Horse, 1980) or take complete childrearing responsibilities for their grandchildren (Shomaker, 1989).

In return for meeting these family responsibilities, Native American elders expect to be respected and cared for when they become too frail to care for themselves. In fact, the traditional Navajo practice of giving grandchildren to grandparents served this purpose (Shomaker, 1989).

It appears that social support for Native Americans increases with availability and proximity to family members. Thus, those on reservations provide more social support because of living arrangements that ensure that there are more family members living nearby. At the same time, since unemployment and poverty are widespread on reservations and among urban Native Americans, the income from the elders' pensions or Social Security makes a significant contribution to the family's survival and thereby ensures interaction with family (Williams, 1980).

Elderly Native Americans are a source of strength for many families and are the recipients of support from their younger family members. Unfortunately, the family portrait is by no means rosy for the Native American population. Poverty, alcoholism, conflicts over acculturation, and despair wreak havoc all too frequently in the Native American family. Poorer health and mental health status of this population, coupled with fewer resources that could help them cope, make for greater stress (Yee, 1989). Despite the strengths of elderly Native Americans and their families, considerable outside resources and support are required to get this population closer to the quality of life many white, middle-class elderly have come to enjoy.

Native Americans have traditionally had rigid gender roles. Women had responsibility for expressive functions in the family such as "kin-keeping." In contrast, men were concerned with breadwinner activities such as employment. The oldest-old Native American still retains many traditional gender roles, but gender roles for the young-old are changing. For instance, among the Navajo, women are increasingly concerned with breadwinner activities while elderly men have lost their traditional roles but have not replaced lost roles. Middle-aged Native American women are taking on more tribal leadership positions than in the past (Hanson, 1980). Older Native Ameri-

From Barbara W. K. Yee, "Gender and Family Issues in Minority Groups," *Generations: Gender & Aging*, Vol. 14(3), 39-42, 1990. Copyright © 1990 by American Society on Aging, 833 Market Street, Suite 512, San Francisco, CA 94103. Reprinted with permission of author and publisher.

can men have experienced the most role changes (John, 1988).

ASIANS & PACIFIC ISLANDERS

The Asian and Pacific Islander population is a very diverse group (Markides and Mindel, 1987; Gelfand and Barresi, 1987; Yee, 1989). In many respects they do not constitute a group at all since they vary on a number of critical characteristics such as language, immigration history, American response to their arrival or presence, and resulting socioeconomic and social adaptation (Yee and Hennessey, 1982).

Immigration history itself promotes diversity in the Asian and Pacific Islander population in part because immigration laws regulated the number and types of people allowed in the United States. As a result, immigration laws have directly influenced Asian family patterns by restricting availability of marital partners or by creating quotas on the flow of Asians and Pacific Islanders. These waves of Asian immigrants and their American children have characteristics and needs that are quite diverse, including the ability to speak English and acculturation to a variety of American ways such as gender roles or family patterns (see Mindel et al., 1988).

Despite this diversity, Asian and Pacific Islander families share some cultural themes, evidenced both in values and behavior, which have implications for the role of the elderly in the family. Individuals and their families express cultural themes in a variety of ways, depending upon level of acculturation and a unique combination of other factors.

Confucian philosophy generates a specific role for each person in the family and society. Every person has a prescribed status, with all relationships of the subordinate-superordinate type: husband-wife, parent-child, or teacher-pupil. This implies that elders have more authority than younger members of the family and that women have a secondary role to men.

Asians who came to the United States as young or early-middle-aged persons have grown old in this country and as a result have become acculturated toward less traditional family relationships (Yee, 1989). Moreover, their American adult children, while they have not completely adopted all American ways, are somewhere between the American norm and their more traditional ethnic counterparts—thereby creating a real gender gap (Osako and Liu, 1986). The generational gap is lessened of course for Asian and Pacific Islander families with longer periods of residence and acculturation in the United States—with traditional elders becoming less traditional, and adolescents or young adults adopting a more bicultural synthesis of both American and Asian values or behaviors (Ho, 1987).

Newly transplanted families, the Southeast Asian refugees being a prime case in point, must deal with the more egalitarian expectations between men and women, older and younger, as well as cope with the greater power of women and younger members of the family (that is, paycheck and duties in the household). This situation often bolsters the more egalitarian role of wives and younger family members but creates family conflicts at the same time (Yee, 1989).

Second, the needs of the family take precedence over the needs of a given individual, and interdependence or obligations and responsibilities are a lifelong characteristic of traditional Asian and Pacific Islander families. Divorce was relatively infrequent among Asian elders because keeping the family together was a more significant goal than spousal happiness. Since interdependence is a lifelong process, increasing dependency with old age is not frowned upon by traditional Asians (Liu, 1986). Thus generational differences in gender and age roles or expectations within the Asian family could be a source of possible conflict.

AFRICAN-AMERICAN FAMILIES

The black population is becoming increasingly diverse. There is a growing middle class that is highly educated and represented in the highest occupational ranks, while blacks are disproportionately represented among the poor and illiterate (see Markides and Mindel, 1987, Gelfand and Barresi, 1987; Yee, 1989). Black family patterns have been influenced by African cultural roots, socialization patterns developed under slavery, effects of racism and discrimination, current socioeconomic and social circumstances, and a whole host of other factors (see McAdoo, 1988).

The African family has traditionally been organized around kinship rooted in blood ties. In contrast, American family kinship revolves around marital ties between spouses. Stability of the African family was not dependent upon the stability of marriages, rather the family kept together by blood ties (Sudarkasa, 1988). Slavery served to modify certain aspects of African family traditions, but emphasis on blood ties, strong bonds of obligation among kinsmen (especially to the mother or grandmother), and strong role of family elders were maintained (McAdoo, 1988).

Black males are stereotyped to be irresponsible, criminalistic, hypersexual, and lacking in masculinity. Staples (1988a) argues that some of these stereotypes become self-fulfilling prophecies because American society prevents black males from reaching the American dream through proper channels. Black women have been viewed as the backbone of the black family. The black dyad had been described as more egalitarian because the female was not economically dependent upon the male throughout the period of slavery and through the present.

Economic and educational factors put additional stress on marital relationships. The rate of divorce among blacks is twice that of whites (Ho, 1987). Among blacks, there is a smaller eligible pool of males considered desirable potential mates. The ratio of single, college-educated males is estimated to be from 2 women for every male to as low as 38 women for every male (Staples, 1988b). These differences can perhaps be traced to the historical practice of black families sending their daughters to college to become school teachers rather than being domestic servants, but not sending sons.

Jackson (1978) reports that grandmothers interact more with the grandchildren from their daughters than with the grandchildren from their sons. Younger grandparents were more likely to share residences with grandchildren than were older ones. Regardless of living arrangement, the majority of grandparents helped with childcare. In contrast to Hill and Shakleford (1978), Jackson (1978) found that grandparents preferred having their grandchildren living near, but not with them. Perhaps a social class or regional sample difference could account for this disparity.

The grandparent factor in black life is thought to be critical. For instance, black women take in relatives at twice the rate of white age peers during the middle-age period (Beck and Beck, 1989). This suggests that black middle-aged women provide both economic and social support for both younger and older relatives (Malson, 1983). Black middle-aged and elderly women over their lifetimes have been a significant source of strength and support for the black family.

HISPANIC FAMILIES

The Hispanic populations share the Spanish language, but their migration histories differ (see Markides and Mindel, 1987; Gelfand and Barresi, 1987; Yee, 1989). For instance, there are generational differences in language and acculturation for Mexican-Americans. The majority of Puerto Rican and Cuban elderly are foreign-born. Despite these differences, one noted gerontologist (Bastista, 1984) suggests that there are more similarities between the Mexican, Puerto Rican, Cuban, and other Hispanic groups than similarities between the Hispanics and the white middle-class population.

Three generalizations can be made about Hispanic families (see Applewhite, 1988). First, the Hispanic population as a whole has a very strong extended-family orientation. The family is viewed as a warm and nurturing place that offers security and a sense of belonging. The Hispanic family includes close friends and children's godparents, who traditionally share social support privileges and family responsibilities. Designation of specific functions and responsibilities among different generations by sex ensured survival of the family.

The second generalization is that there is sex grading. Machismo can take many forms, ranging from the head of the household, breadwinner, major decision maker, requiring total obedience by spouse and children, to his providing for protection and being responsible for dependent family members. Marianismo, the self-sacrificing mother and wife, is the complementary role traditional Hispanic women are often said to play. The extent to which elder Hispanics actually play these roles depends on individual personalities, acculturation, and period of the life cycle in which they find themselves.

The third generalization is that there is a pattern of age and grading that can be found in all Hispanic populations. The young are subordinate to their elders. Elders are viewed as wise, knowledgeable, and deserving of respect. Bacerra (1988) argues that these family roles resulted from the division of labor that occurred as a result of biological functions such as pregnancy and childrearing, for women, and protector for more physically powerful males working the fields or hunting. The elderly assumed their special roles after they could no longer do hard physical labor, taking on functions that helped assure family continuity by being transmitters of accumulated wisdom, nurturers of small children, religious teachers, or family historians. Respect was given to elderly members of the family in return for past labor and for maintenance of family continuity functions during their later years.

In a study of Mexican, Puerto Rican, and Cuban women 55 and older, Bastista (1984) found that there was an acceptance of aging and the realities of aging. Bastista also found consensus about the age and gender norms among Mexican, Puerto Rican, and Cuban women, with cultural sanctions for recognition of one's own aging and appropriate modification of one's attitudes and behavior so as to be consistent with and proper for one's age taking place sometime during the fifth and sixth decades of life. Age-inappropriate behavior and attitudes were more strictly sanctioned for women who deviated than for men. Bastista (1984) also observed that gender influenced the context of conversation, while age determined the content of conversation.

CONCLUSIONS

Two broad-ranging generalizations can be made regarding gender and family issues in minority groups. First, there is much diversity within each minority group. This diversity of family patterns has grown larger over the course of the residency in the United States (Mindel et al., 1988). More egalitarian family patterns are typically seen among the young-old, who typically are American-born or else came to this country during their younger years, during which their job participation directly influenced their family roles. The second generalization is that the subgroups that make up each ethnic category share more similar life experiences with each other than with white, middle-class families (Bastista, 1984; Yee and Hennessey, 1982). Shared cultural roots and experiences with racism provide some bases for these similarities. Likewise, similarities may be produced across minority families as a result of their shared experiences as minority individuals in America.

The diversity in the minority elderly population creates a need to tailor programmatic service-delivery efforts to reflect their heterogeneous nature. Likewise, systematic longitudinal research efforts should be undertaken to explore how different patterns of adaptation occur during later life for these various ethnic groups and to control generational, socioeconomic, and cultural differences among ethnic groups that may cloud the picture.

Minority elders have been identified as being at greater risk for poorer mental and physical health. In spite of these circumstances, many minority elders show enormous sources of strength throughout their lives and into old age and have managed to adapt to what life has fairly or unfairly sent their way.

REFERENCES

Applewhite, S. R., ed., 1988. *Hispanic Elderly in Transition*, New York: Greenwood Press.

Bacerra R. M., 1988. "The Mexican American Family." In C. H. Mindel, R. W. Habenstein, and R. Wright, eds., *Ethnic Families in America: Patterns and Variations*, 3d edition. New York: Elsevier.

Bastista, E., 1984. "Age and Gender Linked Norms Among Older Hispanic Women." In R. Anson, ed., *The Hispanic Older Woman*, Washington, D.C.: National Hispanic Council on Aging, U.S. Government Printing Office.

Beck, R. W. and Beck, S. J., 1989. "The Incidence of Extended Households Among Middle-Aged Black and White Women." *Journal of Family Issues* 10:147–68.

Gelfand, D. E. and Barresi, C. M., eds., 1987. *Ethnic Dimensions of Aging*. New York: Springer.

Hanson, W., 1980. "The Urban Indian Woman and Her Family." *Social Casework* (Oct.) 476–83.

Hill, R. and Shakleford, L., 1978. "The Black Extended Family Revisited." In R. Staples, ed., *The Black Family: Essays and Studies*. Belmont, Calif.: Wadsworth Publishing Co.

Ho, M. K., 1986. *Family Therapy with Ethnic Minorities*. Newbury Park, Calif.: Sage.

Jackson, J., 1978. "Black Grandparents in the South." In R. Staples, ed., *The Black Family: Essays and Studies*. Belmont, Calif.: Wadsworth Publishing Co.

John, R., 1988. In C. H. Mindel, R. W. Habenstein, and R. Wright, eds., *Ethnic Families in America: Patterns and Variations*, 3d edition. New York: Elsevier.

Koh, Y. K. and Bell, W. G., 1987. "Korean Elders in the United States: Intergenerational Relations and Living Arrangements." *Gerontologist* 27:66–71.

Liu, W. T., 1986. "Culture and Social Support." *Research on Aging* 8:57–83.

McAdoo, H. P., ed., 1988. *Black Families*, 2d edition. Newbury Park, Calif.: Sage.

Malson, M., 1983. "The Social-Support Systems of Black Families." *Marriage and Family Review* 5:37–57.

Markides, K. S. and Mindel, C. H., 1987. *Aging and Ethnicity*. Newbury Park, Calif.: Sage.

Mindel, C. H., Habenstein, R. W. and Wright, R., 1988. *Ethnic Families in America: Patterns and Variations*, 3d edition. New York: Elsevier.

Osako, M. M. and Liu, W. T., 1986. "Intergenerational Relations and the Aged Among Japanese Americans." *Research on Aging* 8:128–55.

Red Horse, J. G., 1980. "American Indian Elders: Unifiers of Indian Families." *Social Casework* (Oct.) 490–93.

Shomaker, D. J., 1989. "Transfer of Children and the Importance of Grandmothers Among the Navajo Indians." *Journal of Cross-Cultural Gerontology* 4:1–18.

Sudarkasa, N., 1988. "Interpreting the African Heritage in Afro-American Family Organization." In H. P. McAdoo, ed., *Black Families*, 2d edition. Newbury Park, Calif.: Sage.

Staples, R., 1988a. "The Black American Family," In C. H. Mindel, R. W. Habenstein, and R. Wright, eds., *Ethnic Families in America: Patterns and Variations*. 3d edition. New York: Elsevier.

Staples, R., 1988b. "An Overview of Race and Marital Status." In H. P. McAdoo, ed., *Black Families*, 2d edition. Newbury Park, Calif.: Sage.

Williams, G. C., 1980. "Warriors No More: A Study of the American Indian Elderly." In C. L. Fry, ed., *Aging in Culture and Society.* New York: Praeger.

Yee, B. W. K., 1989. "Loss of One's Homeland and Culture During the Middle Years." In R. A. Kalish, ed., *Coping with the Losses of Middle Age.* Newbury Park, Calif.: Sage.

Yee, B. W. K., 1989. *Variations in Aging: Older Minorities.* Texas Consortium of Geriatric Education Centers Publication.

Yee, B. W. K. and Hennessey, S. T., 1982. "Pacific/Asian American Families and Mental Health." In F. U. Munoz and R. Endo, eds., *Perspectives on Minority Group Mental Health.* Washington D.C.: University Press of America.

Barbara W. K. Yee, Ph.D., is an Assistant Professor in the Department of Graduate Studies, School of Allied Health Sciences, University of Texas Medical Branch, Galveston, Tex.

3 Developments in Research on Black Families: A Decade Review

Robert Joseph Taylor
University of Michigan

M. Belinda Tucker
University of California, Los Angeles[**]

Linda M. Chatters
University of Michigan[*]

Edith Lewis
University of Michigan[***]

The literature on black families from the past decade is reviewed. An overview of topics and issues of importance to black families considers (a) black families in relation to their age, gender, and family roles, (b) substantive issues of relevance to black American families, including social support and psychological well-being, and (c) an examination of recent demographic trends in black family structure. The conclusion provides comments on research on black families and recommendations for future efforts.

The past ten years have witnessed a tremendous increase in the diversity and breadth of research on the family lives of black Americans. Despite this impressive growth, significant limitations persist in the dissemination of these efforts and their integration into the corpus of family life literature. It is frequently the case that books investigating black family issues are not well publicized and, as a consequence, remain relatively obscure. Other works that employ predominantly black samples fail to use the term *black* (or other racial designations) in their title (e.g., Furstenberg, Brooks-Gunn, and Morgan, 1987; Thompson and Ensminger, 1989), thus making it difficult to locate these materials. Similarly, it is not uncommon that research on black families is overlooked in major reviews of family life research.

As with all social science, research and writing on black families transpires within a larger social and political context that influences the nature and direction of inquiry, as well as the interpretation and application of findings. The area of black family studies has been particularly sensitive to the impact of various competing paradigms or orientations that have served both to identify significant areas of inquiry and to frame the nature and scope of debate on issues of black family life (Allen, 1981; Farley and Allen, 1987). Although extant models of black family life emphasize their resilient-adaptive features (Farley and Allen, 1987), remnants of the pathological-disorganization or cultural deviant perspective on black families are evident in several current writings (e.g., Anderson, 1989; Schoen and Kluegel, 1988), as are frameworks that place inordinate emphasis on the social problems facing

---

School of Social Work and Institute for Social Research, University of Michigan, Ann Arbor, MI 48109-1285.

[*]School of Public Health and Institute for Social Research, University of Michigan, Ann Arbor, MI 48109-2029.

[**]Center for Afro-American Studies, University of California, Los Angeles, 160 Haines Hall, 405 Hilgard Avenue, Los Angeles, CA 90024-1545.

[***]School of Social Work, University of Michigan, Ann Arbor, MI 48109-1285.

From Robert Joseph Taylor, Linda M. Chatters, M. Belinda Tucker, and Edith Lewis, "Developments in Research on Black Families," *Journal of Marriage and the Family*, Vol. 52: 993-1014, 1990. Copyright © 1990 by National Council on Family Relations, 3989 Central Avenue Northeast, Suite 550, Minneapolis, MN 55421. Reprinted by permission.

black Americans (e.g., Jaynes and Williams, 1989, chap. 10). These works stand in contrast to emerging research that (*a*) employs resilient-adaptive perspectives on black families, (*b*) examines a broad range of topics and their interrelationships, and (*c*) illuminates the diversity of family life among black Americans (Hill et al., 1990).

The scope of research and writing dictates a selective approach to reviewing literature on black families. In an attempt to address the breadth of concerns in a fairly comprehensive manner, several priorities have been adopted in providing an overview of topics and issues of importance to black families. First, this article almost exclusively relies on material that has been published since the last decade review (Staples and Mirande, 1980), and priority is given to more recent research. Second, topics such as family violence and family policy, which are examined in other articles in this volume, are not discussed here. The organizational structure of the review is as follows: the first section considers black families in relation to their age, gender, and family roles; the second focuses on substantive issues of relevance to black American families, including social support and psychological well-being; and the third section examines recent demographic trends in black family structure. The conclusion provides final comments on research on black families and recommendations for future efforts.

LIFE COURSE ISSUES

This section of the literature review addresses distinct family issues related to life course position. Research reviewed in this section examines black children and racial socialization, the period of adolescence, gender and role behavior among black couples, role strain among black women, the salience of the provider role among black men, and informal support networks of elderly black adults.

Black Children

One of the most researched areas addressing children in black families is that of racial socialization (Spencer, Brookins, and Allen, 1985). Black parents, like all parents, play a pivotal and crucial role in instructing their children on how to participate successfully as citizens in the wider society. The general goals of the socialization process are to provide children with an understanding of roles, statuses, and prescribed behaviors within society and an appreciation of their position within the social structure (Thornton, Chatters, Taylor, and Allen, 1990). For the most part, parental socialization values mirror those of the wider community and society, and in turn, societal agents (e.g., schools, religious institutions) reinforce the socialization themes that are expressed in the family context. However, for black parents, racial prejudice and discrimination are important intervening factors in this process. For black Americans, socialization occurs within a broader social environment that is frequently incompatible with realizing a positive self and group identity.

In the 1980s, there was much speculation about the manner in which parents and the family environment functioned as a buffer between the child and this hostile social climate (Jackson, McCullough, and Gurin, 1988; Peters and Massey, 1983). During this period, several studies examined family socialization techniques (Bowman and Howard, 1985; Peters, 1985; Spencer, 1983) as intermediaries between the child and the immediate context. The process of explicit racial socialization is clearly a distinctive childrearing activity that black parents engage in as an attempt to prepare their children for the realities of being black in America. However, recent studies suggest that close to a third of black parents do not report conveying racial socialization messages to their children (Bowman and Howard, 1985; Thornton et al., 1990). Among those who do, the family sometimes provides specific socialization messages stressing a proactive orientation toward existing social inequalities (Bowman and Howard, 1985; Peters, 1985). For some black parents, issues of race are a central concern in raising their children. Their efforts involve explicit preparation for their unique situation and experiences as black Americans (Peters, 1985) or an attempt to forewarn their children concerning the nature of the broader social environment (Harrison, 1985).

Bowman and Howard (1985) and Thornton et al. (1990) identified various structural factors that were significantly correlated with whether or not parents imparted racial socialization messages to their children. Differential patterns of socialization emerged, particularly with regard to sex of the child and of the parent. Black male adolescents were more likely to be cautioned about racial barriers, whereas young women were more likely to be socialized with reference to issues of racial pride (Bowman and Howard, 1985). Reflecting differences for men and women (Thornton et al., 1990), fathers who were older and who lived in the Northeast (versus the South) were more likely to impart race-related socialization strategies to their children, while being widowed or never married decreased the probability of this practice. Mothers who resided in neighborhoods in which the racial composition reflected roughly equal numbers of blacks and whites were more likely to socialize their children racially than were mothers who lived in all-black areas. Mothers who had never been married were less likely, while highly educated, older women were more likely to familiarize their children with racial realities. Among the many unexplored topics in the area of racial socialization, there remains scant information concerning the conflict between the socialization messages of the family and society and the manner in which these differences are resolved.

Adolescence

Historically, literature on the nature of adolescence has had as its primary focus the variety of challenges and problems that face this group, and the general depiction of adolescence is that it is a developmental period characterized by conflict and transition. What is unique to the study of black adolescents is the extent to which being black and adolescent has come to be viewed as synonymous with a variety of social problems. Even a cursory examination of the statistics on physical and mental health, educational attainment, teenage pregnancy and parenting, crime (as perpetrator and victim), substance abuse, and job and employment patterns attests to the fact that these problems are both numerous and significant.

What is not evident in the literature on this group is an appreciation for the diversity of black youth as individuals who come from different family, neighborhood, and community settings and socioeconomic backgrounds (Jones, 1989). Black youth are monolithically portrayed as urban, low-income, plagued by a multitude of problems, and lacking in the resources and/or motivation to effect change in their lives. Further, by restricting the scope of research on black adolescents to social problems and/or "problem youth," we have learned relatively little about issues of motivation, personality and psychological development, cognitive and moral development, identity and self-esteem, attitude formation, family relationships with parents and siblings, family socialization issues—in short, issues for which there exists an established and burgeoning literature regarding white youth.

Married Couples

A collection of research findings suggest that gender distinctions in the provider and homemaker roles are not as rigid in black families as they are in white families (Beckett and Smith, 1981; Ericksen, Yancey, and Ericksen, 1979). Black women have historically had higher levels of participation in the paid labor force than white women, and black men are more likely than white men to endorse the view that women should be employed (Huber and Spitze, 1981). The involvement of black women in the provider role may reflect a wider acceptance of women's labor force participation among blacks generally and/or reflect an economic necessity in relation to the precarious and uncertain conditions that characterize the employment and earning patterns of black men within particular segments of the labor market. With regard to the homemaker role, black husbands are more likely than their white counterparts to share housework and child care (Ericksen et al., 1979). Greater levels of egalitarianism in the division of household labor among black couples is maintained when the analysis controls for wife's employment status, relative earning power, and sex-role attitudes (Ross, 1987). Despite the fact that black households are more egalitarian, gender differences in contributions to household work indicate that black women still perform the majority of the traditional chores of cooking, cleaning, and laundry, and are more likely than black men to feel overworked (Broman, 1988a).

Black Women

As noted in other sections of this review, the status and position of black women in relation to general issues such as psychological well-being (Brown and Gary, 1985, 1987), informal support networks (H. McAdoo, 1980) and extended-family households (Beck and Beck, 1989) is well represented in the literature. One of the more interesting areas of research among this group addresses the correlates and consequences of role strain. Thompson and Ensminger (1989) argue that among poor, black women, long-term single parenting represents a chronic stressor. Two studies examined the correlates of role strain within the areas of parenting, economic concerns, and household maintenance among black mothers (Lewis, 1988, 1989). With regard to the parental role, black mothers who had a current partner, fewer children in the household, and extended kin who lived some distance away but not out of state were less likely to report strain in this area. Black mothers who indicated that they had someone to help with child care were less likely to report role strain in the area of household maintenance. Women who had a current partner, earned higher incomes, and were older were less likely to report experiencing economic role strain. An examination of the multiple roles of middle-aged and elderly black women found that traditional social roles of parent and spouse did not significantly affect their psychological and physical health (Coleman, Antonucci, Adelmann, and Crohan, 1987).

Black Men

In contrast to the volume of work focused on the position of black women, the role of black men in families is one of the most conspicuously neglected areas of family research. The absence of a reliable knowledge base on the role of black men in families has resulted in a portrayal of black men as peripheral to family and as performing poorly in the family roles of spouse and father (Allen, 1981; J. McAdoo, 1981). A few studies have investigated the saliency of the provider role and perceptions of role performance among black men. Cazenave found that the role of economic provider was a frequently cited familial role among both middle-income black fathers (1979) and blue-collar black men (1984). Among middle-income black fathers, the goal of exceeding the socioeconomic status of their own fathers (who had low incomes and irregular employment) was central to their self-perceptions of being better providers for their families (Cazenave, 1979). Other research (Taylor, Leashore, and Toliver, 1988) found that personal income and age were positively associated with the likelihood that black men perceived themselves as being good providers for their families. Provider role strain, however, was found to affect life happiness adversely among a sample of married black fathers (Bowman, 1985). The centrality and significance of the provider role for this group is supported by the findings that having a higher personal income is associated with the probability of being married among black men (Tucker and Taylor, 1989) and satisfaction with family life among black husbands (Ball and Robbins, 1986a).

Research efforts examining the affective roles and functions of men in black families are exceedingly rare. Limited work among lower-middle to middle-class families suggests that black men are highly involved in the parental and childrearing role (J. McAdoo, 1981) and are successful in that capacity, as evidenced by their producing children who are well adjusted and positively motivated on several indicators (Allen, 1981). In addition, research indicates that both black fathers and mothers are involved in the racial socialization of children (Thornton et al., 1990).

Black Elderly

A vast majority of research on the family life of elderly blacks has addressed their informal social support networks. An analysis of the correlates of support from extended family (Taylor, 1985) found that for those elderly persons with children, gender, income, education, region, and familial interaction were all significant predictors of the frequency of support. Among the childless elderly, however, having an available pool of relatives was of singular importance. Gibson and Jackson (1987) found that the support resources of older black adults were tailored to their individual needs, specifically in relation to age and physical and functional health status. Family members figured prominently in the support networks of the elderly. Adverse changes in the economic viability of black families are viewed as potentially jeopardizing these support resources.

Two sets of analyses found that sociodemographic and family factors influenced the size and composition of informal helper networks of elderly blacks (Chatters, Taylor, and Jackson, 1985, 1986). Marital status was particularly important, with married older blacks having larger helper networks consisting of immediate family. Unmarried elderly persons had smaller networks that comprised a wide variety of individuals. The significance of region for the size and composition of the helper network was particularly intriguing and suggested that Southern residents had larger networks that were more likely to include a diverse group of helpers (see Taylor, 1988a, for a review of this literature).

SUBSTANTIVE ISSUES

This section of the literature review examines research and writings on extended-family household arrangements, intergenerational relations, informal social support networks, social support and psychological well-being, and family therapy.

Extended-Family Households

Existing research has consistently documented that blacks are more likely to reside in extended-family households than are whites (Angel and Tienda, 1982; Beck and Beck, 1989; Farley and Allen, 1987; Hofferth, 1984; Tienda and Angel, 1982). A longitudinal analysis of the incidence of extended-family households among middle-aged women (Beck and Beck, 1989) revealed that 6 out of 10 black women experienced some form of household extension during the period from 1969 to 1984. Racial comparisons revealed that the higher proportion of extended households among black women was primarily due to the presence of grandchildren residing within their households (Beck and Beck, 1989).

Racial differences in household composition are sustained even in the presence of controls for socioeconomic status. Farley and Allen (1987) found that, when they controlled for income, extended living arrangements were twice as common among black compared to white households. In contrast, marital status emerges as an important predictor of household extension. Research suggests that both blacks and whites who are not married have a higher probability of residing in an extended household (Beck and Beck, 1989; Farley and Allen, 1987).

Extended-family arrangements are recognized to have important economic benefits and are viewed as an effective mechanism for pooling limited economic resources. The practice of "doubling up" in extended households has an important bearing on the economic welfare of the family and, in comparison to direct cash transfers, is generally a less expensive method of providing for needy relatives. Angel and Tienda's (1982) research on sources of household income suggests that among blacks, the relative contributions of a wife, adult children, and non-nuclear relatives constitute a greater portion of the total household income than is the case among whites. Because of the generally lower earnings of black heads of households, supplemental income from family members was required to achieve a desired standard of living or, in many cases, simply to meet daily needs.

Other supportive benefits have been examined in relation to extended-family household arrangements, and in particular, the presence of non-nuclear adults within the household has been associated with the reallocation of employment and domestic responsibilities. Research suggests that another adult in the household (who assists with child care and other household duties) may help alleviate the burden associated with caring for an impaired family member or provide the opportunity for a single parent with a young child to pursue educational goals and obtain employment outside the home (Hogan, Hao, and Parish, 1990).

Intergenerational Relations

The majority of recent research on intergenerational relationships within the black population has been concerned with the exchange of assistance across generations. In particular, several studies have examined the role that adult children play in the support networks of elderly black adults and the assistance that black grandmothers provide to children and grandchildren. Elderly black adults who had children had a greater likelihood of receiving support from extended-family members (Taylor, 1985, 1986) and church members (Taylor and Chatters, 1986a). Similarly, elderly black adults who were parents had a larger helper network (Chatters et al., 1985) and utilized more informal helpers in response to a serious personal problem (Chatters, Taylor, and Neighbors, 1989). Adult children, daughters in particular, were selected most frequently by older black adults as the person who would help them if they were sick (Chatters et al., 1986). In contrast, childless elderly persons were more likely to rely upon brothers, sisters, and friends (Chatters et al., 1986). Despite these substitutions, childless elderly adults were still at a distinct disadvantage with regard to the size of their informal helper networks. An investigation of the use of informal helpers during an emergency demonstrated that the parent-child bond is important across the life course. Younger adults tended to rely heavily on their parents, older adults relied on their adult children, and middle-aged black adults tended to depend on both their parents and children (Taylor, Chatters, and Mays, 1988).

Racial comparisons of the grandparent role reveal that, in comparison to whites, black grandparents take a more active part in the parenting of grandchildren (Cherlin and Furstenberg, 1986). The greater involvement of black grandparents may be due to several circumstances. First, the greater probability of blacks residing with grandchildren and in three-generation households (Beck and Beck, 1989) provides increased opportunities for involvement in active grandparenting (Hogan et al., 1990). Second, a higher incidence of marital (i.e., separation, divorce), employment (i.e., layoffs, unemployment) and health (i.e., morbidity and mortality) events among blacks (Cherlin and Furstenberg, 1986) may have important consequences for both household arrangements and family child-care responsibilities. Finally, it may be the case that there are explicit cultural norms in support of extended-family relations in operation among black Americans (Sudarkasa, 1981).

Research indicates that mothers of black teenage parents play a prominent role in the lives of their children and grandchildren. The assistance that adolescent mothers receive from their extended family generally and their own mothers in particular has a positive impact on their educational and economic achievement and parenting skills and their children's development (Brooks-Gunn and Furstenberg, 1986; Stevens, 1984, 1988; M. Wilson, 1989).

Recent and accelerating changes in family structure (e.g., increase in nonmarital childbearing, shortened length of time in marriage) among blacks may have important consequences for intergenerational relationships (Burton and Dilworth-Anderson, in press). Burton and Bengtson (1985) investigated the role perceptions and concerns of women who experienced, in a normative sense, early (median age 32 years) vs. on-time (median age 46 years) entry into the grandmother role. The pattern of early grandmotherhood tended to result from two generations of teenage pregnancy: their own and their daughter's. "Early" grandmothers expressed significant discomfort in their role as a result of the inordinate caretaker burdens and childrearing responsibilities for both their adolescent child and grandchild and the role incongruency arising from being young and a grandmother.

Informal Social Support

Extended family networks. During the past decade, one of the most significant areas of research in the black family literature has concerned the role and functioning of the extended family in informal support networks. Indeed, much of the research focusing on intergenerational relationships and the family lives of elderly black adults has addressed questions that pertain, either directly or indirectly, to informal support networks. Several recent literature reviews that are concerned with extended-family networks in relation to childhood development (M. Wilson, 1986, 1989) and aging black adults (Taylor, 1988a) attest to the significance of this substantive area.

Taylor (1986) found that both family and demographic factors were important predictors of receiving support from extended-family members among black Americans. With regard to family variables, having an available pool of relatives, frequent interaction with family members, and close familial relationships were predictors for receiving support from extended family. A recent study examined the level of familial involvement among two groups of black adults who reported that they did not receive assistance from their extended families (Taylor, 1990). Multivariate analyses contrasting individuals who had never received assistance (support-deficients) with those who reported that they had never needed assistance (self-reliants) indicated that self-reliants reported significantly higher levels of familial involvement. Dressler, Hoeppner, and Pitts's (1985) examination of household structure in a black community found evidence of diverse household forms that varied on the basis of gender of household head and level of integration in extended networks, and that were related to one another through mutual interaction and support exchange. Collectively, these findings underscore the importance and pervasiveness of extended-family members in the support networks of black Americans.

Two studies investigated the use of informal helpers specifically in relation to a serious personal problem that the respondent had experienced (Chatters et al., 1989; Neighbors and Jackson, 1984). Neighbors and Jackson's (1984) investigation of informal and professional help utilization revealed that 8 out of 10 respondents enlisted informal help solely or in conjunction with professional assistance. Chatters et al. (1989) found that being female, having higher income, and maintaining greater levels of contact with family were all predictive of larger informal helper networks. Significant differences by problem type indicated that respondents with interpersonal, economic, and emotional problems utilized smaller networks than persons who indicated that they had a physical health problem.

Friendship and church support networks. Emergent research has investigated the role of friends and church members in the informal support networks of black Americans. Several studies have indicated that friends, neighbors, coworkers, and in-laws are important sources of assistance for black Americans (Brown and Gary, 1987; Chatters et al., 1986, 1989; Dressler, 1985; Ellison, 1990; Jackson and Berg-Cross, 1988; H. McAdoo, 1980; Malson, 1983; Oliver, 1988; Taylor, Chatters, and Mays, 1988; Ulbrich and Warheit, 1989). However, it is generally agreed that kin are more prevalent in informal networks than non-kin (Chatters et al., 1986, 1989). An analysis of the use of kin and non-kin during an emergency revealed that older blacks were more likely than younger blacks to use non-kin (Taylor, Chatters, and Mays, 1988). Among elderly black adults, those who indicated that they were not affectively close to their families, and the childless elderly, had a higher probability of having helper networks comprised of friends (Chatters et al., 1986).

Marital status has shown a significant predictive relationship with the composition of support networks. Unmarried elderly black adults apparently compensated for the absence of a spouse by using other relatives and non-kin in their informal helper networks (Chatters et al., 1985, 1986). In comparison to married respondents, divorced elderly blacks were more likely to use friends and neighbors as helpers, widowed persons were more likely to utilize friends, and the never-married were more likely to select neighbors (Chatters et al., 1986).

The past few years have witnessed an emergence of interest in the area of religion and families, and specifically, the role and functions of religious institutions as a surrogate for the family. The majority of this research has addressed these issues among black Americans. This area of work is particularly relevant for this racial group because blacks consistently display higher levels of religiosity than whites (see Taylor, 1988b), and religious participation has been found to buffer psychological distress among blacks (Brown and Gary, 1987). Church members have been found to be a critical source of support among blacks. Dressler (1985) found that church members were important sources of assistance in coping with stress associated with racism, marital difficulties, and psychological problems. In an investigation of church support networks, church attendance, church membership, and subjective religiosity were positively related to the receipt of support from church members, whereas being Catholic (as opposed to Baptist), divorced (as opposed to married), older, and female were negatively associated (Taylor and Chatters, 1988). Similarly, research among elderly blacks notes the importance of church attendance as a predictor of both the frequency and the amount of support received from church members (Taylor and Chatters, 1986a). Taylor and Chatters (1986b) examined concomitant support to elderly blacks from family, friends, and church members. Observed patterns of support revealed that if elderly blacks received help from church members, it was likely that family and friends were also part of the network. An examination of the types of support provided indicated that church members provided advice and encouragement, help during sickness, and prayer (Taylor and Chatters, 1986b).

Psychological Well-being

A long tradition of work has explored the nature and correlates (i.e., family and marital life influences) of subjective well-being (SWB) among the general population. However, relatively few investigations have explored SWB and its correlates among black adults (Chatters, 1988).

Marital status was not significantly associated with psychological distress (i.e., reports of significant personal problems) among a national sample of black Americans (Neighbors, 1986) or an urban sample of black women (Brown and Gary, 1985). Among black women with school-age children, however, those who lived with a spouse or another adult had lower levels of psychological distress than those who were the only adult in the household (Thompson and Ensminger, 1989).

With regard to the impact of marital status on reports of life satisfaction, happiness, and other indicators of psychological well-being, married blacks generally express higher levels of well-being than their unmarried counterparts (Broman, 1988b; Jackson, Chatters, and Neighbors, 1986; Zollar and Williams, 1987). Broman (1988b) found that separated and divorced statuses were both negatively associated with life satisfaction, and further, being divorced was negatively related to family life satisfaction. Among black adults who were 55 years and older, persons who were widowed and separated had lower levels of happiness as compared to married individuals (Chatters, 1988). Marital status, however, was not significantly related to self-esteem or perceived control among middle-aged and older black women (Coleman et al., 1987). Further, Ball and Robbins (1986b) found that while marital status was not related to reports of life satisfaction among women, for men being married was associated with generally lower levels of satisfaction (see Chatters and Jackson, 1989, for a comprehensive review of subjective well-being research among black adults).

Although the diverse effects of parental status on psychological well-being have been routinely investigated among whites, these issues remain a neglected research area among blacks. Preliminary evidence suggests that while being a parent is associated with lower levels of happiness and satisfaction and higher levels of anxiety among whites (McLanahan and Adams, 1987), it is unrelated to SWB among blacks. Parental status was unrelated to (*a*) both life satisfaction and family life satisfaction (Broman, 1988b) and (*b*) self-esteem and perceived control among middle-aged and older black women (Coleman et al., 1987). In addition, black parents with children residing in the home had lower levels of psychological distress than their childless counterparts (Reskin and Coverman, 1985).

Social Support and Psychological Well-being

A growing collection of research findings suggests a connection between involvement in extended-family support networks and mental health and psychological well-being. Black adults with supportive family and friendship relations were found to have heightened self-esteem and personal efficacy (Hughes and Demo, 1989). Similarly, reported satisfaction with social support from family and friends significantly reduced psychological distress among both employed and unemployed black women (Brown and Gary, 1988). Among blacks who were experiencing an economic crisis (Neighbors and LaVeist, 1989), those who received financial assistance reported lower levels of psychological distress; the primary sources of financial aid were family and friends. The literature is somewhat equivocal concerning the effects of gender on social support and the relationship between structural characteristics of support networks and well-being. With regard to gender differences, Brown and Gary (1987) found that perceived support from family buffered psychological distress, but only among women. In contrast, Dressler (1985) found that this relationship existed solely among men. In several studies, structural aspects of supportive networks, such as frequency of contact between network members (Thomas, Milburn, Brown, and Gary, 1988), number of extended kin (Dressler, 1985), and proximity of relatives (Warheit, Vega, Shimizu, and Meinhardt, 1982) failed to influence psychological distress. Brown and Gary (1987), however, found that the number of proximate relatives reduced distress among black women. Antonucci and Jackson's work (1989) on older black adults suggests that the potential for feelings of dependency and exploitation in support relationships are diminished when social exchange are governed by normative rules and expectations regarding reciprocity. The notion of reciprocity is a useful framework for examining supportive behaviors across the life course as well as how involvement in supportive behaviors may be related to positive individual outcomes (e.g., personal competency, perceptions of control, successful adaptation to aging).

Family Therapy

The decade of the 1980s has focused specific attention on the role of ethnicity and race in family intervention. The family therapy literature among black Americans reflects the renewed interest in the impact of race and culture. An edited volume addressing social work practice among black American famlies (Logan, Freeman, and McRoy, 1990) critiques past perspectives on and orientations toward the family (particularly with regard to issues of diversity in family forms). Further, this work attempts to develop a framework for practice that is grounded in current literature on the black family and addresses the culturally specific needs of black families. Robinson's recent work (1989) suggests that race has a definite and significant impact on the clinical treatment of black families. She presents a framework and a specific treatment strategy for working with black clients, incorporating issues of (*a*) the racial identity congruence of the client, (*b*) the implications of race in the presenting problem, and (*c*) the racial awareness of the clinician. Wilson (1986) suggests that intervention approaches within black extended families should recognize the validity of extended-family forms, clarify the role relationships among family members and generational patterns of influence, and assess members' resources in developing and realizing the goals of family therapy. Barbarin's (1983) work proposes a model of coping among black families and elaborates classes of variables specific to black Americans that may affect the process of adaptation (i.e., appraisal, behavioral strategies, and access to coping resources and support). These and other recent efforts reflect an attempt to (*a*) acknowledge the cultural distinctiveness of black families, (*b*) make explicit the broader social context and its impact on the presentation of problems and the therapeutic relationship, and (*c*) propose specific therapy and intervention approaches that are appropriate for black clients and families. Finally, Boyd-Franklin's (1989) critique of various models of family therapy underscores the importance of identifying the historical, social, and political variables that have an impact on family process and outcome.

DEMOGRAPHIC TRENDS IN FAMILY STRUCTURE

In the past three decades, American families have experienced a number of substantial demographic changes. These demographic trends include declining rates of marriage, later ages at first marriage, higher divorce rates, an increase in female-headed households, a higher proportion of births to unmarried mothers, larger percentages of children living in female-headed families, and a higher percentage of children living in poverty (Jaynes and Williams, 1989; W. Wilson, 1987). Although these changes have been experienced by both blacks and whites, black families have disproportionately suffered their impact. This section of the review examines these demographic trends in black family structure. In particular, this section presents research investigating fertility patterns, well-being of black children, teenage pregnancy, adolescent mothers and fathers, single-parent families, demographic constraints on marriage among blacks, interracial marriage, and the black underclass.

Fertility

One of the major trends in fertility over the past few decades among both blacks and whites is the increase in the percentage of unmarried women who give birth (Farley and Allen, 1987; Garfinkel and McLanahan, 1986; Jaynes and Williams, 1989). In 1960, the proportion of out-of-wedlock births among blacks was 22%. By 1984, almost 6 of 10 black babies were born to unmarried mothers, whereas among whites, 1 birth in 8 occurred to an unmarried woman (Farley and Allen, 1987; Jaynes and Williams, 1989). This increase in the percentage of out-of-wedlock births among blacks was due to two demographic changes (Farley and Allen, 1987; Jaynes and Williams, 1989). First, the age at which black women marry has risen and the overall length of time they are married has shortened. Consequently, among black women the length of time in which a nonmarital pregnancy can occur has increased, while the period of marital childbearing has shortened. Second, there has been a greater decline in the fertility rate of married black women than of unmarried black women. This difference in fertility rates results in an increase in the percentage of total births to unmarried black women. Therefore, it is erroneous to interpret the increase in the percentage of births to unmarried black women as a rise in their birth rate. In reality, the birth rates of unmarried black women actually declined during the seventies and early eighties (Farley and Allen, 1987, Table 4.1).

Children's Well-being

Three aspects of black children's well-being are addressed: living arrangements, foster care, and childhood poverty.

Living arrangements of children. The increasing number of female-headed families has important implications for the living arrangements of black children. In 1985, half (51%) of all black children (persons under age 18) lived with their mothers but not with their fathers (Jaynes and Williams, 1989). The incidence of single-father families among blacks is very low; only 2% of black children lived in these households in 1980 (Sweet and Bumpass, 1987). In addition, it has been projected (Bumpass, 1984) that 86% of all black children are likely to spend some time in single-parent households.

Foster care. In addition to the high proportion of children residing in female-headed household, black children are more likely than whites or Hispanics to reside with neither biological parent. Although the practice of informal adoption among black extended families absorbs many children, a disproportionate number of black children live in institutions, in group homes, and with foster families. Research on foster care is limited by a lack of high-quality national data and the failure of many states and communities to keep relatively current and reliable information. Available research, however, has noted several consistent findings (Jenkins and Diamond, 1985; Morisey, 1990). First, black children have a higher likelihood of being placed in foster care because of neglect (e.g., leaving children without adequate supervision, inadequate housing, nutrition). Second, it has been estimated that black children are three times more likely to be in foster care than white children. Last, black children remain in foster care for longer periods of time and, consequently, are more likely to undergo multiple placements. Because of the developmental risks associated with long-term residence in the foster care system, this is a high-risk group that deserves serious attention from both researchers and policymakers (see NBCDI, 1989, for a more detailed examination of black children in foster care).

Childhood poverty. In the last two decades, the rate of poverty among black children has increased dramatically, and in 1986, close to half of all black children lived in poverty (Zill and Rogers, 1988). The high incidence of poverty among black children is partially due to the lower earnings of black men relative to white men, higher rates of female-headed households among blacks, and a decline in the real value of government cash transfers directed at children. Within the larger group of individuals and families in poverty, there are those for whom poverty status may be of a temporary nature. Consequently, researchers delineate between those individuals who have temporary "spells" of poverty in contrast to persons and families who are persistently poor (Bane and Ellwood, 1986).

Research on the duration of poverty status suggests that while long-term poverty is a rare occurrence for whites, it is much more common among the black population (Ellwood, 1988). Duncan and Rodgers (1988) investigated the length of childhood poverty during a 15-year period, using data from the Panel Study of Income Dynamics. Fewer than one in seven black children lived comfortably above the poverty line during the entire 15-year period. Further, almost a quarter of black children were poor for 10 of those 15 years. Blacks accounted for almost 90% of the children who were poor during at least 10 out of 15 years. Length of poverty was longer for black children who lived in families in which the household head was disabled and for those who resided with a single parent. Living in poverty places a large proportion of black children in jeopardy for serious health problems, low educational achievement, and minimal labor market participation (Jaynes and Williams, 1989).

Zill and Rogers (1988), argue that two recent changes in black American families are beneficial for children's well-being: a reduction in the proportion of families that have large numbers of children and an increase in the educational level of parents. Although a black child is presently more likely to live in a single-parent family than a comparable child was in the '60s and '70s, the child's mother has a higher probability of having completed high school or attended college.

Teenage Pregnancy

Although adolescent pregnancy affects every

racial and income group, it has a disproportionate impact on black teenagers. Estimates for 1984 indicate that 41% of black females and 19% of white females became pregnant by the age of 18 (Furstenberg, Brooks-Gunn, and Chase-Lansdale, 1989). Two demographic patterns in the last 25 years help explain the rate of pregnancy and nonmarital births among black teenagers: relatively high rates of sexual activity among teenagers and a decreasing incidence of marriage among blacks generally and among younger blacks in particular.

With regard to sexual activity, data from the National Longitudinal Study of Youth (NLSY) reveal that young unmarried black females (ages 15 to 19) were more likely to have engaged in sexual intercourse than their white counterparts. In 1982, 53% of black females in this age group had engaged in sexual activity, as compared to 40% of white females (Hayes, 1987). It is important to note that although a higher percentage of young black females engage in sex, they have intercourse less frequently than their white counterparts (Zelnik, 1983). NLSY data also reveal large gender differences in the age of initiation of sexual activity among blacks. Among black males, 42.4% of those who were 15 and 85.6% of those who were 18 years of age indicated that they were sexually active. The corresponding percentages among black females were 9.7% and 59.4%, respectively (Hayes, 1987).

Because of the inconsistent use of contraceptives, a substantial number of sexually active black and white teenagers eventually become pregnant (Hayes, 1987). Black teenagers are less likely to use a contraceptive method than are white teens (Hayes, 1987; Moore, Simms, and Betsey, 1986; Zelnik and Shah, 1983), but these differences are substantially reduced when age of sexual initiation is controlled (Zelnik, Kantner, and Ford, 1981). Among teenagers who use some form of contraception, however, black females are more likely to use oral contraceptives and white females are more likely to use withdrawal (Moore et al., 1986).

A nonmarital pregnancy can result in one of several outcomes, including abortion, adoption, and childbearing outside of marriage. Black teenagers are less likely to terminate a pregnancy by abortion than are white teenagers (Farley and Allen, 1987; Hayes, 1987). Since black teenagers had a higher incidence of unintended pregnancy, however, their abortion rate in 1981 was twice as high as the rate for white girls aged 15 to 19: 68.9 per 1,000 women compared with 35.8 per 1,000 (Hayes, 1987). With regard to adoption, available data indicate that despite the high levels of unintended pregnancy, 9 out of 10 black and white teenagers kept and raised their children (Bachrach, 1986; Hayes, 1987).

Black adolescents are more likely to give birth outside of marriage than white adolescents. In 1984, the rate of nonmarital childbearing among persons 15–19 years old was 87 per 1,000 unmarried black women compared to 19 per 1,000 white women. Between 1970 and 1984, however, the rate of nonmarital childbearing decreased by 10% among blacks, whereas among whites it increased by 74% (Farley and Allen, 1987; Hayes, 1987). Consistent with the fertility data presented earlier, the declining rates of marriage among blacks have contributed to the high rate of nonmarital childbearing among black adolescents. In 1960, almost a third of black women 18–19 years old were married, whereas in 1984 less than 3% were married. Consequently, by the mid-1980s, almost all children born to adolescent mothers were out of wedlock (Furstenberg et al., 1987). For a more thorough examination of adolescent pregnancy and sexual behavior, refer to the work of Furstenberg et al. (1987), Furstenberg et al. (1989), Hayes (1987), Hofferth and Hayes (1987), and Moore et al. (1986).

Adolescent Mothers

In the past decade researchers have investigated several consequences of adolescent pregnancy for the mother. In particular, research has examined issues such as family structure, family size, educational achievement, and labor force participation. Early marriage is strongly associated with early childbearing and there is a high incidence of divorce among persons who marry at young ages (Hayes, 1987; Sweet and Bumpass, 1987). Furstenberg and colleagues' (1987) 17-year follow-up of a sample of adolescent mothers (mostly black) found that among those who had married early, approximately two of three of their marriages had been dissolved. With regard to family size, the adolescent mothers in this study tended not to have a large number of children.

About a fifth never had a second child (20.8%), two-fifths had one additional birth (41.3%), and one-fourth had two more children (26.0%).

The interruption of school with a birth generally decreases the educational attainment of young girls. This decrease in educational attainment, however, is smaller for black adolescents than for their white counterparts. Furstenberg et al. (1987) found that many of the adolescent mothers in their sample resumed their education after the birth of the first child. Most of the educational attainment following the birth of a child took place 6 or more years later. The educational attainment of this group, however, was still significantly lower than that of comparably aged black women who postponed childbearing.

Early childbearing has important implications for eventual labor force participation and economic attainment. In comparison to mothers who have children later in life, early childbearers have a lower likelihood of finding stable employment and a greater tendency to go on welfare (Furstenberg et al., 1989). These differences are more notable at younger ages, but many early childbearers recover from these interruptions later in life (Furstenberg et al., 1989). For instance, the rate of welfare use among the respondents in the Furstenberg et al. (1987) sample decreased substantially as the women reached middle age. Racial variations in the labor force participation of black and white early childbearers indicate that black mothers accumulate more work experience than their white counterparts, and the difference in work experience between early and late childbearers is smaller among blacks (Hayes, 1987; Hofferth and Hayes, 1987).

Adolescent Fathers

Research on adolescent pregnancy and parenting demonstrates the relative scarcity of work examining the role of adolescent fathers (Hendricks and Montgomery, 1983). This absence of information hampers a comprehensive understanding of teenage pregnancy and parenting (Lerman, 1986; Marsiglio, 1989; Parke and Neville, 1987). Methodological critiques of this literature (Parke and Neville, 1987: 146) include issues of sampling (e.g., determining appropriate age ranges, use of volunteer samples, samples from clinic or service agency–based populations), method (e.g., reliance on self-report and proxy questionnaires vs. other methods), and design (e.g., inclusion of appropriate comparison groups, use of longitudinal data). Reservations in the use of volunteer samples reflect the concern that such samples are biased toward adolescent males who are more accepting of parental responsibilities. This concern is particularly crucial if attitudes about early childbearing vary for distinct subgroups of the population (i.e., higher acceptance of early childbearing and out-of-wedlock births among black Americans) (e.g., Marsiglio, 1987).

The emergent literature on black adolescent fathers suggests a greater appreciation for the diversity of this population group in relation to the developmental aspects of adolescence (Parke and Neville, 1987) and their individual enactment of the fatherhood role. Black adolescent fathers have distinctly different patterns of fatherhood experiences (i.e., age at paternity, timing of fatherhood in relation to work and educational experiences, number of children, length of fatherhood experience, relationship with child's mother, marital experience). A study of attitudes among unwed black adolescent fathers (Hendricks and Montgomery, 1983) suggests that parenthood was desirable, and in retrospect, fathers indicated being prepared for that role. In an earlier investigation (Hendricks, Howard, and Caesar, 1981), black adolescent fathers were less sanguine and reported problems in interpersonal relationships and in social and economic areas (i.e., educational and occupational).

Marsiglio's (1987) examination of initial living arrangements, marital experiences, and educational outcomes for adolescent fathers found that young black men were more likely than Hispanics or whites to have had a nonmarital first birth and were least likely to live with that child. However, in comparison to other adolescent fathers, blacks were more likely to complete high school. Adolescent fathers have a higher probability of living apart from their partner and/or child than do nonadolescent fathers (Danziger and Nichols-Casebolt, 1988), and this is particularly the case among black adolescent fathers (Lerman, 1986; Marsiglio, 1987). However, a recent report among a sample of teenage-mother families (Danziger and Radin, 1990) suggests that father's absence from the home does not necessarily reflect noninvolvement in parenting; minority fathers were more likely to be involved than were white fathers. Separate analyses for minority teen-mother families (predominately black) indicated that fathers were more likely to be involved if they were younger (roughly 6 out of 10 minority fathers were under 21 years of age), if they had been employed in the last year, and if their child was younger.

Female-Headed Households

As compared to whites, black families are considerably less likely to be headed by a married couple and more likely to be headed by single females. In 1980, one in four black households was headed by a single female (27.2%). In the past 20 years there has been a significant increase in the proportion of female-headed households among both blacks and whites. Among blacks the increase in female-headed households is due primarily to a decreasing propensity to marry among young black men and women. This declining likelihood of marriage is strongly linked to the high levels of unemployment and low earnings of young black men (Wilson and Neckerman, 1986).

Black female-headed families are one of the most impoverished groups in America. Among black Americans, 53% of female-headed families were in poverty, as compared to 15% of male-headed families (Farley and Allen, 1987). Similarly, in 1985, black female-headed families were twice as likely to have incomes at the poverty level than were white female-headed families (Jaynes and Williams, 1989). Jaynes and Williams (1989: 525) and McLanahan and Booth (1989) have identified several mechanisms that explain the disproportionate degree of poverty of black female-headed families. First, many black families rely on the income of two employed adults to remain out of poverty. Simply because of its reliance on a sole wage earner, a single-parent family has a higher likelihood of being poor. Second, because black women have lower incomes than black men (Farley and Allen, 1987), among single-parent families, those with a female head are more likely to be poor than those with male head. Third, young black women who form single-parent households generally come from poor households and often lack the skills to generate high earnings. Fourth, because of the scarcity of inexpensive child care and lack of health insurance associated with lower-status occupations, many black single mothers of young children cannot earn enough from employment to justify working outside the home. Fifth, Aid to Families with Dependent Children (AFDC, or welfare) and food stamps accounted for 28% of the income for black female-headed households (Garfinkle and McLanahan, 1986, Table 2); AFDC benefits are recognized to be woefully inadequate. Sixth, child support and alimony payments to single mothers are meager, accounting for only 3.5% of the income of black single mothers (McLanahan and Booth, 1989). Finally, the birth of a child may disrupt the educational or job experiences of the mother and reduce future earning potential.

Several studies have suggested that there are important intergenerational consequences with regard to the subsequent socioeconomic and marital status of children who live with mother-only families as compared with two-parent families. These studies indicate that among black children, those who live with their mothers only generally do less well on several social indicators than those who live with two parents. There is some evidence to suggest that black children who reside with one parent are less likely to be in school at the age of 17 and less likely to graduate from high school (McLanahan, 1985). Daughters of black single mothers were found to be at a higher risk of establishing a female-headed household at the age of 16 than were daughters of two-parent black households (McLanahan, 1988). This risk was increased if the marital disruption of the parents occurred when the child was older (15-16) as opposed to younger (12 or less). Controlling for income reduced but did not eliminate the risk of a daughter establishing a single-parent household (McLanahan, 1988). In another analysis (McLanahan and Bumpass, 1988), black daughters who spent part of their childhood in a single-parent family because of marital disruption (i.e., divorce, separation) or because the parent never married were 36% more likely to have a teenage birth, 52% more likely to have a premarital birth, and 32% more likely to have a marital disruption. The effects of residing in a single-parent family on these various outcomes were much more pronounced among whites than blacks. In addition, Hogan and Kitagawa (1985) found that black adolescent girls from single-parent families were more likely to be sexually active and to have premarital births than adolescents from two-parent households. It is important to note that this collection of findings is not definitive (Jaynes and Williams, 1989), and it remains to be seen whether some other variables are more important than family structure in determining the future socioeconomic and marital status of black children.

Garfinkle and McLanahan (1986) argue that the negative intergenerational consequences of residing in single-parent families may be attributed to economic deprivation, maternal employment, and the absence of a residential father. Since black female-headed families have such a high incidence of poverty, it is not surprising that their offspring fare worse in adulthood than children from two-parent families. It is also important to note that extended-family involvement may help mitigate some of the differences between being raised in single versus two-parent households.

Constraints on Marriage

Rapidly changing marriage patterns among African Americans has spawned a renewed focus on the determinants of marriage behavior. The long-established pre-1950 pattern of blacks marrying earlier than whites has been replaced by an increasingly divergent pattern of blacks marrying later than whites (Cherlin, 1981). Between 1975 and 1985, the proportion of black women who had ever married declined sharply from nearly 80% to 65% (compared to an 89% to 82% drop among whites) (Norton and Moorman, 1987). Also, the percentage of black women who were divorced increased from 22% to 31% (compared to 18% to 27% among whites) (Norton and Moorman, 1987).

The decline in expectation of marriage for black women has been particularly striking. When Rodgers and Thornton (1985) used annual synthetic cohorts to estimate proportions of groups expected to marry by age 44, they found that between 1970 and 1979, the proportions had declined to approximately 90% for white men and women, as well as black men. However, the proportion of black women expected to marry declined from the already low figure of 86% to 76%, meaning that by 1980, one-quarter of the existing population of black women were not expected to have married by their 44th birthday. Projecting proportions of later cohorts likely to every marry (by projecting cumulative marriage probabilities), Rodgers and Thornton (1985) estimated that close to 90% of white males and females and 86% of black males born in 1954 will have married by their 45th birthday; but only 70% of black females born in 1954 are expected to marry. In contrast, 94% of black women born in the 1930s eventually married.

Among the consequences of these trends are an increase in the number of female-headed households, an increased burden of childrearing for women, and an increase in the percentage of women and children living in households with incomes below the poverty level. Concerns about the societal consequences of having large numbers of young males unattached to the traditional socializing structures have also been raised (Rossi, 1984).

Theories of causation. Significant changes in the distribution between the sexes have been posited as a possible factor in these shifts in marital patterns in the general population. Known as "marriage squeeze" among demographers, it is hypothesized that a decrease in the availability of marriage partners for female members of the "baby boom" has led to delays in marriage and lower marriage rates, particularly for women (Glick, 1981; Rodgers and Thornton, 1985; Schoen, 1983). This shortage of partners is the result of the ever-increasing cohort sizes that characterized the post–World War II baby-boom years, coupled with the tendency of women to marry men who are two to three years older. Baby-boom women were therefore seeking husbands from older and numerically smaller cohorts. Although the marriage squeeze phenomenon affected blacks as well as whites, it also served to exacerbate the impact of the long-standing black male shortage that is due primarily to differential mortality rates. The black sex ratio has been steadily decreasing since the 1920s, and some have suggested that this prolonged shortage of men has led to a broadening of mate selection standards among black women. Spanier and Glick (1980) found that black women compared to white women were more likely to marry men who were previously married, less educated, and older.

Guttentag and Secord (1983) have argued that imbalanced sex ratios (i.e., the number of men per 100 women) have had major societal consequences. Male shortages, in particular, have been accompanied by higher rates of singlehood, divorce, out-of-wedlock births, adultery, and transient relationships; less commitment among men to relationships; lower societal value on marriage and the family; and a rise in feminism. Guttentag and Secord (1983) have asserted that the extended male shortage in the black American population is a major contributor to marital decline among blacks and an increasing out-of-wedlock birth rate. There is some empirical support for these theories. Tucker's (1987) analysis of sex ratios for five ethnic groups (including blacks) found fairly substantial associations between sex ratio and percentage divorced and separated, percentage of single women aged 25-34 (peak marriage ages), and percentage of households with female heads and no husbands. Using international data, South (1986) found female shortage to be associated with lower female marriage and fertility rates, higher age at marriage among women, and higher female literacy, divorce, and crime involvement (South and Messner, 1987). U.S. sex ratio studies have typically relied on census data, which are biased by an undercount of black men. Even when corrected for coverage errors, the black ratio remains about five points below that of whites, and therefore, in the view of Guttentag and Secord (1983), still likely to have significant effects on social structure. Yet, Tucker and Mitchell-Kernan (in press) argue that sex ratio is only one component of the constraints on mate availability that have resulted in declining marriage among blacks. That is, numerical availability is further qualified by an individual's *potential* for relationship formation, which is shaped by willingness or ability to enter into relationships with the opposite sex (e.g., heterosexual, noninstitutionalization), attractiveness (how one measures up on the basis of specific sociocultural preferences—e.g., economic status, physical features); and eligibility (whether one fits the socioculturally prescribed definitions of eligibility—e.g., same race). Although there is little research that explores how these three factors might differentially affect black marriage behavior, sociologists and economists have been particularly concerned about the relationship between the economic condition of black males and black family structure. William Wilson (Wilson, 1987; Wilson and Neckerman, 1986) and Darity and Myers (1986-87) have argued that the increasing economic marginality of black males makes them less attractive as potential husbands, since they are constrained in the ability to perform the provider role in marriage. Views of the economic incentive associated with marriage may undergo change when the societal inclination for women to marry men of higher (or at least equal) socioeconomic status is coupled with the substantial joblessness, underemployment, and decreasing educational attainment that are disproportionately characteristic of major segments of the black male population. These factors reduce the likelihood that marriage will occur, as well as undermine the stability of existing partnerships. There is some support for these economic arguments. Testa, Astone, Krogh, and Neckerman (1989) found that employed fathers in inner-city Chicago were twice as likely as nonemployed fathers to marry the mother of their first child. Also, Tucker and Taylor (1989) found that, among men, personal income was positively associated with the probability of marriage but unrelated to the probability of being involved in a nonmarital romantic relationship.

Interracial Marriage

Overall, interracial marriage involving black Americans remains relatively rare. In 1988, only 4.6% of black males' marriages and 2.1% of black females' marriages included partners of other races. Yet these figures can overshadow significant geographic differences in outmarriage behavior (Tucker and Mitchell-Kernan, 1990). According to the 1980 Census, intermarriage rates among blacks ranged from a low of .6% among black females in the South to 12.3% among black males in the West (U.S. Bureau of the Census, 1985). Furthermore, as Tucker and Mitchell-Kernan (1990) point out, there is evidence of a rather dramatic rise in outmarriage in Western states. One out of every six black men in the West who married for the first time between 1970 and 1980 (i.e., more recent marriages) married women of another race.

Overall, as well as by region, intermarriage for black females remains about one-quarter the male level. Lieberson and Waters (1988) used 1980 Census data to calculate odds ratios representing the tendency to marry in one's ethnic group versus marrying out of one's ethnic group (i.e., percentage in/percentage out) and have determined that black women have the highest overall odds of any ethnic group in the United States of marrying another black when they marry for the first time:

32,998 (as compared to 3,468 for Puerto Rican women; 743 for Mexican women; and 16 for American Indian women). However, the odds of black women under 25 years of age marrying a black man drops to 8,602 (in contrast to a ratio of 115,660 for black women aged 55 to 64 years). Therefore, although blacks still remain relatively unlikely to marry persons of other races, the likelihood of interracial marriage among younger blacks had increased substantially by 1980. Intercensal estimates from the Current Population Surveys indicate that the level of interracial marriage among blacks increased 1.1 percentage points for males as well as females between 1981 and 1988. It seems likely that interracial marriage rates will continue to rise for black Americans.

Tucker and Mitchell-Kernan (1990) examined the structural factors that are associated with black interracial marriage, using 1980 census data for Los Angeles County (where black interracial marriage rates are relatively high). They found that the predictors of interracial marriage were virtually identical for black men and black women: interracially married blacks compared to those who married within the race tended to be younger, were more likely to have been married previously, and had greater spousal age differences (both younger and older). Additionally, interracial marriage seemed to be associated with living away from your place of birth, coupled with having been raised in a more racially tolerant region of the country. These findings suggested that social control (from the community of origin) still strongly supports black marriage within the race. Schoen and Wooldredge (1989), examining marriage choices in North Carolina and Virginia, found a greater likelihood of intermarriage among more highly educated black men.

The rate of interracial marriage has implications for mate availability, particularly in the West, where outmarriage among black men is relatively high and quite different from the black female outmarriage rate. Moreover, marriage squeeze in the general population may account for an increased tendency for white women to consider black men as mates (Guttentag and Secord, 1983). Further declines in the marital expectations for black women will occur should black men define their pool of eligible mates as including nonblacks, while black women limit their mate choices to those of the same race.

Black Underclass

During the past decade, a significant body of research has addressed the development of a black underclass. Much of this work, as it relates to family issues, investigates topics that have been previously discussed in this review (e.g., the increase in female-headed households, poverty and family structure). However, a remaining issue germane to our review of research on black families is the increasing economic marginality of black men. Recent research efforts have examined the growing economic marginality of black men in relation to the underclass. Black men have a higher likelihood than white males of being unemployed and working part-time (Farley and Allen, 1987; Jaynes and Williams, 1989). Black men are disproportionately employed in low-wage jobs, unprotected by seniority, and work in industries that are particularly sensitive to business downturns (Jaynes and Williams, 1989).

As noted previously in this review, the declining economic status of black men has important ramifications for family structure. The precarious economic situation of black men is a major predictor of the decreasing rates of black marriage (W. Wilson, 1987; Wilson and Neckerman, 1986). Additionally, the decreasing rate of marriage among blacks is an important contributing factor in the substantial increases in both nonmarital births and female-headed households (Farley and Allen, 1987). Collectively, these findings reinforce the argument that black family structure and the economic situations of black men and women are inextricably linked (see Danziger and Weinberg, 1986; Ellwood, 1988; Glasgow, 1981; and W. Wilson, 1987, 1989, for detailed discussions of underclass issues).

CONCLUSION

Although the scope of this review makes it difficult to propose specific recommendations for research, it is useful to summarize four general trends in research on black families and to suggest how they might influence future research directions. First, there was phenomenal growth in this area, reflected in both the quantity and quality of efforts to examine the nature of black family life, as well as the manner in which black families were regarded in the social scientific community. The increase in volume of research encouraged replication, debate, synthesis, and the generation of new efforts. Further, black family researchers acknowledged the value orientations that framed their work, as well as the political ramifications of research (Dilworth-Anderson, Johnson, and Barton, in press; Fine, Schwebel, and James-Myers, 1987).

Second, investigations of black families during this decade demonstrated greater conceptual, methodological, and analytic sophistication. Conceptually, research displayed a greater appreciation for the relationships between macro-level and micro-level influences in relation to black family phenomena (e.g., Staples, 1985). With regard to sample selection, design, and analytic frameworks, important improvements were made, including the availability of nationally representative samples of black respondents, the development of adequate samples of blacks within comparative studies, the use of nonclinical groups of respondents, greater efforts to recruit and utilize groups that are difficult to locate, and the development of appropriate comparative frameworks (i.e., black to white and within-black contrasts).

Third, as a result of the first two trends, a more balanced depiction of black family life emerged. Research increasingly reflected an appreciation for variability in the status of black families overall, as well as within particular social strata. As a result, a more precise understanding emerged concerning the operation of relevant causative factors for particular family phenomena and the specific consequences for individual families. Finally, related to the recognition of diversity in black family status and form, the past decade saw the establishment of black families within the legitimate body of family research. It can be argued that with few exceptions, the raison d'etre of research on black families was not to explore basic questions of family functioning, but to explain black families in comparison to white, middle-class families.

The racial comparative rationale and framework that guided this research was increasingly called into question by numerous researchers (many of whom identified this problem prior to the 1980s). Central among their criticisms is that the exercise of simple racial comparisons in which white behaviors are designated as the standard or baseline invariably indicates the presence of deficiencies in blacks. Further, black behaviors have no inherent significance other than the extent to which they differ from that of whites. Rather than advancing the legitimate task of generating knowledge concerning commonalities across racial groups, the simple and routine application of comparative frameworks ultimately denies the significance of differences for informing the scientific enterprise and ignores the mechanisms through which observed disparities are manifested. A comprehensive understanding of the impact of race on any phenomena is fundamentally incompatible with such an orientation and framework for research.

At this point, we consider some implications of these general trends for the current state of research on black families. First, continuing research on black families must consider the impact and interrelationships among factors that operate at varying levels (i.e., micro- versus macro-level) and potentially manifest themselves through diverse behaviors and phenomena. For example, additional work is needed to examine the linkages between changes in family structure (e.g., nonmarital adolescent births) and alterations in family relationships and functioning (e.g., changes in the grandparent role) or household structure (e.g., multigeneration household arrangements). Second, it is clear that research on black families must occur within expanded disciplinary frameworks. The use of an interdisciplinary approach is an important corrective to viewing black family phenomena in isolation and separate from other perspectives. For example, in research on black adolescence, it may be productive to team a professional in the area of child welfare and social policy with a researcher whose areas of expertise include human development. The dual concentration on issue of both applied and basic research will bring a clearer and more comprehensive focus to the examination of black adolescence. This expanded perspective will provide important information about black adolescence as a developmental stage (i.e., by identifying commonalities across youth), the varied ways that being young and black relate to one's position within the social structure (i.e., by distinguishing experiences unique to black youth), and the relationship between social location and developmental phenomena.

Finally, the tendency to view black families as a collection of the problems and challenges they face has diverted attention from important and basic issues of family function, structure, and relationships and restricted the research focus to that of "problem black families." This caution is particularly relevant for current considerations of the black underclass, whose position and status in society are especially urgent and compelling. Among both lay and scientific communities, there exists a real concern for the serious difficulties and problems that face significant numbers of black families. Certainly, to deny the existence of these problems or to underestimate their impact would be both naive and irresponsible. Likewise, to permit their existence to dominate or restrict the research agenda and/or compromise the research process in relation to black families would be equally detrimental. As students of African American families we would do well to remember that our attempts to understand and address phemonena (including those identified as social problems) that are of relevance to black families requires the application of our best scientific efforts to specify their character and identify causes and consequences and the exercise of the scientific method in the most precise and scrupulous manner possible.

NOTE

The authors acknowledge the assistance of Cheryl Burns and Rukmalie Jayakody for bibliographic search and acquisition. They are deeply indebted to Harold W. Neighbors, Sandra K. Danziger, James S. Jackson, and Michael C. Thornton for comments on earlier drafts of the manuscript. This work was supported in part by FIRST Awards to the first and second authors from the National Institute of Aging (Nos. R29 AG 06856 and R29 AG 07179), and a Research Scientist Development Award to the third author from the National Institute on Mental Health (No. K01 MH00681). Address correspondence to Robert J. Taylor, School of Social Work, University of Michigan, Ann Arbor, MI 48109.

REFERENCES

Allen, Walter R. 1981. "Moms, dads, and boys: Race and sex differences in the socialization of male children." Pp. 99-114 in Lawrence E. Gary (ed.), Black Men. Beverly Hills, CA: Sage.

Anderson, Elijah. 1989. "Sex codes and family life among poor inner-city youths." Annals of the American Academy of Political and Social Science 501: 59-78.

Angel, Ronald, and Marta Tienda. 1982. "Determinants of extended household structure: Cultural pattern or economic model?" American Journal of Sociology 87: 1360-1383.

Antonucci, Toni, and James Jackson. 1989. "Successful aging and life course reciprocity." Pp. 83-95 in A. M. Warnes (ed.), Human Aging. London: Hoder and Stoughton.

Bachrach, Christine A. 1986. "Adoption plans, adopted children, and adoptive mothers." Journal of Marriage and the Family 48: 243-253.

Ball, Richard E., and Lynn Robbins. 1986a. "Black husbands' satisfaction with their family life." Journal of Marriage and the Family 48: 849-855.

Ball, Richard E., and Lynn Robbins. 1986b. "Marital status and life satisfaction among black Americans." Journal of Marriage and the Family 48: 389-394.

Bane, Mary Jo, and David T. Ellwood. 1986. "Slipping into and out of poverty: The dynamics of spells." Journal of Human Resources 21: 1-23.

Barbarin, Oscar A. 1983. "Coping with ecological transition by black families: A psychological model." Journal of Community Psychology 11: 308-322.

Beck, Ruby W., and Scott H. Beck. 1989. "The incidence of extended households among middle-aged black and white women: Estimates from a 5-year panel study." Journal of Family Issues 10: 147-168.

Beckett, Joyce O., and Audrey D. Smith. 1981. "Work and family roles: Egalitarian marriage in black and white families." Social Service Review 55: 314-326.

Bowman, Philip. 1985. "Black fathers and the provider role: Role strain, informal coping resources and life happiness." Pp. 9-19 in A. W. Boykin (ed.), Empirical Research in Black Psychology. Rockville, MD: NIMH.

Bowman, Philip, and Cleopatra Howard. 1985. "Race-related socialization, motivation, and academic achievement: A study of black youth in three-generation families." Journal of the American Academy of Child Psychiatry 24: 134-141.

Boyd-Franklin, Nancy. 1989. Black Families in Therapy: A Multisystem Approach. New York: Guilford.

Broman, Clifford L. 1988a. "Household work and family life satisfaction of blacks." Journal of Marriage and the Family 50: 743-748.

Broman, Clifford L. 1988b. "Satisfaction among blacks: The significance of marriage and parenthood." Journal of Marriage and the Family 50: 45-51.

Brooks-Gunn, Jeanne, and Frank F. Furstenberg. 1986. "The children of adolescent mothers: Physical, academic, and psychological outcomes." Developmental Review 6: 224-251.

Brown, Diane R., and Lawrence E. Gary. 1985. "Social support network differentials among married and non-married black females." Psychology of Women Quarterly 9: 229-241.

Brown, Diane R., and Lawrence E. Gary. 1987. "Stressful life events, social support networks, and physical and mental health of urban black adults." Journal of Human Stress 13: 165-174.

Brown, Diane R., and Lawrence E. Gary. 1988. "Un-

employment and psychological distress among black American women." Sociological Focus 21: 209-220.
Bumpass, Larry L. 1984. "Children and marital disruption: A replication and update." Demography 21: 71-81.
Burton, Linda M., and Vern L. Bengtson. 1985. "Black grandmothers: Issues of timing and continuity of roles." Pp. 61-77 in Vern L. Bengtson and Joan F. Robertson (eds.), Grandparenthood. Beverly Hills, CA: Sage.
Burton, Linda M., and Peggye Dilworth-Anderson. In press. "The intergenerational family roles of aged black Americans." Marriage and Family Review.
Cazenave, Noel A. 1979. "Middle-income black fathers: An analysis of the provider role." Family Coordinator 28: 583-593.
Cazenave, Noel A. 1984. "Race, socioeconomic status, and age: The social context of American masculinity." Sex Roles 11: 639-656.
Chatters, Linda M. 1988. "Subjective well-being evaluations among older black Americans." Psychology and Aging 3: 184-190.
Chatters, Linda M., and James S. Jackson. 1989. "Quality of life and subjective well-being among black adults." Pp. 191-214 in R. L. Jones (eds.), Adult development and aging. Berkeley, CA: Cobb and Henry Publications.
Chatters, Linda M., Robert J. Taylor, and James S. Jackson. 1985. "Size and composition of the informal helper network of elderly blacks." Journal of Gerontology 40: 605-614.
Chatters, Linda M., Robert J. Taylor, and James S. Jackson. 1986. "Aged blacks' choices for an informal helper network." Journal of Gerontology 41: 94-100.
Chatters, Linda M., Robert J. Taylor, and Harold W. Neighbors. 1989. "Size of the informal helper network mobilized in response to serious personal problems." Journal of Marriage and the Family 51: 667-676.
Cherlin, Andrew J. 1981. Marriage, Divorce, Remarriage. Cambridge, MA: Harvard University Press.
Cherlin, Andrew J., and Frank F. Furstenberg, Jr. 1986. The New American Grandparent: A Place in the Family, a Life Apart. New York: Basic Books.
Coleman, Lerita M., Tony C. Antonucci, Pamela K. Adelman, and Susan E. Crohan. 1987. "Social roles in the lives of middle-aged and older black women." Journal of Marriage and the Family 49: 761-771.
Danziger, Sandra K., and Ann Nichols-Casebolt. 1988. "Teen parents and child support: Eligibility, participation, and payment." Journal of Social Service Research 11: 1-20.
Danziger, Sandra K., and Norma Radin. 1990. "Absent does not equal uninvolved: Predictors of fathering in teen mother families." Journal of Marriage and the Family 52: 636-642.
Danziger, Sheldon H., and Daniel H. Weinberg (eds.). 1986. Fighting Poverty: What Works and What Doesn't. Cambridge, MA: Harvard University Press.
Darity, William, and Samuel L. Myers. 1986-87. "Public policy trends and the fate of the black family." Humboldt Journal of Social Relations 14: 134-164.
Dilworth-Anderson, Peggye, Leanor Boulin Johnson, and Linda M. Burton. In press. "Reframing theories for understanding race, ethnicity, and families." In Pauline Boss, William Doherty, Ralph La Ross, Walter Schumm, and Suzanne Steinmetz (eds.), Sourcebook of Family Theories and Methods: A Contextual Approach. New York: Plenum Press.
Dressler, William W. 1985. "Extended family relationships, social support, and mental health in a Southern black community." Journal of Health and Social Behavior 26: 39-48.
Dressler, William, Susan Haworth Hoeppner, and Barbara J. Pitts. 1985. "Household structure in a Southern black community." American Anthropologist 87: 853-862.
Duncan, Greg J., and Willard L. Rodgers. 1988. "Longitudinal aspects of childhood poverty." Journal of Marriage and the Family 50: 1007-1021.
Ellison, Christopher G. 1990. "Family ties, friendships, and subjective well-being among black Americans." Journal of Marriage and the Family 52: 298-310.
Ellwood, David T. 1988. Poor Support. New York: Basic Books.
Ericksen, Julia A., William L. Yancey, and Eugene P. Ericksen. 1979. "The division of family roles." Journal of Marriage and the Family 41: 301-313.
Farley, Reynolds, and Walter R. Allen. 1987. The Color Line and the Quality of Life in America. New York: Russell Sage Foundation.
Fine, Mark, Andrew I. Schwebel, and Linda James-Myers. 1987. "Family stability in black families: Values underlying three different perspectives." Journal of Comparative Family Studies 18: 1-23.
Furstenberg, Frank F., Jr., Jeanne Brooks-Gunn, and Lindsay Chase-Lansdale. 1989. "Teenaged pregnancy and childbearing." American Psychologist 44: 313-320.
Furstenberg, Frank F., J. Brooks-Gunn, and S. Philip Morgan. 1987. Adolescent Mothers in Later Life. New York: Cambridge University Press.
Garfinkel, Irwin, and Sara S. McLanahan. 1986. Single Mothers and Their Children: A New American Dilemma. Washington, DC: Urban Institute Press.
Gibson, Rose C., and James S. Jackson. 1987. "The health, physical functioning, and informal supports of the black elderly." Milbank Quarterly 65: 421-454.
Glasgow, Douglas. 1981. The Black Underclass. New York: Vintage Books.
Glick, Paul C. 1981. "A demographic picture of black families." Pp. 106-126 in Harriette P. MacAdoo (ed.), Black Families. Beverly Hills, CA: Sage.
Guttentag, Marcia, and Paul F. Secord. 1983. Too Many Women: The Sex Ratio Question. Beverly Hills, CA: Sage.
Harrison, Algea. 1985. "The black family's socializing environment." Pp. 174-193 in Harriette P. McAdoo and John L. McAdoo (eds.), Black Children. Beverly Hills, CA: Sage.
Hayes, C. D. (ed.). 1987. Risking the Future: Ado-

lescent Sexuality, Pregnancy, and Childbearing (Vol. 1). Washington, DC: National Academy Press.

Hendricks, Leo E., Cleopatra Howard, and Patricia Ceasar. 1981. "Help-seeking behavior among select populations of unmarried adolescent fathers: Implications for human service agencies." American Journal of Public Health 71: 733-735.

Hendricks, Leo E., and Teresa Montgomery. 1983. "A limited population of unmarried adolescent fathers: A preliminary report of their views on fatherhood and the relationship with the mothers of their children." Adolescence 18: 201-210.

Hill, Robert B., Andrew Billingsley, Eleanor Ingram, Michelene R. Malson, Roger H. Rubin, Carol B. Stack, James B. Stewart, and James E. Teele. 1989. Research on African-American Families: A Holistic Perspective. Boston: William Monroe Trotter Institute.

Hofferth, Sandra L. 1984. "Kin networks, race, and family structure." Journal of Marriage and the Family 46: 791-806.

Hofferth, Sandra L., and C. D. Hayes (eds.). 1987. Risking the Future: Adolescent Sexuality, Pregnancy, and Childbearing (Vol. 2). Working Papers and Statistical Reports. Washington, DC: National Academy Press.

Hogan, Dennis P., Ling-Xin Hao, and William L. Parish. 1990. "Race, kin networks, and assistance to mother-headed families." Social Forces 68: 797-812.

Hogan, Dennis P., and Evelyn M. Kitagawa. 1985. "The impact of social status, family structure, and neighborhood on the fertility of black adolescents." American Journal of Sociology 90: 825-855.

Huber, Joan, and Glenna Spitze. 1981. "Wives' employment, household behaviors, and sex-role attitudes." Social Forces 60: 150-169.

Hughes, Michael, and David H. Demo. 1989. "Self-perceptions of black Americans: Self-esteem and personal efficacy." American Journal of Sociology 95: 132-159.

Jackson, Jacqueline, and Linda Berg-Cross. 1988. "Extending the extended family: The mother-in-law and daughter-in-law relationship of black women." Family Relations 37: 293-297.

Jackson, James S., Linda M. Chatters, and Harold Neighbors. 1986. "The subjective life quality of black Americans." Pp. 193-213 in F. M. Andrews (ed.), Research on the Quality of Life. Ann Arbor: Institute for Social Research, University of Michigan.

Jackson, James, Wayne McCullough, and Gerald Gurin. 1988. "Family, socialization environment, and identity development in black Americans." Pp. 242-256 in H. McAdoo (ed.), Black Families (2nd ed.). Beverly Hills, CA: Sage.

Jaynes, Gerald David, and Robin M. Williams, Jr. (eds.). 1989. A Common Destiny: Blacks and American Society. Washington, DC: National Academy Press.

Jenkins, Shirley, and Beverly Diamond. 1985. "Ethnicity and foster care: Census data as predictors of placement variables." American Journal of Orthopsychiatry 55: 267-276.

Jones, Reginald L. (ed.). 1989. Black Adolescents. Berkeley, CA: Cobb and Henry Publishers.

Lerman, Robert I. 1986. "Who are the young absent fathers?" Youth and Society 18: 3-27.

Lewis, Edith A. 1988. "Role strengths and strains of African-American mothers." Journal of Primary Prevention 9: 77-91.

Lewis, Edith A. 1989. "Role strain in black women: The efficacy of support networks." Journal of Black Studies 20: 155-169.

Lieberson, Stanley, and Mary C. Waters. 1988. From Many Strands: Ethnic and Racial Groups in Contemporary America. New York: Russell Sage Foundation.

Logan, Sadye M. L., Edith M. Freeman, and Ruth G. McRoy. 1990. Social Work Practice with Black Families. White Plains, NY: Longman.

Malson, Michelene. 1983. "The social-support systems of black families." Marriage and Family Review 5: 37-57.

Marsiglio, William. 1987. "Adolescent fathers in the United States: Their initial living arrangements, marital experience, and educational outcomes." Family Planning Perspectives 19: 240-251.

Marsiglio, William. 1989. "Adolescent males' pregnancy resolution preferences and family formation intentions: Does family background make a difference for blacks and whites?" Journal of Adolesent Research 4: 214-237.

McAdoo, Harriette. 1980. "Black mothers and the extended family support networks." Pp. 125-144 in L. F. Rodgers-Rose (ed.), The Black Woman. Beverly Hills, CA: Sage.

McAdoo, John L. 1981. "Black father and child interactions." Pp. 115-130 in Lawrence E. Gary (ed.), Black Men. Beverly Hills, CA: Sage.

McLanahan, Sara S. 1985. "Family structure and the reproduction of poverty." American Journal of Sociology 90: 873-901.

McLanahan, Sara S. 1988. "Family structure and dependency: Early transitions to female household headship." Demography 25: 1-16.

McLanahan, Sara, and Julia Adams. 1987. "Parenthood and psychological well-being." Annual Review of Sociology 13: 237-257.

McLanahan, Sara S., and Karen Booth. 1989. "Mother-only families: Problems, prospects, and politics." Journal of Marriage and the Family 51: 557-580.

McLanahan, Sara S., and Larry Bumpass. 1988. "Intergenerational consequences of family disruption." American Journal of Sociology 94: 130-152.

Moore, Kristin A., Margaret C. Simms, and Charles L. Betsey. 1986. Choice and Circumstance: Racial Differences in Adolescent Sexuality and Fertility. New Brunswick, NJ: Transaction Books.

Morisey, Patricia G. 1990. "Black children in foster care." Pp. 133-147 in Sadye M. L. Logan, Edith M. Freeman, and Ruth G. McRoy (eds.), Social Work Practice with Black Families. New York: Longman.

National Black Child Development Institute. 1989. Who Will Care When Parents Can't? A Study of

Black Children in Foster Care. Washington, DC: National Black Child Development Institute.

Neighbors, Harold W. 1986. "Socioeconomic status and psychologic distress in adult blacks." American Journal of Epidemiology 124: 779-793.

Neighbors, Harold W., and James S. Jackson. 1984. "The use of informal and formal help: Four patterns of illness behavior in the black community." American Journal of Community Psychology 12: 629-644.

Neighbors, Harold W., and Thomas A. LeVeist. 1989. "Socioeconomic status and psychological distress: The impact of financial aid on economic problem severity." Journal of Primary Prevention 10: 149-165.

Norton, Arthur J., and Jeanne E. Moorman. 1987. "Current trends in marriage and divorce among American women." Journal of Marriage and the Family 49: 3-14.

Oliver, Melvin L. 1988. "The urban black community as network: Towards a social network perspective." Sociological Quarterly 29: 623-645.

Parke, Ross D., and Brian Neville. 1987. "Teenage fatherhood." In Sandra L. Hofferth and C. D. Hayes (eds.), Risking the Future: Adolescent Sexuality, Pregnancy, and Childbearing (Vol. 2). Washington, DC: National Academy Press.

Peters, Marie. 1985. "Racial socialization of young black children." Pp. 159-173 in H. McAdoo and J. McAdoo (eds.), Black Children. Beverly Hills, CA: Sage.

Peters, Marie, and G. Massey. 1983. "Chronic vs. mundane stress in family stress theories: The case of black families in white America." Marriage and Family Review 6: 193-218.

Reskin, Barbara F., and Shelly Coverman. 1985. "Sex and race in the detriments of psychophysical distress: A reappraisal of the sex role hypothesis." Social Forces 63: 1038-1059.

Robinson, Jeanne B. 1989. "Clinical treatment of black families: Issues and strategies." Social Work 34: 323-329.

Rodgers, William L., and Arland Thornton. 1985. "Changing patterns of first marriage in the United States." Demography 22: 265-279.

Ross, Catherine E. 1987. "The division of labor at home." Social Forces 65: 816-833.

Rossi, Alice S. 1984. "Gender and parenthood." "American Sociological Review 49: 1-10.

Schoen, Robert. 1983. "Measuring the tightness of the marriage squeeze." Demography 20: 61-78.

Schoen, Robert, and James R. Kluegel. 1988. "The widening gap in black and white marriage rates: The impact of population composition and differential marriage propensities." American Sociological Review 53: 895-907.

Schoen, Robert, and John Wooldredge. 1989. "Marriage choices in North Carolina and Virginia, 1969-71 and 1979-81." Journal of Marriage and the Family 51: 465-481.

South, Scott J. 1986. "Sex ratios, economic power, and women's roles: A theoretical extension and empirical test." Journal of Marriage and the Family 50: 19-31.

South, Scott J., and S. F. Messner. 1987. "The sex ratio and women's involvement in crime: A cross-national analysis." Sociological Quarterly 28: 171-188.

Spanier, Graham B., and Paul C. Glick. 1980. "Mate selection differentials between whites and blacks in the United States." Social Forces 58: 707-725.

Spencer, Margaret. 1983. "Children's cultural values and parental child-rearing strategies." Developmental Reviews 3: 351-370.

Spencer, Margaret, Geraldine Kearse Brookins, and Walter Recharde Allen. 1985. Beginnings: The Social and Affective Development of Black Children. Hillsdale, NJ: Lawrence Erlbaum Associates.

Staples, Robert. 1985. "Changes in black family structure: The conflict between family ideology and structural conditions." Journal of Marriage and the Family 47: 1005-1014.

Staples, Robert, and Alfredo Mirande. 1980. "Racial and cultural variations among American families: A decennial review of the literature on minority families." Journal of Marriage and the Family 42: 157-173.

Stevens, Joseph H., Jr. 1984. "Black grandmothers' and black adolescent mothers' knowledge about parenting." Developmental Psychology 20: 1017-1025.

Stevens, Joseph H., Jr. 1988. "Social support, locus of control, and parenting in three low-income groups of mothers: Black teenagers, black adults, and white adults." Child Development 59: 635-642.

Sudarkasa, Niara. 1981. "Interpreting the African heritage in Afro-American family organizations." Pp. 37-53 in Harriette P. McAdoo (ed.), Black Families. Beverly Hills, CA: Sage.

Sweet, James A., and Larry L. Bumpass. 1987. American Families and Households. New York: Russell Sage Foundation.

Taylor, Robert J. 1985. "The extended family as a source of support for elderly blacks." Gerontologist 26: 630-636.

Taylor, Robert J. 1986. "Receipt of support from family among black Americans: Demographic and familial differences." Journal of Marriage and the Family 48: 67-77.

Taylor, Robert J. 1988a. "Aging and supportive relationships among black Americans." Pp. 259-281 in James Jackson (ed.), The Black American Elderly: Research on Physical Health. New York: Springer.

Taylor, Robert J. 1988b. "Structural determinants of religious participation among Black Americans." Review of Religious Research 30: 114-125.

Taylor, Robert J. 1990. "Need for support and family involvement among black Americans." Journal of Marriage and the Family 52: 584-590.

Taylor, Robert J., and Linda M. Chatters. 1986a. "Church-based informal support among elderly blacks." Gerontologist 26: 637-642.

Taylor, Robert J., and Linda M. Chatters. 1986b.

"Patterns of informal support to elderly black adults: Family, friends, and church members." Social Work 31: 432-438.

Taylor, Robert J., and Linda M. Chatters. 1988. "Church members as a source of informal social support." Review of Religious Research 30: 193-203.

Taylor, Robert J., Linda M. Chatters, and Vickie Mays. 1988. "Parents, children, siblings, in-laws, and non-kin sources of emergency assistance to black Americans." Family Relations 37: 298-304.

Taylor, Robert J., Bogart Leashore, and Susan Toliver. 1988. "An assessment of the provider role as perceived by black males." Family Relations 37: 426-431.

Testa, Mark, N. M. Astone, Marilyn Krogh, and Kathryn Neckerman. 1989. "Employment and marriage among inner-city fathers." Annals of the American Academy of Political and Social Science 501: 79-91.

Thomas, Veronica, Norweeta G. Milburn, Diane R. Brown, and Lawrence E. Gary. 1988. "Social support and depressive symptoms among blacks." Journal of Black Psychology 14: 35-45.

Thompson, Maxine S., and Margaret E. Ensminger. 1989. "Psychological well-being among mothers with school-age children: Evolving family structures." Social Forces 67: 715-730.

Thornton, Michael, Linda M. Chatters, Robert J. Taylor, and Walter R. Allen. 1990. "Sociodemographic and environmental influences on racial socialization by black parents." Child Development 61: 401-409.

Tienda, Marta, and Ronald Angel. 1982. "Headship and household composition among blacks, Hispanics, and other whites." Social Forces 61: 508-531.

Tucker, M. Belinda. 1987. "The black male shortage in Los Angeles." Sociology and Social Research 71: 221-227.

Tucker, M. Belinda, and Claudia Mitchell-Kernan. In press. "Sex ratio imbalance and Afro-Americans: Conceptual and methodological issues." In Reginald Jones (ed.), Advances in Black Psychology. Berkeley, CA: Cobb and Henry.

Tucker, M. Belinda, and Claudia Mitchell-Kernan. 1990. "New trends in black American interracial marriage: The social structural context." Journal of Marriage and the Family 52: 209-218.

Tucker, Belinda, and Robert J. Taylor. 1989. "Demographic correlates of relationship status among black Americans." Journal of Marriage and the Family 51: 655-665.

U.S. Bureau of the Census. 1985. 1980 Census of the Population, Subject Reports: Marital Characteristics. Washington, DC: Government Printing Office.

Warheit, George, William Vega, D. Shimizu, and Kenneth Meinhardt. 1982. "Interpersonal coping networks and mental health problems among four race-ethnic groups." Journal of Community Psychology 10: 312-324.

Wilson, Melvin N. 1986. "The black extended family: An analytical consideration." Developmental Psychology 22: 246-259.

Wilson, Melvin N. 1989. "Child development in the context of the black extended family." American Psychologist 44: 380-385.

Wilson, William Julius. 1987. The Truly Disadvantaged. Chicago: University of Chicago Press.

Wilson, William Julius (ed.). 1989. "The ghetto underclass: Social science perspectives." Annals of the American Academy of Political and Social Science 501: 8-192.

Wilson, William Julius, and Kathryn J. Neckerman. 1986. "Poverty and family structure: The widening gap between evidence and public policy issues." Pp. 232-259 in Sheldon H. Danziger and Daniel H. Weinberg (eds.), Fighting Poverty: What Works and What Doesn't. Cambridge, MA: Harvard University Press.

Ulbrich, Patricia M., and George J. Warheit. 1989. "Social support, stress, and psychological distress among older black and white adults." Journal of Aging and Health 1: 286-305.

Zelnik, Melvin. 1983. "Sexual activity among adolescents: Perspectives of a decade." In Elizabeth McAnarney (ed.), Premature Adolescent Pregnancy and Parenthood. New York: Grune and Stratton.

Zelnik, Melvin, John Kantner, and Kathleen Ford. 1981. Sex and Pregnancy in Adolescence. Beverly Hills, CA: Sage.

Zelnik, Melvin, and Farida K. Shah. 1983. "First intercourse among young Americans." Family Planning Perspectives 15: 64-72.

Zill, Nicholas, and Carolyn C. Rogers. 1988. "Recent trends in the well-being of children in the United States and their implications for public policy." Pp. 31-98 in Andrew J. Cherlin (ed.), The Changing American Family and Public Policy. Washington, DC: Urban Institute Press.

Zollar, Ann Creighton, and J. Sherwood Williams. 1987. "The contribution of marriage to the life satisfaction of black adults." Journal of Marriage and the Family 49: 87-92.

4 Hispanic Families in the 1980s: A Decade of Research

William A. Vega
University of California, Berkeley

A selective literature review covering the period of 1980 until early 1990 suggests certain changes within the knowledge base about Hispanic families in the continental United States. While the long-standing interest in cultural patterning of gender roles and family process continues, a "social adaptation" approach is evident in the demographic and migration research literature. The focus of this approach is on formative effects of environment on family structure, and the role played by family networks in facilitating international immigration and socioeconomic incorporation. The research of the 1980s also underscores gender role flexibility, which has accompanied the movement of women into the labor force, as well as effects of acculturation in multigenerational Hispanic populations. Despite an increase in empirical research, there remains much conjecture about family socialization patterns and differences in attitudes and values across cultures. The available evidence favors an interpretation that Hispanic families are increasingly vulnerable to marital disruption, but that familism—defined as either face-to-face interaction or supporting behaviors—remains a more typical feature of Hispanic families than of non-Hispanic white families. It is also evident that different Hispanic ethnic groups have had dissimilar experiences in family viability, and comparative research is needed to clarify contributory factors.

This review considers research on the Hispanic family in the United States that has appeared in print during the 1980s. The scope of the review includes studies in articles and books on families of Mexican, Puerto Rican, and Cuban origin. The coverage is selective and limited primarily to those studies that represent original research or contribute new theory to the arena of Hispanic family research. Other literature reviews that have appeared during this time period are not covered, except in instances when they involve a new synthesis of theory or information.

A change of research perspectives occurred in the 1980s, owing in great part to the social events and conditions experienced during this decade. Massive immigration and internal migration have had far-reaching consequences for family formation and structure among Hispanics. However, this situation is not unprecedented. Rather, it represents the latest chapter of cyclical trends in American ethnic history (Muller and Espenshade, 1985). In this regard, contemporary research perspectives may aid us in demythologizing the Hispanic family in the past, present, and future. They may also help us to understand better how families change in response to new and challenging social situations and cultural influences.

Since the contemporary research literature derives its discourse and imagery from the research of the past, it is not possible to partition this review completely from the abiding theoretical questions that have occupied students of the Hispanic family for decades. Current research is driven by these enigmas. For example, the long-standing debate about whether depictions of traditional family values, behaviors, and structure

---

Department of Social and Administrative Health Sciences, School of Public Health, Warren Hall, University of California, Berkeley, CA 94720.

are either accurate or relevant has not diminished, despite persistent attempts to put it aside (Staples and Mirande, 1980). Similarly, the ramifications of multigeneration acculturation on family functioning are not well understood, despite numerous attempts to conceptualize the process. It is clear that, while we understand more, we still don't have enough of the right kind of information to adequately explain the complexity and volatility of Hispanic families. In the 1980s, empirical research with an emphasis on "social adaptation" has become the alternative to earlier simplistic formulations of Hispanic families and reflects the most prominent social facts about Hispanic society in the past decades, including migration, immigration, acculturation, socioeconomic incorporation, minority group status, and the entry of women into the labor force. This review critically summarizes what has been learned in the past decade and points out deficiencies in theory and analytical perspectives. It also outlines new directions for future research.

THE STATUS OF THE HISPANIC POPULATION

The dramatic changes that have occurred during the 1980s place Hispanics into a demographic trajectory wherein they can be expected to become the largest ethnic minority group in the continental United States shortly after the turn of the century. Of course, the Hispanic population is not unitary, but is composed of numerous Spanish-speaking ethnic groups whose cultural origins are rich and diverse. Overall, between 1980 and 1988, there was an increase of 34.4% in the size of the Hispanic population (U.S. Bureau of the Census, 1988). This represented a total population in 1988 of 19,431,000. Most of this increase was fueled by immigration from Mexico. Indeed, the Mexican-descent population increased by 39.9% between 1980 and 1988 to a total of 12,110,000. The traditional Southwestern enclaves of Mexican descent have now been transcended, making way for Mexican Americans to become a national minority group. Puerto Ricans, Cubans, and other Latin Americans each increased by proportions of at least 25% during the same period of time. However, Cubans and Puerto Ricans remained essentially regional populations. The states of California, Texas, New York, and Florida contain almost three-quarters of the Hispanic population in the continental United States.

The proportion of Hispanic families below the poverty level has increased slightly to a 1987 level of 25.8% compared to a non-Hispanic level of 9.7% in that same year. Furthermore, Hispanic fertility was 29% higher than non-Hispanic white fertility in 1980 (Bean and Tienda, 1987), a discrepancy that is primarily attributable to women of Mexican origin because they have the highest fertility levels and they are the largest Hispanic ethnic group. On the other hand, Cuban women had fertility rates slightly below those of non-Hispanic white women (Perez, 1986). Mainland Puerto Ricans have high fertility rates, are most likely to have female-headed households with children, and have the lowest family income (Moore and Pachon, 1985: 62).

Some important conclusions are reached by Bean and Tienda (1987) in their monumental review of 1980 census data. Among the most pertinent is their challenge to the long-held supposition that Hispanic families are more stable than non-Hispanic white families. They report negligible variations in rates of marital disruption between non-Hispanic whites, Mexican Americans, and Cuban Americans, but Puerto Rican rates that are much higher than those of the other groups. Although other investigators (Frisbee, Opitz, and Kelly, 1985) had reported lower divorce rates for Mexican Americans, Bean and Tienda point out that when separation is included in marital disruption, such differences disappear. Further, Angel and Tienda (1982) report that non-nuclear family members are more likely to contribute to household income in Hispanic households precisely because there is a higher percentage of female-headed households in Mexican (19.9%) and Puerto Rican (38.6%) than in non-Hispanic white households (14.1%). Therefore, having other adults living in the household or contributing to its maintenance may be indicating an erosion of Hispanic family strengths, even though traditional cultural expectations may be motivating this supportive behavior.

The census data suggest two important trends for Hispanics between the 1960 and 1980 census: (*a*) the average size of Hispanic households is decreasing, and (*b*) marital disruption is increasing. Frisbee (1986) points out that Mexican American and Cuban American marital stability is inversely related to educational attainment, but among Puerto Ricans, educational attainment increases marital stability. Moreover, the lifetime fertility of Hispanic-origin women varies strongly with educational attainment. As noted by Bean and Tienda (1987), "If lower education tends generally to make for higher fertility, and if the Spanish origin women are relatively more concentrated in the lower educational categories, it is not difficult to see why higher fertility persists within many of the groups" (p. 224).

In summary, we have the profile of a Hispanic population that is increasing at a much faster rate than the non-Hispanic population but continues to experience substandard levels of educational attainment and family income. It is likely that the continental Hispanic population will continue these demographic trends (Bean, Schmandt, and Weintraub, 1989; Hayes-Batista, Schink, and Chapa, 1988). The primary contributory factor to population growth will be immigration. Despite the passage of the Immigration Reform and Control Act of 1986, it is unlikely that either legal or undocumented immigration will be markedly curtailed. Moreover, there is some evidence that undocumented immigrants form Mexico are more likely to arrive with the anticipation of becoming permanent residents, and an increase of women and families is noticeable in a migratory stream that was formerly dominated by men (Passel and Woodrow, 1984).

FAMILY STRUCTURE AND
SOCIOECONOMIC CONDITIONS

The morphological characteristics of the Hispanic family are increasingly understood to be a response to socioeconomic conditions. Griswold del Castillo (1984) notes that while the extended family was an "ideal type" in the second half of the 19th century, Mexican Americans were no more likely than non-Hispanics to have extended families. Furthermore, the vicissitudes of life on the frontier rendered families highly susceptible to disruption and reformulation. This required great resourcefulness on the part of both men and women, and gender roles were not highly differentiated. Indeed, by 1870 in Los Angeles, almost 38% of Mexican-descent families were headed by females, with similar proportions found in San Antonio and Santa Fe (p. 32). Griswold del Castillo concludes, "The Mexican American family has had to be flexible, pluralistic, and adaptive to survive" (p. 132).

The parallels between this historical situation and the current research on the Hispanic family are illuminating. Portes and Bach (1985) note that 75% of Cubans and 50% of Mexican Americans reported some or a great deal of help from relatives during their first three years of postimmigration residence. The use of families for migration and adaptation has been assessed in two important studies, which conclude that binational, intercommunity linkages are sustained through resilient family network ties (Alvarez, 1987; Massey, Alarcon, Durand, and Gonzalez, 1987).

Chavez, in two articles (1985 and 1988), traces the ties between family structure and legal residence. In one study (1985) he contrasts undocumented and documented Mexicans on direction of family extension and finds that 76.6% of undocumented families are extended laterally, which indicates a predominance of households where "the additional relative is of the same kinship generation, for example, a brother, sister, cousin" (p. 323). Among legal immigrants, less than half were in lateral extension, and in contrast, 30.6% were up-extended—that is, residing in a household that included a mother, father, aunt, or uncle. Among the undocumented, only 5.3% were up-extended. Among legal residents there is a tendency for families to reunify as members are brought in from Mexico or these households expand because of marriage and childbearing.

Among undocumented immigrants the process is more complex, because some migrants choose to go home, usually after one year. Others stay, which is indicated by the dramatic increase from 22% to 42.4% in simple family households among those migrants staying longer than one year. Simple family households are defined as conjugal units and any of their children. This indicates a rapid rate of family formation even among the undocumented group (see also Browning and de la Garza, 1986). This profile of flexibility in family formation resonates with the historical evidence cited previously. Both illustrate the requirement for adaptive capacities within Hispanic families in dealing with the exigencies of economic marginality, labor market pressures, and physical relocation. Moreover, as noted by Chavez in another article (1988), undocumented migrants "living in households comprised of families more often viewed their employment as permanent than did their single counterparts" (p. 102). This tendency was true of even recent arrivals. Naturally, as the family has offspring who are native-born U.S. citizens, the long-stay perspective is reinforced and the family becomes "binationalized."

Muschkin and Myers (1989) report that recent migrants from Puerto Rico have an overrepresentation of disrupted families, and cohabitation seems more common for second-generation families (p. 500). On the other hand, families on the island are more likely to be intact (Bird and Canino, 1982). This difference has preoccupied some researchers who believe that such variations "point to the need to explore the variations in ecological settings and the different locales of challenge in which Puerto Ricans (single and families) strive to make the most of difficult economic and social circumstances" (Pelto, Roman, and Liriano, 1982: 43). In fact, these authors report finding a variety of "household structures, extra-household ties, and general patterns of helpful exchange" (p. 54); and they add that similar findings would probably be common if research designs were sensitive to their identification. Disrupted families that are headed by females are seen as an outcome of highly stressful environments where unemployment is common. Nevertheless, it would be enlightening to study variations in family stability across Hispanic ethnic groups within the same social ecology.

Cultural Maintenance and Family Functioning

Changing cultures is an adaptive process, and acculturation is also idiosyncratic, producing distinctive levels of change in individual family members (Vega, Hough, and Romero, 1983). For example, cultural values and behaviors as well as ethnic identification may differ intergenerationally (Keefe and Padilla, 1987; Szapocznik and Hernandez, 1988). Historically, immigrants have represented a bulwark of resistance to acculturation, and it has been expected that their family processes would deviate most markedly from "American" families. However, it is not accurate to juxtapose Latin American ethnic cultures with American culture as if they are truly discrete or static. Culture change is a worldwide phenomenon, and wide intracultural variations can be expected in all complex Western societies, including those in Latin America. It remains an empirical question whether specific cultural differences between Hispanics and non-Hispanics are responsible for systematic variations in familism, gender roles, or family process. Much of the literature of the 1980s, especially the literature about Mexican Americans, is devoted to exploring these interrelated issues.

Familism and Social Support

The belief that Hispanics are more family-oriented than Anglos has been a consistent theme in the social science literature for decades. In fact, this line of reasoning has been a cornerstone of the extended traditional family stereotype and is linked to many of the pejorative images that have beset discussions of the Hispanic family. Because this stereotype has been so controversial and the empirical evidence so inconsistent, contemporary researchers have continued their quest for conceptual precision and empirical evidence that could clarify this issue (Alvirez, Bean, and Williams, 1981). As noted by Zinn (1982–83: 225), "The literature on familism among Chicanos reflects a mixed bag of assumptions, approaches, findings, and interpretations."

In a reflective article culminating extensive field research, Keefe (1984: 65) notes that despite the adaptive requirements of acculturation and urbanization, Mexican Americans are still credited with enjoying large extended-family networks and that this perception is "somehow related to real behavior patterns (authors see values variously as cause, effect or reinforcing agent)." From her own research, Keefe describes differences in family network and support patterns between Mexican Americans and non-Hispanics. One of the most noteworthy variations is the tendency for Mexican Americans to participate in relatively large kin networks and to engage in high rates of visiting and exchange. This pattern was true for immigrant and non-immigrant Mexican Americans. On the other hand, non-Hispanics maintained ties with fewer kin, and often these relationships were long-distance contact situations. Corresponding differences were found in the greater willingness of Mexican Americans to agree that the family should be the resource for dealing with problems. However, both ethnic groups strongly valued kin relationships and acknowledged that there are disadvantages to maintaining strong ties (Keefe, 1984: 67). The difference seems to lie in the geographic propinquity of Hispanic extended kin networks, which facilitates visiting and exchange behaviors, whereas non-Hispanics are more readily satisfied with long-distance relationships while restricting intimate contact to the nuclear family. The Mexican American family, then, is more multiplex, since it is more likely to be available and used to meet instrumental and affective needs. In this sense, it should be considered more extended.

Confirmatory empirical findings sustain much of what Keefe has elaborated. Mindel (1980) concludes that non-Hispanics migrate away from kin networks and Hispanics migrate toward them. He attributes these differences to cultural traditions, in that "close kinship ties are not merely a convenient form of aid but a well-known, enjoyable, and expected set of practices and attitudes" (p. 32). However, he somewhat qualifies the "family-as-resource" perspective by stating that kin networks are more likely to meet social-emotional needs than instrumental ones. Three separate empirical studies have also reported the tendency for Mexican American immigrants to have smaller social networks available than second-generation offspring have, and to rely on family more exclusively for emotional nurturance and problem solving (Golding and Burnam, 1990; Griffith and Villavicencio, 1985; Vega and Kolody, 1985). However, the second generation has broader social networks available because these consist of multigeneration kin and friend contacts.

Griffith and Villavicencio (1985) report that education and income were the best predictors of "more available support and more contact with network members." This finding is provocative, because it throws into question the appropriateness of comparing Hispanic and non-Hispanic patterns of familism without appropriate controls for socioeconomic differences across groups. There are no studies comparing patterns of middle-class Hispanics and non-Hispanics, which would be illuminating for predicting the future of Hispanic familism. There is also no consensus about the context of extended-family support. The historical case has been made for kinship networks as exchange systems for people who are economically marginal, but recent writings have been more likely to confirm emotional support as the main outcome of familism (Valle and Bensussen, 1985).

Markides, Hoppe, Martin, and Timbers (1983), in their three-generation study, concluded that older Mexican Americans and non-Hispanics had good relationships with family members. However, the Mexican American elderly were more likely to expect more from their children and not receive it. It may be that the acculturation process has created distinctive intergenerational expectations. However, in a later article, Markides, Boldt, and Ray (1986) reconfirmed the familistic orientation of Mexican Americans by noting that the family is the dominant source of advice and help in all generations.

These findings underscore the complexity of linking affiliational patterns with their underlying motives. The reasons why family members prefer contact with each other can have multiple and simultaneous rationales, and these are difficult to capture in descriptive studies using a limited theoretical framework. Similarly, relationships between expressed values and actual behaviors cannot be precisely understood without taking heed of how interpersonal transactions occur in the process of daily living. Some familial interactions may be instrumental, others may be symbolic, while others may be inescapable. Given the tendency for Mexican Americans to lean toward socially desirable answers, great care must be taken in the design of research in order to determine what people really mean, not just what they are saying, and whether their behaviors are consistent with normative expressions.

Gender Roles

Gender roles in the Hispanic family continue to be a primary area of conjecture and research in the 1980s. Paul Kutsche (1983) provides a detailed ethnographic description of Hispanic families in northern New Mexico that is a "throwback" to the traditional ethnographic literature. He describes the patriarchal model as follows: "The double standard of responsible adult behavior is quietly rampant in New Mexico, so a man who keeps his family well and is directly known to other men to indulge himself away from home is tacitly admired" (p. 154). On the other hand, "the wife owes her husband absolute sexual fidelity and, like Caesar's wife, also the appearance of it" (p. 159). Nevertheless, despite this type of gender stereotyping, Kutsche notes that strict gender roles deviate from the traditional division of labor when men are away working for extended periods. Under these circumstances, "either sex will do any job without hesitation" (p. 154). He also notes that childrearing is a joint parental obligation.

It is very common in the contemporary literature, as it was in the past, to find descriptions of the Hispanic family that contain references to continuity in traditional cultural expectations as well as evidence of female role transformations that openly challenge male dominance or a notion of a culturally ordained division of labor (Gonzalez, 1982; Zinn, 1982). For example, in a historical review, Zinn (1980) found that availability of employment was the most important determinant of whether Mexican American women worked or not. Similar findings have been reported for Puerto Rican women in New York (Moore and Pachon, 1985: 104). In describing gender roles in Puerto Rico, Bird and Canino (1982) restate the familiar "machismo" cultural motif. Nevertheless, family decision-making is described as either a joint process of both parents or primarily the job of the mother. As implied by Ybarra (1982a), an understanding of flexibility in gender roles within the Hispanic family has been obfuscated by the reliance on monocausal explanations (e.g., machismo) "for all changes that occur within the family structure" (p. 42). The result, she states, is the tendency for the Hispanic family to be studied in "a vacuum," while the social context of behavior and gender roles is ignored. The implication is that Hispanic families are adaptive, and gender role expectations will change as social conditions require. In Ybarra's empirical study of gender roles among Mexican Americans, she found a range "from a patriarchal (role-segregated) structure to an egalitarian (or joint-role) structure, with many combinations of these two polar opposites evident" (Ybarra, 1982b: 172).

In a rare example of a comparative ethnographic study, Kelly and Garcia (1989) contrast the experience of Cuban women in Miami and immigrant Mexican women in Los Angeles. These authors conclude that despite similar gender role expectations about female employment in both groups, their outcomes differed as a result of economic and political conditions in the two study sites. Immigrant Mexican women in Los Angeles find themselves in a process of "proletarianization," where their labor is required for family survival, whereas many Cuban women left the labor force when short-term goals of improving living standards were attained. In many ways, women entering the labor force remains a culturally anomalous behavior, requiring constant negotiation, conflict, and justification. Indeed, these authors conclude that Hispanic women attain greater personal autonomy via external employment. However, when this occurs in the context of socioeconomic marginality, employment is often a sign of family vulnerability.

Employment may also be a marker of individual vulnerability for married working women. Canino and associates (1987) find much higher depressive symptom levels among married women than among married men who are working full-time in Puerto Rico, and as a consequence, these investigators conclude, "Employment status does represent a different social role for married men and women" (p. 455).

Family Process

Within the contemporary literature, attention has increasingly turned toward improving our understanding about how family process characteristics of Hispanic families are being affected by living in a multicultural environment. Martinez (1986) offers a theoretical model for conceptualizing family socialization that is based on two fundamental statements. First, "individuals are members of multiple social groups" (p. 266), and therefore, they can be aware of and even participate in multiple social systems simultaneously. This predisposes them to be opportunistic and adaptable. Second, "membership in social systems is further assumed to be progressive, and in this sense the model is developmental" (p. 266). That is, the individual is a member of a family, that family lives in a community, and this has implications for social affiliations of all types. Therefore, membership will radiate to multiple groups and institutions whereby the individual is shaped by these experiences and is influenced by the broader social environment as well. This framework stresses the "interconnective relationships of the individual, the family and society." Regrettably, this type of model does little to identify which extrafamilial factors will provoke specific types of family changes.

Starting from similar theoretical premises and writing about the Cuban family, other researchers (Szapocznik and Hernandez, 1988) report from clinical and empirical studies that, typically, adult immigrants acculturate at a rate that is much slower than that of their children, a difference that leads to profound intergenerational conflicts. In turn, these conflicts are aggravated by parental efforts to gain control over their children. Eventually children can move even farther in the direction of rejecting parental expectations. In short, dramatic differences in cultural orientation exacerbate normal intergenerational strains to produce unique parenting problems and family vulnerability among Cuban Hispanics. Evidently, the process could be generalizable to other Hispanic ethnic groups as well.

Among the relatively few comparative studies about Hispanic family process, most have focused on family dynamics and marital experience. For example, family cohesion and adaptability were compared among a sample of non-Hispanics and Mexican Americans by using the Family Adaptability and Cohesion Scale (Vega et al., 1986). Overall, families in both samples functioned well and had similar family process characteristics, on the basis of the circumplex model of Olson, Russell, and Sprenkle (1980). However, the characteristics of low-acculturation Mexican American families differed from both high-acculturation Mexican American and non-Hispanic white families. For example, low-acculturation parents were more likely to be low in stress and to be satisfied with family life and spouse personality during the stage of raising preadolescent children, which was the focus of this study.

In quite a different type of empirical research, the sources of marital strain among Mexican American women were compared to those for non-Hispanic women (Vega, Kolody, and Valle, 1988). The sources of marital strain were found to be very similar in both cultural groups. However, the less acculturated Mexican Americans, most of whom were low-income housewives, were more likely to experience marital strain based on nonreciprocity of spouse but were less likely to experience frustrations about spouse's ability to provide adequately for them. Nonreciprocity involves circumstances where the spouse insists on having his own way and will not give in to his wife's wishes. However, this study restricted the selection of marital strain items only to those used in a previous study with a non-Hispanic community sample.

Another comparative study of family roles found few differences in perceptions about siblings' and parents' roles between Mexican American and non-Hispanic children. An important aspect of this study is that it controlled for the socioeconomic status of the families. Birth-order dynamics were similar for all children except the last-born, which suggests that the values operating in family dynamics, and especially in the socialization of children, differed little in both ethnic groups (Jaramillo and Zapata, 1987). These authors conclude that their findings further disconfirm the idea that Hispanic families are categorically discrete from non-Hispanic families.

DISCUSSION AND CONCLUSION

Despite the passage of time, the shortage of empirical studies on the Hispanic family noted by Ramirez and Arce in their highly cited literature review (1981) continues to persist. Notwithstanding several important demographic studies, the need for new empirical research is most evident in the case of the Cuban American family. However, even within the expansive literature on Mexican Americans, there remains much conjecture and recitation of old work, with few new hard facts on which to base a viable resynthesis of heuristic models. Most of the studies reported in the literature must be considered "exploratory or first-level research" (Rothman, Gant, and Hnat, 1985: 211), lacking comprehensive theoretical grounding for a continuing program of investigation. Given the noncomparability of most contemporary findings about the Hispanic family, and the lack of a consistent conceptual grounding, it is difficult to develop hypotheses about cultural similarities or differences in family process that may exist among Cubans, Puerto Ricans, or Mexican Americans. Several recommendations that could help in overcoming this impasse are summarized below.

1. Historical, ethnographic, and empirical studies are needed that investigate the relationship of family characteristics to social and economic incorporation. Complementary studies using a common theoretical framework would be most enlightening, especially comparative studies, which permit using ethnographic and historical information to design empirical field studies, as well

as to interpret the results of those studies (Alvarez, 1987).

2. Researchers should be circumspect about overgeneralizing from idiosyncratic samples, and replications (or partial replications) of carefully done research using common instrumentation and designs would help establish convergent validity and reliability in Hispanic family research.

3. Since virtually all empirical research is currently limited to cross-sectional studies, it is very difficult to assess dynamic family processes. Developmental theoretical models and prospective multivariate designs are needed to establish causal links between designated independent variables (e.g., SES, labor markets effects, cultural factors) and predicted changes in family relations, structure, or processes.

4. Care should be taken not to confuse assenting statements in interviews about family values and normative expectations with actual behavior. Values can be countervailing. Values can be retained that are conflicting or that neutralize actual behavior. For example, see the account by Weeks and Cuellar (1981) about the Hispanic elderly in their field study who believed they should be able to count on family ties for support but failed to seek such assistance because of the more closely held value of self-reliance, which inhibits help-seeking from family members.

5. Specific ethnic group membership and the intergenerational and acculturation characteristics of samples should be measured and reported in all types of research. These are potentially confounding factors that can seriously limit the generalizability or interpretation of empirical studies (Trevino, 1988).

6. Systematic ethnographic studies are needed regarding language and the role it plays in preserving family practices, familism, intergenerational cohesion, and ethnic identity (Moore and Pachon, 1985; Portes and Rumbaut, 1990).

7. More attention should be paid to current developments in non-Hispanic theory and research, such as the work reported in this volume. The Hispanic family research literature reflects isolation and will benefit from the introduction of new perspectives and analytical paradigms. In conducting this review, it was apparent to me that a great deal of exciting family research is appearing in books about migration and adaptation rather than within journals about family process.

8. Hispanic family research should encompass the study of the rapidly increasing population of Central and South Americans in the United States (Suarez-Orozco, 1989) and the implications of settlement patterns for intermarriage and cultural dissemination between members of different Hispanic ethnic groups (for an excellent recent example of appropriate procedures, see Jiobu, 1988).

9. Family strengths and the role of culture in sustaining these should be studied with empirical methods rather than by conjecture.

An important limitation of this review is the exclusion of the literature on fertility regulation and family planning, which may be an increasingly important area of research in the 1990s. Nonetheless, despite a moderate yield of new studies in the last decade, there is an encouraging movement toward social-environmental conceptual frameworks that transcend the long-debated limitations of emic cultural models of family life among Hispanics. This trend has facilitated a wide-ranging discourse regarding antecedent and contemporary processes that have contributed to the social adaptation of Hispanic families in American culture. It has also opened the path for more sophisticated study designs and methodological procedures.

References

Alvarez, Robert. 1987. Families: Migration and Adaptation in Baja and Alta California from 1800 to 1975. Berkeley: University of California Press.

Alvirez, David, Frank Bean, and David Williams. 1981. "The Mexican American family." In C. H. Mindel and R. W. Habenstein (eds.), Ethnic Families in America. New York: Elsevier Press.

Angel, Ronald, and Marta Tienda. 1982. "Determinants of extended household structure: Cultural pattern or economic need?" American Journal of Sociology 6: 1360–1383.

Bean, Frank, Jurgen Schmandt, and Sidney Weintraub. 1989. Mexican and Central American Population and U.S. Immigration Policy. Austin: University of Texas Press.

Bean, Frank, and Marta Tienda. 1987. The Hispanic Population of the United States. New York: Russell Sage Foundation.

Bird, Hector, and Glorisa Canino. 1982. "The Puerto Rican family: Cultural factors and family intervention strategies." Journal of the American Academy of Psychoanalysis 10: 257–268.

Browning, Harley L., and Rodolfo O. de la Garza. 1986. Mexican Immigrants and Mexican Americans. Austin, TX: Center for Mexican American Studies.

Canino, Glorisa J., Martiza Rubio-Stipec, Patrick Shrout, Milagros Bravo, Robert Stolberg, and Hector R. Bird. 1987. "Sex differences and depression in Puerto Rico." Psychology of Women Quarterly 4: 443-459.

Chavez, Leo. 1985. "Households, migration, and labor market participation: The adaptation of Mexicans to life in the United States." Urban Anthropology 14: 301-346.

Chavez, Leo. 1988. "Settlers and sojourners: The case of Mexicans in the United States." Human Organization 47: 95-108.

Frisbie, W. Parker. 1986. "Variation in patterns of marital instability among Hispanics." Journal of Marriage and the Family 48: 99-106.

Frisbie, W. Parker, Wolfgang Opitz, and William R. Kelly. 1985. "Marital instability trends among Mexican Americans as compared to blacks and Anglos: New evidence." Social Science Quarterly 66: 587-601.

Golding, Jacqueline, and Audrey Burnam. 1990. "Stress and social support as predictors of depressive symptoms in Mexican Americans and non-Hispanic whites." Journal of Social and Clinical Psychology 9: 268-286.

Gonzalez, Alex. 1982. "Sex roles of the traditional Mexican family." Journal of Cross-Cultural Psychology 13: 330-339.

Griffith, James, and Sandra Villavicencio. 1985. "Relationships among acculturation, sociodemographic characteristics, and social supports in Mexican American adults." Hispanic Journal of Behavioral Sciences 7: 75-92.

Griswold del Castillo, Richard. 1984. La Familia. Notre Dame, IN: University of Notre Dame Press.

Hayes-Bautista, David E., Werner O. Schink, and Jorge Chapa. 1988. The Burden of Support. Stanford, CA: Stanford University Press.

Jaramillo, Patricio, and Jessie T. Zapata. 1987. "Roles and alliances within Mexican-American and Anglo Families." Journal of Marriage and The Family 49: 727-735.

Jiobu, Robert. 1988. Ethnicity and Assimilation. Albany, NY: SUNY Press.

Keefe, Susan. 1984. "Real and ideal extended familism among Mexican Americans and Anglo Americans: On the meaning of 'close' family ties." Human Organization 43: 65-70.

Keefe, Susan E., and Amado M. Padilla. 1987. Chicano Ethnicity. Albuquerque: University of New Mexico Press.

Kelly, Patricia F., and Anna Garcia. 1989. "Power surrendered, power restored: The politics of home and work among Hispanic women in Southern California and Southern Florida." In L. Tilly and P. Guerin (eds.), Women and Politics in America. New York: Russell Sage Foundation.

Kutsche, Paul. 1983. "Household and family in Hispanic Northern New Mexico." Journal of Comparative Family Studies 14: 151-165.

Markides, Kyriakos S., Joanne S. Boldt, and Laura A. Ray. 1986. "Sources of helping and intergenerational solidarity: A three generations study of Mexican Americans." Journal of Gerontology 41: 506-511.

Markides, Kyriakos S., Sue K. Hoppe, Harry W. Martin, and Dianne M. Timbers. 1983. "Sample representativeness in a three-generation study of Mexican Americans." Journal of Marriage and the Family 45: 911-916.

Martinez, Marco A. 1986. "Family socialization among Mexican Americans." Human Development 29: 264-279.

Massey, Douglas, Rafael Alarcon, Jorge Durand, and Umberto Gonzalez. 1987. Return to Aztlan. Berkeley: University of California Press.

Mindel, Charles H. 1980. "Extended familism among urban Mexican Americans, Anglos, and blacks." Hispanic Journal of Behavioral Sciences 2: 21-34.

Moore, Joan, and Harry Pachon. 1985. Hispanics in the United States. Englewood Cliffs, NJ: Prentice-Hall.

Muller, Thomas, and Thomas J. Espenshade. 1985. The Fourth Wave. Washington, DC: Urban Institute Press.

Muschkin, Clara, and George C. Myers. 1989. "Migration and household family structure: Puerto Ricans in the United States." International Migration Review 23: 495-501.

Olson, David H., Candyce S. Russell, and Douglas H. Sprenkle. 1980. "Circumplex Model of Marital and Family Systems: II. Empirical studies and clinical intervention." In J. P. Vincent (ed.), Advances in Family Intervention, Assessment, and Theory (Vol. 1). Greenwich, CT: JAI Press.

Passel, J. S., and K. A. Woodrow. 1984. "Geographic distribution of undocumented aliens counted in the 1980 census by state." International Migration Review 18: 642-671.

Pelto, Pertti, Maria Roman, and Nelson Liriano. 1982. "Family structures in an urban Puerto Rican community." Urban Anthropology 11: 39-58.

Perez, Lisandro. 1986. "Immigrant economic adjustment and family organization: The Cuban success story reexamined." International Migration Review 20: 4-20.

Portes, Alejandro, and Robert L. Bach. 1985. Latin Journey. Berkeley: University of California Press.

Portes, Alejandro, and Ruben G. Rumbaut. 1990. Immigrant America: A Portrait. Berkeley: University of California Press.

Ramirez, Oscar, and Carlos Arce. 1981. "The contemporary Chicano family: An empirically based review." In A. Barron (ed.), Explorations in Chicano Psychology. New York: Prager.

Rothman, Jack, Larry Gant, and Stephen A. Hnat. 1985. "Mexican American family culture." Social Service Review 59: 197-215.

Staples, Robert, and Alfredo Mirande. 1980. "Racial and cultural variations among American families: A decennial review of the literature on minority families." Journal of Marriage and the Family 42: 887-903.

Suarez-Orozco, Marcelo. 1989. Central American Refugees and United States High School: A Psychosocial Study of Motivation and Achievement. Stanford,

CA: Stanford University Press.

Szapocznik, Jose, and Roberto Hernandez. 1988. "The Cuban American family." In C. H. Mindel, R. W. Habenstein, and R. Wright (eds.), Ethnic Families in America. New York: Elsevier Press.

Trevino, Fernando. "Uniform minimum data sets: In search of demographic comparability." American Journal of Public Health 78: 126-127.

U.S. Bureau of the Census. 1988. Population Characteristics. Current Population Reports, Series P-20, No. 438. Washington, DC: Government Printing Office.

Valle, Ramon, and Gloria Bensussen. 1985. "Hispanic social networks, social support, and mental health." In William A. Vega and Manuel Miranda (eds.), Stress and Hispanic Mental Health. DHHS Pub. No. 85-1410. Rockville, MD: NIMH.

Vega, William A., Richard Hough, and Annelisa Romero. 1983. "Family life patterns of Mexican Americans." In G. J. Powell (eds.), The Psychosocial Development of Minority Group Children. New York: Brunner/Mazel.

Vega, William A., and Bohdan Kolody. 1985. "The meaning of social support and the mediation of stress across cultures." In William A. Vega and Manuel Miranda (eds.), Stress and Hispanic Mental Health. DHHS Pub. No. 85-1410. Rockville, MD: NIMH.

Vega, William A., Bohdan Kolody, and Ray Valle. 1988. "Marital strain, coping, and depression among Mexican-American Women." Journal of Marriage and the Family 50: 391-403.

Vega, William A., Thomas Patterson, James Sallis, Philip Nader, Catherine Atkins, and Ian Abramson. 1986. "Cohesion and adaptability in Mexican-American and Anglo families." Journal of Marriage and the Family 48: 857-867.

Weeks, John R., and Jose Cuellar. 1981. "The role of family members in the helping networks of older people." Gerontology 21: 388-394.

Ybarra, Lea. 1982a. "Marital decision-making and the role of machismo in the Chicano family." De Colores 6: 32-47.

Ybarra, Lea. 1982b. "When wives work: The impact on the Chicano family." Journal of Marriage and the Family 44: 169-178.

Zinn, Maxine B. 1980. "Employment and education of Mexican American women." Harvard Educational Review 50: 47-62.

Zinn, Maxine B. 1982. "Chicano men and masculinity." Journal of Ethnic Studies 10: 29-44.

Zinn, Maxine B. 1982/3. "Familism among Chicanos: A theoretical review." Humboldt Journal of Social Relations 10: 224-238.

5 Diversity and Community: Right Objectives & Wrong Arguments

Frank F. Wong

Prologue: An Allegory or a Fairy Tale?

Once upon a time a proud people lived on the top of a mountain. From that summit, it seemed, they could see everything everywhere. Daily clouds obscured the distant horizon but occasionally they would glimpse a huge mountain far in the distance. These momentary revelations notwithstanding, they were content in believing that the whole world was what they could see on their own mountain. Because of this they did not realize that their mountain was in reality a foothill, one of many that circled the huge mountain in the distance. Nor did they know that other people on other foothills shared the same belief that what they saw from their own summit was the whole world, everything everywhere, even though it was but one of many foothills.

One day a terrible cataclysm struck the land. A violent tremor shook their foothills until they began to crumble. All the proud peoples had to descend from their particular mountain to seek refuge in the lowlands at the base of the huge mountain. There they discovered that other peoples from other foothills had also descended to the lowlands to escape the wrath of nature. Now suddenly the land became quiet, the clouds lifted, and all the peoples could see for the first time the huge mountain in all of its towering glory whereas before they had known it only in part through a fleeting glimpse.

But nature was not finished with these people. A great flood came thundering into the valley, and all the peoples scrambled onto higher land on the side of the huge mountain to escape the deluge. Day after day the floodwaters rose. All of the peoples realized that they would need to ascend the mountain together to save themselves. But as they began to climb, great disputes broke out between the different peoples, for each had their own idea about how best to climb the mountain. After all, each of the peoples had long believed that they had seen everything everywhere and therefore they knew everything everywhere. It was difficult for them to admit that they had seen only a portion of the huge mountain and only from the angle of vision of their particular foothill.

As the floodwaters continued to rise, the clamorous disputes yielded to the urgencies of survival. Despite their different points of view, they had one thing in common: They had to climb the hill to survive. As they debated their dilemma, they came to a new revelation. Each of the different peoples knew a different part of the huge mountain—one knew where the rockslides were, one knew where water was to be found, another knew the passage through difficult terrain. Now they came to a new vision of everything everywhere, a new vision of truth. They realized that they had been looking differently at the same mountain, and, once they exchanged views with the common purpose of climbing to the mountaintop of truth, they developed a more complete understanding of the mountain than any of them had developed separately. They formed a community of climbers and began the difficult ascent. They are still climbing and we do not know the end of the story.

A Duel in the Dark: the Debate about Diversity and Community

When a respected member of the Redlands faculty resigned an elected faculty position because he believed that my advocacy of cultural diversity was racist and a challenge to fundamental tenets of the academic community, I was deeply troubled. The troubling part was not the clash of faculty and administration or the ad hominem accusation; academic administrators learn to live with that. I was troubled because it had come after many hours of debate in which I sought to understand his view and he, I think, sought to understand mine.

Those hours of debate, in retrospect, were like a duel in the dark: The thrust and parry of our arguments seemed to go past each other—we stabbed thin air, our mutual anger mounted, the misengagement was complete. I've listened since to many discussions of diversity and community, and I am reminded each time of that incident. I have even come to regard it as a metaphor for the larger debate, a debate that too often becomes a "duel in the dark."

From Frank F. Wong, "Diversity & Community: Right Objectives and Wrong Arguments," from *Change*, Vol. 23(4): 50-54, 1991. Reprinted with permission of the Helen Dwight Reid Educational Foundation. Published by Heldref Publications, 1319 Eighteenth St., N.W., Washington, D.C. 20036-1802. Copyright © 1991.

What came to trouble me more about the incident was something else. I began to suspect that there was validity to some parts of his argument. Perhaps both of us were standing on our respective foothills arguing about the shape of a mountain we saw from different perspectives. No wonder there was confusion in the dialogue, no wonder the debate lacked engagement.

Gradually, I've come to this uncomfortable conclusion: Those of us who advocate cultural diversity too often have the wrong end of the argument when it comes to the issue of forming community, while those who've been skeptical of cultural diversity in the name of defending a traditional academic community have the right end of the argument but have argued it wrongly. Until we understand this, we will continue to talk past each other in mounting futility and frustration. It does not help that each side tends to talk only with those of like mind, and attend its separate conferences to explore separate foothills.

What do I mean when I say that cultural diversity advocates have the wrong end of the argument with respect to community? A community needs a shared sense of purpose. It also needs a set of shared activities that rest upon a broader sense of possibilities of shared human experience. Something in common needs to exist for community to flourish. This something in common is what we often call tradition. Diversity cuts in the other direction. Diversity divides, it fragments, it attacks tradition, it will often undermine a sense of common purpose.

We may wish to believe, as I heard it said at a recent conference on "Making Diversity Work," that the more diversity you have, the fewer problems you have. But on campuses where hate crimes have escalated, where student ethnic groups have begun to attack each other, where arguments over the traditional canon have made enemies of colleagues, it is not convincing. We cannot fall into the trap of arguing that diversity in and of itself is good and ignore the importance of commonality, coherence, unity, connectedness, and community.

Those of us who support cultural diversity will often argue for a multicultural community without acknowledging that the very term may be an oxymoron; "many cultures" is likely to mean many communities, and a rhetorical conjunction of the terms will not bring about a shared sense of purpose. Our arguments tend to imply, even if we do not explicitly state, that every culture has its own validity; when we argue for cultural pluralism it comes dangerously close to cultural relativism. Then the Allan Blooms of the world nail us to the wall. We argue that tradition and meaning must be deconstructed into many traditions and many meanings, but neglect to reconstruct anything in their place. So we open students' minds without giving them something to close on.

We will often argue, correctly, for the inclusion of the new scholarship in women's studies, ethnic studies, and international studies, but our rhetoric sometimes echoes the exclusionary tones of those whom we oppose. So we label our adversaries as Eurocentric, reactionary, or backward looking, and by creating these steroetypes we do unto them as they have done unto us—we don't need to deal with their arguments because they don't belong to the right group.

When we complain about the exclusion of our fields of study and the exclusion of our groups from positions of influence, we are inclined to make it an issue of power, which in some respects it certainly is. But our complaints about power conflict with concerns about community, so inadvertently we find ourselves again on the wrong side of the argument, even though our concerns are right. Challenging the power of those in power does not contribute to a sense of community.

What then are the right sides of the community argument that our adversaries make so wrongly? The academic conservatives argue that our colleges and universities should be concerned primarily with truth rather than power, understanding rather than political advocacy. This indeed comes closer to the fundamental reason for being of our institutions than do our arguments about political competition. This is not to say that one can address the challenges of diversity without concern for academic politics, but there needs to be a larger community context for these politics to proceed in a healthy manner and it is unwise to ignore that context in the name of self-interested politics. For an academic community, it is more appropriate to build a sense of shared purpose around the pursuit of truth than around the pursuit of politics.

Academic conservatives are also on the right side of the argument when they associate truth with universalism rather than relativism. The ultimate test of truth is that it applies to everything everywhere anytime, which is to say that it is universal. For the theoretical physicists, the inconsistencies between relativity theory and quantum theory offend their sense of truth and so they seek a unified field theory to reconcile them. While the knowledge explosion and academic specialization have shattered any sense of the comprehensive unity of knowledge of a kind sought by medieval theologians, our quest for more limited truths is still driven by our impulse to find order, explanation, coherence, unity, and ultimately some proximate universalism.

The problem with relativism is that it leads all too easily to separatism. If each group has its own truth, and each group's truth is equally valid, and there are no wider standards to deal with the differences, you will then have difficulties in creating a sense of community. At UCLA, where every student ethnic group has its own newspaper advocating its own separate cause, some of these difficulties have surfaced.

The inherent pluralism of American society, bred by the multiple immigrant origins of its people, has avoided separatist anarchy through a larger universalist vision of human rights applying to all people regardless of religion or racial origin. This vision was established in the Declaration of Independence and institutionalized in the Bill of Rights.

Allan Bloom is on the right side of the argument when he suggests that Western civilization has set the standard with its insistence that cultural claims be universal, applying to all civilized human beings and not just to those in a particular time and place. But he and other academic conservatives argue this case wrongly when they presume that their view of the Western tradition is equivalent to universalism. To make the claim is not the same as to establish its validity, which is where the conservative's argument breaks down. When Bloom rejects the relativism and separatism of some extreme forms of women's studies and ethnic culture studies, he is right; when he refuses to test seriously the universalist claims of his view of the Western tradition against the findings of the new scholarship in women's and ethnic studies, he abandons his own criteria for truth.

The hypocrisy of this approach is similar to the hypocrisy that has occurred in the history of this nation when the principles of equal opportunity enunciated in the Declaration of Independence and the Bill of Rights are extended to some groups but not to others, even though their application is claimed to be universal. To make universalist claims and fail to be inclusive of subcultures and other cultures is truly to stand on a foothill, thinking it's the highest mountain, believing you can see everything everywhere.

The feminist philosopher Elizabeth Minnich neatly punctures the universalist claims of conventional wisdom in the social sciences when she points out that what is defined as normal for human beings is said to be similar to what is defined as normal for males, while what is called abnormal for human beings is similar to what is called abnormal for females. The false equation between male behavior and all human behavior is unmasked. Carol Gilligan makes the same case when she shows that moral development theory from Freud to Kohlberg is essentially male moral development theory—theory that does not adequately account for or explain female behavior with respect to moral response. The Gilligan and Minnich challenges are based on the failure of earlier theories to be inclusive of the experience of women; they assume that truth should be universal and not relative. It must describe the huge mountain of experience, not just its separate foothills.

Academic conservatives are on the right side of the argument when they stress the importance of maintaining high and consistent standards of quality as our student population becomes increasingly diverse in its cultural backgrounds. But as in the case of their emphasis on truth, their argument is defective when they concern themselves only with standards in the abstract and not with how those standards are applied and whether their application is truly universal and therefore equitable. To advocate consistent admissions standards is entirely appropriate; to assume that SAT scores and high school grade point averages are a fair and equitable measure for all students, including those with different cultural backgrounds, is inappropriate.

Standards, like truth, should be inclusive rather than exclusive. Wise advocates of cultural diversity like John Slaughter recognize the importance of associating diversity with quality rather than pitting diversity against standards of excellence. Diversity, says Slaughter, is the point at which excellence and equity intersect.

Capturing Community for Diversity: Finding the Highest or the Lowest Common Denominator?

In setting out to capture the flag of community for the cause of diversity, it is important to recognize that at many, if not most, institutions of higher education the traditional sense of community no longer exists. Even before the issue of cultural diversity became the topic of the day, for at least a quarter of a century colleges and universities were breaking up into subcultures that had nothing to with gender, race, or ethnicity—indeed, breaking away from collegiality that had shaped the mythic ideal of the academic community. The forces that caused this erosion of the academic community include the increasing professionalization of the faculty, the specialization of academic research and graduate training, and the bureaucratization of administrative functions. The domination of the curriculum by professionalized and increasingly autonomous departments led to the fragmentation of the curriculum, which in turn led to a call for coherence in the form of the general education movement.

Indeed, the hallmark of American higher education has been its diversity—intellectual, social, and institutional—as the country reached for broader, more democratic access to our colleges and universities. Given this history of increasing, pervasive diversity, it is reasonable to ask, Why is it that the additional diversity, represented primarily by women and ethnic groups, is now so troubling and vexatious to the academic community?

Perhaps it is because this new cultural diversity more directly challenges a traditional culture of academe, a culture shaped by Anglo-European influences. African-American studies, women's studies, Hispanic-American studies, and Asian-American studies have raised serious questions about the inclusiveness of that Anglo-European tradition in ways that did not occur when higher education admitted war veterans after World War II or when federal and state financial aid opened university doors to families with limited financial means. While earlier new groups to higher education willingly accepted assimilation on the traditional academic culture's terms, the new groups have refused to do so. Instead, they have argued for the right to contribute to the redefining of that tradition on the terms of their own insights and arguments about their own experience.

If our institutions already have an eroded sense of community and now confront a more contentious and fundamentally challenging diversity, what hope can we have that the flag of community can be captured by the cause of cultural diversity? No one said that the climb up the mountain would be easy. But then we should remember that necessity often inspires invention. Perhaps if we understood the sheer necessity of the effort, we'd find unexpected resources for creative responses to this challenge. Let me suggest three ways in which we might regard this situation as an opportunity and not just as an overwhelming problem.

First, we should regard the challenge of cultural diversity as a crisis confronting our institutions in their entirety. It is a crisis of such urgency and complexity as to require the cooperative efforts of all major parties within our institutions. No institution can effectively address these issues without the involvement of faculty, students, administration, and staff. The faculty must take the lead in clarifying the intellectual issues, in reshaping the curriculum, and in devising new pedagogies; no academic department is without responsibility or opportunity in this area. Students must help to reshape the social climate so that minority students do not feel devalued and segregated. Administrators must keep the issue on the university agenda, order priorities accordingly, and provide needed resources. Student life offices, athletic departments, admissions and financial aid, academic support units, cultural programming offices—all must be involved in addressing the new cultural diversity. Staff have their own special role in conveying the style and attitude of the institution as they serve students.

There are many problems confronting universities that can be resolved by one office or another, one sector of the university or another. But cultural diversity is not that kind of problem. Because it is a community-wide problem, it must summon the coordinated efforts of *all* sectors of the community. In the process of doing so, it may just serve to restore some sense of common purpose, something of the lost community still envied by our collegial instincts. The climb up the mountain will be more successful if it is a community effort. The need to climb together can generate a community focus not present without the challenge of the climb.

Second, we should not think of cultural diversity as an end or good in itself. We should think of cultural diversity as a necessary means to a larger purpose. Increased cultural diversity will happen; it is written in the demographics. Of course we must insist that access to all levels of our institutions be fair and equitable so that the diversity is pervasive and not segregated. But as many campuses are now learning, increased access creates new problems, not the least of which is our inability to unite around larger goals. Our own rhetoric may contribute to that inability when we talk about "celebrating diversity" or "affirming differences."

What we need is a way of talking about diversity within the context of those things human beings share in common. We need to pursue an understanding of diversity within the imperatives of universality. With such a perspective, the end and objective of confronting diversity on our campuses is a higher and more integrated community. It is not a multicultural community that we seek; it is an *intercultural* community, where different groups engage each other with united purpose. We seek not a community of the lowest common denominator, where differences are tolerated and sometimes sullenly accepted, but a community of the highest common denominator, where difference is an enriching resource that leads us to a fuller understanding of what is universally true.

We need to create an academic community where people with different cultural backgrounds view each other as having similar needs, similar aspirations, and similar problems but with different ways of manifesting them. In this kind of community, different clothes, different accents, different music, different habits, different skin color, and different self-presentation are viewed with interest and curiosity rather than hostility and suspicion. In such a community, cultural differences are regarded not as a dehumanizing stereotype but as an intriguing variation that we seek to understand. In so doing we enlarge both our understanding and our humanity.

Such a community would rest upon the insight of the artist who seeks the expression of the universal in the particular. It is the insight revealed by Toni Morrison in *Beloved,* when we understand the humanity of the slave through her writing, even though we are not black nor have been enslaved. It is the insight we gain from Manuel Puig in *Kiss of the Spider Woman,* when we understand the humanity of homosexuals, even though we have no such experience. It is the insight we learn from Maxine Hong Kingston in *Woman Warrior,* when we understand the humanity of women struggling for respect in a male-dominated society and of immigrant families torn across two cultures.

But communities require more than shared, high-minded objectives. They also require shared daily activity. It is here that we find our third opportunity. In seeking to create a new academic community out of cultural diversity, we should turn to the activities that are most widely shared and address the cultural diversity issues within them. Because it is the faculty that sets the intellectual tone for a university, we should focus on their primary shared activity: teaching. It is in the classroom that faculty and students engage each other, where teaching and learning, the primary functions of the university, converge.

We need fresh ways to present our subject matter so that the conceptual pitfalls around cultural diversity do not become embedded in the way students learn. Social science courses that purport to describe human behavior in general should be critically examined to see if they describe behavior only in a particular culture. Studies of culture should not take place in isolation or in separation, but in either a comparative context or in relationship to other contemporaneous cultures. We need more courses in comparative religion, comparative history, comparative literature, comparative politics, and comparative psychology. In such courses the tests of difference and commonality should be jointly applied so that students gain a vision of the variation of common humanity. The spirit that infused Joseph Campbell's approach to mythology should underlie our study of humanities and social sciences.

We need fresh ways to understand how the way we teach may adversely affect the way students from different cultural backgrounds learn. We should be mindful of Uri Triesman's discovery that the performance of African-American students in math classes at UC-Berkeley was more a result of how they were taught than the level of their intellectual ability. If students feel socially alienated, their learning is impaired.

The teaching that we do is like giving students the techniques for climbing the proverbial mountain of truth. In familiar terrain, students will be able to climb alone; in unfamiliar terrain, the security of the group is important if not essential. Both in climbing and teaching about climbing, we should have the appropriate humility that our condition requires. We should no longer confuse our foothills with the mountain. We should know that the climb is difficult and still ahead of us. And we should know that there may be many paths that lead to the same mountaintop, and we should not confuse the paths for the place to which they lead us.

A Conclusion in Five Epigrams

Let me conclude with five epigrams that summarize my observations. First, diversity without community becomes anarchy. Second, community without diversity becomes fantasy, if not anachronism. Third, community with diversity is an act of creation rather than an act of tradition; perhaps it is an act of recreating tradition. It is more an act of morality than an act of politics. Fourth, mountain climbing takes great individual effort but is fundamentally a team sport. Fifth, it is up to us to finish our story—not as a fairy tale, but as an allegory.

Frank F. Wong is vice president for academic affairs at the University of Redlands.

6 The Study of Ethnic Minority Families: Implications for Practitioners and Policymakers

Peggye Dilworth-Anderson and Harriette Pipes McAdoo[*]

An overview of some major research issues about ethnic minority families is provided. The discussion focuses on conceptual, theoretical, and methodological concerns in the study of ethnic minority families. These concerns are discussed in relation to their influence on developing and implementing interventions for ethnic minority families. The information provided can help both researchers and practitioners.

In many ways the study of the family is very personal regardless of the fact that most researchers believe they approach the subject with great objectivity. Researchers' conceptual and theoretical perspectives are influenced by their personal life history, family of origin, value orientation, and group identification within the culture. In the discussion on paradigms for the sociology of knowledge Merton (1968) states that the existential basis of thinking which provides the context for the production of knowledge, is influenced by one's social and cultural characteristics. Therefore, one's social position, class, generation, and occupation as well as values, ethos, climate of opinion, and type of culture can affect the production of knowledge. Butler (1987) asserts that researchers bring with them the baggage of a group experience, including cultural, social, and historical variables. They think as their group thinks, using certain words that have meaning for their group. Such baggage has an impact on the avenues of approach to the surrounding world of the creators of knowledge.

Adams (1985) suggests that depending on the value system of the researcher, practitioner, or family it is possible that they will not agree on what is considered a problem or a solution. Therefore, whether a phenomenon is viewed as a problem or a solution may not be an objective reality at all but may be determined by the observer's values. Fine, Schwebel, and James-Myers (1987) state that scientific activity, and how it is perceived by society, depends on the values which are currently manifested by scientists and society. Therefore, the different conceptual frameworks and theoretical perspectives used to develop research questions and interpret information about families reflect not only the personal values of the researcher but the overriding cultural ones as well.

The purpose of this article is to discuss how conceptual approaches, theoretical perspectives, and methodological procedures used in the study of ethnic minority families influence interventions and policy decisions that address the needs of these families. A major focus is on how the values and attitudes of researchers serve as antecedents for developing and perpetuating particular conceptual and theoretical frameworks. These frameworks are discussed in regard to how they are used to create the knowledge base that both researchers and practitioners use.

Conceptual Approaches and Theoretical Perspectives

In a study of two groups of behavioral scientists, Krasner and Houts (1984) examine whether the value-laden view of science or the traditional value-free position influences basic assumptions in scientific research. The results of the study show that behavioral scientists basically

---

[*]Peggye Dilworth-Anderson is Professor of Child Development and Family Relations, School of Human Environmental Sciences, University of North Carolina at Greensboro, Greensboro, NC 27412. Harriette Pipes McAdoo is Professor of Social Work, School of Social Work, Howard University, Washington, DC 20059.

Key Words: ethnic minority families, family functioning, family relations, methodology, theoretical perspectives.

operate from a value-laden perspective. They also suggest that theoretical perspectives and major changes in scientific thinking reflect basic value assumptions of researchers rather than logical fact finding. In a discussion on the history of science, Kuhn (1970) writes about the value-laden nature of scientific inquiry. Ultimately, value-laden research compromises and threatens the conceptual and theoretical integrity of a science or discipline.

Allen (1978), in discussing applicable theories of black family life, describes the limitations of particular conceptual frameworks and theoretical perspectives, because they fail to include the unique and distinct characteristics of black people. Allen asserts that conceptual approaches such as structural-functionalism do not focus on the dynamic, change-oriented perspective of black family life. Using this approach, ethnic minority families are viewed as incapable of mobilizing energies and resources within their own infrastructure to create and maintain family strengths. These types of approaches promote a comparison of the socioeconomic conditions between black and white families to determine how well they function. Thus, the value systems of researchers reflect those in the general society which view one's income, occupational, and educational levels as primary determinants of family functioning. When black families deviate from acceptable norms established by different socioeconomic levels in white families, then the black families are viewed as deviant or pathological. Researchers pay little or no attention to those characteristics of the black family that are positive or adaptive, regardless of socioeconomic status. Characteristics of the black family that more closely define it are not viewed as researchable if they cannot be compared to similar ones in white families. As Fine et al. (1987) state, if researchers consider factors other than socioeconomic status (i.e., support, caring, loyalty) to be important indices of the quality of family life, then researchers must acknowledge that there may be a whole host of other, more valid measures of family stability among blacks.

Wilson (1986) suggests that when basic assumptions about black people in general were challenged in American society's sociopolitical arena in the 1960s and 1970s (as reflected by replacing the term Negro with black) researchers began to critically rethink how to study the black family. As a result, conceptual frameworks and theoretical perspectives that encouraged examining and interpreting dysfunctional, pathological, or maladaptive aspects about the black family were replaced with approaches that can lead to understanding both positive and negative aspects of family relations. Therefore, the interactional-situational, cultural variant, and developmental (life-course) approaches are more often being employed by researchers. The interactional-situational approach allows researchers to focus on interpersonal relationships and socialization patterns within the family (Allen, 1978). The family is thus seen as capable of influencing its members as opposed to only functioning according to structural factors in the society as the structural-functionalist approach emphasizes. The cultural variant perspective allows for studying the black family as a distinctive cultural form with an African heritage that has shaped the value and belief systems within the family (Nobles, 1978). The developmental (life-course) perspective focuses on examining the family according to normal or abnormal transitions. Therefore, the sequencing of family life can be studied according to a group's historical, cultural, and social position in the society (Eider, 1984). As Allen (1978) suggests this approach allows the researcher to view the black family structure and process against the critical sociohistorical backdrops of slavery, emancipation, and urbanization.

Methodology and Ethnic Minority Families

Inappropriate or weak conceptual and theoretical frameworks can lead to methodological problems when conducting research on ethnic minority families. Although numerous problems exist, three are discussed: sample selection, definition of concepts, and unit of analysis. These problems, are discussed because they are seen as having the greatest impact on the knowledge base used by practitioners to provide interventions to ethnic minority families. In reviewing the literature, the most frequently recurring problem is that of *sample selection*. Jackson (1985) asserts that the majority of empirical studies on the black family have been based upon haphazardly selected, conveniently available samples of blacks and their families. These types of samples create problems with external validity which limit generalizing the findings to the larger population. Peters (1981) asserts that many studies do not specify the race or culture of samples, thus ignoring culture specific influences. When more than one race is included, minorities are often described as "others," especially if they are not black. Further, many studies on minority families fail to include those that are nonproblematic and middle class. Overall, the family literature is replete with inadequate and biased samples of ethnic minority families.

In regard to the problem of *definition of concepts*, Wilson (1986), in his analytical discussion on the black extended family, states that defining the family exclusively as a nuclear unit limits understanding of black family life. (This also applies to other ethnic minority families where the extended kin system defines family relations, particularly among Hispanics and Native Americans.) Wilson further asserts that the normative belief about the nuclear family is often inconsistent with everyday family functioning because other family forms exist and members function well within them. Therefore, when minority families do not conform to the traditional nuclear family unit, such as found in single-parent, multigenerational, kin/fictive-kin households, researchers often exclude these various family structures from studies assessing competence or positive family functioning. Peters (1981) suggests that when minority families are studied, researchers are not interested in process or how various influences affect them, but the central concern is intervention. Becavar and Becavar (1988) assert that we need to examine the variety of family forms which may be supportive of normal growth and development for both adults and children in all families.

As equally important as the other problems is the one that addresses the *unit of analysis* researchers use to analyze black family life. Mitchell and Register (1984) and Staples and Mirande (1980) have suggested that once the black family is defined according to how it empirically functions and not from a theoretical notion of how it should function, then researchers are more likely to employ the appropriate unit of analysis. Given that family relations among blacks and other ethnic minority families primarily operate within an extended kin context, the unit of analysis should focus on the extended kin network. Therefore intergenerational relations, the sharing of multigenerational households, consanquineal relations, and the kin network need to be incorporated in conceptual and theoretical approaches. The unit of analysis would then reflect the process and context of family functioning. Thus, the focus of analysis would continue to use the nuclear unit when appropriate, but more importantly, the extended kin system would be seen as another way to analyze and interpret family relations.

Research evidence does show that major characteristics of family relations are missed when the individual, as opposed to a dyadic or group unit of analysis, is used to explain any family structure that has a high level of intergenerational relations and a viable extended kin network (Hagestad & Neugarten, 1985; Thompson & Walker, 1982). If, however, researchers continue to focus on the nuclear family unit as the context in which optimal family functioning occurs, then extended kin systems may be overlooked as a unit to assess family functioning.

Implications for Practice and Policy

The approaches researchers use to study ethnic minority families influence the interventions implemented by practitioners and the knowledge base developed by policy makers to address family needs. If the pathology or deficit approach to understanding the black family is accepted, then practitioners and policymakers would most likely support developing and providing programs that address changing these families to fit the criteria of success used by white families. Culturally defined strengths indicative of ethnic minority family life would not be addressed.

When information on these families is collected using the structural-functionalist approach, researchers create a knowledge base about them that focuses on how socioeconomic conditions and other major societal factors influence family functioning. The black family would be seen as quite mechanistic in its ability to survive in the American society. Little or no information using the structural-functionalist approach addresses the dynamic and adaptive characteristics of the black family that practitioners can use.

If more culturally sensitive approaches such as the interactional-situational, cultural variant, or developmental are used, then practitioners and policymakers would have available information that allowed them to address dynamic relations between individuals and within the family system as a whole. Further, sociohistorical and cultural characteristics would also be used as well as how certain stages of the family life cycle may better represent how and why families function a certain way. Contextual and process factors would be considered as a part of providing interventions.

Conclusions

Practitioners and policymakers are faced with the challenge of addressing "real" issues and needs. However, if researchers continue to create a knowledge base that is not culturally sensitive at all levels of the research process, inappropriate policies and interventions may be designed for ethnic minority families based on information researchers provide.

When researchers design studies with both racial and cultural sensitivity, practitioners are encouraged to do the same in addressing the needs of those they serve. If, for example, black children and teenagers are not seen as deviations from normal children, interventions can be designed to incorporate their unique racial and cultural background. Further, the nuclear family will not be viewed as the structure in which families function best. Instead, when researchers examine the extended kin system which basically defines ethnic minority families, then practitioners can better utilize a family system that is working. Interventions will be designed to address a kin system, and not nuclear units.

REFERENCES

Adams, B. (1985). The family: Problems and solutions. *Journal of Marriage and the Family*, 47, 525-529.

Allen, W. (1978). The search for applicable theories of black family life. *Journal of Marriage and the Family*, 40, 117-131.

Becavar, D. S., & Becavar, R. J. (1988). *Family therapy: A systematic integration*. Boston, MA: Allyn and Bacon, Inc.

Butler, J. S. (1984). Social research and scholarly interpretation. *Society*, 24(2), 13-18.

Elder, G. (1984). Families, kin, and the life course: A sociological perspective. In R. D. Parke (Ed.), *Advances in child development research: The family* (pp. 80-135). Chicago, IL: University of Chicago Press.

Fine, M., Schwebel, A., & James-Myers, L. (1987). Family stability in black families: Values underlying three different perspectives. *Journal of Comparative Family Studies*, 18, 1-23.

Hagestad, G. O., & Neugarten, B. L. (1985). Age and the life course. In R. H. Binstock & E. Shanas (Eds.), *Handbook of aging and the social sciences* (2nd ed., pp. 35-61). New York: Van Nostrand Reinholt Company.

Jackson, J. (1985). *Methodological considerations in the study of the black family*. Paper presented at a conference, The black family: Contemporary issues and concerns, Pennsylvania State University.

Krasner, L., & Houts, A. (1984). A study of the value systems of behavioral scientists. *American Psychologist*, 39, 840-850.

Kuhn, T. (1970). *The structure of scientific revolutions*. (2nd ed.). Chicago, IL: University of Chicago Press.

Merton, R. K. (1968). *Social theory and social structure*. New York: The Free Press.

Mitchell, J., & Register, J. (1984). An exploration of family interaction with the elderly by race, socioeconomic status and residence. *The Gerontologist*, 24, 48-54.

Nobles, W. (1978). Toward an empirical and theoretical framework for defining black families. *Journal of Marriage and the Family*, 40, 679-688.

Peters, M. (1981). Parenting in black families with young children: A historical perspective. In H. McAdoo (Ed.), *Black families* (2nd ed., pp. 221-224). Newbury Park, CA: Sage Publications.

Staples, R., & Mirande, A. (1980). Racial and cultural variations among American families: A decennial review of the literature on minority families. *Journal of Marriage and the Family*, 42, 157-173.

Thompson, L., & Walker, A. (1982). The dyad as the unit of analysis: Conceptual and methodological issues. *Journal of Marriage and the Family*, 44, 889-900.

Wilson, M. N. (1986). The black extended family: An analytical consideration. *Developmental Psychology*, 22, 246-256.

Chapter 2 Multicultural Vignettes: Variations on a Theme

> But "glory" doesn't mean 'a nice knock-down argument' Alice objected.
> When I use the word, Humpty Dumpty said—it means just what I choose it to mean—neither more or less (Carroll 1946, 94).

While a broad, macro-perspective is needed as a base to understand others, a closer micro-inspection of personal perceptions with their assigned meanings permit knowledge otherwise unobtainable. Kaleidoscopic vignettes in Chapter 2 offer an opportunity to look at individuals and groups where they live—from the inside out. Why do we believe cultural diversity issues can best be understood when viewed from within the family? We borrow from the words of Mead and Heyman in their classic, *Family,* to answer this question.

> Through the family we have a common heritage. This heritage provides us with a common language that survives and transcends all the differences in linguistic form, social organization, religious belief, and political ideology that divide man. And as men must irrevocably perish or survive together, the task of each family is also the task of all humanity. This is to cherish the living, remember those who have gone before, and prepare for those who are not yet born (1965, 11).

After a brief discussion of the Hmong people and their culture, Thao provides an intriguing description of Hmong marriage customs including the meaning of marriage, mate selection, and establishing the validity of a marriage. The grounds for and defenses against divorce along with the rights of married women in the Hmong society are analyzed. The difficulties confronting the Hmong as they attempt to cope with unfamiliar and, to them, strange state laws regarding marriage, divorce, and the rights of married women are discussed.

Many persons may be unaware that Native American tribal governmental officials actually function as representatives of domestic-dependent nations within the United States. O'Brien provides a glimpse into the workings of all levels of tribal government including the legislative, judicial, and social service provider roles. Attempts by tribes to maintain culture and independence while at the same time trying to interface with the dominant American culture provide constant threats to traditional tribal philosophies and customs.

While culture may make some difference in the degree of family cohesion and adaptability, such variations reside within the range of well-functioning and resilient families. Vega et al. found that both low-income Mexican-American and middle-income Anglo families exhibited healthy family functioning during the life stage of rearing adolescent children. In fact, when high-acculturation Mexican-American parents were compared with Anglos, their perceptions of family cohesion and adaptability were practically indistinguishable.

Contrary to popular misconceptions and stereotypes about sexual attitudes of blacks, Timberlake and Carpenter concluded from their research that middle-class black adults hold moderate and well-informed views of sexuality. Their findings challenge the view that sexual knowledge leads to increased sexual activity. In fact, three-fourths of their sample believed that parent-child discussions about sexuality should start before the child begins first grade. Finally, the educational level was found to be more important in determining differences and similarities in sexual attitudes than sex, age, or marital status.

Historically, family social scientists have believed that ethnically-mixed heritage persons who were products of an intermarriage tended to adopt a single ethnic identity. However, in a study of mixed-heritage Japanese-American and Hispanic college students, Stephan and Stephan found that three-fourths of the part-Japanese and almost one-half of the part-Hispanic students listed a multiple ethnic identity rather than a single ethnic identity. The authors suggest that traditional ethnic boundaries are being eroded by intermarriage.

Lastly, few social demographers have attempted to explain black-white differences in childlessness as a by-product of education, age at marriage, and economic opportunities. Boyd challenges unfounded assumptions with his findings that when high-status black couples find their progress toward assimilation into the dominant social institutions impeded, they often choose voluntary childlessness. Using U.S. Census data, he found that among college-educated, high-status couples, blacks delay marriage longer and report higher rates of voluntary childlessness than comparable white couples.

7 Hmong Customs on Marriage, Divorce and the Rights of Married Women

T. Christopher Thao

In this paper, I offer to do a comparative study of Minnesota laws and of Hmong customs on marriage, divorce, and the rights of married women. When I refer to the Hmong here, I am talking about the Hmong of Laos whom I know best although the introduction to the Hmong in the following passages is broader in scope.

This paper will be divided into two parts. The first part will deal with the basic rules governing each area of study, e.g. Hmong marriage in its own perspective as I understand it. The second part will be an analytical discussion of the pros and cons of the two, hoping to give the readers an insight into Hmong customs in the areas of study.

Hmong family is an extended family. The word "family" is used to connote the inclusivity of those that are referred to. For example, all Hmong are one family; all members of the Thao and Kue clans are a family. However, when the word "family" is used in connection with kinship structure, it would include all persons sprung from a traceable ancestor and who constitute a lineage.

The word "family" as used in the context of this paper is different from how it is defined above. I will use it to include only individuals who are two generations apart or less. For example, my family members are descendants of my grandparents, including both males and females. I explicitly exclude other categories of kinship to make it easier to understand.

Introduction to the Hmong

The Hmong are a people whose origin is not known, but they are found to live in Southern China, North Vietnam, Laos, and Thailand. Most Hmong live in Southern China with a population of about five million. Hmong in Indochina originally emigrated from Southern China and after 1975 again emigrated from Laos, in the thousands, to the United States and other western countries.

Few Americans knew about the Hmong before 1975 when Hmong came to seek refuge in American cities. More than sixty thousand Hmong of Laos have settled in California, Minnesota, Wisconsin, and other states within the union.

Hmong are as confused as Americans as to why they are here in the United States. They knew that Americans were their friends during the Indochina war; they thought that Americans would help them to win and that they were winning, until Americans began to disappear from Laos. American withdrawal from Indochina took Hmong by surprise and left them unprepared, without adequate warning. After the Americans were gone, Hmong had two choices: to be re-educated by the Communists or to be re-educated by their American ally.

Generally, Hmong have not been exposed to modernization because they have lived far removed from educational centers. Few Hmong were afforded the benefit of higher education. Thus, some people referred to them as "ancient people". Perhaps, Hmong are not "ancient", but they are the disadvantaged who have not had an equal opportunity.

Hmong culture

In Hmong culture, the basic structure is what anthropologists refer to as the "clan", which is patrilineal in character. It is informal. Members of the clan include all individuals who carry the same clan name, whether born or married into it. Each member is presumed to be related to the other members and they refer to one another as brothers. The clan name is used in the same manner as a surname but really it is an identity.

A clan usually is composed of more than one lineage, which may be divided into several sub-lineages or groups. The lineage, as used here, refers to a group of people who share a common ancestor. A sub-lineage is a sub-group of the lineage which is further subdivided into families.

A clan leader is not traditionally elected into office. He is designated representative of the clan at the time and place where such a representative is requested. His role is assumed and his authority is based customarily by implied consent which may be revoked by noncompliance of clan members. As one

From T. Christopher Thao, "Hmong Customs on Marriage, Divorce and the Rights of Married Women." In *The Hmong World*, ed. Brenda Johns and David Strecker. New Haven, CT: Yale Center for International and Area Studies Copyright © 1986 by Yale Southeast Asia Studies. Reprinted by permission.

can imagine, the clan leader risks his personal reputation. Thus, the tasks of a clan leader are temporary in nature.

A clan leader could very well be a lineal leader, the leader of a lineage of which he is a member. This lineal leader may be elected into office, but usually is appointed by a retiring leader. His authority by far is more substantial and surpasses that of the clan leader. Because he has a direct tie to the members of the lineage, he is respected by the lineal members. His actions are binding on the members of his lineage during his tenure in office.

Relationship between clans follows the doctrine of laissez-faire, incorporating a practice similar to the doctrine of good faith and credit as found among the states in the United States. When a problem is exclusively internal within a clan, other clans could not get involved, except upon request, but would recognize the actions of that clan as valid and final. Each clan enjoys complete autonomy with regard to its internal matters. Problems between clans are resolved by mutual agreement with recommendations from other clan leaders, who may be called on as impartial parties.

The strength of a relationship between any two clans is measured by intermarriage, propinquity, and good faith. Because marriage is not only a bond between the two individuals but also between the two clans, it naturally becomes a factor in measuring the strength of their relationship. Propinquity is very important in mate selection as well as in maintaining trust between the two clans. The relationship is a two-way street and both clans are to exert their best effort to maintain it. Good words must go hand in hand with good deeds.

Resolving disputes

As mentioned above, each clan has complete autonomy with regard to its internal matters. There are exceptions, however. Hmong are also receptive to other means of resolving their disputes. For example, a marriage dissolution hearing may be held before the leader of another clan if one of the parties so decides. Hmong also have had experiences with the Lao Royal Government and other peoples in the past and therefore are willing to accept changes.

While Hmong were in Laos, they were practically autonomous in civil matters and sometimes in criminal matters too. The government peacefully allowed Hmong to retain their traditions, customs, and practices. During the 1960s and early 1970s, Hmong, under the leadership of former General Vang Pao, created two courts in the city of Long Cheng. These two courts had jurisdiction over civil and criminal matters which came before them. Should the problem not be resolved, the parties could appeal to General Vang Pao.

Hmong could also choose to bring suit in the judicial system which was established and run by the Lao Royal Government. However, a case brought before the government courts became subject to the law of the land and Hmong customs would not be taken into consideration. Hence, Hmong often chose to resolve their disputes among themselves.

Part One
I. HMONG CUSTOMS ON MARRIAGE

A. HMONG MARRIAGE

Marriage, by Hmong standards, is a way of life. One is expected to get married some day during one's youth and to raise a family of one's own. Heaven, according to the Hmong, created man and woman to love, to care for, to share, and to help one another. Hmong believe that this is the purpose for which man and woman were created, not to be alone or to be single, but to be together in unity. That unity is marriage.

The bond of marriage can be created only between a man and a woman. Marriage between persons of the same sex is not only impermissible but impossible, because marriage should produce offspring. Hmong belief in marriage can be traced back to a legend called "Poj Cuag Ob Nus Muag" in which it was necessary for a brother to wed his sister in order for human reproduction to continue. See Vang, "Hmong Marriage Customs: A Current Assessment", in *The Hmong in the West: Observations and Reports*, Downing and Olney, eds., pp. 29-47, published by the Center for Urban and Regional Affairs, University of Minnesota, 1982.

There are several ways in which marriage can take place in Hmong culture. The preferred way is through an informal marriage proposal by the man to the woman, accompanied by a gift. The acceptance of the gift by the woman signifies the voluntariness of the parties and serves the same purpose as an engagement ring.

Once the agreement is secured, the man would ask his parents for permission to marry the girl or woman. If his parents consent to the marriage, they will find two able mediators or go-betweens who will go to the girl's parents with a formal marriage proposal. Upon the mediators' arrival at the girl's parents' residence, they will announce their mission and request permission to enter the home. The girl's parents will also find two able mediators who would come to the negotiation table with the other mediators. (Sometimes, one mediator on each side is permissible.)

The formal marriage proposal, although presented orally, consists of several important terms. One of those terms is the promise to love the girl, evidenced by the willingness to pay a bride price. One deals with the possible breach of that promise and its consequences. Another would be about dissolution remedies. If there is any objection to the terms of the proposal, negotiation will continue until both parties reach mutually agreeable terms. If no objection is made, the proposal will become a binding contract between the two parties, the young man and his family on one side and the girl and her family on the other, witnessed by the mediators themselves.

Sometimes, the contract is written and made available to the parties. The signatures of the parties and of the witnesses usually are affixed on the document itself. (The young man and woman may or may not sign the contract because in Hmong culture signatures of their parents would be sufficient to bind both of them.) A feast will commemorate the successful negotiation of the marriage. Friends, relatives and people in the community would be invited.

A less preferred way is elopement, which usually is the result of a situation in which the young man and woman are in love, but their parents do not consent to their marriage. Sometimes the young man's family may seek elopement in order to enjoy an advantage in the marriage negotiation which will follow. This is especially true when the girl's family is known to be very aggressive and demanding in marriage negotiation. The girl may also seek elopement in order to get out of an unwanted engagement or a similar plight.

Elopement poses special problems because literally the marriage takes place in secrecy. The situation looks like a cohabitation between the man and the woman. Since Hmong cannot imagine cohabitation, the situation must resolve itself properly into a marriage. Therefore, the man is trusted in good faith to formally propose a marriage agreement and to set a date for a wedding. Go-betweens are still required to mediate any differences between the parties, to assure the bride's parents that the girl will be loved, and to witness the commencement of the marriage in accordance with custom.

Two other ways are engagement and exclusive negotiation. Engagement is a process in which the parents of the young man and woman negotiated the terms of the marriage before an actual marriage negotiation; however, it is subject to the final decision of the young man and woman. It is like a matching process except that it would foreclose any other negotiation between the girl's parents and a prospective groom. This is why some girls seek elopement.

Exclusive negotiation is an actual marriage negotiation except that the young man and woman do not have any say or that either or both the young man and woman would be pressured into accepting the marriage. It is sometimes referred to as a "given for marriage" which has prompted many people to say that the girl is in fact sold. Hmong do realize that this form of marriage is very unfair and for most Hmong it has become obsolete.

Another form of marriage is that of a man marrying his older brother's widow. Of course, both parties must consent to the marriage if it is to take place. The purpose of this practice is to preserve the identity of the children born as issues of the marriage. Many Hmong marriages took place with this form of arrangement.

The bride price

The word "bride price" is a western term, and it is not literally accepted as such within the Hmong community. The term must be interpreted within the context of Hmong culture in order to appreciate its meanings. For the Hmong, the bride price represents two things: it is a symbolic recognition of the hardship of raising the girl, and it is a consideration for a promise to love.

The hardship of raising a child is very substantial. The amount of money received by the bride's family would never compensate the parents for their effort, but it is merely a symbol that recognizes the effort. Thinking that the money is a bride price can be unjustifiably misleading. As Hmong put it, "ib tog luj neeg thiab ib tog luj nyiag los yeej tsis tau", or "even if one end of the balance scale is filled with money and the other with the person, it still cannot be done."

Secondly, the bride price represents a valued consideration for a promise to love. Usually the girl's parents will ask the man's family during the marriage negotiation whether they would promise to love the girl. The man's family will answer in the affirmative. For a consideration thereof, the girl's family will request a monetary value in lieu of the oral promise. The money which has changed hands will be held much like a security, e.g., should the promise be breached by the man's family, the money will be forfeited. On the other hand, if the girl fails to properly play her role as a good wife, the money will be returned in full or in part.

Validity

The validity of a marriage is measured by community standards. If a relationship looked like a marriage, was negotiated as one, and was intended as such, it must be a marriage. Proof of such a marriage may be given by the marriage negotiators themselves or by the village chief verifying that a marriage exists between the parties in question.

There are some marriages in Minnesota that are valid under Hmong customs, but they are considered terminated under Minnesota law. Polygamous, underaged, and common law marriages are examples. Polygamy was legal in Laos and Thailand, so some Hmong men had more than one wife. Once in the United States, they had to keep one wife and divorce the others. However, such divorces are not final under Hmong custom.

Hmong do not prohibit underaged marriage. In fact, many Hmong were married when they were about fifteen and sixteen and some are still getting married at those ages, although the trend is changing.

Their customary marriage has carried over into the United States, and so most marriages among the Hmong in this country are still initiated in this manner before obtaining a legal marriage in accordance with American law. An interval may elapse between the time when a couple is married according to Hmong custom and the time when a legal marriage takes place. In the meanwhile, husband and wife are validly married to one another by Hmong standards, and yet they are not validly married at law.

Competency generally is not a problem in Hmong marriage. If a bride price is received and the mediators have exchanged their vows, customarily by drinking wine together and by exchanging some money, a marriage is valid. This was true even for a marriage created by an exclusive negotiation.

Generally speaking, a marriage may be invalid if it falls within a cultural prohibition such as a marriage between clan members, i.e., ancestor and descendant, brother and sister, uncle and niece, etc., and members of related clans. Members of related clans do not marry because both clans are related historically in some cultural context. An example of this would be members of the Thao and Kue clans (who generally accept the legendary theory that the Kues were members of the Thao clan but became disengaged with that clan due to some mysterious events). However, the problem is enforcement: no sanction can be imposed upon violators. A marriage in violation of such prohibitions would be likely to be condemned rather than to be declared invalid. Therefore the system depends largely on the willingness of the people to conform.

If the husband is missing but not yet considered dead, the wife must wait for a reasonable period of time before she can remarry, usually three to five years. On the other hand, if the husband is missing and presumed dead, the wife may remarry. There is a practice according to which the wife must set aside a sum of money that will enable the husband to marry another woman should he ever come back.

In sum, validity is not a problem because Hmong marriage always involves some form of negotiation. Elopement is the only form of marriage that poses special problems of validity when the girl's parents challenge it.

B. HMONG DIVORCE

Hmong believe in the family. The family remains the most respected institution today as it was years ago, and couples are encouraged to maintain good marital relationships. They put their family ahead of their individual needs. Hence, divorce is very uncommon. Divorced women are thought to possess certain moral defects, and young men and women are cautioned not to get involved with them. Parents become outraged when their children get divorced. Because fault is the basis of divorce, the parties would usually develop animosity toward one another, and the likelihood of reconciliation would become extremely remote. Although child visitation is not forbidden, the noncustodial parent would not see his or her children for quite a long time.

The process of a divorce begins with an oral communication from one of the couple directly to the leader of the lineage of which they are members or to a leader of another clan or lineage. The leader before whom the petitioner appeared would set a date for a hearing on the matter. The parties are given oral notice of the hearing (including members of their respective families, if the hearing is before a leader outside of the husband's clan). He would also call one or more competent individuals in his lineage or clan whom he trusts to give him good advice to come to the hearing.

At the hearing, the petitioner would be personally given an opportunity to present his or her side of the matter. S/he may call witnesses to testify. The respondent would also have an opportunity to do the same. If required, the parties can make additional arguments or present additional facts before the presiding leader makes his decision. The presiding leader may question the parties and their witnesses in order to obtain all relevant facts of the case. There is no rule governing the hearing besides the leader's common sense of how to conduct the hearing and the forum is generally open to the public.

After the leader has heard all arguments, he will receive advice from the people whom he has called, sometimes from the relatives of the parties as well. If there is hope of saving the marriage, he will advise the parties and give his reason(s). He will also explain the problems of the case to the parties, inform them of their rights, and narratively compare the case to other cases so that the parties know what to expect should a divorce go through. Generally, the parties are given a couple of days to think through and to consult with their respective relatives.

Finally, if the parties come back being assured that a divorce is best for both parties, the leader will allow them to be divorced. A proclamation is publicly made, and thereafter the marriage will be considered terminated.

Grounds and defenses

Hmong divorce is based on fault. The petitioner must show that there exist reasonable ground(s) for which the marital relationship should be terminated, and must be able to convince the presiding leader as such. Adultery, impotency, and insanity, as well as cruel and inhuman treatment, are some of the grounds for a divorce.

Adultery is thought to be the result of temptation and uncontrollable impulses. Generally, it is believed that a marital affair is a product of two individuals, although intentional affairs are not ruled out. Rationalization of this theory rests on the simple fact that God created men and women to be with one another. It is essential that men have feeling toward women in order that one may have a desire for the other. Such is the nature of mankind. The burden of proof is on the petitioner to show that adultery committed by the other spouse exceeded a tolerable threshold.

The threshold factors are not clear for a generalization to be made. However, it is conceivable that at least the totality of the circumstances and the accused spouse's fulfillment of his or her responsibilities in the family should be considered.

Impotency is difficult to prove, but if it is proved, a divorce is likely to be granted. It is reasonably expected that a marriage should produce offspring and if one of the spouses is impotent, the marriage would be childless. Thus, a divorce must be granted. Proved insanity would also result in a divorce. Common sense tells us that insanity of one spouse is an unreasonable burden to be placed on the shoulders of the other spouse.

Cruel and inhuman treatment is recognized as a basis for divorce. Again, Hmong seem to establish a threshold defense in this area. For example, there is spousal discipline, which is distinguishable from spousal abuse. Abuse, as used in the Hmong cultural context, is comparable to the concept of family violence as it is understood in contemporary American life in which bodily harm or fear of bodily harm must be shown. Spousal discipline, on the other hand, seems to fall within the doctrine of laissez-faire in which each clan would have complete autonomy over it.

If a Hmong wife comes to you with a bruise in the eye, she may have been abused. However, if the wife initiated the fight, e.g., she took a bat intending to hit her husband and then her husband punched her in the eye because of it, this would not be an abuse situation. Rather, it would be considered a disciplinary action . . . to teach her. Although he has not intended it as such, the practical effect of the black eye is, nevertheless, a lesson to her.

Long-term separation and desertion are considered deliberate and unjustifiable acts which are grounds for divorce. The spouse who left the home or initiated the separation forfeited his or her right to claim a valid marriage. Hmong have been able to utilize these two concepts in the United States to benefit both parties; however, these concepts remain unacceptable in their cultural settings.

C. THE RIGHTS OF MARRIED HMONG WOMEN

When a Hmong woman gets married, her husband takes her into his paternal home. Traditionally, an acceptance ceremony will be performed just outside of his parents' doorstep. The ceremony is both to publicize their acceptance of the new bride into the family and also to comply with the practice of ancestor worship. Another explanation of the ceremony is that it is an invitation of the bride's soul to enter the home. The ceremony is functionally the same as that of the groom carrying the bride over the threshold as Americans customarily do.

This transformation changes a married woman's status and imposes certain obligations on her. She now becomes subject to the rules within her husband's home which may be very different or even unfair to her personally. She cannot rightfully refuse, as other members of the family could not, to sublet their dwelling place to a relative of the family. Looking at the circumstances, she has limited independence and she should obey rules and cooperate with members of her new family.

When I say that a married woman in Hmong culture has limited independence, I mean that she has no superior rights over members of her new family. The rights of an individual family member are expressed in terms of the ability of the family to provide. For example, one has the right to expect an equally reasonable share of the family pie and no more. This means that a married woman must make an adjustment in her new home regardless of whether she was rich or poor before her marriage. Another limitation is the fact that she should cooperate with members of her new family. She should be willing to tender the fruit of her labor toward the welfare of the family. In sum, the welfare of the family is central and the rights and responsibilities of each family member are inseparable from those of the family.

Notwithstanding the general rule above, a married woman has a right under her marriage contract to be loved and she is entitled to a special relationship with her husband. It is fair to say that she cannot be ignored or neglected by members of her new family. That right is a privilege, in other words, and it cannot be waived under any circumstances.

Her liability is limited to the contributable value of her services. As she cannot rightfully demand a greater share of the family pie, liability cannot be wrongly imposed upon her beyond what she can reasonably bear. If she has completely tendered her earned income toward the family welfare, she will be exempted from further liabilities. If she has retained a portion of her income, she may be required to bear a reasonable amount of liability. A married woman with no income is not liable.

A married woman's rights to property, marital or non-marital, is similar to community property in the United States. *Black's Law Dictionary* 254 (5th ed. 1979). She has a joint interest with her husband, but she may not validly transfer her interest without her husband's consent. Property that each of the spouses owned before their marriage becomes marital property.

II. MARRIAGE, DIVORCE, AND THE RIGHTS OF MARRIED WOMEN: THE PROVISIONS OF MINNESOTA LAWS

A. CONTRACT FOR MARRIAGE

"Marriage, so far as its validity in law is concerned, is a civil contract between a man and a woman, to which consent of the parties, capable in law for contracting, is essential." *Minn. Stat.* Section 517.01 (1984). "Marriage is a contract between a man and a woman" explicitly excludes marriage between people of the same sex. *Baker v. Nelson,* 291 Minn. 310, 191 N.W. 2d 185 (1971). The contract is "sui generis", creating relationship and status as husband and wife for the parties and responsibilities and duties over which they have no control. 11A Dunnell 2d, *Marriage* Section 1, 266 (3rd ed. 1978). Marriage involves the man, the woman, and the state. Neither consent of the parties, although it is essential, nor a license from the state in itself would create a marriage. It is the product of both.

The relation is confidential in nature and fiduciary in its character. *Knox v. Knox,* 222 Minn. 477, 25 N.W. 2d 225 (1946). A decision by the husband to share the family home with his relatives may be vetoed by the wife and vice versa. The responsibilities and duties of the parties to one another are subject to state law. For example, people normally do not think about alimony when they get married, but the law implies this duty on the married couple.

Validity

The validity of a marriage is determined by the law of the place where it is consummated. If it is valid at the time and place where it is made, it is valid anywhere. In re *Kinkead's Estate,* 239 Minn. 27, 57 N.W. 2d 631 (1953). A marriage obtained by fraud and perjury is presumed to be valid. Common law and underaged marriages contracted in another state, if they are valid in that state, are valid in Minnesota. Common law marriage status may be obtained by Minnesota residents, if the couple moved into a common law state and established their reputation there before returning to live in Minnesota. *Laikola v. Engineered Concrete,* 277 N.W. 2d 653, 658 (Minn. 1959).

A contract for marriage may not be valid if the marriage is not solemnized. *Minn. Stat.* Section 517.04 (1984). Regardless of whether the person who solemnized the marriage had actual authority, a marriage is valid if it was solemnized in good faith. *Minn. Stat.* Section 517.17 (1984). Solemnization may be performed by a justice of the peace, a judge, a minister, or a licensed individual.

Anyone eighteen years of age or older is capable of contracting for marriage in Minnesota. A female with consent of her parents and of a judge may contract for marriage at the age of sixteen, but a man must be eighteen in order to contract for marriage. A secret or fraudulently induced marriage by minors without their parents' consent is not void until annulled, however. See *Raske v. Raske,* 92 F. Supp. 248 (D. Minn. 1950).

The parties must also have mental capacity to contract for marriage. Mental capacity is a question of fact and a person committed into a state hospital is capable of contracting. Op. Att'y Gen., 1008 (September 22, 1969).

Minn. Stat. Section 517.03 (1984) sets out marriages that are prohibited in Minnesota. Bigamy is one. The law recognizes only one spouse at a time so one who knowingly marries a married person does it at his or her own peril. However, if that person faithfully believed that his or her marriage was legal but for the discovery of its illegality at a later date, he or she would be conferred the same rights as a legal spouse. *Minn. Stat.* Section 518.055 (1984). Despite the illegality of a marriage, if paternity is proven, children born to the couple would be legitimate. Op. Att'y Gen. No. 46, 124 (1934).

The statute also prohibits marriage between ancestor and descendant, brother and sister, uncle and niece, aunt and nephew, and first cousins. However, the law explicitly recognizes marriage between first cousins in "aboriginal culture". The term "aboriginal culture" is not defined, but the clue is that such marriage must be an "established custom" in that particular culture. *Minn. Stat.* Section 517.03 (1984).

The prohibition of remarriage of a divorced person within six months after the termination of the prior marriage has been abolished by Minnesota Law of 1978, Chapter 772, Section 19. See Bowen, *The 1978 Marriage and Divorce Act,* 48 Henn. Lawyer 6 (November-December 1978).

B. MINNESOTA DIVORCE

Divorce in Minnesota is sometimes referred to as no-fault. The basic rule is that fault should not be considered in a divorce proceeding and that a person should be free to make his or her own choice of whom to marry. Judge Bowen argued that divorce in Minnesota is not "pure" no-fault but "it moves closer . . . by limiting the evidence basis for finding of irretrievable breakdown". *Bowen,* supra. What it means is that the burden of proof has been reduced to a minimum: the proof of irretrievable breakdown. The parties may still have to show the cause(s) of the breakdown but not the parties' fault.

It is a matter for the court to consider whether in fact the marriage relationship has broken down. *Hagerty v. Hagerty,* 281 N.W. 2d 386 (Minn. 1979). There are two ways in which a court can find a marriage breakdown: 180 or more days of separation or the existence of serious marital discord adversely affecting the attitude of one or both of the parties toward the marriage. The former is not hard to prove, but the parties may find it difficult to wait for 180 days. The latter is not hard to wait for, but the parties may find it difficult to tell their story to the court.

In a divorce that involves contested child custody, the court will look into the best interest of the child(ren). If the child has the mental capacity to decide or if the parties can be persuaded to agree to a particular arrangement, the problem will not be difficult for the court. Usually, the court will appoint a guardian *ad litem* who will have the responsibility of advising the court with respect to child custody, support, and visitation. The court may have to do an independent investigation, which the court would not want to do, and to consult with professionals about custodial arrangement. Some commentators on the subject suggested that the child should be provided with an attorney in addition to the appointment of the guardian ad litem. See *A Kid Needs a Good Attorney, Too,* 36 Bench and Bar of Minn. No. 5, 31 (1979).

If child custody is awarded to a spouse, the court will also provide reasonable visitation rights to the non-custodial spouse unless the court has found that such visitation rights would endanger the child's life or health. Child support and spousal maintenance, if any, are determined without regard to misconduct. Child support is necessary for the upkeep of the child and spousal maintenance is provided to a spouse who has little financial ability to sustain his or her life.

The division of marital property should be "just and equitable" and is made without regard to marital misconduct. The law presumes substantial contribution by both parties toward the acquisition of marital property "while they were living together as husband and wife". See *Minn. Stat.* Section 518.58 (1984). The court may equitably divide non-marital property to assure adequacy and fairness. Homestead and household furnishings may be awarded exclusively to one spouse without prejudice upon either party. In *Carlson v. Olson,* 256 N.W. 2d 249 (1977), the court awarded one-half of a man's non-marital property acquired during a lengthy cohabitation to his cohabitant as an "irrevocable gift".

Today, there is a trend toward marriage mediation as an alternative to litigation in court. Although mediation does not always resolve marital problems, some people have found it to be satisfactory, including members of the bar. See Note, *Don't Fight It Out . . . Work It Out!,* Ram. Barister 3 (May 1983); Baxter, *Divorce Mediation: A Constructive Way to Negotiate,* 1 Minn. Fam. L. J. 223-228 (1983); Kisson, *A Primer on Marriage Dissolution Settlements,* Minn. Trial Lawyer 6-7 (November-December 1983); and Spector,

Dissolution ... Method of Settlement, 1 Minn. Fam. L. J. 107-109 (November 1982). Some attorneys seemed to suggest that settlement should be a number one priority rather than contesting the issues in court.

C. THE RIGHTS OF MARRIED WOMEN IN MINNESOTA

Every married person retains the same identity and enjoys the same protection in Minnesota law as if that person were single. A married woman can bring an action in her own name in court, including an action for protection or redress against her husband. Marriage creates a marital status and obligations between the married partners, but it does not change or affect the individual's rights. *Minn. Stat.* Section 519.01 (1984).

A married woman retains ownership of property she acquired before the marriage, or after a decree of legal separation, or property excluded as marital property under a valid antenuptial agreement. Minn. Stat. Section 519.02 (1984). She may contract with anyone and she will be legally bound under the terms of the contract. If she committed an offense against another person or against the state, she will be held responsible for her own action. Her property, real or personal, shall be made available to her creditors as if she were a single person and her personal property may be made available to her husband's creditors as if she were a party to the contracts or debts.

The statue provides an exception to the stated rule above. Neither a contract between a husband and wife nor the granting of power of attorney from one to the other related to the transfer of interest in real property from one to the other is generally valid. There exist narrow circumstances in which such transactions may be valid, but they are not important to consider in connection with this paper. *Minn. Stat.* Section 519.06 (1984).

If a husband deserts his wife, the wife may be entitled to a divorce should such desertion last more than one year. Similarly, if the husband is insane for ten years or more, the wife may be entitled to a divorce and to ownership of marital property. This does not mean that she cannot get a divorce earlier, but if she does get a divorce early (e.g. a divorce under *Minn. Stat.* Section 518), she may not be entitled to ownership of the marital property.

As mentioned above, a married person has the right to appear before court for an order of protection and for redress against her husband under *Minn. Stat.* Section 518B.01 et seq. (1984). An order of protection is one in which, upon hearing the complaint, the court may restrain an abusing party from committing acts of domestic abuse in the home. A wife may bring an action against her husband for damages resulting from a tort committed by him. See *Janke v. Janke,* 292 Minn. 296, 195 N.W. 2d 185 (1972); *Busch v. Busch Construction, Inc.,* 262 N.W. 2d 37 (Minn. 1977); and Note, *Interspousal Recovery Rights: Minnesota Supreme Court 1971-1972,* 57 Minn. L. Rev. 996 (1973).

A married woman is not liable for debts incurred by her husband, if such liability is not incurred for the buying of necessities for the maintenance of their home. A tort committed by a husband cannot be imputed to his wife. See *Christensen v. Henn. Transp. Co.,* 215 Minn. 394, 10 N.W. 2d 406 (1943). A wife is primarily responsible for her own debts, whether necessities or not. See *Busch,* supra. Necessities include "household articles and supplies furnished to and used by the family". *Minn. Stat.* Section 519.09 (1984). It may be reasonably construed that "household articles and supplies" cover automobiles, a suitable dwelling place, clothing, food, and other items which are indispensable for the sustenance of human life. Necessities arguably do not include financial support a wife has contributed to the living expenses of her husband while he was studying in medical school. See *DeLa Rosa v. DeLa Rosa,* 309 N.W. 2d 775 (Minn. 1981).

Part Two
AN ANALYTICAL DISCUSSION

A. MARRIAGES

The general rule of law in Minnesota is that if a marriage is valid at the time and place where it is consummated, it is valid everywhere. Common law marriage has been abolished in Minnesota since 1946, but the extent of the legislative abolition does not go beyond the boundaries of this state. A common law marriage consummated outside of Minnesota in accordance with the law of that state is valid in Minnesota (see *Laikola,* supra), but for a marriage consummated in Minnesota to be valid, it must be contracted.

American common law marriage is "one not solemnized in the ordinary way but created by an agreement to marry, followed by cohabitation". *Black's Law Dictionary* 251 (5th ed. 1979). The elements of common law marriage are: (a) a positive mutual agreement, (b) to enter into a marriage relation, (c) cohabitation sufficient to warrant a fulfillment of the necessary relationship of man and wife, and (d) an assumption of marital duties and obligations. Id.

Hmong marriage proceeds with a marriage proposal, from a man to a woman or from a man's family to a woman's family. Such a proposal is subject to a final and mutual agreement between the parties in order for it to be binding and for a marriage to take place. Once an agreement is reached by the parties and after a feast, or a wedding dinner, in commemoration of the event has taken place, the woman moves with the man into his parents' house where cohabitation would begin. The marriage would also be witnessed by at least two mediators. All these comply with American common law marriage, save a certificate of marriage. A Hmong marriage that validly took place in Laos or in Thailand according to Hmong customs is valid in Minnesota. Even though proof of Hmong marriage cannot be originally documented, evidence from the spouses' immigration papers should be sufficient. Congress has the delegated power to regulate immigration and a congressional enactment is supreme over the law of the states. Should a marriage be considered valid for immigration purposes, it must be valid under state law. See 8 *U.S.C.* section 1101 et seq.

It does not follow, however, that every Hmong marriage in Minnesota is valid. Polygamy, underaged marriage, and other Hmong marriages may not be valid. Polygamy may be construed as a form of bigamy and therefore it is contrary to the United States' public policy, even though such marriage would be valid under the law of the place where it took place. For example, some Hmong men had more than one wife, which was legal in Laos and Thailand, before coming into the United States. These men had to divorce one of their wives so that they could come to the United States. These divorces are not recognized at all in Hmong culture, but they are considered terminated under U.S. law.

It does not matter how many wives a person has, there is only one wife recognized under the law of Minnesota: the one documented on paper. This rule does not fully resolve the problems of Hmong polygamous marriage. What about a Hmong woman who has knowingly gotten married to a married Hmong man in Thailand, and who nevertheless has come to the United States as the only wife? What rights does the first wife have against her husband? What rights does the second wife have against her husband? Suppose the man acknowledges that he has two wives?

In Minnesota, a woman who knowingly marries a married man does not enjoy the protection of *Minn. Stat.* section 519.055 (1984). She cannot be a putative spouse. Applying Minnesota law to Hmong polygamy, the first wife cannot be denied a putative spouse status. She was first in time. Her rights are superior to any other woman who later get married to her husband.

The second wife can remain as the legal wife, but since she was second in time, her rights should be inferior to those of the first wife. If she is not happy with the status, she can get a divorce. The marriage should not be annulled because it was valid at the time and place where consummated.

If the husband acknowledges that he had two wives and that he divorced his first wife only to enter the United States, he has committed a fraud which would render him deportable under U.S. immigration law. He has no other alternative but to argue that he has fully divorced the first wife.

The same is true of Hmong underaged marriages. The law of Minnesota provides that a man must be at least 18 years of age and a woman must be at least 16 years of age in order to contract for marriage. Hmong marriages often take place while the parties are about fifteen or sixteen years of age, although the trend is changing; therefore it is safe to say that Hmong underaged marriage consummated in Minnesota fails to comply with the law. Underaged marriage, however, may also be successfully argued as cohabitation. The parties may raise their ages so that their marriage can be legalized. Also, if the parties want to remain married, knowing that their marriage is legally impermissible, they could wait until both parties attain legal age or go to get married in another state. Minnesota law does not discourage any such practice.

A Hmong marriage consummated in Minnesota according to Hmong customs would not automatically be valid even though both the man and the woman are over 18 years of age. In order for such a marriage to be recognized in Minnesota, it must be contracted and be solemnized. Hmong marriage is unlawful in Minnesota although it fulfills American common law requirements and may be valid under the law of other states. Even though Hmong in the United States may not be U.S. citizens, their marriage is, unlike that of American Indians which is specifically excluded, subject to the law of the state of Minnesota.

On the other hand, an invalid marriage under Hmong customs may be valid in Minnesota. For example, a marriage between members of a clan who are only distant relatives would be valid. Also, a marriage between members of two related clans would not violate Minnesota law. Realizing the prospect of changes which would clearly abridge the status quo of their marriage customs, Hmong are very nervous.

There are some similarities in Hmong marriage customs and Minnesota law. Hmong utilize the family structure in the marriage process. The family initiates a marriage proposal and negotiates on its terms. Hmong engage mediators to represent them during negotiation, to witness the marriage, and to carry out Hmong marriage customs. A feast is prepared in commemoration of the event and people in the community are invited to help celebrate the beginning of a new life for the new couple.

Minnesotans utilize the government in the marriage process. The state becomes a party to the marriage. Minnesota law provides that a marriage be solemnized by someone in front of at least two witnesses. Normally, a date is set for a wedding so that relatives and friends can come to honor the new marriage.

A Hmong mediator has the knowledge and the skills required under Hmong marriage custom. He is a leader in the community and has status. A justice of the peace or a judge, on the other hand, is a trained person in the law. A minister is also trained in his own field and is a leader in his religion. It is arguable that Hmong mediators would be qualified to be licensed under Minnesota law for the purpose of the solemnization of marriage.

There are some advantages and disadvantages in Hmong marriage. The advantages are that parents are highly involved in the mate selection process. They oversee the negotiation of a marriage proposal, making sure that their son or daughter will not be taken for granted or taken advantage of and that the marriage will last. Once a marriage has taken place, the families from both sides contractually are obligated to help the new couple build and maintain a good marital relationship. Of course, this is possible because Hmong parents do want their children to be happy after they are married because their children are their future security.

There are disadvantages too. Excessive family involvement can kill a marital relationship. Some parents are too close to their children and are afraid to let go. Bringing a new bride into an old home may not bring harmony but may bring tension. Each party has his own expectation of a new bride, including the new bride herself. Sometimes the marriage partners are pressured into the marriage and they are pressured to maintain a good marital relationship. They may not love one another but for the interests of their respective parents.

The recognition of first cousin marriage in Minnesota statute is not contrary to Hmong custom. First cousins are allowed to marry if they are from two different clans. This is an established custom. Hmong culture is likely to be an "aboriginal culture" as it is defined in the statute.

Hmong do not recognize legal separation and cohabitation. When Hmong talk about long-term separation, they refer to situations in which the spouses do not sleep together as husband and wife for a period of time, even though they are living under the same roof. Hmong cannot perceive legal separation. The question is: why would they want to be husband and wife if they cannot live together? There cannot be a status between being single and being married. You are either one or the other.

Hmong also feel that Minnesota law imposes an unreasonable burden on the married person. They see it as only for a perfect couple: those that have no marital problems. Hmong perceive the law to be very rigid and it regulates every aspect of family life, leaving little room for disagreement and spousal discipline. Personal tolerance is not accounted for in the law.

Hmong antenuptial agreements or marriage contracts may be unenforceable in Minnesota courts for two reasons. First, the young man and young woman may have been in their infancy and not intelligent enough to have made such a binding contract. Secondly, their parents negotiated the marriage for them and an agreement between their parents would not necessarily serve their best interests. I feel that Hmong minors could get their marriages annulled in proper circumstances.

Another area of Hmong marriage that poses special problems to the Hmong as well as to Minnesota law is elopement. Can a minor legally in custody of her parents run away just to get married? Can her parents rightfully apprehend her and take her back? Or can they retain her against her will? Should they call the police? What should the police do? Should the police detain the young man or should the police let the young man go? Is it a kidnapping or an elopement?

B. DIVORCES

Traditionally, Hmong divorces involve not only the individuals but their respective families too. The spouses probably have gone through many sessions of counseling before they decide to give up the marriage. Since fault is the basis for a divorce, the parties would toss the liability of fault between themselves. It is like a ball game in which there are two teams playing against one another. The presiding leader and his friends are like the judges whose job is to keep scores of the teams. the parties that score the most win. It is seemingly unjust or unfair. It does not take into consideration all the individuals' rights.

On the other hand, Hmong may not find no-fault divorce an alternative to theirs. It is 180 degrees from theirs. How could it be fair to reward the spouse, whose misconduct caused the family breakdown, child custody, child support, property rights, and alimony? The law, although fair on the face of it, practically benefits women more than men. For example, child custody often is awarded to the mother rather than to the father. A wife whose marital misconduct caused the marriage to be terminated may be awarded alimony. She may also be awarded homestead rights, household goods and furnishings, as well as substantial other property.

Hmong are frightened when they see a divorced woman living with a boyfriend while receiving alimony from her ex-husband. At the same time, she may live in the house that was bought during the marriage. It seems as though once you are married, you give the other person a license to take a bite out of your financial resources for as long as you live.

They also see their customs becoming useless. To the Hmong, the question in child custody cases is not which of the parents would better care for the children but how the identity of the children would be better preserved. The practical effects of this system benefit the men more than the women because Hmong culture is patrilineal. Hmong do realize, of course, that women are physically and emotionally attached to their children and their relationship with the children may be stronger.

Hmong are concerned whether their divorce process can ever be used. Since the family was involved in the negotiation, has become party to the marriage, and is obligated to help build and maintain a good marital status, it would like to have some say in the divorce process. Hmong wish to utilize the resources within their community, such as their lineal and clan leaders, in order that after a divorce, there would still be harmony between the two families and clans.

C. THE RIGHTS OF MARRIED WOMEN

Minnesota law protects the property interests of the marriage partners while Hmong customs do not. In Minnesota, a married person can own property in his or her own name. A woman can transfer her interest in her property without the consent of her husband. She is treated in law as though she is unmarried. A married Hmong woman only has a joint interest in property. She may not validly transfer her interest without her husband's consent. A married person in a Hmong community is always a married person.

A married Hmong woman would not be liable for debts, whether they are incurred for the buying of necessities, if she does not have an income or if she has wholly rendered her income toward the family. This does not mean that she can freely pledge the credit of her family members for unjust debts. Traditionally, a Hmong woman does not pledge the credit of her family beyond her authority because such action is clearly improper. A married woman in Minnesota is liable for her own debts and the "just" debts of her husband. However, she may be in very bad financial circumstances so as to render the debts uncollectible by creditors.

A married Hmong woman does have a right to take her husband to the clan or lineal leader of the family for other good causes but rarely for damages. It is believed that both the husband and the wife could only own joint interest in property and therefore it does not make sense for the husband to pay his wife damages. In Minnesota, both the husband and the wife can own separate property and so it does make sense for one to pay damages to the other. Besides, most personal risks can be insured against in Minnesota, and a wife would have a valid claim against the insurance company when her husband committed a tort against her.

CONCLUSION

Hmong customary marriage could be construed as a form of common law marriage and thus is prohibited from taking place in Minnesota; however, marriages that were validly made in Laos, Thailand, and common-law states in the United States would be valid. Cultural differences between Hmong and Minnesotans do exist which would require different judicial treatments of Hmong marriage. Marriages between distant clan members would be an area which the courts will find difficult to deal with, e.g., a preference toward upholding the law would be legitimate but at the same time it would directly abridge Hmong customs. In fact, it may be an act of cultural extinction.

Hmong marriage processes could be maintained, but they must not proceed in such a way as to violate the law. Negotiation between parents is permissible to the extent that such negotiation does not deprive the marrying individuals of their rights and is for the best interests of the individuals. Antenuptial agreement can be validly made binding on the individuals as long as they are competent at law to enter into such an agreement.

Can the law accommodate a Hmong divorce process? I think that it can. The judicial system in the United States is established to resolve disputes between people who cannot live peacefully together. Also, the courts do encourage settlements between the parties. Hmong families can proceed with whatever process they choose, their own or that which is available in the courts. However, a divorce granted by Hmong leaders could not be treated by the courts as a valid divorce; it may be treated as a recommendation or be looked upon as a marriage dissolution agreement which may be incorporated into the divorce decree by the court.

In the meantime, while Hmong hesitate to follow the American judicial system, attorneys representing Hmong clients in divorce cases should encourage them to settle, especially to settle in the institutions existing within their community.

The rights of married Hmong women are subject to change. It is commercially impractical for a woman in the United States to pledge the credit of her family members when she contracts for goods or services. She cannot be exempted from her husband's debts which she had notice of or when such debts were incurred for the buying of necessities. A married woman is better protected by the law rather than by Hmong custom against a tort committed by her husband, and it is economical to insure against the risk of tort rather than to have the debts rest on an individual's shoulders.

8 Tribal Governments

Sharon O'Brien

The dispatcher notifies the Reno Sparks, Nevada, tribal police officer of a robbery in progress. The Navajo healthcare worker drives for an hour over the mesa to make certain an elderly women is properly taking her prescribed medication. The Quinault tribal biologist attends a national conference to discuss with other experts the latest techniques in salmon hatching. Banging down his beaded gavel, the Sac and Fox judge grants the couple's divorce petition. The Mississippi Choctaw Chief has requested the council to examine the feasibility of constructing a bingo hall on tribal lands. The Yakima delegation is in Washington, D.C. to lobby its congressional representatives for support against the proposed location of a nuclear-waste dump near their reservation in Washington state.

The scenarios sketched above illustrate the numerous roles tribal governments perform daily throughout Indian country. For thousands of years, tribes have served their people, providing for their safety, health, and economic well-being. Their structures, processes, and methods of governing have changed; the responsibilities have not. To best appreciate the current challenges faced by the more than six hundred tribal governments in the continental United States and Alaska, one must first understand the past pressures that tribes have endured.

Historically, tribal governments varied considerably in structure and complexity. The smaller bands of the Basin and California regions approximated truly direct great democracies. The Muscogee Confederacy of the Southeast, on the other hand, possessed an elaborate system of checks and balances guided by a dual clan and town system.

Contact between Indians and non-Indians altered in varying degrees—but without exception—the philosophy, structure, and powers of these traditional governments. The immigrants valued property, material progress, and individualism. Indian nations, with their extensive lands and resources, were both the source of and the obstacle to the attainment of the non-Indians' goals. Tedious negotiations with people who did not view land as a commodity to be sold, who cared little for the individual amassment of wealth, and who practiced consensus decision-making precluded the quick attainment of lands by the non-Indian. The federal government responded to this obstinacy with measures to destroy tribal cultures and sovereignty.

The federal government, like its European predecessors, initially recognized tribes as independent nations, with exclusive sovereignty over their external and internal affairs. England negotiated more than 500 treaties with tribes and the United States more than 370. Recognition for tribal rights declined, however, as the greed for Indian lands intensified and the power balance tipped favorably towards the United States, jeopardizing the tribes' ability to maintain their traditional structures and powers. Tribal governments, such as those of the Choctaw, Cherokee, and other Indian nations of the Southeast, responded to internal tribal demands and changed their governments, modeling them after those of their white neighbors. Other tribes, such as the Lakota (or Sioux), were subjected to continuous federal policies designed to undermine their leaders and governments.

By the late 1800s, the federal government's decision to solve the "Indian problem" by assimilating Indians into the dominant society had emasculated not just the government of the Lakotas, but most other tribal governments. Congress' unilateral decision in 1871 to end treaty-making with the Indian nations deprived tribal governments of a voice in their relationship with the federal government. The virtual extinction of the buffalo and other game, a forced reliance on federal rations, and the allotment of reservation lands severely disabled the tribal governments' ability to secure their people's economic well-being. The authority of the Bureau of Indian Affairs agent and the establishment of Indian police forces and courts usurped the tribal government's responsibility to provide for public order and justice. Federal regulations outlawing tribal religious practices, efforts to convert tribes to Christianity, policies to extinguish Indian languages, and the teaching of American values through education obscured the philosophical sources of traditional governments. Federal actions were indeed changing tribes from self-sufficient nations into wards.

By the 1930s, when Congress passed the Indian Reorganization Act, tribal governments had nearly ceased to exist. The Indian Reorganization Act of 1934 offered tribes constitutions drafted by the Bureau of Indian Affairs (BIA) and congressional funds for economic development. Although many experts praised the act for its resuscitation of tribal governments, others criticized it as assimilationist, charging that the government provided tribes with Western-derived political institutions rather than improving traditional systems.

Congressional support of tribal governments, however limited or misdirected, ended in the 1950s and early 1960s with the passage of several termination bills—legislation

From Sharon O'Brien, "Tribal Governments," *National Forum : The Phi Kappa Phi Journal*, Vol. 71(2): 18–20, 1991. Copyright © 1991 by the Honor Society of Phi Kappa Phi. Reprinted by permission of author and publisher.

intended to solve the ever-present Indian problem by abrogating the federal government's relationship with tribes and integrating their lands and peoples into the surrounding states. Pursuant to this objective, Congress terminated its relationship with 109 communities, bands, and tribes before again altering its policies toward tribal governments in the mid-1970s. Congress' current approach toward tribal governments is to acknowledge and promote tribal self-determination. The implementation of this policy has translated into increased funds and training that enable tribal governments to administer programs and services formerly operated by the Bureau of Indian Affairs.

Congress refers to its relationship with tribes as a government-to-government relationship, a term signifying the inherent sovereignty of each party. As sovereigns, tribal governments receive their authority to operate from their own people, not from the United States Constitution as do state governments. (This has led one judge to write that tribal governments, in effect, have a status higher than states.) No longer viewed as wards, tribal governments are recognized by Congress and the states as the official representatives of domestic dependent nations.

As domestic dependent nations, tribes possess the inherent sovereignty to exercise all governmental power unless extinguished by treaty or congressional legislation or unless it is a power that is inconsistent with the tribes' dependent status. In practical terms this means that tribes have retained, with some limitations, the authority to structure their own governments, to administer justice, to regulate domestic relations, to manage and develop their lands and resources, to conduct businesses, and to tax individuals and commercial enterprises.

Differing cultures, histories, resources, and leadership abilities have created a diverse collection of tribal governments, each with its own structure, governing style, objectives, and tribal programs. Approximately half of all tribes operate according to the guidelines of the Indian Reorganization Act. Other tribes, such as the Onondaga and the Seneca of New York, the Yakima of Washington, and several Pueblos, have retained much of their traditional structures.

In general, tribal governments are headed by a council, referred to by some tribes as a legislature, or a business committee. Council members are usually elected, although such tribes as the Warm Springs of Oregon and the Miccosukee of Florida have a combination of elected officials and traditional band or clan chiefs. A community's cultural values may also be apparent in the council's composition, for instance in the ratio of young to old, educated to non-educated, and men to women council members. Governing styles and procedures differ too. The discussion of an economic-development proposal by one tribal government may continue informally for months until the council has achieved a clear consensus. A neighboring tribe's consideration of a similar proposal may last a shorter time, with discussions occurring according to Robert's Rules of Order, and the final decision determined by majority vote.

Although many are patterned after non-Indian institutions, most tribal governments do not possess clearly separated branches of government. Especially in smaller tribes, the council may be responsible for various, if not all, executive, legislative, and judicial functions. The independence and power of the executive (referred to as a chairperson, chief, governor, or president, depending on the tribe) is determined by a tribe's history, constitution, and mode of election. The relocated Five Civilized Tribes of Oklahoma, who historically have possessed strong executives, elect their principal chiefs by popular vote. The Menominees of Wisconsin have ceded the election of the chairperson to their legislature.

More than 140 tribal governments have established separate judicial systems. These courts vary considerably in complexity, independence, and cultural orientation. Tribal legal systems may include one court or several, such as separate criminal, civil, family, or conservation courts. The Navajo Nation has developed the most elaborate system, consisting of an attorney general's office, a variety of specialized courts, and more than twenty codes, including laws pertaining to commercial enterprises and child welfare. On small reservations, the council may serve as the court of first and last resort. Other tribal constitutions vest the council with the right to hear appeals. A few tribes, such as the Lakota, have established a special supreme-court level to decide appeals from any of the several member reservations. Judicial review, a right not given to all tribal courts, and the selection process of judges, elected by the people or appointed by the council, are other factors affecting the independence of tribal judicial systems.

Whatever the particular system, most tribal courts employ and apply a combination of traditional and Anglo-derived procedures and laws. For example, tribal regulations on the Blackfeet reservation require all lawyers and judges to speak the native language and to be members of the tribal bar; other reservations require lawyers and judges to be members of the state bar, while still others provide a more informal conflict-resolution process staffed by respected leaders who may or may not have formal legal training.

Tribal courts no longer exercise complete criminal and civil jurisdiction over all matters and individuals within their territory. Criminal and civil jurisdiction in Indian country is today a patchwork of exclusive and concurrent authority exercised by tribal, federal, and state governments. The federal government has assumed criminal jurisdiction over Indians committing any of fourteen major crimes. In addition, two recent Supreme Court decisions have ruled that the exercise of tribal criminal jurisdiction over anyone but a member is inconsistent with the tribes' status as domestic dependent nations. These court cases and laws, in combination with federal legislation limiting the penalties levied by tribal courts to one year in jail or $5000 in fines, has severely undermined the ability of tribal governments to protect their people and others living on the reservation. Tribes have retained most civil jurisdiction over Indians and non-Indians within their boundaries. Civil-dispute settlement, marriage, divorce, zoning, and taxation are inherent powers properly exercised by all tribal governments. The Agua Caliente have passed zoning laws for their reservation lands, parts of which are located in Palm Springs, California. The Jicarilla Apache tax energy companies located on their property. Tribal courts, as clarified by the Indian Child Welfare Act of 1978, possess primary jurisdictional rights over state courts in procedures involving the custody and adoption of enrolled Indian children.

Historically, states had no jurisdiction over tribal lands. In the last thirty years, however, the federal government has allowed state governments to exercise increased authority within reservation boundaries. In 1953, Congress granted five (later six) states the authority under Public Law 280 to assume criminal and civil jurisdiction over most reservations within their borders. And as mentioned above, state courts now have the power to try nonmembers for criminal acts committed on the reservation. The states are also permitted to tax and regulate non-Indians hunting and fishing on non-Indian lands within reservation boundaries.

Ironically, as the courts chip away at the edges of tribal autonomy, Indian governments are developing into increasingly experienced and well-trained social-service providers. The Muscogee Creeks of Oklahoma own and operate their own hospital. Head Start, alcoholism, and elderly programs are basic services provided by tribal governments throughout Indian country. Support for cultural activities, the supervision of government housing programs, and job training are among other services administered by tribes.

Given the limited resource base of most reservations, the provision of social services and programs depends heavily upon the availability of federal funding. In communities where unemployment ranges from 20 to 80 percent and half of all jobs are tied to federal programs, budget reductions can have disastrous consequences. Attempting to free themselves from dependence on federal dollars, tribal governments have initiated a variety of entrepreneurial projects. Tribes fortunate enough to have mineral, timber, or fishery resources are investing considerable efforts, both individually and jointly, in their sustained exploitation. The Mescalero Apache, along with forty-three other tribes, compose the membership of Council of Energy Resource Tribes (CERT)—an organization that provides technical assistance to tribes in the development of their oil, gas, and coal reserves. The Pacific Northwest tribes are especially knowledgeable and proficient in all facets of the salmon industry, from hatcheries to processing. Washington tribes now raise more than 30 percent of all salmon produced in the state.

The introduction of gaming operations in Indian country in the last two decades has offered many tribal governments, particularly those poor in land and resources, an opportunity to infuse needed jobs and money into the tribal economy. The tribal council of the Wisconsin Oneidas, to mention one of the more successful examples, has constructed a profitable bingo operation and hotel near Green Bay. With revenue generated from these businesses, the council has supplemented and improved the tribe's educational services, health and elderly care, and economic-development programs.

In addition to their responsibilities to provide social services, ensure public safety, initiate economic development, regulate zoning and taxation, and protect members' rights, tribal governments possess one other extremely important obligation—defense of the tribe's sovereignty and culture. Tribal survival depends on more than improving tribal programs and services. Nor is tribal survival simply an issue of retaining the language, traditions, and crafts. Tribal governments must also adapt to and meet outside pressures while maintaining internal cohesion and integrity.

How does a tribal government reinforce its culture's traditional respect for the environment and engender responsibility for collectivity when surrounded by an alien culture that praises domination of the environment, measures progress and self-worth in terms of individual materialism, and emphasizes rights over responsibility?

It is this underlying and constant contradiction that forces tribal governments to analyze every decision for the long-term impact on the tribe's culture and independence, as well as for its pragmatic benefits. Decisions that for state and local governments involve primarily issues of funds and support have greater and more wide-reaching consequences for tribal governments. For example, a tribal council is in the process of establishing a judicial system. Should it resurrect the tribe's traditional mediation model or install an adversarial system? The former is more culturally attuned but may deter investments by outside companies. Should resources be left undeveloped in keeping with traditional teachings, exploited by a tribal business, or leased to individual tribal members? Should a tribal government with limited resources request the county police to provide law and order on the reservation? How does a council balance the need for protection and safety against the potential loss of tribal authority to the state? Should a tribal business strive for maximum efficiency and profits, or sacrifice some degree of both to employ more tribal members?

It is this fundamental tension between two cultures, exacerbated by limited resources, that most challenges tribal governments today. Whether tribes can meet and survive this challenge is perhaps best answered by reference to a letter written by Benjamin Franklin in 1751:

> It would be a very strange thing if Six Nations of ignorant savages should be capable of forming a scheme for such a union, and be able to execute it in such a manner as that it has subsisted for ages, and appears indissoluble; and yet that a like union should be impracticable for ten or a dozen English colonies.

Franklin's reference is to the Iroquois Confederacy, a political alliance of the Mohawk, Oneida, Seneca, Cayuga, and Onondaga nations (the Tuscarora joined later), which continues to operate today. Scholars estimate that the Iroquois established their confederacy around 1200 A.D. Whether the Iroquois Confederacy, or the All Indian Pueblo Council, composed today of the nineteen Pueblos of New Mexico, deserves the honor as the oldest continuing political institution in the United States, remains unknown. What these institutions do illustrate is the cultural tenacity, human resourcefulness, and political ability of indigenous governments to survive.

SHARON O'BRIEN is the acting chair of and an associate professor in the Department of Government and International Studies at the University of Notre Dame.

9 Cohesion and Adaptability in Mexican-American and Anglo Families

William A. Vega
San Diego State University

Thomas Patterson,* James Sallis,* Philip Nader,* Catherine Atkins,* and Ian Abramson*
University of California-San Diego

This article reports data from a community sample of Anglos and Mexican Americans concerning two dimensions of family functioning: cohesion and adaptability. The Family Adaptability and Cohesion Evaluation Scales–II (FACES) were used with a sample of 294 parents with school-age children who were taking part in a large community-based health promotion project. In addition, an acculturation measure was used in order to test for differences that might be attributable to intracultural variation among Mexican Americans. No significant differences in mean scores or distributions were detected between ethnic groups for cohesion or adaptability, even when acculturation was controlled. Next, a circumplex model was used to test for differences in distribution within a 16-cell matrix of family types. It was found that the distribution of scores for both ethnic groups fell predominantly within two quadrants of the model that predict well-functioning families during this stage of the life course (childrearing, with children reaching adolescence). Some differences were found in the distribution of scores into the three regions of the model (balanced, midrange, and extreme), with Anglos somewhat more likely to be represented in the balanced region and Mexican Americans more likely to be either midrange or extreme. However, tests for acculturation effects indicated that intracultural variation among Mexican Americans accounts for these differences, with low-acculturation respondents more likely to score outside of the balanced region. Implications of the findings are discussed within the explanatory framework of the circumplex model and related to national findings.

To date, research concerning family functioning has not identified a "normative" family type, despite a voluminous literature focusing on various morphological and functional characteristics of families (Litwak, 1960; Moroney, 1980; Parsons, 1968; Sussman, 1959; Van de Ban, 1967). Historically, a strong emphasis in the family literature has been toward clinical descriptions of disorganized and pathological families and the identification of associated correlates (Bell and Bell, 1982; Glueck and Glueck, 1962; McCord and McCord, 1958; Redl and Wineman, 1951; Rosen, 1970). The interest in identifying factors and process associated with well-functioning families in the general community, paradoxically, is much more difficult to find. The purpose of this article is to examine two important dimensions of family functioning, cohesion and adaptability, through the use of the Family Adaptability and

All correspondence concerning this article should be directed to the first author.

Department of Mexican American Studies, San Diego State University, San Diego, CA 92182.

*Division of General Pediatrics, M031F, University of California-San Diego, La Jolla, CA 92093.

Cohesion Evaluation Scales–II (FACES) (Olson, Russell, and Sprenkle, 1982). The data were collected in a community study that included Anglo and Mexican-American respondents who volunteered to participate in a large health promotion project.

These family dimensions were selected for study because they emerged as core concepts after an extensive review of the literature conducted by Olson, Russell, and Sprenkle (1979, 1980) and have been incorporated by these investigators into a comprehensive circumplex model suitable for sociocultural and clinical research. *Family cohesion* is defined by the authors of the FACES as the emotional bonding that family members have toward one another. *Adaptability* is defined as the ability of a marital or family system to change its power structure, role relationships, and relationship rules in response to situational and developmental stress. Cohesion and adaptability are independent constructs measured with an integrated 30-item scale that requires rater judgments about aspects of group behavior and functioning that set the social and affective climate of family life (for specific examples, see the FACES–II items listed in the Appendix).

As noted by Staples and Mirande (1980) in their decennial review of the literature on minority families, research and models describing the Mexican-American family fall into three historical groupings. First, sociocultural researchers, such as Madsen (1964) and Heller (1966), depicted the Mexican-American family as very traditional in structure and values and characterized by an extended patriarchal structure with rigid sex roles best exemplified by *machismo*. This view of the family, in turn, was criticized as being overly ethnocentric with a strong Anglo-American bias, a tendency underscored by the emphasis on pejorative descriptions of the Mexican-American family as featuring a static, nonadaptive, and ultimately pathological family structure.

The second wave of literature, which was authored principally by scholars of Mexican-American descent (Mirande, 1977; Montiel, 1970; Romano, 1973) and fueled by the controversy noted above, focused on positive depictions of Mexican-American families, including their adaptive capacities and the supportive content of parental roles (Vega, Hough, and Romero, 1983). However, there was no effort to discredit the notion that some Mexican-American families, especially those strongly oriented toward Mexican culture, are characterized by hierarchical structure, male dominance, and ascribed sex roles. Moreover, the point was forcefully argued that Mexican-American families are no less capable of functioning well than are Anglo families, and a strong tone of resentment was evident in rejecting the notion that Mexican-American culture was being equated with maladjustment. However, most of this literature is in the form of critical essays, not exploratory or confirmatory research (for a complete review of this literature see Griswold, 1984; Ramirez and Arce, 1981).

Several articles based upon empirical research that have appeared since 1970 contradict the premises of the earlier literature. These isolated research investigations are certainly not definitive, remain few in number, and have limited sample sizes. Thus the external validity of these studies remains in question. However, they have been quite consistent in finding little evidence to support the patriarchal model as the prototype of the Mexican-American family. For example, these studies have not found inflexibility in the division of labor (Grebler, Moore, and Guzman, 1970) or exclusively male dominance in decision-making (Cromwell and Cromwell, 1978; Ybarra, 1982; Zinn, 1980), and egalitarian family dynamics are normative. Furthermore, in cross-cultural comparisons, no important differences were found between Anglos and Mexican Americans on key variables such as marital satisfaction covarying with family size, wife's labor-force participation, or conjugal power (Bean, Russell, and Marcum, 1977).

Obviously, far more descriptive research is required before we can fully appreciate the complexity of the Mexican-American family, with its many nuances, and the factors and processes contributing to its changing character. The vast internal differentiation of the Mexican-American population along geographic and socioeconomic vectors, combined with relentless immigration, requires investigators to depict their samples carefully in terms of demographic markers, especially with regard to acculturation levels and their moderating effect on variables of interest. For example, recent cross-sectional studies indicate that familism, and hence the availability of social support, increases with each generation living in this country (Golding, Burnam, and Timbers, 1985; Keefe, Padilla, and Carlos, 1979; Vega and Kolody, 1985), a finding that seems to contradict earlier views that posited a simple acculturation effect wherein the highest levels of familism (the tendency to favor family interaction and social support over other alternatives) would correlate with "Mexicanness" (and Mexican birth) and attenuate in subsequent generations. Parenthetically, the effects of acculturation in Mexican-American families on empirically measured aspects of family functioning is unknown.

In an effort to provide more information on these issues, the analysis that follows permits cross-cultural comparison within the context of this study and with national norms. Furthermore, our results are interpreted on the basis of the circumplex model of family types that is reported to have value for predicting satisfaction with family life and low stress. We also examine the relationship of acculturation level with both family cohesion and adaptability.

As a starting point for the analysis, three hypotheses are tested in order to determine whether or not cross-ethnic differences really exist in familial cohesion and adaptability. These hypotheses extend and complement existing empirical research on Mexican-American families.

1. Mexican-Americans and Anglos will report a similar level of family cohesiveness.
2. Mexican-Americans and Anglos will report a similar level of family adaptability.
3. Acculturation will show no relationship to family adaptability and cohesiveness.

METHODS

Subjects

The data were gathered as part of a large health behavior change study known as the San Diego Family Health Project (Nader et al., 1986). The premise of the sample selection procedure is that the family is the basic unit of socialization, and the family influences formation of health habits. Families were recruited through grade schools in nigh-density Mexican-American neighborhoods and from schools in high-density Anglo neighborhoods. Fifth and sixth grade students were asked to take home information describing the project to their parents and to return forms indicating whether or not they had an interest in the project. Comparisons on key variables (socioeconomic status, nativity, language use, household composition, smoking, diet and exercise habits) indicated no important differences between those who entered the Family Health Project and non-participating families within the respective ethnic groups (Atkins et al., 1985).

The subjects (parents and children) were given a comprehensive baseline assessment and were randomly assigned by school selection to intervention and control conditions. The assessment battery included numerous behavioral and physiological measures, including the FACES. The FACES was administered only to parents. The cohort included 147 adults of Mexican descent and 147 Anglos, and the sample included husbands and wives. The mean age of Anglo respondents was 38.5, and Mexican-descent respondents averaged 36.6 years of age. The socioeconomic status for Mexican Americans was significantly lower than that of Anglos, and men in both groups were about two years older than their spouses. Also, the Mexican-American group included many immigrants along with native-born respondents. Because of this situation, careful comparisons were made to assure language equivalency of the interview instrument, including back-translation and use of expert judges. Furthermore, respondents who were illiterate had the questions read to them.

Acculturation was measured with a modified version of the widely used scale developed and validated by Cuellar, Harris, and Jasso (1980), which permits us to measure this construct as a unidimensional continuum. The typologies that are identified with the use of this scale are "very Mexican," "bi-cultural," and "fully Anglo acculturated." The measure, as used in this research, has a potential range of 1 to 5 points, with the higher scores representing the most acculturated.

The Circumplex Model

The circumplex model of family functioning (Russell, 1979; Sprenkle and Olson, 1978) serves as the conceptual basis of the FACES. As seen in Figure 1, cohesion and adaptability are dual axes, with four ranges on each continuum (note that these ranges are different from the circumplex ranges discussed below). The two inner ranges typically indicate high functioning (shown as "balanced") and the outer two ranges indicate low functioning (shown as "extreme"). The normative data base indicates that, overall, about two-thirds of families usually score in the balanced range; however, the distribution varies, depending on life course factors (these issues are more fully reviewed below, in the discussion section). The circumplex model consists of a 4 × 4 matrix with 16 family typologies. The original research by Russell established the construct validity of the model.

Portner (1980) and Bell (1982) developed the prototype of the FACES in order to measure family cohesion and adaptability as required by the circumplex model. Development of the FACES-II was motivated by the need for a shorter measure with simple sentences and a 5-point response scale that retained empirical reliability as well as construct and discriminant validity.

Stratified random sampling has been used in collecting normative data for the FACES, and the data base includes 2,682 respondents in 40 states. The version of the FACES-II that was utilized in this research is a 30-item measure composed of two subscales; the cohesion subscale consists of 16

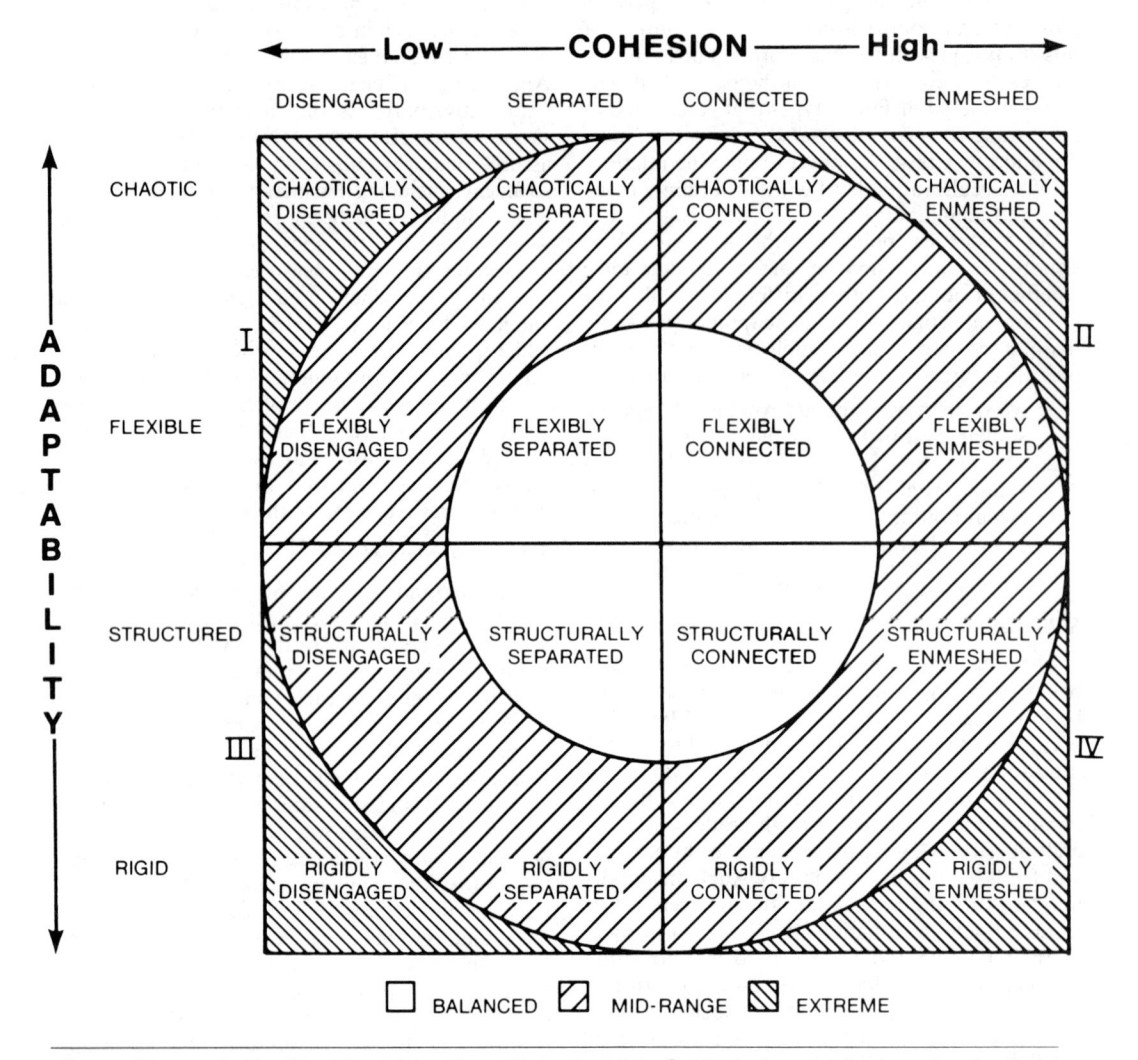

FIG. 1. CIRCUMPLEX MODEL WITH 16 TYPES OF MARITAL AND FAMILY SYSTEMS

[Figure: Circumplex Model diagram showing a 4x4 grid with Cohesion (Low to High: Disengaged, Separated, Connected, Enmeshed) on the horizontal axis and Adaptability (Chaotic, Flexible, Structured, Rigid) on the vertical axis. The 16 cells are labeled: Chaotically Disengaged, Chaotically Separated, Chaotically Connected, Chaotically Enmeshed; Flexibly Disengaged, Flexibly Separated, Flexibly Connected, Flexibly Enmeshed; Structurally Disengaged, Structurally Separated, Structurally Connected, Structurally Enmeshed; Rigidly Disengaged, Rigidly Separated, Rigidly Connected, Rigidly Enmeshed. Quadrants labeled I, II, III, IV. Legend: Balanced (inner circle), Mid-Range, Extreme (outer corners).]

Source: Olson et al., Families: What Makes Them Work. Copyright © 1983 by Sage Publications, Inc. Reprinted by permission.

items and the adaptability, 14 items (see Appendix). The cohesion dimension is measured on the basis of eight concepts: emotional bonding, family boundaries, coalitions, time, space, friends, decision-making, and interest and recreation. The adaptability dimension comprises six concepts: assertiveness, leadership, discipline, negotiation, roles, and rules. The FACES-II was derived from an original list of 90 items through the use of factor analytical procedures.

It should be noted that both cohesion and adaptability are found to vary across the family cycle and that family types used in the circumplex model (such as "rigidly disengaged" or "flexibly connected") are neither static nor equivalent to diagnostic categories. For example, cohesion is found to be highest at early stages in the family cycle; it decreases as children reach adolescence and thereafter, but rises again as children leave the home. Similarly, adaptability also decreases as families move through the childrearing years and increases again when the children leave the home. This means that we expect to see the same families change "types" within the model as they progress through the family cycle. Since these changes often represent functional adaptation, the circumplex family types can only be interpreted in the context of normative data, which establishes associations between family types at each life cycle stage and family resources, stress levels, coping ability, and marital and familial satisfaction. These issues are treated in greater detail in the discussion section, where normative data are used to interpret the results presented below.

National norms for cohesion include a range of 16 to 80, with a mean of 64.9; 8.4 is the standard deviation. The range for adaptability is also 16 to 80, with a mean of 49.9 and a standard deviation of 6.6. Internal consistency was tested in the present sample by using Cronbach's alpha (Cronbach, 1960), and the results for each subscale and ethnic subsample combination are as follows: Anglos, .75 (adaptability) and .77 (cohesion); Mexican Americans, .80 (adaptability) and .79 (cohesion). Both sets of results are well above Cronbach's criterion for reliability.

RESULTS

Initial statistical tests were conducted to determine whether gender differences existed by ethnic subsample for either cohesion or adaptability, which would necessitate a discrete analysis for males and females. However, no statistically significant differences were found, so the gender subsamples were merged for the analyses that follow.

The analyses include three stages. First, both cohesion and adaptability are analyzed separately in order to determine their distributions for both ethnic groups and for testing the hypotheses. Second, cohesion and adaptability are combined into the circumplex model in order to determine the distributions by ethnic group into three regions, balanced, midrange, and extreme; and this analysis is also done with controls for acculturation level. Finally, the results are analyzed within the matrix to examine ethnic distributions by types (individual cells and quadrants). From an intuitive perspective, we expected differences to emerge because we are comparing quite distinct cultural and sociodemographic groups. For example, the Mexican-American respondents tend to be low in income and marginally educated (less than high school) and many are immigrants, while the Anglos generally are middle-class and very well educated (at least some college). All respondents resided in homogenous social areas corresponding to their ethnic and socioeconomic status. Acculturation effects were tested by splitting the acculturation measure at its midrange (i.e., 2.5), thereby dichotomizing the distribution into low and high acculturation. This procedure was used because of the bimodal distribution of acculturation scores on the Cueller, Harris, and Jasso scale.

In order to test the first null hypothesis we compared Anglos to Mexican Americans on the cohesion subscale of the FACES–II. As Table 1 shows, the means for Anglos and Mexican Americans are 62.84 and 63.69, respectively. We conducted t tests that revealed no statistically significant difference in means; therefore the null hypothesis for cohesion was not rejected. The subsample means are very close to the national norm as well (64.9).

Similarly, the tests for differences in adaptability yielded means of 49.55 and 50.41 for Anglos and Mexican Americans, respectively, again with no significant difference in mean scores. The null hypothesis for family adaptability was not rejected. The national norm is 49.9, also quite close to the subsamples in this research.

TABLE 1. COHESION AND ADAPTABILITY SCORES FOR ANGLOS AND MEXICAN AMERICANS

Subscale	Anglos	Mexican Americans[a] All	Low Acculturation	High Acculturation
Cohesion				
Mean	62.84	63.69	63.83	63.34
SD	7.71	8.90	9.05	9.05
Enmeshed	8%	11%		
Connected	23%	25%		
Separated	43%	43%		
Disengaged	26%	21%		
Adaptability				
Mean	49.55	50.41	50.54	49.93
SD	6.44	8.24	8.20	8.93
Chaotic	17%	28%		
Flexible	16%	11%		
Structured	46%	36%		
Rigid	21%	25%		

[a]Note that proportional distributions for acculturation levels were not calculated because of small cell sizes.

The influence of acculturation on both cohesion and adaptability scores among Mexican Americans was examined. Table 1 indicates that high- and low-acculturation groups have practically identical mean scores on both subscales, with no statistical differences. Again, the null hypothesis is not rejected for the effects of acculturation on family cohesion and adaptability among Mexican Americans.

Another way of understanding the distribution of FACES scores is to compare the proportions falling into the different levels of cohesion and adaptability, controlling for ethnicity and the acculturation level of respondents. These results, also shown in Table 1, indicate no important differences in the cohesion distribution within the four levels: enmeshed, connected, separated, and disengaged. About two-thirds of both subsamples fall into either the separated or disengaged levels. Separated is the most important level for both, containing 43% of the families. On the other hand, some differences are notable when we compare the distribution of adaptability levels, with Mexican Americans more likely to be chaotic or, to a lesser extent, rigid. Anglos are more likely to be structured or slightly more likely to be flexible. However, about two-thirds of both subsamples are either structured or rigid.

On the basis of the sociocultural literature that has compared normative and value orientations across these cultural groups (Madsen, 1964; Heller, 1966), we would have expected Anglos to be high on adaptability and low on cohesion, and Mexican Americans to be primarily represented high on cohesion but with low adaptability. The Anglos are likely to fall into mid to low cohesion levels and the Mexican Americans into mid to low adaptability levels. Somewhat surprisingly, the Anglos are less flexible than expected and the Mexican Americans have less cohesiveness than we would have predicted on the basis of previous research.

The next analysis examined the distribution by ethnic group into the three regions of the circumplex model: balanced, midrange, and extreme. The criteria for placement into the balanced range is that both cohesion and adaptability scores fall into the two middle ranges on their respective continuums (cohesion: connected or separated; adaptability: flexible or structured). For the midrange, one score had to fall in the middle ranges and one outside of it. The extreme region was attained when both cohesion and adaptability were in the extreme ranges. Table 2 shows the results of these comparisons.

Anglos are somewhat more likely to be represented in the balanced region, and the difference across ethnic subsamples is about 8%. On the other hand, the Mexican-descent respondents are slightly more likely to be either at the midrange or extreme, both with differences of about 4%. However, when we assessed intraethnic differences by acculturation, dichotomizing the Mexican-descent group into high and low acculturation, we found that most of these differences were accounted for by the low-acculturation group. In fact, there were no differences at all between the high-acculturation Mexican Americans and Anglos in the balanced range (48%), but there was an 11% difference between the low-acculturation subsample (37%) and the other two. Obviously, these differences imply that corresponding discrepancies will also be found in the midrange and extreme ranges across subsamples. There is a tendency for the distribution in the extreme range to show a gradual increase, with the high-acculturation subsample having the highest score (24%). Acculturation is related to variations in family functioning, with low-acculturation respondents less likely to be represented in the balanced region of the circumplex model.

Our final analysis, shown in Table 3, gives the individual cell and quadrant distributions by ethnic group. Note that the four cells in the upper left correspond to Quadrant I in the circumplex model (Fig. 1), the four cells in the upper right correspond to Quadrant II, the lower left to Quadrant III, and the lower right to Quadrant IV.

Both ethnic subsamples are most likely to be represented in Quadrant III, which represents mid to low levels of cohesion (separated-disengaged) and adaptability (structured-rigid); Anglos, 53%, and Mexican Americans, 46%. On the other hand, both subsamples are least likely to be repre-

TABLE 2. DISTRIBUTION OF ANGLOS AND MEXICAN AMERICANS INTO REGIONS OF THE CIRCUMPLEX MODEL

Model Region	Anglos	Mexican Americans All	Low Acculturation[a]	High Acculturation
Balanced	48%	40%	37%	48%
Midrange	32%	36%	38%	30%
Extreme	20%	24%	24%	22%

[a]Note that this column totals less than 100% because of rounding.

TABLE 3. DISTRIBUTION OF ANGLOS AND MEXICAN AMERICANS WITHIN CIRCUMPLEX MODEL (WITH CUTPOINTS IN FACES SCORES FOR RESPECTIVE CELLS)

		COHESION			
A D A P T A B I L I T Y	Characteristic	Disengaged (56.9 or below)	Separated (57.0–65.0)	Connected (65.1–73.0)	Enmeshed (73.1 and above)
	Chaotic (56.1 or above)	Anglos 0% Mexican Americans 0%	Anglos 1% Mexican Americans 7%	Anglos 10% Mexican Americans 12%	Anglos 6% Mexican Americans 8%
	Flexible (50.1–56.0)	Anglos 3% Mexican Americans 1%	Anglos 13% Mexican Americans 11%	Anglos 0% Mexican Americans 0%	Anglos 0% Mexican Americans 0%
	Structured (44.0–50.0)	Anglos 9% Mexican Americans 5%	Anglos 25% Mexican Americans 18%	Anglos 10% Mexican Americans 11%	Anglos 2% Mexican Americans 2%
	Rigid (43.9 or below)	Anglos 14% Mexican Americans 16%	Anglos 5% Mexican Americans 7%	Anglos 2% Mexican Americans 2%	Anglos 0% Mexican Americans 0%

Note: The cutpoints in FACES scores are those of Olson and associates; respondents in this study were sorted accordingly.

sented in Quadrant IV, which includes mid to high levels of cohesion (connected-enmeshed) but low levels of adaptability (structured-rigid). Although there are differences in the overall distributions across groups, the patterning of the distributions is similar for both Mexican Americans and Anglos.

When we review the individual cells, perhaps the most striking finding is the absence of respondents in either group who score in the following matrix typologies: (*a*) disengaged-chaotic; (*b*) flexible-connected; (*c*) flexible-enmeshed; and (*d*) rigid-enmeshed. One type (chaotic-disengaged) is most closely associated with seriously disorganized families and runaway behavior among children (Bell, 1982). We have no easy explanations for this patterning, except to say that it certainly speaks to the general similarity in family patterns across cultural groups in this study. A further illustration of this tendency is that for both ethnic subsamples the cell with the highest frequency is the separated-structured, which is a "balanced type," and the extreme type with highest frequency is also the same (rigid-disengaged). Since these families are in the midstages of childrearing, we anticipated finding (on the basis of national norms) a higher proportion of families falling into the high cohesiveness and adaptability cells but were surprised not to find it in either subsample.

DISCUSSION

Our findings are fundamentally in accord with other recent community studies that have found no major differences between Mexican Americans and Anglos in comparisons on dimensions of family functioning such as, in this instance, cohesion and adaptability. Even comparisons controlling for acculturation did not produce differences in groups, and all the null hypotheses were confirmed. Slight differences were detected in the distribution of scores into the four levels of adaptability, with Mexican Americans being more likely to score at the extreme high end of adaptability, indicating very high flexibility in dealing with issues of family structure and role content. This means, for example, that the family is likely to have a greater ability to try new ways of dealing with problems or shifting responsibilities from person to person.

We are most impressed by the similarity of the overall patterning within the circumplex model for the ethnic subsamples in this research, and by the further similarity between our overall distribution within the circumplex model when compared with national data reported by Olson et al. (1985: 190) for families in these life stages. Families, according to their model, are depicted as existing within four life course stages: in Stage 1 are couples without children, in Stage 2 are families with young children, in Stage 3 are families with adolescents, and in Stage 4 are older couples. By their criteria, families in our research should fit with Stages 2 and 3; and according to normative data, most families should fall into Quadrant II or III. In fact, 69% of Anglo and 66% of Mexican-American respondents fall into either of these two quadrants.

These distinctions are very important because levels of cohesion and adaptability vary across the life course, and this implies fluctuating distributions within the circumplex model. Moreover, the coping abilities of well-functioning families also shift over time, indicating the relativity of the three ranges of family types (balanced, midrange, and extreme). For example, when using independent measures of coping and stress, Olson et al. (1985) found that families falling in the "extreme" range of the circumplex model during Stage 2 are better copers than families falling into the balanced range. Therefore, in this instance, it is preferable to be "extreme." It is important to remember that the ranges do not necessarily represent a continuum of well-functioning to dysfunctional families, but rather a construct for understanding family dynamics over the life cycle.

This caveat is especially pertinent for interpreting our results in that one-fifth of Anglos and one-fourth of Mexican Americans scored in the extreme range. The work of Olson et al. (1985) indicates that the "extreme" family type is probably more satisfied with family life during the child-rearing stage and has "greater skill in communicating, resolving conflict, and managing financial affairs; utilizing friends and family for support, and more satisfaction with their partner's personality" (p. 197), and they are more likely to be conventional. The only exceptions to this tendency may be chaotic-disengaged or enmeshed-rigid types, which were completely absent in our sample. Furthermore, most of our families within both ethnic subsamples fell into Quadrant II or III, which correspond with high satisfaction and low stress in family Stages 2 and 3, according to results concerning the predictive value of the circumplex model. These are areas we intend to explore in future studies, because we postulate that families that function well will be more successful at changing their health habits.

The tendency for couples to move into Quadrant III as their children move into adolescence, as documented in the normative data, was attributed by Olson et al. (1985) to the lowered interest in and/or ability of couples to be together, with the husband more likely to be invested in career pursuits and the wife in childrearing (or employment), thus decreasing the level of cohesion (closeness) and moving the family toward greater structure or even rigidity (low adaptability). Since the research project required families to have at least one child in either the fifth or sixth grade, we also found the greatest proportion of families in Quadrant III. This distribution is associated with salutory effects on family well-being and couple satisfaction.

The differences noted above are important because the construct validity of the circumplex model is based on several criteria: normative distributions, convergent validity derived from independent measures of family functioning and satisfaction within cross-sectional samples, and the clinical predictive value of the typologies. Our results, taken at face value, would seem to indicate that, overall, our sample families are scoring in a "healthy families" configuration. However, we find one difference between our results and those reported by Olson et al., in that our proportion of families located in Quadrant II is smaller. One possible explanation has to do with the regional culture of the study site. San Diego, California, with its residential instability, rapid population growth, and sprawling suburbs, is a world of commuters and of short- and long-staying migrants. Since the culture of the region is characterized by rapid social change and segmentation in interpersonal relationships, we conjecture that low cohesion may emerge from the lifestyle and experience of the individual respondents, each operating daily in quite independent spheres of activity.

Low adaptability is more difficult to explain because, at least on the surface, the environment would seem to require the opposite. However, it may be that low adaptability serves to compensate for low cohesion in this context by providing continuity of expressive and instrumental support through highly patterned role behavior, thus offsetting the destabilizing effects of other environmental factors. Also, the national norms derived by Olson et al. (1985) represent a middle-to-upper-middle-class sample of Lutherans, which could be hypothesized to have higher normative integration and family orientation than general community samples. Again, these explanations are offered only as speculations. Our findings could result from sample atypicality, although we are unable to identify any viable explanation of how this could operate to produce this relatively minor difference in distribution.

The use of the FACES in this study underscores several important points of theoretical and methodological interest. As mentioned earlier, no consensus exists concerning the qualities of well-functioning families, and research studies have identified a wide range of "normal" family types. Olson and colleagues explicitly recognize that cultural factors can moderate the predictive value of the circumplex model, especially in circumstances where family members share cultural definitions of appropriate family structure and role content. When the FACES is used with highly diverse ethnic groups in a community study, as we have done, generalizations can only be made with caution. Since the FACES was not specifically designed to tap cross-cultural differences, there may be nuances of family functioning that are beyond the scope of circumplex model and limit its predictive value when used with normative data derived from multiethnic populations. This indeterminacy raises the issue of whether the model is currently more useful for identifying pathological features in clinical interventions. Only future validation research can resolve these questions.

A final note of caution concerns the nature of our sample. Since our study relies on volunteer family participation in a health project, biases could exist in the types of families entering our sample. It would be logical to infer that families with high motivation and expressive support would be more likely to join our project, and this could produce a systematic effect that limits the external validity of our findings. Obviously, use of the FACES in future cross-sectional research with Mexican Americans and Anglos is warranted.

CONCLUSION

In summary, there are no important differences between low-income Mexican-American and middle-income Anglo parents in their perception of global levels of family cohesion and adaptability. Using normative data as a basis for comparison, we would not expect differences in overall coping ability or family satisfaction between our subsamples either. Within both subsamples, most families fall within areas of the circumplex model that are associated with successful coping. The differences that exist across and within groups tend to be those of degree rather than of kind. For example, although acculturation tends to accentuate the differences in the proportions falling into balanced, midrange, or extreme ranges, the fact is that most of the Mexican-American families fall into the quadrants with range combinations most predictive of healthy family functioning during these family stages, and the same is true for the Anglo families. Interestingly, when high-acculturation families among Mexican Americans are compared to Anglos, they are virtually indistinguishable within the criteria of the circumplex model. Since the research is descriptive, we are unable to provide etiological evidence regarding the relationship between acculturation and family functioning.

These results suggest that culture makes a difference in family cohesion and adaptability within the circumplex model, but these variations remain within the criteria of well-functioning and resilient families. We consider this research exploratory, and we intend to continue with repeated measures to determine the test-retest reliability of these findings and to identify correlates that may be related to different facets of family activities. We are especially concerned about health behavior change and how family cohesion and adaptability are related to facilitating these goals. The intuitive appeal of the circumplex model used in this research is that it has face validity and multiple applications, as well as potential cross-cultural sensitivity for identifying normal and pathological families. It may have predictive value as well. We encourage replication of our research with other multiethnic samples in order to explore the prospects and limitations of this model for the coherent interpretation of family dynamics.

REFERENCES

Atkins, Catherine, Thomas Patterson, Beatriz Roppe, James Sallis, and Philip Nader. 1985. Health Habits and the Decision to Volunteer for a Family Health Project. Paper presented at the annual meeting of the American Psychological Association, Los Angeles (August).

Bean, Frank, Curtis Russell, and John Marcum. 1977. "Familism and marital satisfaction among Mexican Americans: The effects of family size, wife's labor force participation, and conjugal power." Journal of Marriage and the Family 39: 759-767.

Bell, Richard. 1982. Parent-Adolescent Interaction in Runaway Families. Unpublished doctoral dissertation, University of Minnesota, St. Paul.

Bell, L., and D. Bell. 1982. "Family climate and the role of the family adolescent: Determinants of adolescent functioning." Family Relations 31: 519-527.

Cromwell, Vicky L., and Ronald E. Cromwell. 1978. "Perceived dominance in decision-making and conflict resolution among Anglo, black, and Chicano couples." Journal of Marriage and the Family 40: 749-759.

Cronbach, Lee J. 1960. Essentials of Psychological Testing. New York: Harper.

Cuellar, Israel, L. Harris, and R. Jasso. 1980. "An acculturation scale for Mexican American normal and clinical populations." Hispanic Journal of the Behavioral Sciences 2: 199-217.

Glueck, Sheldon, and Eleanor Glueck. 1962. Family Environment and Delinquency. Boston: Houghton Mifflin.

Golding, Jacqueline, Audrey Burnam, and Diane Timbers. 1985. Acculturation and Distress: Social Psychological Mediators. Paper presented at the annual meeting of the American Psychological Association, Los Angeles (August).

Grebler, Leo, Joan Moore, and Ralph Guzman. 1970. The Mexican American People. New York: Free Press.

Griswold, Richard. 1984. La Familia: Chicano Families in the Urban Southwest, 1848 to the Present. Notre Dame, IN: University of Notre Dame Press.

Heller, Celia. 1966. Mexican American Youth: Forgotten Youth at the Crossroads. New York: Random House.

Keefe, Susan, Amado Padilla, and Manuel Carlos. 1979. "The Mexican American extended family as an emotional support system." Human Organization 38: 144-152.

Litwak, Eugene. 1960. "Occupational mobility and extended family cohesion." American Sociological Review 25: 9-21.

Madsen, William. 1964. The Mexican Americans of South Texas. New York: Holt, Rinehart and Winston.

McCord, Joan, and William McCord. 1958. "The effects of parental role models on criminality." Journal of Social Issues 14: 66-75.

Mirande, Alfredo. 1977. "The Chicano family: A reanalysis of conflicting views." Journal of Marriage and the Family 39: 747-756.

Montiel, Miguel. 1970. "The social science myth of the Mexican American family." El Grito: A Journal of Contemporary Mexican American Thought 3: 56-63.

Moroney, M. 1980. Families, Social Services, and Social Policy. DHHS Pub. No. (ADM) 80-846. Washington, DC: U.S. Government Printing Office.

Nader, Philip, James Sallis, Joan Rupp, Catherine Atkins, Thomas Patterson, Michael Buono, William Vega, Karen Senn, Ian Abramson, Bea Roppe, and Robert Kaplan. 1986. "The Family Health Project: Reaching families through the schools." Journal of School Health 56: 227-231.

Olson, David H., Hamilton McCubbin, Howard Barnes, Andrea S. Larsen, Marla J. Muxen, and Marc A. Wilson. 1983. Families: What Makes Them Work. Beverly Hills, CA: Sage.

Olson, David H., Candyce S. Russell, and Douglas H. Sprenkle. 1980. "Marital and family therapy: A decade review." Journal of Marriage and the Family 42: 973-993.

Olson, David H., Candyce S. Russell, and Douglas H. Sprenkle. 1980. "Circumplex model of marital and family systems, II: Empirical studies and clinical intervention." In John P. Vincent (ed.), Advances in Family Intervention, Assessment, and Theory (Vol. 1). Greenwich, CT: JAI Press.

Olson, David H., Candyce S. Russell, and Douglas H. Sprenkle. 1982. "The circumplex model of marital and family systems, VI: Theoretical update." Family Process 22: 69-83.

Parsons, Talcott. 1968. "The normal American family." In Marvin B. Sussman (ed.), Sourcebook in Marriage and the Family. New York: Houghton Mifflin.

Portner, Joyce. 1980. Parent-Adolescent Interaction of Families in Treatment. Unpublished doctoral dissertation, University of Minnesota, St. Paul.

Ramirez, Oscar, and Carlos Arce. 1981. "The contemporary Chicano family: An empirically based review." In A. Barron (ed.), Explorations in Chicano Psychology. New York: Praeger.

Redl, Fritz, and David Wineman. 1951. Children Who Hate. New York: Free Press.

Romano, Octavio I. 1973. "The anthropology and sociology of Mexican Americans: The distortion of Mexican American history." In O. Romano (ed.), Voices: Readings from El Grito. Berkeley, CA: Qunito Sol Publications.

Rosen, L. 1970. "The broken home and male delinquency." In Marvin Wolfgang et al. (eds.), The Sociology of Crime and Delinquency. New York: John Wiley and Sons.

Russell, Candyce S. 1979. "Circumplex model of marital and family systems, III: Empirical evaluation of families." Family Process 18: 29-45.

Sprenkle, Douglas H., and David H. Olson. 1978. "Circumplex model of marital systems, IV: Empirical study of clinical and non-clinical couples." Journal of Marriage Therapy 4: 59-74.

Staples, Robert, and Alfredo Mirande. 1980. "Racial and cultural variations among American families: A decennial review of the literature on minority families." Journal of Marriage and the Family 42: 887-903.

Sussman, Marvin B. 1959. "The isolated nuclear family: Fact or fiction?" Social Problems 6: 333-340.
Van de Ban, A. W. 1967. "Family structure and modernization." Journal of Marriage and the Family 29: 771-773.
Vega, William, Richard Hough, and Annelisa Romero. 1983. "Family life patterns of Mexican Americans." In Gloria Powell, Joe Yamamoto, Annelisa Romero, and Armando Morales (eds.), Psychosocial Development of Minority Group Children. New York: Brunner/Mazel.
Vega, William, and Bohdan Kolody. 1985. "The meaning of social support and the mediation of stress across cultures." In William Vega and M. Miranda (eds.), Stress and Hispanic Mental Health: Relating Research to Services Delivery. Washington, DC: National Institute of Mental Health.
Ybarra, Lea. 1982. "When wives work: The impact on the Chicano family." Journal of Marriage and the Family 44: 169-177.
Zinn, Maxine B. 1980. "Employment and education of Mexican American women: The interplay of modernity and ethnicity in eight families." Harvard Educational Review 50: 47-61.

APPENDIX

ITEMS IN THE FAMILY ADAPTABILITY AND COHESION EVALUATION SCALES-II

1. Family members are supportive of each other during difficult times.
2. In our family, it is easy for everyone to express his/her opinion.
3. It is easier to discuss problems with people outside the family than with other family members.
4. Each family member has input in major family decisions.
5. Our family gathers together in the same room.
6. Children have a say in their discipline.
7. Our family does things together.
8. Family members discuss problems and feel good about the solutions.
9. In our family, everyone goes his/her own way.
10. We shift household responsibilities from person to person.
11. Family members know each other's close friends.
12. It is hard to know what the rules are in our family.
13. Family members consult other family members on their decisions.
14. Family members say what they want.
15. We have difficulty thinking of things to do as a family.
16. In solving problems, the children's suggestions are followed.
17. Family members feel very close to each other.
18. Discipline is fair in our family.
19. Family members feel closer to people outside the family than to other family members.
20. Our family tries new ways of dealing with problems.
21. Family members go along with what the family decides to do.
22. In our family, everyone shares responsibilities.
23. Family members like to spend their free time with each other.
24. It is difficult to get a rule changed in our family.
25. Family members avoid each other at home.
26. When problems arise, we compromise.
27. We approve of each other's friends.
28. Family members are afraid to say what is on their minds.
29. Family members pair up rather than do things as a total family.
30. Family members share interests and hobbies with each other.

Source: David H. Olson, Joyce Portner, and Richard Bell, in Olson et al. (1983).

10 Sexuality Attitudes of Black Adults[*]

Constance A. Timberlake and Wayne D. Carpenter[**]

This study considers the sexuality attitudes of a black middle-class sample (N = 124). Categories assessed include beliefs and attitudes in the following: communication regarding sexuality information, adolescent contraception, adolescent pregnancy, nonmarital intercourse, responsibility for contraception and pregnancy, abortion, pornography, and masturbation. ANOVAs were performed on individual questions and groupings according to sex, age, education, and marital status. Results suggest that the participants are well-informed, moderate, and consistent in their beliefs. Implications of the study are useful for both researchers and practitioners.

In the area of sexuality, liberals and conservatives are often worlds apart. Yet with regard to educating their children, both agree that parents should be the primary sexuality educators (Gordon & Snyder, 1989; Koop, 1988). This is especially true in light of the preponderance of information and concern regarding teen pregnancy. The research described in this article is directed to the family professional. Family professionals have been aggressive in their commitment to enhance the quality of family life by designing and implementing sexuality educational programs, and more thoroughly preparing future family professionals. However, a disproportionate amount of knowledge is inherited and reflects the attitudes, beliefs, and behavior of the "traditional" family which has not, by and large, reflected nor included the full spectrum of the black family (Billingsley, 1988). For example, the literature reflects that the sexuality attitudes of black adults has yet to be an area of study. Family professionals must possess information that is both relevant and current to the population being served, if they are to design and implement programs that will take into consideration nuances that may not exist in the traditional "white" model.

At present, the adolescent pregnancy rate in the United States is twice that of France, England, and Canada; three times that of Sweden; and seven times that of the Netherlands. There are approximately 1.3 million children now living in the United States with 1.1 million teenage mothers. Two thirds of these children were born to mothers under the age of 18. Black American adolescent females have the highest birthrate among teenagers in the developed world. When compared to white adolescents, black adolescents are four times more likely to give birth to babies from a union of unmarried parents. Of all black births today more than half are born to unwed mothers (Hill, 1989).

Often overlooked are the statistics which indicate that while pregnancy rates for minority teenagers are higher than for white teenagers, the birthrate is increasing for whites while holding relatively stable for minorities (National Center for Health Statistics, 1986). Nevertheless, these statistics are alarming, especially when one considers the long-term effects of adolescent pregnancy on the family.

The quality of family life in the United States is largely determined by education and economic resources. Adolescent parents often suffer in both these areas. Statistics indicate that among all teenagers who give birth; one third of black teen mothers and 45% of white teen mothers will not complete high school (Children's Defense Fund, 1988). An adolescent female loses 2 years of schooling as a consequence of early parenting (BOCES Regional Planning Center, 1987).

When a teen mother or father drops out of school without the skills and resources to earn a decent living, the economic costs are high to both the individual and society. The individual loses potential earning power and often becomes dependent upon society for support. Seventy-five percent of all single mothers under age 25 live in poverty. Women who were teenagers when their child was born, are less than 23 years of age, and are head of households account for two thirds of the young families who live in poverty. Of the children who are poor, 80% are white and 91% are black (Children's Defense Fund, 1988). The Center for Population Options estimates that teenage childbearing cost the United States $16.65 billion in 1985 in Aid to Families with Dependent Children (AFDC), food stamps, and Medicaid benefits (BOCES Regional Planning Center, 1987).

Noting such statistics, it is clear that past and present programs to abate the problem of black adolescent pregnancy have not been effective. Such programs have often neglected to draw on the strengths of the two most important social systems available to blacks: the family and the church (Hill, 1972).

Frazier (1963) noted that the black church has historically been the most important source of support and guidance for blacks and their families, and is a major means of communication in the black community. Yet as important as the black church may be, it is parents that play the most important role in the sexual development of their children. Unaware of the teaching roles they play in such development, parents often avoid direct communication with their children regarding sexuality. However, crucial aspects of sex education are taught indirectly, so that by the time children are 3 or 4 years of age they have received considerable information about sexuality (Darling & Hicks, 1982). Walters and Walters (1983) concur stating, "Throughout childhood, parents and children elicit behaviors and respond to each other in ways that contribute to the form and

---

[*]Supported, in part, by the Office of Research and Graduate Studies, Syracuse University.
[**]Constance A. Timberlake is an Associate Professor and immediate past Chair, Department of Child & Family Studies, Syracuse University, Syracuse, NY 13244-1250. Wayne D. Carpenter is a Counselor, Western New England College, Springfield, MA 01119.

Key Words: adolescent pregnancy, black sexuality attitudes.

substance of the growing child's sexual attitudes" (p. 11).

In Fox's (1979) review of the literature on the family's influence upon adolescent sexual behavior, several important points emerge: (a) Not many children receive direct instruction from their parents about sexuality, sexual intercourse, or fertility regulation. (b) Parental verbal communication about sex may forestall or postpone a child's sexual activity. (c) Among those daughters who are sexually active, parental verbal communication appears related to more effective contraceptive practice on the part of the child. Children also gain sexual information from school and peers, but it must be kept in mind that such information always occurs in the context of the attitudes and knowledge that already have been provided by their families (Walters & Walters, 1983).

It is clear that parental attitudes play an important role in the sexual development of children. Ladner (1971) observed that misinformation based on "folk tradition" was often disseminated by mothers and grandmothers. Therefore, she cautioned that individuals who are concerned about adolescent pregnancy broaden their interest to include parents. Fox (1979) suggests that programs likely to be inefficient and ineffective arise from policies which both ignore the familial context of teenage sexual behavior or fail to enlist the familial base of the teenager.

This being the case, some have advocated the critical importance of sex education for *parents* in order to help them be more knowledgeable and effective sexuality teachers (Darling & Hicks, 1982; Staples, 1972; Timberlake & Carpenter, 1986). However, an appreciation of the cultural, ethnic, and preexisting parental attitudes toward sexuality is necessary to develop an effective education program that meets the needs of today's parents and their children. Without such knowledge, there is the risk of developing and implementing educational programs that may attempt to mold differing ethnic groups into idealized models as suggested by Staples (1988).

In partnership with 50 black churches, the authors were interested in developing a model sexuality program for black adults. A literature review revealed a paucity of information regarding sexuality attitudes and beliefs of black adults. It is the purpose of this article to contribute to the literature, knowledge relating to a number of attitudes held by black adults regarding: adolescent birth control and pregnancy, nonmarital intercourse, responsibility for contraception and pregnancy, abortion, pornography, and masturbation.

Method

Initial contact was made with black ministers to secure permission to distribute a questionnaire to their respective parishioners. When permission was received, the researchers delivered packets to the churches for distribution. To increase the size of the sample, the packets were also distributed at the annual conference of the Association of Black Women in Higher Education, Inc., and to parents who had registered for a forthcoming sexuality training program. Thus, this is a nonrandom convenience sample.

The packets included a letter describing the purpose of the survey, the questionnaire, and instructions to complete the questionnaire independently and return the completed questionnaire anonymously via an enclosed stamped envelope. A total of 300 questionnaires were distributed with 124 usable questionnaires returned (41%).

Three fourths of the respondents were female and one fourth were male. Almost one half (46%) were married and living with their spouses; 11% were married and not living with spouse; 16% were divorced; and 3% were widowed. The remaining 24% had never married.

Participants' education was grouped into three categories: some high school to high school graduate (19%), some college to 2-year college graduate (32%), and 4-year college graduate to advanced graduate degree (51%). Annual family income was grouped into four categories: less than $10,000 (8%); $10,000 to $24,999 (29%); $25,000 to $39,999 (26%); and $40,000 or more (37%). Age of participants was grouped into five categories: under 21 years (4%), 21-29 (17%), 30-39 (38%), 40-49 (29%), and 50-59 (12%).

All of the participants had children and/or were the primary child care provider. For the purposes of data analysis, respondents were grouped into four categories: sex, age, education, and marital status. A separate ANOVA was then performed on each of the four categories.

Instrument

The instrument consisted of a questionnaire containing 38 items related to the sexuality beliefs and attitudes of adults. A review of the literature concerning black attitudes and beliefs towards various sexual issues revealed little or no information in this regard. Indeed, most research, until very recently, has focused upon the deviant sexual behavior of blacks (Brown, 1985; French & Wailes, 1982), as opposed to nondeviant behavior, attitudes, and beliefs.

To fill this void items were selected on the basis of areas of concern most frequently raised by black adults who participated in an adult sexuality education program (Timberlake & Carpenter, 1986).

The instrument designed to assess an overview of sexual beliefs and attitudes was subdivided by assigning each of the 38 items into one of the following areas: communication, adolescent birth control, adolescent pregnancy, intercourse, responsibility for birth control and pregnancy, abortion, pornography, and masturbation.

The participants responded to each item by using a 4-point Likert-type scale, reflecting the conservatism of their beliefs. Participants indicated whether they (1) *strongly agreed*, (2) *agreed*, (3) *disagreed*, or (4) *strongly disagreed* with the item statement.

To measure the reliability of the instrument, Cronbach's Alpha was sought. The Cronbach's Alpha is a measure of internal consistency and varies from 0 to 1. When there is no internal consistency in responding to the questions an $\alpha = 0$ is obtained. Whereas, when there is perfect consistency, $\alpha = 1$ is obtained. In the 38 items that were used in this study, Cronbach $\alpha = .94$ was obtained, indicating high internal reliability.

When all eight categories were examined separately, a relatively high internal consistency was established, with the highest being $\alpha = .82$ and the lowest being an $\alpha = .60$. When one takes into consideration the low number of items in each of the categories, these Cronbach Alpha's are acceptable when considering internal consistency.

Participants provided demographic information which included age, sex, marital status, education, current and/or last occupation, and gross income. Participants also provided information regarding the number, sex, and ages of their children.

Results

Do black adults believe in sharing sexual information with children?

When the participants of the study were asked questions as to whether they agreed or disagreed in providing children with sexuality information, an overwhelming percentage (95%) of respondents indicated that fathers should discuss sexual issues with both sons and daughters. This same belief held for mothers discussing sexual issues with their sons as well as daughters (98%). Questions raised by children to which parents do not know the answers should not be ignored (98%), and discussion should begin before the child is in first grade (74%). Moreover, 92% do not uphold the myth that increased sexual knowledge leads to sexual activity.

An ANOVA regarding sexual information and communication revealed no differences with respect to sex, education, and marital status. There was a significant difference ($F = 3.93$, $df = 4$, $p \leq .01$) found for age, with those under age 21 being more restrained in sharing sexuality information as compared with those participants 21 years of age and older.

Regarding individual questions, all respondents agreed that it was acceptable for a child under 5 years of age to hear the words "penis" and "vagina." However, those having 4 or more years of college more strongly indicated the acceptability of using such terms with younger children compared to the other two education groups ($p \leq .05$).

How do black adults feel about teenage birth control? Most black adults (74%) do not believe teenagers regularly use contraceptives when engaged in sexual intercourse. Indeed, black adults favor ready availability of contraceptives for sexually active teens and 75% believe that contraceptives should be made available without parental consent. Asked if their own children were to become sexually active, 97% would want him/her to use contraceptives. No statistical differences were found among the four groups.

Within education groups, items 9 and 12 revealed significant differences. Respondents with a high school education or less expressed a more conservative view than persons with 4 or more years of college, believing that access to contraceptives is a major reason for the increase in sexual activity among teenagers ($p \leq .02$) and that sexually active teens regularly use contraceptives ($p \leq .03$).

Within marital groups, significant differences were found in four of the items. Never Marrieds were significantly more conservative compared to Married With Spouse with respect to providing ready availability of contraceptives ($p \leq .01$), and the availability of contraceptives without parental consent ($p \leq .02$). Moreover, Never Marrieds compared to Married With Spouse, were more likely to believe that the ease of access to contraceptives promotes sexual activity among teenagers ($p \leq .05$).

All marital groups agreed they would want their sexually active teens to use contraceptives. However, there was a significant difference ($p \leq .01$) between the Married Without Spouse and the Never Marrieds, with the former feeling more strongly in favor of such practice.

What do black adults believe to be the reasons behind teen pregnancy? Poor communication with parents was believed to be a factor in teen pregnancy by 56% of the respondents. Seventy percent of the respondents believed the following *not* to be major factors in teenage pregnancy: involvement in ongoing love relationships, lenient standards of behavior imposed by parents, low self-esteem, or a wish to become pregnant. Overall, no significant differences were found between the groups.

Examination of individual questions did reveal significant differences within groups. Males believe more strongly than females ($p \leq .01$) that lenient standards of behavior imposed by parents is a major contributing factor to teen pregnancy. Belief that teens who become pregnant want to do so was held more strongly by those with a high school education or less, compared with those with 4 or more years of college ($p \leq .02$).

How do black adults feel about nonmarital intercourse? Seventy-two percent of the respondents believed it was permissible to engage in nonmarital intercourse; however, this percentage dropped dramatically to 45% when specifically asked about nonmarital intercourse among teens.

With regard to premarital intercourse, education was found to be a significant factor ($F = 4.04$, $df = 2$, $p \leq .02$). When given the statement, "Only married people should engage in sexual intercourse," significant differences were found according to educational background. Those with 4 or more years of college were significantly ($p \leq .001$) more accepting of nonmarital intercourse than those with some college and those with a high school education or less. A strong tendency was also found among the marital groups with the Never Marrieds being more acceptable of nonmarital intercourse than the Married Without Spouse ($p \leq .06$).

Who is responsible for birth control and pregnancy? When asked if birth control is primarily the woman's responsibility, 86% disagreed. Ninety-one percent felt that birth control should be equally shared by both the woman *and* the man. Respondents with 4 or more years of college believed more strongly than those with some college education that responsibility for birth control should be equally shared ($p \leq .02$). With regard to pregnancy, 82% disagreed with the statement "A woman has only herself to blame if she becomes pregnant." Ninety-eight percent of the respondents believed that a man who impregnates an unmarried woman should be expected to participate in any future responsibility of the child.

What are the black attitudes toward abortion? Black adults were divided on their beliefs regarding abortion. A 50-50 split occurred when respondents were asked if abortion should be allowed no matter what the circumstances. Yet only 7% believed that abortion should never be allowed regardless of circumstances. When more specific questions were asked, differences became apparent. Seventy percent of the respondents believed an abortion should be allowed if it were known that the fetus would be born with a serious birth defect or mental retardation. If the mother's life were endangered, 64% would allow an abortion to take place. Sixty-four percent also believed it is permissible for persons under age 18 to have an abortion. When a pregnancy resulted from rape or incest, the number of respondents who would allow an abortion rose to 84%.

An ANOVA revealed education to be a significant factor ($F = 4.09$, $df = 2$, $p \leq .02$). More specifically, those with 4 or more years of college were significantly more in favor of abortions for individuals under age 18 than were persons with some college education ($p \leq .04$). Differences in marital status were also found to be significant with Married With Spouse expressing, more support for abortions for persons under age 18 than Married Without Spouse ($p \leq .05$).

What are the black adult attitudes toward nonviolent pornography? Black respondents were uniformly against pornography. Eight-two percent indicated it is harmful to society; 57% believed it is a major cause of incest, rape, and child molestation; and 65% feel it should not be protected by law. No significant differences were found among the major groupings, nor were there significant differences when individual questions were examined.

What are the attitudes of black adults regarding masturbation? For most blacks (76%), masturbation was perceived as acceptable, normal behavior. Regarding masturbation among children, 90% would not punish a child for masturbation in private, and 71% would not teach their children that masturbation is wrong. A close examination of the data revealed a statistical difference among the educational groups. Respondents with a high school education felt more strongly that children should be taught masturbation is wrong when compared to those with 4 or more years of college ($p \leq .03$).

Discussion

The information gathered in this study comes largely from well-educated, middle-class, urban blacks. As a whole, these participants hold moderate, well-informed, consistent views with regard to sexuality. As such, they are not inclined to believe the many myths related to sexuality that are still prevalent in today's society.

For example, the majority of blacks in this study do not uphold the myth that increased sexual knowledge leads to increased sexual activity. Three quarters of the respondents believe that discussions related to sexuality should begin *before* a child has reached first grade. Furthermore, both parents should be involved in providing sexual information. Indeed, a majority of these blacks believe that a major contributing factor in teen pregnancy is poor communication between parents and children.

Although a majority of the respondents believe it is permissible for adults to engage in nonmarital intercourse, they do not believe teenagers should engage in such activity. For those teens who are sexually active, these black adults have a strong pragmatic belief that contraceptives should be readily available. Indeed, an overwhelming majority would want their own children, if sexually active, to responsibly use contraceptives. Furthermore, the respondents do not adhere to the once dominant belief that birth control is primarily the woman's responsibility. The vast majority believe the responsibility for birth control should be equally shared by men and women. Responsibility for any children born to unmarried parents should also be equally shared.

These blacks do not necessarily favor abortion, per se. However, a majority of them would allow abortions under certain circumstances such as endangerment to the mother's life, if the person were under the age of 18, if the fetus would be born with a serious birth defect or mental retardation, or if the person was a victim of rape or incest. Yet, even so, the degree of support varies with the situation, thus providing a further indication of the complexity of the abortion issue. Hence, it would be a mistake to state that these blacks support abortion, per se, without accounting for the circumstances under which an abortion is being contemplated.

The belief that pornography is not only harmful to society, but also a major cause of such criminal behaviors as incest, rape, and child molestation is held by a large majority of blacks in this study. Moreover, these respondents do not hold the civil libertarian view that pornography should be protected by law.

These black respondents are less conservative, however, regarding their attitudes toward masturbation. It is viewed as acceptable normal behavior. Even where children are concerned, these blacks would not administer punishment for such behavior if done in private, nor would the majority of blacks teach their children that masturbation is wrong.

Implications for Practice

The results of this study have implications for the researcher and family professional, that is, the family practitioner and the family life educator. Family professionals who are uninformed regarding the sexuality attitudes of black adults within their historical context are more likely to create programs that mirror the attitudes and beliefs of the majority population. They run the risk of creating programs that are not effective and indeed, may be in conflict with the intended population. The findings of this study are among the first to provide a knowledge base of sexuality attitudes of black adults that family professionals should consider as they plan and implement sexuality programs for blacks. The findings provide much needed information about the differences and similarities of sexuality attitudes within the black community when differentiated by sex, age, education, and marital status.

One of the more significant findings of the study is that education is a more important factor in determining differences and similarities in sexuality attitudes than are sex, age, or marital status. However, education is not a factor when responses in the area of abortion and pornography are analyzed. The information provided by the study establishes a framework from which professionals can design and implement effective programs for black parents and their children, programs that are sensitive to the difference within the black community and more accurately reflect the full spectrum of sexuality attitudes of blacks. This study provides opportunities for the researcher and family professional to reduce the misconceptions and stereotypes regarding the sexuality attitudes of black adults.

More importantly, according to the findings, the preparation and training of family professionals must increasingly reflect the nuances of racial and cultural diversity within groups. If programs are to be designed to assist black families and subsequently their progeny, family professionals must be cognizant of the similarities and differences. Because black attitudes may differ from those of whites, these differences should not be assumed to be weaknesses but rather considered to be a part of an obviously viable culture. For example, the respondents in this study do not favor abortion per se; they are strongly against pornography, with a significant majority believing pornography is harmful to society and the majority believing that it is a significant contributor to incidents of incest, rape, and child molestation; Never Marrieds are more conservative than Married With Spouse, with respect to having contraceptives readily accessible to teenagers; and black males feel that lenient standards of behavior adopted by parents significantly contribute to teen pregnancy. These findings and others need to be incorporated into sexuality training programs and research efforts relating to the sexuality attitudes of middle class blacks.

Conclusion

This study represents a first step in investigating the sexuality attitudes of today's black middle-class adult. In order to obtain findings which are more amenable to generalization, further research would need to be conducted with larger samples drawn from other geographic regions and differing socioeconomic classes. Additional studies must also investigate the relationship between the expressed attitudes and actual behaviors. The gathering of this information may be significant to the extent that current policies may be positively influenced and thereby enhance the development of more viable programs that will more closely meet the needs of blacks and our society.

REFERENCES

Billingsley, A. (1988). The impact of technology on Afro-American families. *Family Relations, 37,* 420-425.
BOCES Regional Planning Center. (1987, April). Teen pregnancy and parenting: How can schools respond? *Voice, 8,* p. 2. Albany, NY: Albany-Scholaric-Schenectady BOCES.
Brown, S. V. (1985). Premarital sexual permissiveness among black adolescent females. *Social Psychology Quarterly, 48,* 381-387.
Children's Defense Fund. (1988, January/March). *Teen pregnancy: An advocate's guide to the numbers.* Washington, DC: Children's Defense Fund's Adolescent Pregnancy Clearing House.
Darling, C. A., & Hicks, M. W. (1982). Parental influence on adolescent sexuality: Implications for parents as educators. *Journal of Youth and Adolescent, 11,* 231-245.
Fox, G. L. (1979, May-June). The family's influence on adolescent sexual behavior. *Children Today,* pp. 21-25, 36.
Frazier, E. (1963). *The Negro church in America.* New York: Schocken Books.
French, L. A., & Wailes, S. N. (1982). Perceptions of sexual deviance: A biracial analysis. *International Journal of Offender Therapy and Comparative Criminology, 26,* 242-249.
Gordon, S., & Snyder, C. W. (1989). *Personal issues in human sexuality: A guidebook for better sexual health.* Boston: Allyn and Bacon.
Hill, R. B. (1972). *The strength of black families* (1st ed.). New York: Emerson Hall Publishers.
Hill, R. B. (1989). Critical issues for black families by the year 2000. In National Urban League (Ed.), *The state of Black America 1989* (p. 41). New York: National Urban League.
Koop, C. E. (1988). *Understanding AIDS: A message from the surgeon general?* (HHS Publication No. (CDC) HHS-88-8404). Washington, DC: U.S. Government Printing Office.
Ladner, J. (1971). *Tomorrow's tomorrow: The black woman.* New York: Doubleday.
National Center for Health Statistics. (1986). Advanced report of final natality statistics, 1984. *Monthly Vital Statistics Report,* Vol. 35, No. 4, Suppl., July 18, 1986. Hyattsville, MD: Public Health Service.
Staples, R. (1972). Research on black sexuality: Its implication for family life, sex, education, and public policy. *Family Coordinator, 21,* 183-188.
Staples, R. (1988). The Black American family. In C. H. Mindel, R. W. Haldenstein, & R. Wright, Jr. (Eds.), *Ethnic families in America* (3rd ed., pp. 303-324). New York: Elsevier.
Timberlake, C., & Carpenter, W. D. (1986). Adult sexuality training in the black church: An approach toward combatting teenage pregnancy. *Journal of Home Economics, 78,* 29-31.
Walters, J., & Walters, L. H. (1983). The role of the family in sex education. *Journal of Research & Development in Education, 16*(2), 8-15.

11 After Intermarriage: Ethnic Identity among Mixed-Heritage Japanese-Americans and Hispanics

Cookie White Stephan and Walter G. Stephan[*]
New Mexico State University

The ethnic identity of mixed-heritage individuals may have important implications for the future of minority groups in the United States. Both assimilationists and pluralists believe mixed-heritage individuals are most likely to adopt a single ethnic identity. To address this question, the antecedents of individual-level ethnic identity were investigated in two samples of mixed-heritage college students, part-Japanese Americans in Hawaii and part-Hispanics in the Southwest. Seventy-three percent of the part-Japanese and 44% of the part-Hispanics listed a multiple identity on at least one measure of ethnic identity, which suggests that our ethnic boundaries may be eroding through intermarriage. In addition, the antecedents of the identity of these mixed-heritage individuals were investigated.

Ethnic identity, the identification of an individual or group of individuals with a particular ethnic group or groups, is a central issue for social scientists interested in race and ethnicity (Alba and Chamlin, 1983; Glazer and Moynihan, 1975; Greeley, 1971; Horowitz, 1975; Portes, 1984; van den Berghe and Primov, 1974). In this study we explore the ethnic identity of individuals for whom such identity is problematic: persons of mixed heritage.

Empirical investigations have revealed three characteristics of ethnic identity. First, ethnic identity is subjective (Barth, 1969; A. Cohen, 1974; van den Berghe and Primov, 1974). It is not just a process whereby groups or individuals judge their ethnicity solely by objective physical criteria or on the basis of the culture in which they were born, although these criteria are often important (Weber, 1961). Individuals typically select an identity from the several ethnic groups to which they have some claim to membership, but ethnic identity can be inconsistent with both the individual's biological heritage and cultural membership. In recognition of the subjective nature of ethnic identity, it is now thought that self-identification is the least ambiguous way of determining where one group ends and another begins (Barth, 1969; Moerman, 1965; Smith, 1980). For example, in an examination of the ethnic identity of a group called the Lue, the investigator argued that "Someone is a Lue by virtue of believing and calling himself Lue and of acting in ways that validate his Lueness" (Moerman, 1965). Second, ethnic identity is often unstable (R. Cohen, 1978; Handleman, 1977; Moerman, 1965; Nagata, 1974; Okamura, 1981; Wilson, 1984). Many individuals change identities in the course of a lifetime or switch identities regularly in different situations. Of the latter circumstance, Paden (1967) wrote, "situational ethnicity is premised on the observation that particular contexts may determine which of a person's communal identities or loyalties are appropriate at a point in time." For instance, in

---

Department of Sociology and Anthropology, New Mexico State University, Box 3BV, Las Cruces, NM 88003.

[*]Department of Psychology, New Mexico State University, Box 3452, Las Cruces, NM 88003.

Malaysia an occupation may identify one as a Chinese, while one's religion may identify one as a Malay. If this is the case, the individual may well "be" Chinese in one situation and Malay in another (Nagata, 1974).

Third, ethnic identity is a joint process, one by which the group or individual and relevant outsiders together determine the individual's ethnic identity (R. Cohen, 1978; Isaacs, 1975; van den Berghe and Primov, 1974). A group or individual's ethnic identity cannot be sustained successfully if it is inconsistent with the identity assigned by others in the society. In particular, physical or cultural attributes may limit options in selecting an ethnic identity. For example, while many Andean Indians choose to "become" mestizos, or mixed-blood individuals, an Indian who spoke only Quechua would not be accepted as a mestizo by either group (van den Berghe and Primov, 1974). The selection process may also be limited if social relations in the society are rigidly organized around the concept of ethnicity, as in South Africa (Paden, 1967).

Ethnic identity is especially likely to arise as an issue at the boundaries between groups (Barth, 1969). At the societal level, the issue of identity must be faced by ethnic groups who live and work among other groups of people. At the individual level, mixed-heritage people must confront the issue of their own ethnic identity. For example, a person in the American Southwest who is part Caucasian and part Native American Indian and who resides in an area that is dominated by Hispanic culture might identify with one or more of these groups.

Anthropologists have led the way in the study of ethnic identity at the societal level (Barth, 1969; A. Cohen, 1974; De Vos and Romanucci-Ross, 1975; Moerman, 1965). Although a number of sociologists have argued for the importance of studies of ethnic identity at the individual level (Alba and Chamlin, 1983; Gist and Dworkin, 1972; Okamura, 1981; Portes, 1984; van den Berghe and Primov, 1974), the level of analysis of this study, few studies of individual-level ethnic identity exist.

ASSIMILATION OR PLURALISM?

One body of research on ethnicity in the United States has largely focused on the relations between ethnic minorities and the majority group. Two dominant positions have evolved from this research, the assimilationist and the pluralist positions. These two positions are often presented as ideal types, against which the circumstances of actual groups can be judged.

Assimilation theorists argue that the United States is indeed a melting pot, minority people having been blended into the majority culture (Gordon, 1964, 1978; Hirschman, 1983; Yinger, 1981). Although the majority culture may become increasingly diverse and enriched by the inclusion of elements of the minority cultures, it is not greatly changed. In the process of assimilation, the minority culture is altered considerably more, losing some of its distinctive values and identity.

By contrast, the pluralists believe that minority groups retain many aspects of their cultures and identities. Some theorists suggest many minorities have rejected the process of assimilation (e.g., Greeley, 1971), sometimes using ethnicity as a means of resource mobilization (e.g., Jenkins, 1983; Olzak, 1983). Others argue the majority culture has tended to exclude minorities of color (Blauner, 1972) or controlled them through the split labor market (Bonacich, 1972, 1975, 1976; Cummings, 1980; Mukabe, 1981), rendering assimilation of these groups impossible.

Assimilation theorists agree that some types of assimilation are more easily achieved than others. A minority group may readily adopt the culture of the majority group, but they may find barriers to other types of assimilation. Because of prejudice and discrimination against physically distinct groups, some minorities may be blocked from entrance into primary group relations with those in the majority, and particularly from intermarriage with them.

Recently new light has been cast on this old debate by consideration of the effects of intermarriage on ethnic identity. Despite the barriers to marital assimilation, the rates of intermarriage among most minority group members in our society are relatively high and increasing (Crester and Leon, 1982). In addition, the children of intermarriages seem particularly likely to marry outside their ethnic groups (Alba and Golden, 1986; Tinker, 1973).

Because the number of mixed-heritage individuals is growing, their ethnic identity is likely to become an important determinant of the assimilation or separatism of many minority groups in the United States (Alba and Chamlin, 1983; Alba and

Golden, 1986; Lieberson and Waters, 1985). If mixed-heritage individuals identify with a single group, some variation of cultural pluralism should continue to exist. However, if such individuals do not identify with a single group, assimilation may be furthered.

Thus, the ethnic identity of mixed-heritage individuals may have implications for the entire field of domestic race relations. Will we continue to be a nation of clearly definable minority and majority groups or will we become a nation in which intermarriage gradually reduces the number of persons who define themselves as members of a specific ethnic group? Put more simply, are our ethnic boundaries eroding through intermarriage?

Recently a few individual-level studies of mixed-heritage people have been conducted (Alba and Chamblin, 1983; Lieberson and Waters, 1985). They show that an increasing proportion of whites report their ancestors to be derived from more than one country or region. Unfortunately, because of the subjective, situational, and reciprocal characteristics of ethnic identity discussed previously, these studies do not demonstrate an increasing incidence of multiple ethnic identification. An individual whose ancestors derived from two different groups may self-identify with one, both, or neither. This problem is particularly acute in the case of white ethnics. Many know their countries of ethnic origin but have no sense of identification with these countries, seeing themselves as only white, Caucasian, or perhaps American. Since ethnic identity is selected rather than assigned, the best way to determine the ethnic identity of mixed-heritage individuals is to ask them. We have found no previous studies that have done so.

While little data exist on the ethnic identity of mixed-heritage individuals, theorists from both the assimilationist and ethnic pluralist positions have argued that mixed-heritage individuals are most likely to identify with a single ethnic group (Gordon, 1964; Greeley, 1971). The major goal of this study is to put this argument to empirical test.

ETHNICITY AND ETHNIC IDENTITY

The second goal of this study is to explore the antecedents of the ethnic identity of mixed-heritage persons. A selective review of the literature on ethnic identity of single-heritage individuals provides a starting point for this exploration.

Weber (1961) argued that identification with an ethnic group is a feeling of consciousness of kind that begins with commonalities of one of two different types, the first of which is commonality of culture. Weber believed that any aspect of culture can be a starting point for the formation of an ethnic group. Although language and religious beliefs may be particularly important factors, styles of living (e.g., economic life, food, clothing, and housing) are also likely to engender feelings of commonality.

Other theorists concur with Weber's premises regarding the importance of culture. For instance, Elkin (1983) theorizes that ethnic identity is learned in the course of family activities, such as the language the family members speak, and their religion, holiday celebrations, and food customs.

The results of empirical work investigating ethnic identity support the importance of language, religion, religious or cultural ceremonies, and food customs in the acquisition of ethnic identity (A. Cohen, 1974; De Vos, 1975; Isaacs, 1975; Nagata, 1974; Portes, 1984; Stevens and Swicegood, 1987; van den Berghe and Primov, 1974). Also, both theory and empirical data suggest that physical proximity to other group members is important to ethnic identity, whether through neighborhood or societal segregation (Elkin, 1983; Handleman, 1977; Nagata, 1974; Portes, 1984).

According to Weber (1961), the second kind of commonality that may lead to identification with an ethnic group is commonality of physical appearance. Other theories (Isaacs, 1975) and research (van den Berghe and Primov, 1974) support Weber's argument regarding the relevance of physical appearance to ethnic identity. Physical characteristics may limit the extent to which people can be accepted as members of a given ethnic group. For example, in the United States a black with dark skin cannot successfully adopt an ethnic identity as a white, but a black with light skin may successfully "pass." Even one's surname may create a barrier to some identities (Isaacs, 1975).

In addition to commonalities of culture and physical appearance, a number of other factors may influence ethnic identity. An individual's lack of commonality of culture and/or appearance with a given group may lead to rejection by the members of that group. For this reason, acceptance by the group in question seems a likely precondition of ethnic identity. It also seems likely that ethnic identity has an important objective or biological component. The percentage of a person's heritage from a given group is likely to influence ethnic identity, with identity increasing in proportion to one's heritage from the group.

Further, ethnicity is frequently an important indicator of stratification in a society. Identity with a given group may be sought in order to increase one's status or power within the larger society (Blalock, 1967; A. Cohen, 1975; Schermerhorn, 1978; van den Berghe and Primov, 1974). One's ethnic identity can influence one's life chances and one's style of life in most societies. Thus, the prestige accorded to an individual's heritage groups may be an important determinant of ethnic identity. At the same time, the desire of people in high-status groups to protect their status may limit the extent to which others are allowed to increase their status by assuming the ethnic identity of the higher-status group.

Finally, psychological identification with the beliefs and values of one parent (Bandura and Huston, 1961; Sears, 1957) may be associated with ethnic identity. To the extent that an individual psychologically identifies with a parent of a given ethnic group, he or she would be expected to identify with that group.

While the above factors have been associated with the ethnic identity of a single heritage individual or group, no data exist as to the antecedents of ethnic identity for persons of mixed heritage. It seems reasonable to suggest that a mixed-heritage person's identity with his or her groups will be based on the same factors that are important to the identity of single-heritage persons. It is thus hypothesized that a mixed-heritage individual's choice of ethnic identity is associated with (*a*) relative exposure to cultural elements such as language, religious affiliation, attendance at religious ceremonies, physical proximity to other members of the group, and family practices such as food customs; (*b*) observable indicators of ethnicity, such as physical resemblance to the various groups; (*c*) perceived acceptance by the relevant groups; (*d*) percentage of biological heritage; (*e*) status indicators, such as the relative status of the group or groups with which one identifies; and (*f*) psychological identification with one's parents. We will present an individual-level test of the antecedents of ethnic identity in two samples of mixed-heritage college student populations.

STUDY 1: JAPANESE-AMERICANS

Method

Respondents. The respondents were 67 University of Hawaii undergraduates who were at least 25% but less than 100% Japanese in heritage. These respondents were selected because intermarriage is common among Japanese in the United States (Labov and Jacobs, 1986; Schwertfeger, 1982). Intermarriage comprises just under 50% of all marriages in Hawaii, with Japanese-American intermarriage a little over 50% (Hawaii State Department of Health, 1987), making ethnic identity an important issue in this population.

A college-age population was selected for two reasons. First, we believe ethnic identity is particularly salient at this time, as students in their newly achieved independent and adult status interact with others from a variety of ethnic groups. Second, this age group contains a much larger portion of mixed-heritage people than do previous generations.

The education, occupation, and income of Japanese-Americans places them above those of other American minorities (Woodrum, 1981). While status differences among groups exist in Hawaii, no group is generally agreed to be highest in status and no group has a numerical majority. The Japanese are among the higher-status groups, yet they share their high position with at least one other group (Caucasians; some observers rate the Chinese similarly high). The Japanese comprise only around 30% of the Hawaiian population (State of Hawaii, 1987).

The respondents were drawn from the population of part-Japanese students in lower-division psychology classes.[1] Most received course credit in an introductory psychology class, although a small number of respondents from another lower-division psychology class were paid $3.00 for their participation. Information was gathered through a questionnaire form that required about 30 minutes to complete. Respondents completed the form in the presence of the first author singly or in small groups (of two to four persons).

Dependent variables. In an attempt to capture the situational and subjective nature of the process, ethnic identity (SUMID) was measured by a combined score of five questions in which the ethnic identity of the respondent in different settings was elicited (Cronbach's alpha = .78).[2] The questions were as follows: "If you were completing a form for the State of Hawaii, such as an employment form, what would you write down if you were asked to give your ethnic group?"; "When you are with your parents and brothers and sisters, which ethnic group do you think of yourself as belonging to?"; "When you are with your classmates at school, which ethnic group do you think of yourself as belonging to?"; "When you are with your closest friends, which ethnic group do you feel you belong to?"; and "With what ethnic group do you identify most closely? Please list the group that you feel really a part of."[3] These items were scattered throughout the 12-page questionnaire. The particular situations were selected because they are common and important settings in which questions of ethnic identity arise. They of course constitute only a sample of possible situations evoking ethnic identity.

Antecedent variables. The antecedent variables largely comprised the respondents' experiences when growing up in their families of origin.[4]

Cultural factors: The respondents were asked about their exposure to each of the ten largest groups in Hawaii (Japanese, Chinese, Caucasian, Korean, Filipino, Hawaiian, Portuguese, Samoan, Vietnamese, and black). Three cultural indices were formed on the basis of only the information regarding exposure to Japanese culture. An index of exposure to Japanese customs (CUSTOM) comprised standardized scores derived from eight items (alpha = .82). These items measured the extent to which, when the respondent was growing up, his or her family had eaten Japanese food and celebrated Japanese holidays and the extent to which the respondent had dated Japanese people, had Japanese friends and neighbors, felt comfortable with Japanese norms and values, and had felt that his or her values and beliefs were similar to those of Japanese people. The second cultural index was formed from the standardized scores of three items measuring the respondent's childhood and current involvement in Eastern religion (RELIGE; alpha = .59). The remaining cultural index consisted of the combined score of three items measuring the extent to which the respondent, the respondent's mother, and the respondent's father spoke Japanese (LANG; alpha = .65).

Physical factors: An index of physical indicators was formed from the combination of two questions regarding physical appearance: "What ethnic group do you feel you most resemble physically?" and "When you are walking through the streets of Honolulu on an average day, what ethnic group would people most identify you with?" (OTH; alpha = .86).

Status factors: One index of status measured the status of the Japanese parent in the family with two questions. One asked who the primary wage-earner in the respondent's family of origin was, and the other asked who the most influential person in the respondent's family was when the respondent was growing up (POWER; alpha = .52). The second indicator of status assessed the subject's perceptions of the ethnic status hierarchy in the society. It consisted of the difference between perceived status of the Japanese and the respondent's other (or highest-status other) ethnic group (DRJ).

Acceptance: The perceived acceptance of the respondent by Japanese people when growing up (AJ) was measured with a single item.

Japanese heritage: Three separate items measured the percentage of the respondent's, the father's, and the mother's Japanese heritage (HERJ, FJ, MJ, respectively).

Parental identification: Parental identification was measured by the sum of the standardized scores from three items. The first two items asked to which parent the respondent had felt closer and more similar when growing up. The third item measured the extent to which the respondent lived with Japanese relatives as a child (PARENT; alpha = .51).

Results

Description of the sample. The respondents ranged in age from 17 to 29, with a mean age of 19.72. There were 44 females and 23 males in the sample. The respondents had lived in Hawaii from 1 to 29 years, with an average residence of 17.87 years. All were U.S. citizens, born in the United States. Most respondents had been raised in Honolulu and most of their parents were Hawaii natives. Age, sex, and length of residence were not associated with ethnic identity. Because so few parents had been born in Japan, this variable also was not associated with ethnic identity.

In addition to their Japanese heritage, the respondents' ethnic heritage was derived from eight other groups: Chinese, Caucasian, Hawaiian, Filipino, Portuguese, Korean, Okinawan, and Hispanic.

Ethnic identity. Eighteen percent of the respondents listed their ethnic identity as Japanese on all five identity measures, 9% listed their ethnic identity as their other group on all five measures, and the remaining 73% listed a multiple identity on at least one measure. No respondents listed the same multiple-identity response on all five measures of ethnic identity. Most of these latter respondents stated single-identity responses to some items and multiple-identity responses to others. Other respondents listed multiple-identity items to all responses, but varied in the particular response they used. Respondents displaying the former pattern were most likely to mention a single identity in response to the question regarding the group to which the respondent felt closest, and least likely to mention a single identity on the question regarding completion of an official form.

The items measuring ethnic identity were coded to measure degree of Japanese identity on the basis of a 5-point scale, from sole identity as Japanese, to multiple identity with Japanese listed first, to an equal emphasis on two or more groups, to multiple identity with Japanese listed last, to sole identity with the respondent's other ethnic group. A positive beta thus signifies a positive association with identity as Japanese.

Analysis. Because of the small sample size, the 11 antecedent variables were first reduced to 7 antecedent variables for each measure of ethnic identity (J. Cohen and P. Cohen, 1975; Tabachnick and Fidell, 1983) by a combination of forward and backward stepwise regression (Hocking, 1976; Pedhazur, 1982). Then the antecedent variables were regressed on the summary index of ethnic identity. To make certain this process produced no distortion of results, all 11 antecedent variables were also regressed on the dependent measure. Because the results were essentially the same, only the former analysis is presented here. The bivariate correlations between variables are shown in Table 1 and standardized and unstandardized estimates from the multiple regression analyses are found in Table 2.

Since the data are correlational, caution must be exercised in causal interpretation. However, it should be noted that the independent variables are largely retrospective items concerning the respondents' childhoods. Thus, with some reservations, we presume that the direction of influence is most likely to be from previous family practice to present ethnic identity. While flaws such as imperfect memory are common to retrospective data, they generally increase error variance and lower the association between variables. However, we cannot rule out the possibility that memories of the past were adjusted to be consistent with current values.

The antecedent variables accounted for 40% of the variance in the summed measure of ethnic identity. The extent to which the respondent was exposed to Japanese customs as a child, his or her involvement in Eastern religion, and the extent to which the Japanese were perceived to have higher status than the respondent's other ethnic group(s) were significantly associated with overall identity as Japanese.

STUDY 2: HISPANICS

Methods

To determine whether similar results might be found with another sample of mixed-heritage individuals, Study 1 was replicated with a sample of part-Hispanic persons from the southwestern United States. Unlike the Japanese in Hawaii, the economic and social status of the Hispanics in the Southwest is not advantaged (Barrera, 1979; Verdugo and Verdugo, 1984). While Hispanic intermarriage rates have traditionally not been high, they are steadily increasing (Cazares, Murguia, and Frisbie, 1984; Crester and Leon, 1982; Schoen and Cohen, 1980; Valdez, 1983), with the sole exception of Puerto Ricans (Gurak and Fitzpatrick, 1982). In the southwestern U.S. the rate is around 16% (Cazares et al., 1984; Valdez, 1983).

The respondents were 104 New Mexico State University undergraduates who were at least 25% but less than 100% Hispanic in heritage. They were drawn from the subject pool of students taking introductory psychology.[5] Hispanics comprise around 50% of the population in the region and around 30% of the population of the university.

The questionnaire was identical to that used in Study 1, with the following exceptions: the ethnic categories were Hispanic, Caucasian, Native

TABLE 1. BIVARIATE CORRELATIONS OF IDENTITY MEASURES AND ANTECEDENT VARIABLES OF HAWAII MIXED-HERITAGE JAPANESE AMERICANS AND NEW MEXICO MIXED-HERITAGE HISPANICS

Variable	SUMID	CUS-TOM	REL-IGE	DRJ/DRH	OTH	POWER	HERJ/HERH	MJ/MH	AJ/AH	LANG	PARENT	FJ/FH
SUMID	—	.49	.32	.37	.29	.15	.15	.03	.45	.31	.18	.06
CUSTOM	.65	—	.13	.28	.22	.14	.14	.24	.45	.35	.16	-.04
RELIGE	.19	.25	—	.02	.01	.02	-.01	.17	.06	.47	.16	-.13
DRJ/DRH	.22	.21	-.13	—	.12	.22	.09	.01	.23	.00	.07	-.04
OTH	.47	.45	.14	.16	—	.30	.22	-.04	.41	.11	.01	.27
POWER	.50	.45	.32	.10	.22	—	.37	.05	.16	-.06	.45	.16
HERJ/HERH	.49	.41	.24	.12	.22	.65	—	.23	.21	.06	.34	.31
MJ/MH	-.13	.02	.15	-.15	.05	.06	.39	—	-.10	.31	.49	-.62
AJ/AH	.49	.66	.16	.15	.43	.26	.36	.00	—	.01	.10	.14
LANG	.47	.55	.40	.04	.26	.49	.40	.09	.36	—	.18	-.09
PARENT	.43	.39	.21	.01	.30	.66	.58	.46	.23	.42	—	-.21
FJ/FH	.60	.37	.15	.23	.19	.53	.50	-.56	.31	.30	.11	—

Note: The Japanese-American data are found above the diagonal and the Hispanic data below the diagonal. Variables are defined as follows:
SUMID = ethic identity.
CUSTOM = exposure to Japanese (Hispanic) customs.
RELIGE = involvement in Eastern religion (Catholicism).
DRJ (DRH) = difference between perceived status of the Japanese (Hispanics) and the respondent's other ethnic group(s).
OTH = physical appearance indicator.
POWER = status of the Japanese (Hispanic) parent in the family.
HERJ (HERH) = percentage of the respondent's Japanese (Hispanic) heritage.
MJ (MH) = percentage of the mother's Japanese (Hispanic) heritage.
AJ (AH) = perceived acceptance by Japanese (Hispanic) people.
LANG = index of the family's Japanese (Spanish) language abilities.
PARENT = identification with the Japanese (Hispanic) parent.
FJ (FH) = percentage of the father's Japanese (Hispanic) heritage.

TABLE 2. STANDARDIZED AND UNSTANDARDIZED ESTIMATES FOR IDENTITY VARIABLES

Variable	Hawaii Mixed-Heritage Japanese-Americans Beta	B	New Mexico Mixed-Heritage Hispanics Beta	B
CUSTOM	.38***	.05	.27***	.04
DRJ/DRH	.26**	1.12	.01	.09
RELIGE	.29***	.09	-.04	-.01
OTH	.17	.69	.18*	.76
POWER	.03	-.18	-.11	-.60
HERJ/HERH	.09	.03	-.14	-.06
MJ/MH	-.12	.02	.17	.03
AJ/AH	—	—	.02	.11
LANG	—	—	.09	.24
PARENT	—	—	.23*	.07
FJ/FH	—	—	.62***	.12
	$R^2 = .40$		$R^2 = .62$	

*$p = .10$. **$p = .05$. ***$p = .01$.

American Indian, and black;[6] eastern religions were omitted and Catholicism was the religion of interest; the language questions referred to Spanish; and questions referred to respondents' and their parents' Hispanic heritage. In addition, the respondents were asked only about their exposure to Hispanic culture. The respondents completed the questionnaire form in groups of two to eight in the presence of a female Caucasian experimenter.

In this study the Cronbach's alpha values were as follows: exposure to Hispanic customs (CUSTOM) = .81; involvement in the Catholic religion (RELIGE) = .81; the language index (LANG) = .71; physical factors (OTH) = .79; status of the Hispanic parent in the family (POWER) = .36; and parental identification (PARENT) = .84.

Results of Study 2

Description of the sample. The respondents ranged in age from 17 to 35, with a mean age of 19.5. Forty percent were female and 60%, male. All were U.S. citizens, born in the United States. Most had been raised in the southwestern part of the country, and almost none had parents who were born in Mexico. As in Study 1, age and sex were not associated with ethnic identity, nor was country of parents' birth. In addition to their Hispanic heritage, the respondents' ethnic heritage was as follows: Caucasian, Native American Indian, and black.

Ethnic identity. Forty-four percent of the respondents listed their identity as Hispanic, 12% listed their identity as their other group on all five identity measures, and 44% listed a multiple identity on at least one measure. As in Study 1, no respondents listed the same multiple-identity response for all five measures of ethnic identity. The most common pattern was to list single-identity responses to some items and multiple-identity responses to others. Respondents were most likely to mention a single identity in response to the question regarding the group to which the respondent felt closest.

Antecedents of identity. Since the sample size was larger than in Study 1, all 11 antecedent variables were regressed on the overall measure of ethnic identity (Table 2; see Table 1 for correlations among variables). The summed ethnic identity variable measured extent of identity as Hispanic.

The antecedent variables accounted for 65% of the variance in the overall measure of ethnic identity. Exposure to Hispanic customs and percentage of father's Hispanic heritage were significantly associated with identity as Hispanic. Physical resemblance to Hispanics and identification with the Hispanic parent were marginally significantly associated with identity as Hispanic. The interaction of percentage of the father's Hispanic heritage and sex of respondent was not significant; thus, father's heritage is important to both male and female respondents.

DISCUSSION

The Ethnic Identity of Mixed-Heritage People

The most important finding of the two studies reported here is that, contrary to the hypotheses of both assimilationists and pluralists, mixed-heritage people commonly have multiple identities. The finding that around three-quarters of the part-Japanese respondents and almost half of the part-Hispanic respondents list a multiple identity on at least one measure of ethnic identity supports the argument that intermarriage is decreasing identification with a single minority group and consequently is reducing pluralism. The finding that no respondent in either sample consistently used a single mixed-heritage identity suggests that mixed-heritage identities are less stable or more sensitive to situational variation than is single-heritage identity.

In both samples, respondents with the same "biological" or cultural ethnic heritage had different ethnic identities. This finding indicates the subjectivity of ethnic identity. The subjectivity and instability of ethnic identity are also shown by the variability of responses to the five measures of ethnic identity. At the same time, there is also stability in ethnic identity, as demonstrated by significant positive correlations among the individual ethnic-identity measures.

A somewhat greater proportion of part-Japanese than part-Hispanic respondents had multiple identities. Intermarriage is more common in Hawaii than in New Mexico. Further, Hawaii is multicultural and southern New Mexico is more bicultural. The result of these differences is that the part-Japanese sample had biological and cultural ties with more groups than the part-Hispanic sample.[7] Thus, Hispanic identity may be higher than Japanese identity because of the greater number of choices of identity available to the part-Japanese as compared to the part-Hispanic respondents.

A consideration of the locally available mixed-heritage labels suggests an alternative interpretation for this finding. In Hawaii, where intermarriage is common, a number of terms are regularly used to designate mixed-heritage people. New Mexico, where intermarriage is less common, lacks a rich and commonly used vocabulary for designating mixed-heritage identity. In New Mexico, this absence of ready labels for mixed-heritage status may make it more difficult for the individual and others to identify the respondent as mixed-heritage.

Antecedents of the Ethnic Identity of Mixed-Heritage People

The data from both samples suggest that the predictors of ethnic identity may be similar for persons of mixed and of single heritage. While the significant associations support many of the hypotheses regarding the antecedents of ethnic identity, only a single similarity exists between the samples in significant antecedents. For both part-Japanese and part-Hispanic respondents, exposure to Japanese or Hispanic customs plays a significant role in ethnic identity as Japanese and Hispanic. This finding supports the contentions of Weber and other theorists that ethnic identity is based on a commonality of culture.

The differences that exist between the specific antecedents of ethnic identity in the two samples seem to be associated with three factors. First, some significant antecedents seem to distinguish an ethnic group from other ethnic groups in the geographic area. Second, other significant antecedents seem to be associated with status advantages. Third, still other significant antecedents seem to be related to differential socialization into the customs of the group.

Distinctiveness. Religion is a significant antecedent of Japanese but not Hispanic identity. Religion may be important for Japanese but not Hispanic identity because Shintoism and Buddhism distinguish the Japanese from most other groups in Hawaii, whereas Catholicism does not similarly distinguish Hispanics in the Southwest.

The finding that physical resemblance is a significant predictor of Hispanic but not Japanese identity may also be associated with distinctiveness. While the Hispanics in New Mexico are physically dissimilar from the Caucasian majority, the Japanese are less distinguishable from other Asian groups in Hawaii.

These interpretations are consistent with research demonstrating that distinguishing characteristics of an individual are likely to become important components of self-identity (e.g., McGuire, 1984; McGuire, McGuire, Child, and Fujioka, 1978; McGuire and Padawer-Singer, 1976).

Status. Differential status is significantly associated with ethnic identity as Japanese but not as Hispanic. Differential status of the Japanese and the respondent's other heritage group is probably important because identity as Japanese frequently constitutes identity with a higher-status group than identity with the respondent's other heritage group. On the other hand, identity as Hispanic is less likely to carry the rewards of high status, relative to identity with the respondent's other heritage group.

Socialization. Identification with the relevant parent and the percentage of father's biological heritage, which are significant predictors of Hispanic but not of Japanese identity, may be related to both socialization practices and status concerns. The respondent's and mother's Hispanic heritage are not significantly associated with ethnic identity. We speculate that father's Hispanic heritage and identification with the Hispanic parent are surrogate measures of cultural exposure. In part-Hispanic families the father may determine the cultural tradition in which the child will be raised. If the father is mostly Hispanic, the child is likely to be reared in a culturally Hispanic home; if not, the child is less likely to be raised as a cultural Hispanic. Since little status advantage accompanies identification with Hispanics in the Southwest, part-Hispanic respondents may be socialized as Hispanic only when the father's ties to Hispanic culture are strong. By contrast, identity with the relatively high-status Japanese in Hawaii provides a status advantage that identity with most other Hawaiian groups does not confer. For this reason, the part-Japanese respondents may be socialized into Japanese culture to provide them an identity with a high-status group, regardless of the father's ethnic heritage.

Several cautionary notes are in order. First, these explanations are speculative. We offer them to suggest hypotheses regarding the origins of differences between groups for exploration in future research. Second, the generalizability of the findings is limited by the fact that both samples consist of relatively small numbers from select populations, college students. The educational level of the sample (most of whom were college freshmen) may make them nonrepresentative of the population of mixed-heritage people of their generation. Finally, these samples are derived from only two geographic locations and may not be representative of part-Japanese and part-Hispanic people overall. For these reasons, the findings reported here cannot necessarily be generalized to other samples of mixed-heritage people.

Conclusions

The major goal of this study was to determine whether persons of mixed heritage are most likely to identify with a single ethnic group. The question underlying this issue is whether we will continue to be a nation of clearly definable ethnic groups, or whether we will come to be a nation in which intermarriage gradually reduces the number of individuals who define themselves as members of a single ethnic group.

The characteristics of ethnic identity, the prevalence of multiple ethnic identity, and the antecedents of ethnic identity help answer this question. The subjectivity, instability, and reciprocal nature of ethnic identity suggest that multiple ethnic identity is a real possibility for persons who are products of intermarriage. The likelihood of this type of identity can be determined through examination of the prevalence of multiple identity among mixed-heritage respondents. The high percentages of the respondents who identified themselves as having a multiple ethnic identity on one or more identity measures in these samples, combined with the increasing numbers of mixed-heritage persons in our society, suggest that ethnic boundaries may be fading, at least for some ethnic minorities.

To determine the factors that might contribute to cultural pluralism, or the continued existence of distinguishable ethnic groups, we can turn to the antecedents of identification with a single group. These findings are pertinent to a minority group's likelihood of maintaining a separate identity from the majority group. The data from the part-Japanese and part-Hispanic respondents suggest two tentative conclusions, one of them quite obvious and the other less so. First, groups that strongly socialize children into the culture of the group appear most likely to preserve their separate identity. Second, these data suggest that ethnic identity may depend only to a limited extent on a set of common variables. Instead, identity may depend upon the specific group and its social context. The factors distinguishing an ethnic minority from other groups in the region, the status of the group, as well as its socialization practices appear to influence identity with a single ethnic minority.

More individual-level studies of a variety of mixed-heritage peoples are needed to validate the finding that multiple identity is common among persons of mixed heritage, and to explore further the antecedents of ethnic identity. Such individual-level studies could help answer critical questions concerning the likely future existence of ethnic boundaries.

NOTES

The authors gratefully acknowledge the support of the Institute of Culture and Communication, East-West Center, John G. Carlson, Anthony J. Marsella, and the Department of Psychology, University of Hawaii at Manoa; and thank Richard Brislin, Malcolm Holmes, and four anonymous reviewers for comments on earlier versions of this article.

1. It is likely that most of the mixed-heritage part-Japanese students in the introductory psychology classes are represented in the sample. Students in the classes received examination points for participation in research projects. Virtually all students seek such points and few opportunities were available when this study was being conducted. We were beseiged with requests from single-heritage students and students from other mixed-heritage backgrounds for permission to participate. To increase our sample as much as possible, the only other lower-division psychology class was approached for respondents. We recruited 8 of about 70 students from the class, very likely a high proportion of those eligible to participate.

2. The response option was open-ended. Each question was coded on a 5-point scale, as follows: Japanese or Japanese-American = 4, Japanese-Other group (e.g., Japanese-Chinese) = 3, the responses "Both" or "Mixed" = 2, Other group-Japanese (e.g., Chinese-Japanese) = 1, Other group or the response "Local" (a response implying psychological identification with Hawaiian people and culture) = 0. The responses were summed to yield a range from 0 to 20, with high scores representing a greater degree of identity as Japanese. Discussion both with respondents and social scientists studying ethnicity in Hawaii assure us that Japanese and Japanese-American are equivalent responses. No respondent stated "American" as an ethnic identity.

3. For a scale designed specifically to measure identity as Japanese, see Meredith (1967) and Matsumoto, Meredith, and Masuda (1970).

4. Complete information on the coding of all antecedent variables and means for all variables can be obtained by writing the authors.

5. As in the first sample, we think that most of the eligible students from the introductory psychology classes are represented in the sample. About 93% of students fill a course requirement through participation in multiple research participation. The small number of opportunities available to students during this session meant that we turned away many ineligible students who were having difficulty filling the requirement.

6. Coding for Study 2 paralleled that of Study 1. On identity items, all ways of designating Hispanic heritage (e.g., Hispanic, Spanish, Mexican, Mexican-American) were treated as equivalent responses. These responses are commonly used in the region to designate an American citizen of Hispanic ancestry. No respondent stated "American" as an ethnic identity.

7. While 93% of the part-Hispanic respondents are derived from only two ethnic groups, and none from more than three, only 73% of the part-Japanese respondents are derived from two ethnic groups, and 6% are derived from four.

REFERENCES

Alba, Richard D., and M. B. Chamlin. 1983. "A preliminary examination of ethnic identification among whites." American Sociological Review 48: 240-247.

Alba, Richard D., and R. M. Golden. 1986. "Patterns of ethnic marriage in the United States." Social Forces 65: 202-223.

Bandura, Albert, and A. C. Huston. 1961. "Identification as a process of incidental learning." Journal of Abnormal and Social Psychology 63: 311-318.

Barrera, Mario. 1979. Race and Class in the Southwest: A Theory of Inequality. Notre Dame, IN: University of Notre Dame Press.

Barth, Fredrik (ed.). 1969. Ethnic Groups and Boundaries: The Social Organization of Culture Difference. London: Allen and Unwin.

Blalock, Herbert M., Jr. 1967. Toward a Theory of Minority-Group Relations. New York: Wiley.

Blauner, Robert. 1972. Racial Oppression in America. New York: Harper and Row.

Bonacich, Edna. 1972. "A theory of ethnic antagonism: The split labor market." American Sociological Review 37: 547-559.

Bonacich, Edna. 1975. "Abolition, the extension of slavery, and the position of free blacks: A study of split labor markets in the United States, 1830-1863." American Sociological Review 81: 601-628.

Bonacich, Edna. 1976. "Advanced capitalism and black/white relations in the United States: A split labor market interpretation." American Sociological Review 41: 34-51.

Cazares, Ralph B., E. Murguia, and W. P. Frisbie. 1984. "Mexican American intermarriage in a nonmetropolitan context." Social Science Quarterly 65: 626-634.

Cohen, Abner. 1974. Urban Ethnicity. London: Tavistock.

Cohen, Jacob, and P. Cohen. 1975. Applied Multiple

Regression/Correlational Analysis. New York: Lawrence Erlbaum.

Cohen, Ronald. 1978. "Ethnicity: Problem and focus in anthropology." Pp. 379-403 in Bernard J. Siegel (ed.), Annual Review of Anthropology, Vol. 7. Palo Alto, CA: Annual Reviews.

Crester, Gary A., and J. J. Leon. 1982. "Intermarriage in the U.S.: An overview of theory and research." Marriage and Family Review 5: 3-15.

Cummings, Scott. 1980. "White ethnics, racial prejudice, and labor market segmentation." American Journal of Sociology 85: 938-950.

De Vos, George. 1975. "Ethnic pluralism: Conflict and accommodation." Pp. 5-41 in George De Vos and L. Romanucci-Ross (eds.), Ethnic Identity: Cultural Continuities and Change. Palo Alto, CA: Mayfield.

De Vos, George, and L. Romanucci-Ross (eds.). 1975. Ethnic Identity: Cultural Continuities and Change. Palo Alto, CA: Mayfield.

Elkin, Frederick. 1983. "Family, socialization, and ethnic identity." Pp. 145-158 in K. Ishwaran (ed.), The Canadian Family. Beverly Hills, CA: Sage.

Gist, Noel P., and A. G. Dworkin. 1972. "Introduction." Pp. 1-24 in Noel P. Gist and A. G. Dworkin (eds.), The Blending of Races: Marginality and Identity in World Perspective. New York: Wiley-Interscience.

Glazer, Nathan, and D. P. Moynihan (eds.). 1975. Ethnicity: Theory and Experience. Cambridge, MA: Harvard University Press.

Gordon, Milton M. 1964. Assimilation in American Life: The Role of Race, Religion, and National Origin. New York: Oxford University Press.

Gordon, Milton M. 1978. Human Nature, Class, and Ethnicity. New York: Oxford University Press.

Greeley, Andrew. 1971. Why Can't They Be Like Us? America's White Ethnic Groups. New York: Dutton.

Gurak, Douglas T., and J. P. Fitzpatrick. 1982. "Intermarriage among Hispanic ethnic groups in New York City." American Journal of Sociology 87: 921-934.

Handleman, Don. 1977. "The organization of ethnicity." Ethnic Groups 1: 187-200.

Hawaii State Department of Health. 1987. Statistical Report. Honolulu: State of Hawaii.

Hirschman, Charles. 1983. "America's melting pot reconsidered." Pp. 397-423 in Ralph H. Turner and J. F. Short, Jr. (eds.). Annual Review of Sociology, Vol. 11. Palo Alto, CA: Annual Reviews.

Hocking, R. R. 1976. "The analysis and selection of variables in a linear regression." Biometrics 32: 1-50.

Horowitz, Donald L. 1975. "Ethnic identity." Pp. 111-140 in Nathan Glazer and D. P. Moynihan (eds.), Ethnicity: Theory and Experience. Cambridge, MA: Harvard University Press.

Isaacs, Harold R. 1975. Idols of the Tribe: Group Identity and Political Change. New York: Harper.

Jenkins, J. Craig. 1983. "Resource mobilization theory and the study of social movements." Pp. 527-553 in Ralph H. Turner and J. H. Short, Jr. (eds.), Annual Review of Sociology, Vol. 9. Palo Alto, CA: Annual Reviews.

Labov, Teresa, and J. A. Jacobs. 1986. "Intermarriage in Hawaii, 1950-1983." Journal of Marriage and the Family 48: 79-88.

Lieberson, Stanley, and Mary Waters. 1985. "Ethnic mixtures in the United States." Sociology and Social Research 70: 43-53.

McGuire, William J. 1984. "Searching for the self: Going beyond self-esteem and the reactive self." Pp. 73-120 in Robert A. Zucker, J. Arnoff, and A. J. Rabin (eds.), Personality and the Prediction of Behavior. New York: Academic Press.

McGuire, William J., C. V. McGuire, P. Child, and T. Fujioka. 1978. "Salience of ethnicity in the spontaneous self-concept as a function of one's ethnic distinctiveness in the social environment." Journal of Personality and Social Psychology 36: 511-520.

McGuire, William J., and A. Padawer-Singer. 1976. "Trait salience in the spontaneous self-concept." Journal of Personality and Social Psychology 33: 743-754.

Matsumoto, G. M., G. M. Meredith, and M. Masuda. 1970. "Ethnic identification: Honolulu and Seattle Japanese-Americans." Journal of Cross Cultural Psychology 1: 63-76.

Meredith, G. 1967. "The ethnic identity scale: A study in transgenerational communication patterns." Pacific Speech Quarterly 2: 57-65.

Moerman, Michael. 1965. "Who are the Lue? Ethnic identification in a complex civilization." American Anthropologist 67: 1215-1230.

Mukabe, Tomoko. 1981. "The theory of the split labor market: A comparison of the Japanese experience in Brazil and Canada." Social Forces 59: 786-809.

Nagata, Judith A. 1974. "What is a Malay? Situational selection of ethnic identity in a plural society." American Ethnologist 1: 331-350.

Okamura, Jonathan Y. 1981. "Situational ethnicity." Ethnic and Racial Studies 4: 452-465.

Olzak, Susan. 1983. "Contemporary ethnic mobilization." Pp. 335-374 in Ralph H. Turner and J. H. Short, Jr. (eds.), Annual Review of Sociology, Vol. 9. Palo Alto, CA: Annual Reviews.

Paden, John N. 1967. "Situational ethnicity in urban Africa with special reference to the Hausa." Paper presented at the African Studies Association meeting. Cited in Jonathan Y. Okamura, 1981.

Pedhazur, Elazar J. 1982. Multiple Regression in Behavioral Research (2nd ed.). New York: Holt, Rinehart and Winston.

Portes, Alejandro. 1984. "The rise of ethnicity." American Sociological Review 49: 383-397.

Schermerhorn, R. A. 1978. Comparative Ethnic Relations (2nd ed.). Chicago: University of Chicago Press.

Schoen, Robert, and L. E. Cohen. 1980. "Ethnic endogamy among Mexican American grooms: A reanalysis of generational and occupational effects." American Journal of Sociology 86: 359-366.

Schwertfeger, Margaret M. 1982. "Interethnic marriage and divorce in Hawaii: A panel study of 1968 first marriages." Marriage and Family Review 5: 49-59.

Sears, Robert R. 1957. "Identification as a form of behavioral development." Pp. 147-161 in Dale B. Harris (ed.), The Concept of Development. Minneapolis: University of Minnesota Press.

Smith, T. W. 1980. "Ethnic measurement and identification." Ethnicity 7: 78-95.

State of Hawaii. 1987. Vital Statistics. Honolulu: State of Hawaii.

Stevens, Gillian, and G. Swicegood. 1987. "The linguistic context of ethnic endogamy." American Sociological Review 52: 73-82.

Tabachnick, Barbara G., and L. S. Fidell. 1983. Using Multivariate Statistics. New York: Harper and Row.

Tinker, John N. 1973. "Intermarriage and ethnic boundaries: The Japanese American case." Journal of Social Issues 29: 49-66.

Valdez, Avelardo. 1983. "Recent increases in intermarriage by Mexican-American males: Bexar County, Texas, from 1971 to 1980." Social Science Quarterly 64: 136-144.

van den Berghe, Pierre L., and G. P. Primov. 1974. Inequality in the Peruvian Andes: Class and ethnicity in Cuzco. Columbia: University of Missouri Press.

Verdugo, Naomi Turner, and R. R. Verdugo. 1984. "Earnings differentials among Mexican-American, black, and white male workers." Social Science Quarterly 65: 417-425.

Weber, Max. 1961. "Ethnic groups." Pp. 303-309 in Talcott Parsons, E. Shils, K. D. Naegle, and J. R. Pitts (eds.), Theories of Society. New York: Free Press.

Wilson, Anne. 1984. " 'Mixed race' children in British society: Some theoretical considerations." British Journal of Sociology 35: 42-61.

Woodrum, Eric. 1981. "An assessment of Japanese American assimilation, pluralism, and subordination." American Journal of Sociology 87: 157-169.

Yinger, J. 1981. "Toward a theory of assimilation and dissimilation." Ethnic and Racial Studies 4: 249-264.

12 Minority Status and Childlessness*

Robert L. Boyd
University of North Carolina at Chapel Hill

> This study applies the Goldscheider-Uhlenberg theory of minority status and fertility to black-white differences in childlessness. It is hypothesized that when integration into dominant societal institutions is impeded, high-status black couples are more likely to be voluntarily childless than comparable white couples. Using census data, the results tend to support this hypothesis, suggesting that among college-educated, high-status couples, blacks delay marriage longer and have higher rates of voluntary childlessness than do white couples. The implications of these findings are discussed and suggestions for further research are noted.

Introduction

Few issues in social demography are as controversial as the debate over black-white differences in childlessness. Central to this discussion is the role of voluntary versus involuntary factors. Black childlessness is generally treated as involuntary due to sexually transmitted diseases, malnutrition, and inadequate health care (Farley 1970). With the exception of Mommsen (1975) and Mommsen and Lund (1977), few analysts view black childlessness as the result of education, contraception, changes in marriage, and economic opportunities. Rather, investigations of racial differences typically focus on involuntary childlessness. In contrast, this study applies the Goldscheider-Uhlenberg theory (Goldscheider and Uhlenberg 1969) to voluntary childlessness. It is hypothesized that when integration into dominant societal institutions is impeded, high-status black couples have higher rates of voluntary childlessness than comparable white couples. Marital childlessness is studied because marriage is traditionally associated with procreation (Veevers 1979).

An increase in childlessness accompanied the U. S. fertility decline of 1880–1930 (Tolnay and Guest 1982). Industrialization, urbanization, lowered mortality, compulsory education, and status gains by women promoted voluntary childlessness (Popenoe 1936; Kiser 1939; Graybill, Kiser, and Whelpton 1958). Lorimer and Osborn (1934) stated that twenty-five to forty percent of childless women in the 1920s were voluntarily childless. Yet malnutrition, sexually transmitted diseases, and inadequate health care were also suspected causes of childlessness (Cutright and Shorter 1979; McFalls and McFalls 1984).

From Robert L. Boyd, "Minority Status and Childlessness," *Sociological Inquiry*, Vol. 59: 331-342, 1989. Copyright © 1989 by the University of Texas Press. Reprinted by permission.

It was also suggested that white childlessness was voluntary (Tolnay and Guest 1982), whereas black childlessness was involuntary (Farley 1970). For example, Thompson (1931) believed poor health reduced the fertility of urban black women around 1920. Kiser (1935) speculated that diseases, including sexually transmitted diseases, were responsible for low fertility among Harlem blacks. The 1935 National Health Survey linked black fetal deaths to sexually transmitted diseases (Kiser 1942, pp. 223-225). Finally, instability of sexual unions and the dearth of available partners caused unintentional childlessness among blacks (Masnick and McFalls 1976).

However, McFalls (1973), Engerman (1977), Meeker (1977), McFalls and Masnick (1981), Davis (1982), and Tolnay (1985; 1986) claim that the extent of black involuntary childlessness is overstated. Davis (1982), for example, shows that both sexual and non-sexual diseases had little impact on black childlessness early in the twentieth century. She argues that during the period, voluntary childlessness became a popular strategy among black women for adjusting to the cyclical and long-term economic shifts of industrial capitalism. Moreover, health improvements during the 1950s and 1960s reduced involuntary childlessness (Farley 1970).

In addition, social and economic gains by blacks during the 1960s led some analysts to argue that the causes of childlessness have become more alike for the two races (Grinderstaff 1976; Mommsen and Lund 1977). Mommsen and Lund (1977) show that white and black childlessness declined after 1950, changed little during the mid-1960s, and increased afterwards. As marital childlessness increased over the 1970s, there was evidence that voluntary childlessness was promoted by urban residence, social mobility, female labor force participation, higher education, and delayed marriage (Veevers 1972; Poston 1976; Poston and Gotard 1977).

Kunz and Brinkerhoff (1969), Veevers (1971), Stokes and Ritchey (1974), Mommsen (1975), Grinderstaff (1976) and Mommsen and Lund (1977) believe racial differences in childlessness will diminish as blacks become more socially and professionally integrated into the larger society. They expect that fertility differences will disappear as the socioeconomic characteristics of the two races converge (Thomlinson 1965, p. 178; Goldscheider 1971, pp. 272-273). Yet minority status is hypothesized to have an independent effect as insecurities related to minority status lower fertility when: (1) the minority group achieves or desires acculturation, (2) there is convergence of minority-majority socioeconomic characteristics, "particularly at the middle and upper social class levels," along with minority ambitions for social mobility, and (3) the minority group has no pronatalist ideology and no norm proscribing contraception (Goldscheider and Uhlenberg 1969, p. 372). Goldscheider and

Uhlenberg believe that lower fertility for blacks vis-a-vis whites occurs when socioeconomic attributes are held constant.

Ritchey (1975) found significant interactions among race, education, and fertility, a finding which supports the Goldscheider-Uhlenberg theory. Conversely, Sly (1970) found no interaction but concluded that minority status influences fertility after assimilation. Johnson (1979) found no differences among college-educated blacks and whites but stated that upwardly mobile blacks who are denied assimilation have below-white fertility due to deliberate fertility limitation. Among the college educated, it has also been observed that family-size preferences and expectations for whites and blacks converge after assimilation (Ryder and Westoff 1971; Stokes, Krader, and Smith 1977).

Investigations that have compared whites and blacks found that at high levels of education and income, black women were more likely to be childless, controlling for age at marriage (Kunz and Brinkerhoff 1969; Kunz, Brinkerhoff, and Hundley 1973). Other studies find that upwardly mobile black couples remain childless to enhance their status (Mommsen 1973; 1975; Mommsen and Lund 1977). Moreover, as early as 1940 there was a positive relationship between childlessness and the educational attainment of married black women (Farley 1970, p. 122). This suggests that voluntary childlessness among married black women rises as education increases, since childlessness due to disease is inversely related to social status (Bogue 1969, p. 726).

The 1926–1935 birth cohort is used to evaluate the minority status hypothesis of childlessness. This cohort was subjected to the Great Depression and World War II and was exposed to new opportunities in the post-war economy (Elder 1974; Hogan 1981). Early family formation and childbearing were encouraged by favorable labor market conditions and unexpectedly high incomes (Easterlin 1978). Yet, for upwardly mobile dual-worker families, economic prosperity gave working wives the incentive to forego childbearing by increasing the opportunity costs of parenthood (Butz and Ward 1979). Moreover, blacks in this cohort finished their education and entered the labor force before the civil rights era. Black couples attempting to enhance their status thus experienced the paradox of (1) systematic discrimination and exclusion from societal institutions and (2) new opportunities due to labor force expansion and rising wages.

Method and Data

It is hypothesized that when their integration into dominant societal institutions is impeded, high-status black couples (white collar, high income, college educated) are more likely to be voluntarily childless than comparable status white couples. A caveat is that "voluntary childlessness" is childlessness due to social rather than biological or pathological factors and only approximates deliberately planned childlessness (Veevers 1973; Poston 1976).

An indirect test is made with a sample that limits involuntary childlessness and increases voluntary childlessness. First, only once-married (husband present) wives (35-44) with spouses employed in urban occupations are considered. These criteria eliminate rural subfecundity and unintentional childlessness due to marital disruption. Using white and black women with similar marital backgrounds (married once, husband present) isolates differences in marriage patterns. Second, only wives in the labor force who married at age 22 or older are included. Third, family income is used, since "wife's contribution to total family income is likely to influence the couple's decision to remain childless" (Poston 1974, p. 300). Fourth, both husband's and wife's education are considered.

In addition, restrictions are applied to decrease women at high risk of infertility due to poor health care and to ensure that only high-status blacks are included in the sample. Only the three highest income categories available (1969 income) are considered: $10,000-$14,999, $15,000-$19,999, and $20,000 + . Median 1969 family income for married couples in the 35-44 age group was $10,879 (U. S. Bureau of the Census 1975, p. 303); thus, the black and white couples studied are middle and upper class.

To further ensure high-status, the sample is restricted to husbands and wives who have at least a high school diploma and husbands with white collar jobs. Wife's occupation is not available in the data, but at the time of data collection, couples perceived their social rank in terms of husband's status (Felson and Knoke 1974).

Data come from the published report *Women by Number of Children Ever Born* (U. S. Bureau of the Census, 1973). This source contains 1970 census data on the fertility of ever-married women by age, race and ethnicity, income, and labor force participation. The manner in which the data are reported restricts the analysis to cross-tabulations. These data are appropriate for the present study because they cover the childbearing years of women born during 1926-1935. Women in this cohort were age 35-44 in 1970. Ages 35-44 are considered the end of a woman's childbearing years, and childlessness after age 35 is an indicator of permanent childlessness due to the "very low birth probabilities observed at age 35 and over" (Rindfuss, Morgan, and Swicegood 1988, p. 123). Studies of permanent childlessness ordinarily use the age categories over 35 to evaluate permanent childlessness because "childbearing is virtually complete by age 35" (Poston 1974, p. 301). Thus 1970 data are acceptable for the analysis.

Table 1

Percent White Couples Childless, Husband's and Wife's Education, and Family Income

Family Income

Education		Median Years Married	$10,000–$14,999 Couples in Cell	Percent Childless Couples	Median Years Married	$15,000–$19,999 Couples in Cell	Percent Childless Couples	Median Years Married	$20,000+ Couples in Cell	Percent Childless Couples
Wife	Husband									
High School	High School	15.4	38,594	15.6	15.7	21,122	22.6	15.9	10,385	24.9
High School	College (1+ yrs)	14.9	33,809	12.9	15.5	29,500	17.5	15.6	22,082	22.0
College (1+ yrs)	High School	15.2	11,957	12.4	15.0	9,356	21.0	15.1	7,798	17.6
College (1+ yrs)	College (1+ yrs)	14.7	51,991	9.8	15.0	65,192	12.0	15.4	91,375	15.5

Source: U. S. Bureau of the Census. 1973. *Women by Number of Children Ever Born.* Census of Population: 1970. Subject Reports. Final Report PC(2)-3A. Pp. 319–333. Washington, D.C.: U. S. Government Printing Office.

Table 2

Percent Black Couples Childless, Husband's and Wife's Education, and Family Income

Education		\$10,000–\$14,999			\$15,000–\$19,999			\$20,000+		
Wife	Husband	Median Years Married	Couples in Cell	Percent Childless Couples	Median Years Married	Couples in Cell	Percent Childless Couples	Median Years Married	Couples in Cell	Percent Childless Couples
High School	High School	12.5	2,125	18.2	13.9	1,083	9.8	[a]	231	29.0
High School	College (1+ yrs)	12.7	1,210	18.2	13.0	756	16.7	14.6	636	26.7
College (1+ yrs)	High School	13.2	1,045	17.3	12.8	932	22.7	[a]	273	26.0
College (1+ yrs)	College (1+ yrs)	12.9	4,194	16.5	13.7	5,521	18.9	14.1	4,946	17.4

[a] Not Available

Source: U. S. Bureau of the Census. 1973. *Women by Number of Children Ever Born*. Census of Population: 1970. Subject Reports. Final Report PC(2)-3A. Pp. 319–333. Washington, D.C.: U. S. Government Printing Office.

Results

Tables 1 and 2 present the sample data, cross-tabulated by race, wife's education, husband's education, and family income. The cells contain the percent childless, the number of wives in each cell, and median years since marriage. The rank-order of the income categories is straightforward. The rank-order of the wife-husband education categories, from lowest to highest is: high school–high school; high school–college; college–high school; and college–college. College–high school is ranked above the opposite combination because of the importance of wife's higher education as a factor in childlessness (Bogue 1969, p. 728).

Racial differences in childlessness were reduced by the sampling restrictions. Among ever-married women 35–44 in the full census, the percent childless was 7.5 percent for whites and 11.4 percent for blacks (U. S. Bureau of the Census 1973, p. 11). In the study sample, the percentages are 15.2 percent for whites (N = 393,161) and 15.6 percent for blacks (N = 23,991). The high percentage childless implies voluntary childlessness, because when "childlessness rises above 10 percent in couples, we may infer that it is either primarily voluntary childlessness resulting from the use of contraceptives or else a result of very irregular exposure to childbearing" (Bogue 1969, p. 726).

Irregular exposure due to divorce is eliminated as a factor, since only once-married, husband-present wives are used. Unfortunately, one cannot explore separations or premarital unions with these data. Median length of marriage also indicates that wives were married during the peak fertility years (early to late 20s). Much of the childlessness in the sample, then, is attributed to deliberate attempts to forgo or delay childbearing.

Table 1 shows that among white couples, childlessness increases as family income rises, except for the education category college–high school. In addition, median time spent in marriage increases as income increases. A longer duration of marriage facilitates high socioeconomic status by giving couples more time to accumulate household resources. Earlier marriage is also encouraged by expectations of high future income.

With the exception of the middle income category, controlling for family income, the percent of childless couples declines as the level of education rises. The highest proportion of childlessness occurs when both spouses are high school graduates. One-fourth of the high school-educated white couples in the highest category are childless. Conversely, the lowest proportion of childless couples is found among couples with some college.

Table 2 shows that among black couples, the relationship between income and childlessness is more complex when education is controlled. When the wife is a high school graduate, percent childless drops from the first to second income category, only to increase sharply for the third. However, when the wife has some college, percent childless rises from the first to second category. Then, if the husband is a high school graduate, percent childless increases from the second to third category; if the husband has some college, childlessness declines. Finally, and similar to white couples, time spent in marriage rises with income. Median duration of marriage is lower for blacks, suggesting that black couples are more likely than white couples to delay marriage.

Among black couples, the relationship of education to childlessness, controlling for income, is again similar to that observed for white couples. High school graduates have the highest proportion of childlessness among the lowest and highest income categories. Moreover, for both blacks and whites the highest percent childless is found to occur among couples in the highest income category. In the middle income category, the lowest percent childless is found among high school graduates and the highest is found among couples where the wife attended college.

A comparison of college educated white and black couples is used to evaluate the minority status hypothesis of voluntary childlessness. In all three income categories, black couples with one or more years of college are more likely to be childless than comparable white couples. Both white and black childlessness increase from the first to second income category. For whites, percent childless increases from the second to third income category, whereas for blacks it declines slightly. Goldscheider and Uhlenberg's theory, then, seems applicable to racial differences in childlessness.

Table 3 shows childlessness according to race, education, and labor force status for ever-married women age 35-44 in 1975 and 1985. These data show a marked increase in childlessness for whites and a decrease for blacks between 1975-1985. These changes occurred at all levels of education and women's labor force participation.

The increase in white childlessness is due to the rise in voluntary childlessness resulting from the factors discussed above. Explanations for the decline in black childlessness are: (1) improvements in the health and socioeconomic status of disadvantaged blacks reduced childlessness due to involuntary causes; and (2) voluntary childlessness among high-status black couples declined as anti-discrimination programs such as Affirmative Action promoted institutional assimilation and minority advancement. These explanations are consistent with Johnson's (1979) argument that assimilation into the larger society is the most important factor in racial differences in reproduction.

Conclusion

Some support for a minority status hypothesis of voluntary childlessness

Table 3
Percent Childlessness by Race, Education, and Labor Force Status,
Ever-Married Women 35-44 in 1975 and 1985

	1975		1985	
	White (N = 9,659)	Black (N = 1,239)	White (N = 12,948)	Black (N = 1,516)
Education				
No Diploma	6.8	8.7	6.3	5.5
High School Diploma	5.3	9.4	8.1	6.5
College (1+ yrs)	7.3	8.9	14.7	7.1
Labor Force Status				
In Labor Force	7.3	10.8	12.3	7.6
Employed	7.3	11.0	12.5	7.6
Unemployed	7.0	8.4	8.7	6.1
Not in Labor Force	4.2	6.1	6.4	2.9
Total	5.8	9.0	9.9	6.5

Sources: U. S. Bureau of the Census. 1976. *Fertility of American Women: June 1975.* Current Population Reports. Series P-20 No. 301. Pp. 11-12. Washington, D. C.: U. S. Government Printing Office; and U. S. Bureau of the Census. 1986. *Fertility of American Women: June 1985.* Current Population Reports. Series P-20 No. 406. Pp. 40-41. Washington, D. C.: U. S. Government Printing Office.

is found. Using a sample designed to exclude involuntary childlessness, control important variables, and include blacks who experienced *de jure* and *de facto* exclusion from dominant societal institutions, the data suggest that blacks tend to have higher rates of childlessness than do whites. Black couples also spent less time in marital unions than their white counterparts because of greater tendency to delay marriage. The results for highly educated black couples, moreover, are consistent with those reported by Mommsen (1973; 1975), who found that to achieve social mobility, such black couples are likely to be voluntarily childless. The conclusions advanced in the present paper, however, must be regarded as suggestive only because of the limitations inherent in the data.

Racial disparities in childlessness deserve attention, because childlessness is making an increasing contribution to fertility decline in the United States. In addition, exploring trends in black and white childlessness provides insight into the way social change affects childbearing for groups holding greatly dissimilar positions in the stratification system. Unfortunately, there is a conspicuous gap in the demographic literature on voluntary childlessness among black couples, mainly because black childlessness has been treated as "unicausal," the result of poor health and sexually transmitted diseases (McFalls and Masnick 1981). It would be simplistic to think that all segments of the black population are similarly affected by involuntary influences on reproduction (Tolnay 1987). Future studies should address this issue by applying theories of race and fertility to black-white childlessness differences, especially with regard to investigating voluntary childlessness by middle and upper class blacks.

ENDNOTE

*This is a revised version of a paper presented at the 1988 annual meeting of the Southern Demographic Association in San Antonio, TX. I thank Peter Uhlenberg for his helpful comments and suggestions. Support was provided by a National Research Service Award training grant from the Carolina Population Center.

REFERENCES

Bogue, Donald. 1969. *Principles of Demography*. New York: Wiley.

Butz, William, and Michael Ward. 1979. "The Emergence of Countercyclical U. S. Fertility." *American Economic Review* 69:318–328.

Cutright, Phillips, and Edward Shorter. 1979. "The Effects of Health on the Completed Fertility of Nonwhite and White U. S. Women Born Between 1867 and 1935." *Journal of Social History* 13:191–218.

Davis, Nancy. 1982. "Childless and Single-Childed Women in Early Twentieth-Century America." *Journal of Family Issues* 3:431–458.

Easterlin, Richard A. 1978. "What Will 1984 Be Like? Socioeconomic Implications of Recent Twists in Age Structure." *Demography* 15:397–432.

Elder, Glen H. 1974. *Children of the Great Depression*. Chicago: University of Chicago Press.

Engerman, Stanley L. 1977. "Black Fertility and Family Structure in the U. S., 1880-1940." *Journal of Family History* 2:117-138.

Farley, Reynolds. 1970. *Growth of the Black Population*. Chicago: Markham.

Felson, Marcus, and David Knoke. 1974. "Social Status and the Married Woman." *Journal of Marriage and the Family* 36:516-521.

Goldscheider, Calvin. 1971. *Population, Modernization, and Social Structure*. Boston: Little, Brown.

Goldscheider, Calvin, and Peter R. Uhlenberg. 1969. "Minority Group Status and Fertility." *American Journal of Sociology* 74:361-372.

Graybill, Wilson H., Clyde V. Kiser, and Pascal Whelpton. 1958. *The Fertility of American Women*. New York: Wiley.

Grinderstaff, Carl F. 1976. "Trends and Incidence of Childlessness by Race: Indicators of Black Progress Over Three Decades." *Sociological Focus* 9:265-284.

Hogan, Dennis P. 1981. *Transitions and Social Change: The Early Lives of American Men*. New York: Academic Press.

Johnson, Nan E. 1979. "Minority-Group Status and the Fertility of Black Americans, 1970: A New Look." *American Journal of Sociology* 84:1386-1400.

Kiser, Clyde V. 1935. "Fertility of Harlem Negroes." *The Milbank Memorial Fund Quarterly* 12:273-286.

———. 1939. "Voluntary and Involuntary Aspects of Childlessness." *The Milbank Memorial Fund Quarterly* 17:50-68.

———. 1942. *Group Differences in Urban Fertility*. Baltimore: Williams and Wilkins.

Kunz, Phillips R., and Merlin B. Brinkerhoff. 1969. "Differential Childlessness by Color: The Destruction of a Cultural Belief." *Journal of Marriage and the Family* 31:713-719.

Kunz, Phillips R., Merlin B. Brinkerhoff, and Vicky Hundley. 1973. "Relationship of Income to Childlessness." *Social Biology* 20:139-142.

Lorimer, Frank, and Fredrick Osborne. 1934. *Dynamics of Population*. New York: Macmillan.

Masnick, George S., and Joseph A. McFalls. 1976. *The Philadelphia Fertility Study*. Final Report to the National Institute for Child Health and Human Development.

McFalls, Joseph A. 1973. "Impact of VD on the Fertility of the U. S. Black Population, 1880-1950." *Social Biology* 20:2-19.

McFalls, Joseph A., and George S. Masnick. 1981. "Birth Control and the Fertility of the U. S. Black Population, 1880 to 1980." *Journal of Family History* 6:89-106.

McFalls, Joseph A., and Marguerite McFalls. 1984. *Disease and Fertility*. Orlando, FL: Academic Press.

Meeker, Edward. 1977. "Freedom, Economic Opportunity, and Fertility: Black Americans, 1860-1910." *Economic Inquiry* 15:397-412.

Mommsen, Kent G. 1973. "Differentials in Fertility Among Black Doctorates." *Social Biology* 20:20-29.

———. 1975. "Black Childlessness: A Preliminary Analysis." Paper Presented at the Annual Meeting of the Population Association of America, Seattle, WA.

Mommsen, Kent G., and Dale A. Lund. 1977. "Zero Parity in the Black Population of the United States." Paper Presented at the Annual Meeting of the Population Association of America, St. Louis, MO.

Popenoe, Paul. 1936. "Motivation for Childless Marriages." *Journal of Heredity* 17:469-472.

Poston, Dudley L. 1974. "Income and Childlessness: Is the Relationship Always Inverse?" *Social Biology* 21:296-307.

———. 1976. "Characteristics of Voluntary and Involuntary Childless Wives." *Social Biology* 23:198-209.

Poston, Dudley L., and Erin Gotard. 1977. "Trends in Childlessness in the United States, 1910-1975." *Social Biology* 24:212-224.

Rindfuss, Ronald R., S. Phillip Morgan, and Gray Swicegood. 1988. *First Births in America: Changes in the Timing of Parenthood.* Berkeley, CA: University of California Press.

Ritchey, Neal P. 1975. "The Effect of Minority Group Status on Fertility: A Reexamination of Concepts." *Population Studies* 29:249-257.

Ryder, Norman B., and Charles F. Westoff. 1971. *Reproduction in the United States: 1965.* Princeton, NJ: Princeton University Press.

Sly, David F. 1970. "Minority-Group Status and Fertility: An Extention of Goldscheider and Uhlenberg." *American Journal of Sociology* 76:443-459.

Stokes, C. Shannon, Kelley W. Krader, and Jack C. Smith. 1977. "Race, Education, and Fertility: A Comparison of Black-White Reproductive Behavior." *Phylon* 38:160-169.

Stokes, C. Shannon, and Neal P. Ritchey. 1974. "Some Further Observations on Childlessness and Color." *Journal of Black Studies* 5:303-309.

Thomlinson, Ralph. 1965. *Population Dynamics.* New York: Random House.

Tolnay, Stewart E. 1985. "Black American Fertility Transition, 1880-1940." *Sociology and Social Research* 70:2-7.

———. 1986. "Family Economy and the Black American Fertility Transition." *Journal of Family History* 11:267-283.

———. 1987. "The Decline of Black Marital Fertility in the Rural South: 1910-1940." *American Sociological Review* 52:211-217.

Tolnay, Stewart E., and Avery M. Guest. 1982. "Childlessness in a Transitional Population: The United States at the Turn of the Century." *Journal of Family History* 7:200-219.

Thompson, Warren S. 1931. *Ratios of Children to Women, 1920.* Census Monograph. Washington, D. C.: U. S. Government Printing Office.

U. S. Bureau of the Census. 1973. *Women by Number of Children Ever Born.* Census of Population: 1970. Subject Reports. Final Report PC(2)-3A. Washington, D. C.: U. S. Government Printing Office, pp. 319-333.

———. 1975. *Historical Statistics of the United States, Colonial Times to 1970.* Washington, D. C.: U. S. Government Printing Office, p. 303.

———. 1976. *Fertility of American Women: June 1975.* Current Population Reports Series P-20. No. 301. Washington, D. C.: U. S. Government Printing Office, pp. 11-12.

———. 1986. *Fertility of American Women: June 1985.* Current Population Reports Series P-20. No. 406. Washington, D. C.: U. S. Government Printing Office, pp. 40-41.

Veevers, Jean E. 1971. "Differential Childlessness by Color: A Further Examination." *Social Biology* 18:285-291.

———. 1972. "Factors in the Incidence of Childlessness in Canada: An Analysis of Census Data." *Social Biology* 19:266-274.

———. 1973. "Voluntarily Childless Wives: An Exploratory Study." *Sociology and Social Research* 57:356-366.

———. 1979. "Voluntary Childlessness: A Review of Issues and Evidence." *Marriage and Family Review* 2:2-26.

Chapter 3   Families Over the Life Cycle

All the world's a stage.
And all the men and women merely players.
They have their exits and their entrances;
And one man in his time plays many parts (Shakespeare 1924, 260).

In "Families Over the Life Cycle," the multifaceted human development perspective of culturally-diverse families emerges. The old view of the "family life cycle" has been shredded and reglued like a collage. Longer lives, more mobility, and changing roles for women and men all contribute to changing family forms and functions throughout the life cycle. Although there is great variability among families, there are certain issues that prevail at specific ages and certain sequences of events that are likely to occur. However, the ways in which particular events are interpreted by culturally-diverse families may be uniquely different. Our task in understanding is to gain knowledge of what reality is for minority families and insight into what that reality means as it functions in White America.

The universality of the grandparent-grandchild linking bond is poignantly portrayed by a Rutgers University student in the beginning article of Chapter 3. Chiang recounts the relationship with her Taiwanese grandfather as the last link to her ancestral China. As for children of all cultures across the ages, the dichotomous nature of the generation gap is revealed as both a wedge and a bridge.

Harrison et al. explore relationships between socialization goals and child outcomes to the status of minority families, the similarity of their challenges from the larger social systems, and their resulting adaptive strategies. Adaptive strategies include family extendedness, role flexibility, biculturalism, and ancestral world viewpoints. The authors suggest such factors foster a positive orientation to the ethnic group and interdependence for children.

Self-descriptions of Black and Hispanic adolescents in a social agency program for pregnant and parenting teens are used by Dore and Dumois to assess the role of cultural differences in the meaning of adolescent pregnancy. Differences found in family functioning, role definitions, and expectations for individual members have important implications for practitioners who work with minority families. The common theme of economic deprivation and social isolation that surfaced strikes a somber chord for society-at-large.

The flow of resources from parents to children in young adulthood is characteristic of modern society. To determine the role of parental financial investments in the educational aspirations and attainments of young adults, Goldscheider and Goldscheider investigated how income and family structure affect black-white differences in intergenerational financial flows. Their findings have implications for both the study of parent-child relationships and the general social stratification process.

Finally, the relationship of ethnicity and gender to various aspects of life for elderly American Indians (Native Americans), Anglos, and Hispanics are highlighted. Harris et al. report a number of gender and ethnic differences in areas of activities, many of which involve traditional sex-role stereotyping. However, few ethnic or gender differences were found on variables related to feelings about aging or family relationships.

13 The Last Link

Sharline Chiang

By the time I met my grandfather for the first time, I was already nine years old. Like an Eastern wind, he flew from Taiwan into our American home. Carrying his carved mahogany cane, he sauntered around our living room, towering over me with his weighty presence.

I remember him looking somber in his black Chee-Pau, a long embroidered jacket made of Oriental silk. Underneath a faded skull cap his black hair was shorn and oiled. The sides looked like pepper against his jaundiced skin, and wrinkles circled his stony eyes like furrows etched across an antique map.

Call him "Goang-Goang," my parents said. That's what Chinese kids called their grandfathers. So I did. But this character looked so foreign in his Chee-Pau, muttering words in a thick Hunan dialect that I could barely understand. I had to wonder—were we really related?

He seemed so foreign as I watched him pickle his own red peppers in our kitchen. He ate them in bunches clamped between bamboo chopsticks and made smacking sounds with his lips. The peppers made my mouth burn and my eyes water, so I spit them out when he wasn't looking. I listened to him slurping at Mai-Tai (a strong Chinese liquor) during dinner. "Not bad, not bad," he would call out. He smoked Long Life brand cigarettes from Taiwan, which smelled like burning maple leaves.

Sometimes he would ask me questions, and I would nod my head pretending to understand. Once I think he asked me how old I was, and I just kept nodding my head. He shook his head and laughed deeply, like a bass drum's echo.

A week later, he left. And it wasn't until I watched his plane take off that I suddenly felt disappointed. Like most American kids, I was raised on the *Brady Bunch*, Big Macs and the Beach Boys. And like most American kids, I was plagued by all-American images.

On television, American grandfathers were always telling stories about their childhood or about wars. They always ate a lot at annual Thanksgiving dinners and then played ball with their grandchildren afterwards. Years later, these two generations, decades apart, could grow to understand and learn from one another. But it seemed as if I knew so little about my grandfather; there was so much about him that I didn't understand.

What was Goang-Goang like as a boy? Did he like sports? Was he a scholar? Did he fight in any wars? How did he raise my mother? I never got any answers to my questions. But looking back, I guess I never asked.

In fifth grade my parents decided to send me to Taiwan to learn Chinese. I left my American school for a year and attended fourth grade in Tapei. Slowly, living with each other in a tiny cinder block apartment, this little American girl and her Goang-Goang became closer. Eventually his words sounded less foreign, and his strange ways became her lifestyle.

Goang-Goang woke up at five o'clock every morning to walk in the park across the street. Sometimes I went with him. We strolled together, eating our steamed sweet rolls. Our breath trailed in clouds in the cool morning air, clinging to the hazy pastel dawn above us.

Later he would walk me to school, holding my hand as we crossed the blaring highway. At night I practiced writing my characters or played with a Rubik's Cube as he worked on his stamp collection.

Sometimes, if we heard a clanking bell outside our window, he would give me a red dollar and say, "Get two! Hurry before he leaves!"

I would dash downstairs and stop the old man who sold fresh baked sweet potatoes out of a tattered tin cart. I'll never forget the taste of them—hot frothy golden sweetness covered in a crisp sticky skin. We ate them by the window in the dark before bed. Our bodies made shadows from the street lights outside. They cast onto the white walls like the silhouette of a young deer nestled against a mountain.

One day, while I was watching a Chinese soap opera and fiddling with my Rubik's Cube, he tossed a red paper bag onto my lap. Inside was a toy made of a long piece of wood. There were eight silver interlocked rings tied onto the wood in a row. An elongat-

From Sharline Chiang, "The Last Link," *Salad Bowl* Vol. 15: 30-32, 1990. Copyright © 1990 by the Department of American Studies, Rutgers/The State University of New Jersey. Reprinted by permission of publisher.

ed oval wand ran through the rings, locked on to the wood by the strings.

"It is original eight-ring Chinese puzzle. Much more challenging than that American toy you play with. It is ancient game, been around for long time," he explained.

"The object is to remove entire wand from all eight locked rings, one at a time. Have patience," he added.

For the rest of the afternoon, I worked on the puzzle. Goang-Goang pickled more red peppers in the kitchen because he knew they were my favorite.

Each day I played with that puzzle, trying to understand how it worked. One ring, two rings, three rings . . . until there was only one left.

"Look Goang-Goang! I got all seven and one ring left!" I cried.

"Puzzle not completely solved until you get past last ring," he said.

Then he held my wrists together and teasingly exhaled a cloud of Long Life smoke in my face. We coughed and laughed together.

I remember now that Goang-Goang never once tried to help me with the puzzle. But looking back, I guess I never asked.

I used to wonder, did Goang-Goang play with the silver-ringed toy when he was my age? Should I picture him growing up in a mud-caked village in Hunan, or did he live near a city, where red lanterns lined the busy streets? It's true we grew closer, but so much about him was still a mystery to me.

After I returned to New Jersey, I inserted myself back into an American lifestyle. I was in a sixth-grade class where I belonged. I missed him at first. I wrote him letters and called him. *When are you coming back to Taiwan? Soon, Goang-Goang, soon.*

Junior high flew by, and I was too busy groveling through adolescence. I didn't try too hard to keep in touch. My Chinese started slackening, so I stopped writing.

Then came high school. My time was invested in term papers, exams, football games, parties, and proms. Soon those days I had spent with Goang-Goang became a faint illusion. I only recalled them as some clipped frames of my childhood lost in a long reel of fading memories.

Two years ago he suffered a severe stroke. My mother flew out to Taiwan.

One night the phone rang. Goang-Goang had died.

That night I cried alone, letting the empty obscurity wash over me in my moonless room. I didn't cry over the sweet potatoes we shared or the silent morning strolls. I didn't cry because I missed the smell of his cigarettes.

I cried because I had forgotten him. I cried because it was too late.

I hadn't tried hard enough to preserve that linking bond we finally shared. I had forgotten everything. And now, eight years later, I suddenly wanted that time back. I wanted those hours, to sit and talk, to listen and understand. I wanted him to see me, to see how I'd grown. I had lost my only chance to kiss the man who had tucked me into bed goodnight. Closing my eyes, I tried to listen for the soothing sound of his deep voice. But only Guilt whispered back, "It's too late."

Did you know how much I loved you, Goang-Goang? Did he know how much I would miss him? How much I wanted to see him again? Looking back, I guess I should have asked.

I tried to look for that puzzle, really, I did. I went through every trunk and box in the basement, but I never found it. Sometimes it's hard for me to believe that I've really lost it forever, that I'll never see it again. It bothers me, knowing somewhere out there is a lost puzzle that will never be solved.

14 Family Ecologies of Ethnic Minority Children

Algea O. Harrison
Oakland University

Samuel Q. Chan
University Affiliated Program, Children's Hospital of Los Angeles

Melvin N. Wilson
University of Virginia

Raymond Buriel
Pomona College

Charles J. Pine
Sepulveda VA Medical Center and UCLA School of Medicine

HARRISON, ALGEA O.; WILSON, MELVIN N.; PINE, CHARLES J.; CHAN, SAMUEL Q.; and BURIEL, RAYMOND. *Family Ecologies of Ethnic Minority Children.* CHILD DEVELOPMENT, 1990, **61**, 347–362. This article discusses a proposed interconnectedness between the ecologies of ethnic minority families, adaptive strategies, socialization goals, and child behavioral outcomes. The ethnic minority groups included are African American, American Indian/Alaskan Native, Asian Pacific Americans, and Hispanics. Demographic information on population size, geographic area of concentration, and preferred identity terms is provided. It is argued that adaptive strategies, including extendedness of families and role flexibility, biculturalism, and ancestral worldview, emerge from the ecological challenges of ethnic stratification status. These adaptive strategies foster the child-rearing goals of positive orientation to the ethnic group and socialization for interdependence, which in turn enhance the developmental outcomes of cognitive flexibility and sensitivity to discontinuities among ethnic minority children.

Using an ecological framework, this article explores the relation between ecologies of ethnic minority families, adaptive strategies, socialization goals, and developmental outcomes for ethnic minority children. The article is divided into four sections: (*a*) demographic information on ethnic minority families, (*b*) a discussion of the strategies groups have used to adapt to their social status, (*c*) a presentation of socialization goals that have emerged from the adaptive strategies, and (*d*) a discussion of child outcomes. The theoretical conceptions of the ecological orientation extend beyond the behavior of individuals to encompass functional systems both within and between settings, nested structures, and a complex interaction between the developing person and the environment (Bronfenbrenner, 1979). In short, an ecological perspective considers how the individual develops in interaction with the immediate social environment and how aspects of the larger social context affect what goes on in the individuals' immediate settings (Garbarino, 1982). Ethnic minority families in America have faced similar ecological challenges from larger social systems and have developed similar adaptive strategies.

Adaptive strategies refer to observable social behavioral cultural patterns that are interpreted as socially adaptive or maladaptive within the social nexus (DeVos, 1982). Importantly, when a strategy is effective in facilitating adaptation for a minority group, it involves some aspect of the dominant culture's

Except for the first two, authors are listed in the order of joining the project. Special thanks to Charles Nakamura, Hector Myers, Barbara Rogoff, Teresa LaFromboise, Kenyon Chan, Sue Gottschalk, and unknown reviewers for their helpful comments in the preparation of this manuscript. Requests for reprints should be sent to Algea O. Harrison, Department of Psychology, Oakland University, Rochester, MI 48309-4401.

mores and the knowledge that one is a minority at some specified level in a social hierarchy (DeVos, 1982). As members of groups learn which strategies are effective and appropriate, they also learn how best to inculcate these competencies in their children (Ogbu, 1981). The socialization goals of a people are partially derived from their cultural knowledge of their adult tasks, of essential competencies for adequate functioning, and of the methods of transmitting these competencies to succeeding generations (Ogbu, 1981). These cultural patterns are a part of the family ecologies of ethnic minority groups. Family ecology refers to important family functionings that are a reflection of the interactions between the family as a social system and other societal institutions and systems. The family ecologies of ethnic minority children will differ somewhat from those of majority children, where compromising with minority group status is not needed. Consequently, the family ecologies of ethnic minority, when compared to majority, families have the potential of differential outcomes in the development of children. This is especially true if development is viewed as a person's evolving conception of the ecological environment, one's relation to it, as well as one's growing capacity to discover, sustain, or alter its properties (Bronfenbrenner, 1979).

The aim of this article is to explore the interconnectedness between the status of ethnic minority families, adaptive strategies, socialization goals, and child outcomes. Historically, ethnic minority children were not included in samples of subjects studied for establishing normative trends or investigating theoretical questions. Most often data on ethnic minority children came from comparative studies with a controversial deficit explanation (Harrison, Serafica, & McAdoo, 1984; McLoyd & Randolph, 1985). Currently, social scientists are aware of the methodological and conceptual shortcomings of those studies. This article offers a different conceptual perspective for considering ethnic minority families and their children.

Issues in the Study of Family Ecologies of Ethnic Minority Children

The discussion is organized around four general questions, the first of which addresses which groups of people we refer to as ethnic minorities. Minority groups are subordinate segments of their respective societies. However, "Once people perceive ethnic differences and ethnic groups compete against each other, the crucial variables in majority-minority relations is the differential power of one group relative to another" (Yetman, 1985, p. 2). Ethnocentrism, competition, and differential power are the salient ingredients for the emergence and initial stabilization of ethnic stratification. Ethnic stratification refers to a system of arrangements where some relatively fixed group membership (e.g., race, religion, or nationality) is used as one of the standards of judgment for assigning social position with its attendant differential rewards (Noel, 1985). This article focuses on groups of people in the position of minorities in America's ethnic stratification system: African Americans, American Indians/Alaskan Natives, Asian Pacific Americans, and Hispanic Americans. Some of these groups are referred to as castelike minorities by Ogbu (1987, p. 258); "minorities incorporated into a society more or less involuntarily and permanently through slavery, conquest, and colonization." Each group's story is different but includes a common element of exploitable resources: (*a*) the enslavement of Africans and, after emancipation, their segregation and perceived inferior status based on race; (*b*) military conflicts over land and territory between American Indians and European Americans, and the forced removal and transfer of Indians to reservations; and (*c*) Asian Americans whose recent immigrants from Indochina sometimes suffer from the same subordination and exploitation endured by earlier immigrants from China, Philippines, and Japan (the latter were incarcerated during World War II); (*d*) Hispanics who were incorporated through conquest and displacement. In this article, we present a brief demographic summary of the current status of each of these groups.

The second question concerns the strategies these minority families use to adapt to their social environments. Historically, the selected ethnic minority groups have suffered from discrimination and racism. Yet they have formed communities, social institutions, and other organizations for adapting and adjusting to these ecological challenges. What are some of the adaptive strategies of these ethnic minority families? These adaptive strategies form the basis of the family ecologies of ethnic minorities.

The third question concerns the relation between families' adaptive strategies and socialization goals. Adults in families have formed beliefs about what it means to be a member of that ethnic group and what behaviors and attitudes are reflective of adaptations to that status (DeVos, 1982; Ogbu, 1981). These beliefs shape the socialization goals and techniques of ethnic minority families. What socialization goals of ethnic minority families derive from their adaptive strategies?

The final question concerns whether there are developmental patterns among ethnic minority children as a function of their family ecologies. In other words, are there any empirically based trends or patterns among ethnic minority children that can be attributed directly or indirectly to distinct cultural behavioral patterns found among their families? The review will be limited to literature in the cognitive area, where research on ethnic minority children is concentrated. However, there are other developmental domains where empirical studies have been completed but are not as expansive or focused on the relation between family ecologies and child outcomes (e.g., Gibbs, Huang, & Associates, 1989; Irvine & Berry, 1986; McShane, 1988; Powell, Morales, Romero, & Yamamoto, 1983; Rogoff, Gauvain, & Ellis, 1984; Spindler & Spindler, 1987). Shortcomings and the lack of relevant information are highlighted and directions for future research are discussed.

Ethnic Minorities

The ecological challenges facing ethnic minorities are not sudden temporary economic calamities, but derive from a long history of oppression and discrimination. Currently it is reported that one-third of the nation, constituting mainly ethnic minorities, are afflicted by the ills of poverty and discrimination (Report on Minorities in Higher Education, 1988). On all of the major social indicators (e.g., employment, housing, health, etc.) of individual and social well-being, gaps persist—and in some instances are widening—between members of minority groups and the majority population (U.S. Department of Commerce Series, 1988). Nevertheless, when confronted with these challenges, ethnic minority families and communities still strive toward goals and accomplishments as they have done historically. Educational achievement, economic development in the community, political power, affordable housing, and maintaining cultural and religious traditions are some of the goals of these groups (U.S. Department of Commerce Series, 1988).

Demographic Status

African Americans, 96% of whom are descendants of slaves, are currently the largest ethnic minority group in the United States (Reed, 1982). Only recently has the term "African American" been preferred by some persons in the group rather than the term "black." American Indians are the smallest ethnic minority group, although there are more than 500 tribes or nations in the United States (LaFromboise, 1988). Typically, American Indians prefer their tribal designation to the term American Indian (Burgess, 1980). Asian Pacific Americans comprise the fastest-growing population group in the United States (Gardner, Robey, & Smith, 1985). This dramatically accelerated growth is attributable to the continuing influx of immigrants and refugees (for a more detailed discussion of Asian American demographics, see Bouvier & Agresta, in press; Gardner et al., 1985; National Indochinese Clearinghouse, 1980; Pan Asian Parent Education Project, 1982; Peterson & Yamamoto, 1980; Powell et al., 1983). Persons in this group prefer ethnic terms that identify their country of origin. Hispanics are projected to become the largest minority group by the turn of the century. The Hispanic population consists primarily of *mestizo* peoples born of the Spanish conquest of the Americas who intermixed with populations indigenous to the geographic areas. Persons in this group also prefer ethnic terms that identify their country of origin, and when it is necessary to refer to themselves collectively, they prefer the terms Latino or *la Raza* (Buriel, 1987). More detailed demographics of the groups are presented in Table 1.

Currently, a majority of ethnic minority families live in urban areas. American Indians were the exception for urban residence patterns, residing mainly in rural areas and on reservations. Demographic trends, however, suggest an increase in the number of American Indians migrating to large metropolitan areas (Snipp & Sandefur, 1988). In 1980, 55% of American Indians resided in urban locations. Also, these ethnic minority families are younger and have higher birthrates in comparison to majority families.

Adaptive Strategies

Ethnic minority status has potent meaning for persons in the group because of the difficulties these groups have experienced in attempting to coexist with the European American culture. Examples are prevalent in history, literature, and psychology of persons with political and social power and members of the intelligentsia creating negative stereotypes for members of other groups (Padilla & O'Grady, 1987). The groups usually targeted for negative attributions and stereotypes are those in economically subservient positions

TABLE 1

Total Number, Composition of Subgroups, and Geographic Location of Ethnic Minority Groups

Ethnic Group	Total Number	Composition of Subgroups	Geographic Concentration
African-American	28.2 million	African-Caribbean, recent immigrants from Africa	South, Northeast
American Indian/ Alaskan Native	1.5 million/ 64,103	Largest tribes: Cherokee, Navajo, Sioux, Chippewa/ Aleuts, Eskimos	Northwest, West
Asian Pacific Americans	10.0 million	Chinese, Japanese, Korean, Vietnamese, Cambodian, Thai, Filipino, Laotian, Lao-Hmong, Burmese, Samoan, Guamanian	West, Northeast
Hispanic	18.8 million	Mexican, Puerto Rican, Cuban, Central and South Americans	Southwest, Midwest, Northeast, Florida, and California

within the society, as well as groups outside the society that are perceived as political, military, and economic threats. These experiences have influenced the individual and group beliefs about what it means to be a member of an ethnic minority group. There is agreement among psychologists that beliefs form an important psychological guide to action (Sigel, 1985); therefore, it is assumed that these beliefs have been a factor in shaping the strategies that members of low-status groups develop.

Adaptive strategies are proposed cultural patterns that promote the survival and well-being of the community, families, and individual members of the group. The term "adaptive strategies" as used refers to observable social behavior, not to personality dynamics (DeVos, 1982). A review of the literature describing the values, attitudes, and behaviors of ethnic minority families highlights the adaptive strategies these groups have in common. Although there are differences in the salience of a strategy, the similarities across family ecologies are striking. Family extendedness and role flexibility, biculturalism, and ancestral worldviews are all part of the life-styles of these groups. Although ethnic minority groups share a commonality in minority status and ethnic stratification, there have been differences in the impact of ecological challenges from the majority population on these groups. Some of the factors that have mediated the experiences of these different groups are motives for coming to America (Suzuki, 1980), time of immigration (Serafica, in press), educational opportunities (Olmedo, 1981), attitude toward educational establishment (Ogbu, 1981), voluntarily or involuntarily coming to America (Harding, 1980), and the American caste system (Ogbu, 1985). Nevertheless, limited access to societal resources has forged a similarity among ethnic minority families. All have had to develop ways of gaining access to European American cultural and social institutions (e.g., educational, medical, political, legal) for services, employment, power, etc.

Family Extendedness and Role Flexibility

The pattern of establishing extended families is an adaptive strategy common to ethnic minority peoples. Although there are traditional and nontraditional types of families in ethnic minority communities, the extended family form is frequently mentioned by social scientists as a typical family structure in ethnic minority communities (Mindel & Habenstein, 1981). For example, Langston (1980) reported that 85% of her African American elderly sample shared their residence with someone who was either a spouse, an adult child, or a grandchild. Nationally, panel and census data analyses (Beck & Beck, 1989; Sweet, 1977) have indicated that 53% of the African American elderly population shared a residence with a relative, as compared to 40% of the white elderly population. In fact, about 10 percent of African American children below the age of 18 lived with their grandparents and 25 percent of young African American adults between the ages of 18–26 lived with their parents (Beck & Beck, 1984, 1989; Sweet, 1977). Three times as many African American children under age 18 lived with their grandparents than white children, whereas the proportion of African American and white young adults living with parents was about equal (Soldo & Lauriat, 1976; U.S. Bureau of the Census, 1989).

The extended family is a problem-solving and stress-coping system that addresses, adapts, and commits available family resources to normal and nonnormal transitional and crisis situations (Wilson, 1989). Family resources involve family members' ability to contribute tangible help, such as material support, income, childcare, and household maintenance assistance, and nontangible help, such as expressive interaction, emotional support, counseling, instruction, and social regulation (Wilson, 1986, 1989). Through patterns of kin contact and interactions that are proximal, available, frequent, and functional (Gibson, 1972), a family provides its members with a sense of group and personal identities, behavioral rules, roles and responsibilities, and emotional affiliations and attachments (Goode, 1964; Schneider, 1968, 1980). Indeed, extended family refers to family composition, structure, and interaction that go beyond the nuclear family unit to include consanguine, affinal, and fictive relationships (Foster, 1984; Wilson, 1986). Wilson (1986, 1989) asserts that in the African American family, experiencing nonnormal changes and events is a primary reason for the formation of extended family support networks. A common stressful situation in the African American community is the lack of adequate adult resources in single-parent family units. The formation occurs when one family unit absorbs another one. Once formed, the extended family occupies most of the family life span. Martin and Martin (1978) describe the characteristics of extended families as found among African Americans as interdependent, bilateral, and multigenerational; headed by a dominant family figure; having a family-based household; reaching across geographical boundaries; and processing a built-in mutual aid system providing material aid and moral support. Historically, the African American extended family system supports a familial tradition that existed throughout the periods of slavery, emancipation, and mass rural southern exodus (Agesti, 1978; Aoyagi, 1978; Flanagan, 1978; Fogel & Engelman, 1974; Genovese, 1976; Gutman, 1976; Martin & Martin, 1978; Meachan, 1983; Nobles, 1978).

Similarly, American Indian families may be characterized as a collective, cooperative social network that extends from the mother and father union to the extended family and ultimately to the community and tribe (Burgess, 1980). Although such a family structure is not as prevalent as it once was (Ryan, 1981), it has not disappeared (Burgess, 1980; LaFromboise, 1988; Medicine, 1981), and it has endured many changes brought about by influences of the European-American culture. The typical family has several forms, but the basic social unit consisted of the man, woman, and their children and is embedded in the community, multigenerational, collateral, and comprised sibling groupings of different types. Generally, a strong extended family system characterizes many urban and rural contemporary American Indian families (Goodluck & Eckstein, 1978; Medicine, 1981; Red Horse, 1983). American Indian patterns of extended family include several households representing significant relatives along both vertical and horizontal lines, therefore assuming village-type characteristics (Light & Martin, 1986; Red Horse, 1983).

In the same manner, among Asian Pacific American families, selected practices have persisted throughout the process of increasing acculturation in successive generations and are further maintained by recent immigrants (Chan, 1986). The traditional Asian Pacific family is characterized by well-defined, unilaterally organized, and highly interdependent roles within a cohesive patriarchal vertical structure (Serafica, in press). Prescribed roles and relationships emphasize subordination and interdependence. Familial and social behaviors are thus governed by esteem for hierarchical roles and relationships and the virtue of filial piety (Tseng, 1973).

Likewise, familism among Hispanics involves strong feelings of identification, loyalty, and solidarity with the parents and the extended family, and behaviors associated with these feelings, such as frequent contact and reciprocity among members of the same family (Marin, 1986; Ramirez & Castaneda, 1974; Sabogal, Marin, Otero-Sabogal, Marin, & Perez-Stable, 1987). Much like the Asian Pacific family, the Hispanic family is characterized by strong familism. In addition, the Hispanic extended family is similar to the African American family in that it is bilaterally organized and includes nonrelative members (e.g., compadres).

It is clear from empirical writings and discussions that the extended family system is a value and ideal among ethnic minorities. Do demographic changes within ethnic minority groups alter the structure and importance of family extendedness to family members? McAdoo's (1978) investigations found that the extended family structure was still prevalent among upwardly mobile African American families, while community activists from the same community noted that its effectiveness was declining among low socioeconomic status families because of the tremendous burdens of contemporary social problems (Height, 1985). Further empirical studies are needed to delineate when, how, and under what conditions extended families are adaptive or serve as a source of conflict. For example, involvement in extended families increases economic resources among low-income families but reduces consumable income among middle- and working-class families. Stack (1981) found that extended family relationships often produced conflictual feelings among young African American females. Young African American females were often torn between their commitment and loyalties to the extended family and their feelings and commitments to their boyfriends. Similar findings were noted by Dressler (1985) in his study of families in a southern community. Extended kin support appeared to be less effective in reducing the risk of depression among young women compared to young men. Opposite-sex differences were found by Brown and Gary (1987) in their sample of urban northern African American families. Young females were provided more benefits from the extended family in comparison to young males. Clearly more systematic studies are needed on how this adaptive strategy functions in modern life for all ethnic minority groups.

In addition, ethnic minority families have used social role flexibility as a coping mechanism out of historic necessity (Munoz & Endo, 1982). Familial social roles can be regarded as flexible in definition, responsibility, and performance. Parenting of younger siblings by older siblings, sharing of the breadwinner role among adults, and alternative family arrangements have been found to be more prevalent in ethnic minority communities than in majority communities (Allen, 1978; Allen & Stukes, 1982).

Biculturalism

A bicultural orientation is not new or unique to ethnic minority groups. Historically, America's formal and informal policies toward non-English-speaking immigrants were to Americanize people as fast as possible (Wagner, 1981). Most immigrant groups go through the process of acculturation, a cultural change that is initiated by the conjunction of two or more autonomous cultural systems (Bing, 1980). For ethnic minorities in America this has presented a problem because of the devaluing of their ethnic culture by the majority culture. Further, the cultures of African Americans and American Indians have been presented frequently from the European perspective rather than from the writings of persons from the respective ethnic group dominating the prevailing perspectives. One of the ways some ethnic minorities have adapted to the conflictual situation is a bicultural orientation to the acculturation process. (See McShane [1983] or McShane & Berry [1986] for an expanded discussion of alternative pathways [e.g., integration, assimilation, rejection, or marginality].)

Szopocznik and Kurtines (1980) proposed that if the cultural context within which acculturation takes place is bicultural, then acculturation will tend to take place along two dimensions. A linear process of accommodating to the host culture is the first dimension, and the second dimension is a complex process of relinquishing or retaining characteristics of the culture of origin. The person learns to function optimally in more than one cultural context and to switch repertoires of behavior appropriately and adaptively as called for by the situation (Laosa, 1977). Although all ethnic groups have expressed biculturalism as an important adaptive strategy (Harrison et al., 1984), a majority of the emipirical investigations of the process have studied Hispanic Americans.

Nonetheless, African Americans and American Indians have a set of beliefs and behaviors that have their origins in their ancestral cultures (Nobles, 1978, 1988; Red Horse, 1983). These cultures are distinct from

European American culture (Myers, 1982) as a result of the desire to continue the values and traditions of previous generations, and the limited access to the larger society and its social institutions. Yet there are no extensive systematic investigations of biculturalism among these two groups.

Shon and Ja (1983) describe two interrelated levels of adaptive cultural transaction as part of Asian Pacific immigrants' experiences. At the first level of physical or material transition, immigrants must consistently struggle to overcome language barriers and to achieve economic security and educational and occupational success. The second level of cultural transition involves cognitive and affective changes in which the family attempts psychologically to incorporate various features of their new environment. One of several empirical questions from this process is whether these families continue to maintain a bicultural orientation or select other pathways of adaptation.

Sabogal et al. (1987) examined the effects of acculturation on three attitudinal components of Hispanic familism: (1) familiar obligations, (2) perceived support from family, and (3) family as referents. They found that attitudes concerning familial obligations and family as referents diminished with increasing levels of acculturation (as measured by language preference and usage), but that perception of family support remained constant. The selective effect of acculturation on familism is further supported by the research of Reuschenberg and Buriel (1988), who used the Family Environment Scale (FES) (Moos, Insel, & Humphrey, 1974) to study Mexican American families who were either short- or long-term arrivals from Mexico or U.S. born. The FES is primarily a behavioral rather than attitudinal scale and can be scored to distinguish between interactions involving only family members and those involving family members and outside social systems. Reuschenberg and Buriel (1988) found that acculturation was related to differences in families' interaction patterns with outside social agencies, but not to internal family system variables. In other words, acculturation may change the way individual family members interact and present themselves to outside agents, but internal family dynamics remain mostly intact. This finding suggests the dual existence of public and private domains of family life among Hispanic Americans. Hispanics often achieve a bicultural adaptation that uniquely combines aspects of European American and Hispanic cultures, leading to behaviors that are not entirely characteristic of either culture (Buriel, 1987). According to Ramirez (1983), the diversity inherent in Hispanics' heritage has provided this group with a worldview that values integration and synthesis of new cultural experiences rather than complete assimilation.

Biculturalism has been the topic of edited books and reviews of empirical studies. The effects of biculturalism have been investigated from the conceptual frameworks of bilingualism and the need for changes in the delivery of mental health services to ethnic minority groups (e.g., Hakuta & Garcia, 1989; Penalosa, 1980; Powell et al., 1983; Ramirez, 1986; Spindler & Spindler, 1987; Serafica et al., in press; Willig, 1985; Wolfson & Manes, 1985). What is needed for more in-depth understanding of biculturalism is more information on the psychological mechanisms involved and the resulting positive or negative effects for individuals as well as the group.

Ancestral Worldviews

American culture is dominated by the belief in individualism, that is, the notion that "each of us is an entity separate from every other and from the group and as such is endowed with natural rights" (Spence, 1985, p. 1288). One of the ways the concept of individualism is incorporated into American cultural heritage is through the lauding of the protestant work ethic as the pathway to success for individuals (Sampson, 1985). The social order of the majority culture is guided by an acceptance of individualism, which is reflected in encouragement and recognition of individual achievements and accomplishments, especially the attainment of material property (Spence, 1985). Given the status of ethnic minorities, generally individualism has not been their pathway to the American Dream. Further, individualism is incompatible with the ancestral worldviews of ethnic minorities.

The indigenous psychology of ethnic minority cultures differs from the majority culture in how interwoven the interest and well-being of the self is with the ethnic group to which one belongs. Self-contained individualism is an indigenous psychology of the majority culture (Heela & Lock, 1981; Nobles, 1978; Ramirez, 1983; Sampson, 1988). In contrast, the degree of fluidity of boundaries between self- and non-self-interests among ethnic minorities is based on a more inclusive conception of the person or self, that is, persons are attached to families, households, communities, and the group (Heela & Lock, 1981; Sampson, 1988). Thus, when confronted in American society with racism, discrimination, occupational barriers, and negative portrayals of the ethnic group, ethnic minorities have used their ancestral worldviews as an adaptive strategy for pathways to achievement and sense of personal worth.

The salience of ancestral worldviews as reflected in spirituality/religiosity and philosophical orientations in contemporary ethnic minority communities is well documented (Garbarino, 1976; Gill, 1982a; Medicine, 1980; Ramirez & Castaneda, 1974; Shon & Ja, 1983; Taylor, 1988; Taylor, Thornton, & Chatters, 1988; Thornton & Taylor, 1988). The term "religiosity" is used in the scholarly orientation to refer to images, actions, and symbols that define the extent and character of the world for the people and provide the cosmic framework for which their lives find meaning, purpose, and fulfillment (Gill, 1982b).

Sudarkasa (1988) and Nobles (1988) have noted that African Americans possess a worldview that is akin to an African belief in collectivism rather than a European belief in individualism. However, research has not been conducted on these concepts among African Americans, and it is not known whether such orientations affect family functioning. On the other hand, research has documented the persistence of some African cultural patterns among contemporary African American families for both rural and urban areas (Sudarkasa, 1988). For example, emphasis on consanguinity, kinship that is biologically based, is a salient feature of African and African American family organization. Researchers have noted the role of religion in enhancing life satisfaction among a national sample of African Americans (e.g., Taylor, 1988).

In American Indian traditions, all aspects of life take on religious significance, and religion and culture are intimately connected (Medicine, 1981; Michaelsen, 1983). American Indians do not share a single dominant religion (Gill, 1982b; Hultkrantz, 1981; Hurdy, 1970), yet a common practice across a variety of American Indian tribal cultures is the quest for a guardian spirit (Garbarino, 1976; Hamer, 1980; Lewis, 1981). The attaining of a guardian spirit is seen as a confidence builder, which at the very least would result in the capability to manage most of life's stresses and demands.

Traditional cultural orientations and values among many Asian Pacific American subgroups are deeply rooted in the doctrines and philosophies of Buddhism, Confucianism, and Taoism; each offers a worldview and prescription for living that emphasizes selected virtues and adherence to codes of behavior. Confucian thought, important to Asian/Pacific families, is guided by a philosophical orientation wherein *harmony* is the core of existence, and persons' obligation is to sustain harmony within the social order (Chan, 1986; Sampson, 1988; Sue & Sue, 1987). The Hispanic value system of familism is supported and reinforced by the pervasive religious practices in the community. For example, the image of the Virge de Guadalupe (the *Mestizo* equivalent of the Virgin Mary) is both a religious and an unofficial national symbol of *la Raza* (Ramirez & Castaneda, 1974).

In short, the worldviews of ethnic minorities have emphasized collectivism or loyalty to the group in some form. One of the interesting empirical questions needing investigation is how prevalent is the regard for collectivism as compared to individualism among ethnic minorities groups. Do attitudes about collectivism predict behavior? What are the contributing factors to intra- and intergroup differences on these dimensions?

Socialization Goals

Adaptive responses to ecological challenges have shaped the family ecologies of ethnic minorities and affected the socialization of children. Socialization refers to the processes by which individuals become distinctive and actively functioning members of the society in which they live (Elkin & Handel, 1984; Zigler, Lamb, & Child, 1982). The family ecologies of ethnic minority children differ from majority children's and partially provide the basis for variations in the context of socialization. The mechanisms for transmittal of the culture are the same for both ethnic minority and majority children (e.g., reinforcement, modeling, identification, etc.). Yet ethnicity is potent in the socialization process of families since it includes group patterns of values, social customs, perceptions, behavioral roles, language usage, and rules of social interactions that group members share in both obvious and subtle ways (Phinney & Rotheram, 1987).

Attribution theory (Dix & Grusec, 1985), distancing theory (which reflects the theories of Piaget, Kelley, & Weiner [Johnson & Martin, 1985; McGillicuddy-DeLisi, 1985]), and social learning theories have provided the conceptual underpinning for the assumption that parental beliefs are important determinants in the socialization process. In addition, other theoretical orientations have expanded beyond the consideration of parental beliefs and behaviors to include the cultural context in which those processes occur (Bronfenbrenner, 1979; Rogoff, 1982). Ogbu's cultural-ecological model of child rearing is a part of this trend and offers a viable conceptual framework for understanding the relation between the strategies ethnic minorities have adopted to meet the group's ecological challenges and the selection of certain socialization goals.

Ogbu (1981) proposes that child rearing in the family and similar micro settings during the periods of infancy, childhood, and adolescence is geared toward the development of instrumental competence. Instrumental competence refers to the ability to perform culturally specific tasks that are required for adult economic, political, and social roles. Indeed, Ogbu (1981, p. 417) notes, "child categories and instrumental competencies resulting from child-rearing techniques eventually develop into adaptive adult categories and instrumental competencies in the population." In the sections that follow, we identify some of the socialization goals espoused by ethnic minority families. We argue that these goals emerge from the adaptive strategies of ethnic minority families identified earlier. The child-rearing goals so identified and described are positive orientation toward ethnic group and socialization for interdependence.

Positive Orientation toward Ethnic Groups

One goal of the socialization practices among ethnic minority families is to foster a positive orientation among children toward their ethnic group as a means of promoting biculturalism and acceptance of the orientations of the ancestral worldview. Children are taught to view their role within the family and society in terms of relationships and obligations to the family (Chan, 1986; Tseng, 1973). In one of the few empirical studies investigating family socialization of ethnic attitudes, Bowman and Howard (1985) offer insightful information regarding the effect on children of parents actively socializing them regarding the consequences of their ethnicity in the larger society. This study of a national sample of African American three-generational families indicated that the manner in which parents oriented their children toward racial barriers was a significant element in children's motivation, achievement, and prospects for upward mobility. Parents of successful children emphasized ethnic pride, self-development, awareness of racial barriers, and egalitarianism in their socialization practices.

A large percentage of ethnic minority children are growing up in homes where English is not the dominant language and where American culture does not govern most aspects of family life, especially child rearing (Gutierrez, Sameroff, & Karrer, 1988). These children are oriented toward the family group as a source of information regarding their ethnic identity and culture. There is a body of literature on socialization of ethnic identification and the social-behavioral correlates of ethnic identity (e.g., Phinney & Rotheram, 1987).

Socialization for Interdependence

Ethnic minority families typically stress interdependence as a socialization goal for children as a logical accompaniment to emphasis on extended families and the ancestral worldview of collectivism. Parents tend to reinforce personality traits that are consistent with this goal. Given ecological challenges for achievement and accomplishment in American society, the pathway for individual and group members of ethnic minorities has been generally through collective actions that open opportunities for individual achievement. Thus socializing children toward interdependence with the group fosters the continuation of that pathway.

Generally, ethnic minority children are taught to think, feel, and act in ways that involve the development of a cooperative view of life, rather than one of a singularly competitive nature (Chan, 1986; Green, Sack, & Pambrum, 1981). Individuals are instructed to view themselves as an integral part of the totality of their family and the larger social structure and experience a social/psychological dependence on others. Cooperation, obligation, sharing, and reciprocity are essential elements of social interaction (Delgado-Gaitan, 1987; Serafica, in press). These values sharply contrast with Western ideals of competition, autonomy, and self-reliance (Sampson, 1988).

Sims (1978, 1979), in an empirical study concerned with sharing among African American children, found that children were more willing to share their toys and possessions when the request was made in the context of group reference. Establishing an ethnic minority reference facilitated more personal concern on the part of children and thus heightened children's motivation to share. Also, sharing was identified as an appropriate behavior of an ethnic group member. Children were probably affected by the expected group norm that sharing and cooperation were to be done with other group members. Although the number of studies on the topic is limited, there is evidence that American Indian and Hispanic American children are more cooperative and conciliatory in resolving potential interpersonal conflicts than are majority children (Delgado-Gaitan, 1987; Kagan & Madsen, 1971; Knight & Kagan, 1977; Osborne, 1985). There are no comparable studies for Asian American children.

Cognitive Developmental Outcomes

How do socialization goals stemming from adaptive strategies of ethnic minority families influence children's cognitive development? The socialization process is complex, and it is difficult to ascribe developmental outcomes to specific factors. The research evidence for these and similar questions is diffuse, sparse, uneven across ethnic minority groups, and lacking for some (McShane, 1988), yet some insights can be obtained from the general literature on ethnic minority children and families. Caution should be exercised in generalizing from group data to individuals within any single ethnic minority group (Laosa, 1977). Further, within-group differences are an important source of variance when studying developmental outcomes on child behavioral measures. Investigators have examined the variables of social class (Carter, 1983; DeVos, 1973; Hakuta, 1987; Shon & Ja, 1983), identification with ethnic culture (Buriel, 1984; McShane, 1983), generation status (Buriel, Calzada, & Vasques, 1982), geographic origin (Shon & Ja, 1983), father absence (Powell et al., 1983; Scott-Jones, 1987), gender (Hare & Castenell, 1985), home environment (Slaughter & Epps, 1987), and geographical habitats (McShane & Berry, 1986) as examples of important determinants of intragroup heterogeneity.

Theories abound explaining the determinants, course, and trends of cognitive development. Currently, the concepts of Vygotsky (1978) are receiving increased attention as a framework for investigating the importance of culture to cognitive development. Vygotsky viewed children as active participants who attempted to master and competently function in the world around them. One of the ways they mastered their world was through the use of auxiliary stimuli. Auxiliary stimuli are introduced as a means of active adaptation and include the tools of the culture into which the child is born, the language of those who relate to the child, and other means produced by the child himself. Thus, Vygotsky concluded that in order to study development in children one must begin with an understanding of two principally different entities, the biological and the cultural.

The ideas of Vygotsky (1978) have been expanded and serve as a source of fresh insights in the area of developmental psychology (e.g., Irvine & Berry, 1986). Bronfenbrenner (1989) summarized the essence of this trend as proposing that the attributes of the person most likely to shape the beginning of the course of one's cognitive development are those that induce or inhibit dynamic dispositions toward the immediate environment, referred to as developmentally instigative characteristics. For an elaborate discussion of these complex ideas, see Bronfenbrenner (1989). In the section that follows, we examine cognitive flexibility and sensitivity to discontinuity as aspects of cognitive development shaped by the socialization goals of ethnic minority families.

Cognitive Flexibility

Researchers have consistently found that ethnic minority families are concerned with biculturalism—or preparing children to function in both the ethnic and nonethnic communities (Harrison et al., 1984; Peters, 1988). Theoretical and empirical evidence (Ramirez, 1983) indicates that biculturalism often involves more than using two cultural modalities in a simple additive manner (Gutierrez et al., 1988). The process of integrating two cultural systems involves greater cognitive and social flexibility that eventuates in a unique synthesis of both ethnic and nonethnic cultures as well as separateness of both cultures. Achieving the new synthesis is a complex process fraught with many obstacles and conflicts.

Biculturalism can be expressed in values, identity, and customs. Nonetheless, bilingualism is perhaps the most investigated indicator (Hakuta & Garcia, 1989). Balanced bilingual children show more cognitive flexibility than monolingual children (McShane & Berry, 1986; McShane & Cook, 1985; Osborne, 1985; Ramirez & Castaneda, 1974; Seifert & Hoffnung, 1985), that is, the ability to detect multiple meanings of words and alternative orientations of objects. Studies also indicate that bilingualism fosters metalinguistic awareness, the cognitive ability to attend to language as an object of thought rather than just for the content or idea (Diaz, 1983). In the same manner, Boykin (1979) investigated cognitive flexibility by exploring whether differences in the format variability of a set of problem-solving tasks affected the problem-solving performance of ethnic and majority school children. He found that African American children as compared to majority children performed better on tasks that were presented in a varied, as opposed to an unvaried, format. The majority children performed equally well with both formats. The differences between the performance of African American and majority children are explained by Boykin with the concept of psychological/behavioral verve. Psychological/behavioral verve is a unique adaptation to the high-energy pace of home experiences that is manifested in one's attitude, orientation, and responsiveness to varied, constantly changing stimulation.

Sensitivity to Discontinuity

Discontinuity has been defined as an abrupt transition from one mode of being and behaving to another accompanied by noticeable differences in social role assignments and expectations (Marcias, 1987). The problems generated by discontinuity between the home environments of ethnic minority children and the school environment are of concern. Discontinuity has the possibility of negative consequences on cognitive functioning because it affects academic achievement and social adjustment (Osborne, 1985; Spindler & Spindler, 1987). Ethnic minority children are more likely to be exposed to discontinuities between their family ecologies and school environment than majority children, whose family ecologies are more likely to be similar to the academic setting. In her studies of the social ecologies of African American children, Holliday (1985) observed that the discontinuity between home, neighborhood, and school facilitated the development of situational problem solving among young persons. In the home and neighborhood, children's roles most frequently demanded problem-solving skills, that is, the ability to recognize, adapt to, circumvent, or change an encountered predicament. In the school environment, however, children's interpersonal skills—the ability to become a participant, to gain leadership, and to cooperate and collaborate—as well as academic excellence were in greatest demand. Continuity between learning environments of home and school is an important element in the performance of children on problem-solving tasks (Delgado-Gaitan, 1987; Laosa & Sigel, 1982; Marcias, 1987). Research studies have found that ethnic minority children show improvements in their achievement levels, memory, and problem-solving abilities when the context of the learning environment is consistent with their background (Boykin, 1979; Hare, 1985; Holliday, 1985; Spindler & Spindler, 1987). This phenomenon is highlighted in the teaching strategies parents use in interactions with children. The teaching/learning strategies used in the home influences how children perform on problem-solving situations in school (Laosa, 1980; Laosa & DeAvila, 1979; Steward & Steward, 1973).

Summary and Discussion

Recent population projections of the increase in the proportion of Americans who are members of an ethnic minority group have heightened the need for social scientists to understand these populations. The purpose of this article was to consider the interconnectedness of ecologies of ethnic minority families, adaptive strategies, socialization goals, and child behavioral outcomes. Ethnic minority groups have adaptive strategies that developed as responses to ecological challenges. The adaptive strategies discussed were family extendedness and role flexibility, biculturalism, and ancestral worldview. Adult members of the group have as their socialization goals fostering a positive orientation to the ethnic group and interdependence for children. Cognitive flexibility and sensitivity to discontinuities in children were viewed as developmental outcomes. We hope that this article will stimulate research that can be utilized by those who educate, parent, socialize, and support ethnic minority children.

Although progress has been made in initiating writings and empirical investigations of ethnic minority families and children, a majority of the publications focus on mental health rather than on developmental issues. There is also unevenness in the quality of the research efforts on ethnic minorities, and the social sciences have serious shortcomings in this area.

In the future, researchers need to attend to the extreme heterogeneity among various ethnic groups. It is important to identify the specific ethnic/demographic characteristics of the group studied in empirical investigations. It is important to note that although the cognitive domain was selected for review because there were more empirical investigations in that area, other aspects of development should be studied using this conceptual framework. Earlier literature on ethnic minority children concentrated on cognitive issues and subsequently has been criticized for narrowness of focus and shortcomings in methodology.

Researchers need to consider level of acculturation, period of immigration, social class, and appropriateness of comparison group in research designs. Failure to do so are principal pitfalls in the study of development among ethnic minorities. Also, social scientists need to take stock of the ethnocentrism biases in the formulation of research questions and interpretations of data from studies of ethnic minority children. Sampson (1988) and Spence (1985) offer insightful comments on the percursors for this tendency. With increased interest in the cultural context of development, there is hope that more culturally sensitive research will yield more insightful information regarding development among ethnic minority children.

Two examples of research designs that may be fruitful are offered. One is to study the socialization practices of different ethnic minority families that are rearing successful children. What are the similarities and differences in their parenting techniques, and what factors account for them? Second, in every culture there are critical social pathways to success. What were the procedures or pathways taken by adult members of the ethnic groups that led to success? What environmental factors and psychological processes can best explain how ethnic group members have managed to succeed? Finally, more effort needs to be directed to the formulation of conceptual models that can best explain the development of ethnic minority children. The models should not only be explanatory, but also suggestive of empirical investigations. These efforts are worthwhile as we continue our attempts to understand human development in a cultural context.

References

Agesti, B. F. (1978). The first decades of freedom: Black families in a southern county, 1870–1885. *Journal of Marriage and the Family*, **46**, 697–706.

Allen, W. R. (1978). Black family research in the United States: A review, assessment, and extension. *Journal of Comparative Family Studies*, **2**, 167–189.

Allen, W. R., & Stukes, S. (1982). Black family lifestyles and the mental health of black Americans. In F. U. Munoz & R. Endo (Eds.), *Perspectives on minority group mental health* (pp. 43–52). Washington, DC: University Press of America.

Aoyagi, K. (1978). Kinship and friendship in black Los Angeles: A study of migrants from Texas. In D. Shimkin, E. Shimkin, & D. Frate (Eds.), *The extended family in black societies* (pp. 277–355). Chicago: Aldine.

Beck, R. W., & Beck, S. H. (1984). Formation of extended households during middle age. *Journal of Marriage and the Family*, **46**, 277–287.

Beck, R. W., & Beck, S. H. (1989). The incidence of extended households among middle-aged black and white women. *Journal of Family Issues*, **10**, 147–168.

Bing, J. (1980). Acculturation as varieties of adaptations. In A. M. Padilla (Ed.), *Acculturation: Theory, models and some new findings* (pp. 9–23). Boulder, CO: Westview.

Bouvier, L. F., & Agresta, A. (forthcoming). Projections of the Asian American population. In J. T. Fawcett & B. Carino (Eds.), *Asian and Pacific immigration to the United States*.

Bowman, P. J., & Howard, C. (1985). Race-related socialization, motivation, and academic achievement: A study of black youth in three-generation families. *Journal of the American Academy of Child Psychiatry*, **24**, 134–141.

Boykin, A. W. (1979). Psychological behavioral verve: Some theoretical explorations and empirical manifestations. In A. W. Boykin, A. J. Franklin, & J. F. Yates (Eds.), *Research directions of black psychologists* (pp. 351–367). New York: Russell Sage.

Bronfenbrenner, U. (1979). *The ecology of human development*. Cambridge, MA: Harvard University Press.

Bronfenbrenner, U. (1989, June). *The ecology of cognitive development: Research models and fugitive findings*. Paper prepared for presentation as the keynote address for the Nineteenth Annual Symposium of the Jean Piaget Society, Philadelphia.

Brown, D. R., & Gary, L. (1987). Stressful life events, social support networks, and the physical and mental health of urban black adults. *Journal of Human Stress*, **13**, 165–174.

Burgess, B. J. (1980). Parenting in the Native American community. In M. D. Fantini & R. Cardenas (Eds.), *Parenting in a multicultural society* (pp. 63–73). New York: Lougman.

Buriel, R. (1984). Integration with traditional Mexican-American culture an sociocultural adjustment. In *Chicano psychology* (2d ed, pp. 95–130). New York: Academic Press.

Buriel, R. (1987). Ethnic labeling and identity among Mexican Americans. In J. S. Phinney & M. J. Rotheram (Eds.), *Children's ethnic socialization* (pp. 134–152). Beverly Hills, CA: Sage.

Carter, J. (1983). *Vision or sight: Health concerns for Afro-American children*. In G. J. Powell (Ed.), *The psychological development of minority children* (pp. 13–25). New York: Brunner/Mazel.

Chan, S. (1986). Parents of exceptional Asian children. In M. K. Kitano & P. C. Chinn (Eds.), *Exceptional Asian children and youth* (pp. 36–53). Reston, VA: Council for Exceptional Children.

Delgado-Gaitan, C. (1987). Tradition and transitions in the learning process of Mexican children: An ethnographic view. In G. Spindler & L. Spindler (Eds.), *Interpretive ethnography of education: At home and abroad* (pp. 333–359). Hillsdale, NJ: Erlbaum.

DeVos, G. A. (Ed.). (1973). *Socialization for achievement*. Berkeley: University of California Press.

DeVos, G. A. (1982). Adaptive strategies in U.S. minorities. In E. E. Jones & S. J. Korchin (Eds.), *Minority mental health* (pp. 74–117). New York: Praeger.

Diaz, R. (1983). Thought and two languages: The impact of bilingualism on cognitive development. In E. Gordon (Ed.), *Review of research in education, Vol. 10*. Washington, DC: American Educational Research Association.

Dix, J. H., & Grusec, J. E. (1985). Parent attribution processes in the socialization of children. In I. E. Sigel (Ed.), *Parental belief systems* (pp. 201–233). Hillsdale, NJ: Erlbaum.

Dressler, W. W. (1985). Extended family relationships, social support, and mental health in a southern black community. *Journal of Health and Social Behavior*, 26, 39–48.

Elkin, F., & Handel, G. (1984). *The child and society: The process of socialization*. New York: Random House.

Flanagan, W. G. (1978, August). *The extended family as an agent of social change*. Paper presented at the Ninth World Congress of the International Sociological Association, Uppsala University, Uppsala, Sweden.

Fogel, R., & Engelman, S. (1974). *Time on the cross* (Vols. 1 and 2). Boston: Little, Brown.

Foster, H. J. (1984). African patterns in Afro-American families. *Journal of Black Studies*, 14, 201–232.

Garbarino, J. (1982). Sociocultural risk: Dangers to competence. In C. B. Kopp & J. B. Krakow (Eds.), *The child: Development in a social context*. Reading, MA: Addison-Wesley.

Garbarino, M. S. (1976). *Native heritage*. Boston: Little, Brown.

Gardner, R. W., Robey, B., & Smith, P. C. (1985). Asian Americans: Growth, changes and diversity. *Population Bulletin*, 40, 4.

Genovese, E. D. (1976). *Roll, Jordan, roll*. New York: Random House.

Gibbs, J. T., Huang, L. N., & Associates (1989). *Children of color*. San Francisco: Jossey-Bass.

Gibson, G. (1972). Kin family network: Overheralded structure in past conceptualizations of family functioning. *Journal of Marriage and the Family*, 34, 13–23.

Gill, S. D. (1982a). *Beyond "the primitive": The religions of non-literate peoples*. Englewood Cliffs, NJ: Prentice-Hall.

Gill, S. D. (1982b). *Native American religions*. Belmont, CA: Wadsworth.

Goode, W. J. (1964). *The family*. Englewood Cliffs, NJ: Prentice-Hall.

Goodluck, C. T., & Eckstein, F. (1978). American Indian adoption program: An ethnic approach to child welfare. *White Cloud Journal*, 1, 3–7.

Green, B. E., Sack, W. H., & Pambrum, A. (1981). A review of child psychiatric epidemiology with special reference to American Indian and Alaska Native children. *White Cloud Journal*, 2, 22–36.

Gutierrez, J., Sameroff, A. J., & Karrer, B. M. (1988). Acculturation and SES effects on Mexican American parents' concepts of development. *Child Development*, 59, 250–255.

Gutman, H. G. (1976). *The black family in slavery and freedom, 1750–1925*. New York: Vintage.

Hakuta, K. (1987). Degree of bilingualism and cognitive ability in mainland Puerto Rican children. *Child Development*, 58, 1372–1388.

Hakuta, K., & Garcia, E. E. (1989). Bilingualism and education. *American Psychologist*, 44, 374–379.

Hamer, J. H. (1980). Acculturation stress and the functions of alcohol among the forest Potowatomi. In J. Hamer & J. Steinwings (Eds.), *Alcohol and native peoples of the north* (pp. 107–153). Washington, DC: University Press of America.

Harding, V. (1980). *The other American revolution*. Los Angeles: Center for Afro-American Studies, University of California, Los Angeles.

Hare, B. R. (1985). Reexamining the achievement central tendency: Sex differences within race and race differences within sex. In H. P. McAdoo & J. L. McAdoo (Eds.), *Black children* (pp. 139–151). Beverly Hills, CA: Sage.

Hare, B. R., & Castenell, L. A. (1985). No place to run, no place to hide: Comparative status and future prospects of black boys. In M. B. Spencer, G. Brookins, & W. Allen (Eds.), *Beginnings: The social and affective development of black children* (pp. 201–214). Hillsdale, NJ: Erlbaum.

Harrison, A. O., Serafica, F., & McAdoo, H. (1984). Ethnic families of color. In R. D. Parke (Ed.), *The family: Review of child development research* (Vol. 7, pp. 329–371). Chicago: University of Chicago Press.

Heela, P., & Lock, A. C. (Eds.). (1981). *Indigenous psychologies: The anthropology of the self*. London: Academic Press.

Height, D. (1985, March). What must be done about children having children. *Ebony*, p. 76.

Holliday, B. G. (1985). Developmental imperative of social ecologies: Lessons learned from black children. In H. P. McAdoo & J. L. McAdoo (Eds.), *Black children* (pp. 53–71). Beverly Hills, CA: Sage.

Hultkrantz, A. (1981). *Belief and worship in Native North America*. Syracuse, NY: Syracuse University Press.

Hurdy, J. M. (1970). *American Indian religions*. Los Angeles: Sherbourne.

Irvine, S. H., & Berry, J. W. (Eds.). (1986). *Human abilities in cultural context*. Cambridge: Cambridge University Press.

Johnson, J. E., & Martin, C. (1985). Parents' beliefs and home learning environments: Effects on cognitive development. In I. E. Sigel (Ed.), *Parental belief systems* (pp. 25–50). Hillsdale, NJ: Erlbaum.

Kagan, S., & Madsen, M. C. (1971). Cooperation and competition of Mexican, Mexican-American, and Anglo-American children of two ages under four instructional sets. *Developmental Psychology, 5*, 32–39.

Knight, G. P., & Kagan, S. (1977). Development of prosocial and competitive behaviors in Anglo-American and Mexican-American children. *Child Development, 48*, 1385–1394.

LaFromboise, T. D. (1988). American Indian mental health policy. *American Psychologist, 43*, 388–397.

Langston, E. J. (1980). Kith and kin; natural support systems: Their implications for policies and programs for the black aged. In E. P. Stanford (Ed.), *Minority aging policy issues for the '80s* (pp. 125–145). San Diego: University Center on Aging, College of Human Services, San Diego State University.

Laosa, L. M. (1977). Cognitive styles and learning strategies research. *Journal of Teacher Education, 28*, 26–30.

Laosa, L. M. (1980). Maternal teaching strategies in Chicano and Anglo American families: The influence of culture and education on maternal behavior. *Child Development, 51*, 759–765.

Laosa, L. M., & DeAvila, E. A. (1979). Development of cognitive styles among Chicanos in traditional and dualistic communities. *International Journal of Psychology, 14*, 91–98.

Laosa, L. M., & Sigel, I. E. (1982). *Families as learning environments for children*. New York: Plenum.

Lewis, R. (1981). Patterns of strengths of American Indian families. In F. Hoffman (Ed.), *The American Indian family strengths and stresses* (pp. 101–107). American Indian Social Research and Development Associates, Inc., P.O. Box 381, Iskta, NM 87022.

Light, H. K., & Martin, R. E. (1986). American Indian families. *Journal of American Indian Education, 26*, 1–5.

Marcias, J. (1987). The hidden curriculum of Papago teachers: American Indian strategies for mitigating cultural discontinuity in early schooling. In G. Spindler & L. Spindler (Eds.), *Interpretive ethnography of education: At home and abroad* (pp. 363–380). Hillsdale, NJ: Erlbaum.

Marin, G. (1986, October). *The process of acculturatism of Latinos in the U.S.* Paper presented at the Second Puerto Rican Convention of Psychology and Mental Health, Rio Piedras, Puerto Rico.

Martin, E., & Martin, J. (1978). *The black extended family*. Chicago: University of Chicago Press.

McAdoo, H. (1978). Factors related to stability in upwardly mobile black families. *Journal of Marriage and the Family, 40*, 761–776.

McGillicuddy-DeLisi, A. V. (1985). The relationship between parental beliefs and children's cognitive level. In I. E. Sigel (Ed.), *Parental belief systems* (pp. 7–24). Hillsdale, NJ: Erlbaum.

McLoyd, V., & Randolph, S. (1985). Secular trends in the study of Afro-American children: A review of child development, 1936–1980. *Monographs of the Society for Research in Child Development, 50*(4–5, Serial No. 211).

McShane, D. (1983). Explaining achievement patterns of American Indian children: A transcultural and developmental model. *Peabody Journal of Education, 61*, 34–48.

McShane, D. (1988). An analysis of mental health research with American Indian youth. *Journal of Adolescence, 11*, 87–116.

McShane, D., & Berry, J. W. (1986). Native North Americans: Indian and Inuit abilities. In J. H. Irvine & J. W. Berry (Eds.), *Human abilities in cultural context* (pp. 385–426). Cambridge: Cambridge University Press.

McShane, D., & Cook, V. (1985). Transcultural intellectual assessment: Hispanic performance on the Wechslers. In B. Wolman (Ed.), *Handbook of intelligence: Theories, measurements, and applications*. New York: Wiley.

Meacham, M. (1983). The myth of the black matriarchy under slavery. *Mid-American Review of Sociology, 8*, 23–41.

Medicine, B. (1980). American Indian women: Spirituality and status. *Bread and Roses, 2*, 14–18.

Medicine, B. (1981). American Indian family: Cultural change and adaptive strategies. *Journal of Ethnic Studies, 8*, 13–23.

Michaelsen, R. S. (1983). "We also have a religion": The free exercise of religion among Native Americans. *American Indian Quarterly, 7*, 111–142.

Mindel, C. H., & Habenstein, R. W. (Eds.). (1984). *Ethnic families in America: Patterns and variations*. New York: Elsevier.

Moos, R. H., Insel, P. M., & Humphrey, B. (1974). *Manual for the Family Environment Scale*. Palo Alto, CA: Consulting Psychologists Press.

Munoz, F. U., & Endo, R. (Eds.). (1982). *Perspectives on minority group mental health*. Washington, DC: University Press of America.

Myers, H. F. (1982). Research on the Afro-American family: A critical review. In B. Bass, G. Wyatt, & G. Powell (Eds.), *The Afro-American family: Assessment treatment and research issues* (pp. 35–69). New York: Grune & Stratton.

National Indochinese Clearinghouse (1980). *Indochinese refugee education guides, general information series.* Washington, DC: National Indochinese Clearinghouse.

Nobles, W. W. (1978). African root and American fruit: The black family. *Journal of Social and Behavioral Sciences,* **20,** 1–18.

Nobles, W. W. (1988). African-American family life: An instrument of culture. In H. P. McAdoo (Ed.), *Black families* (2d ed., pp. 44–53). Beverly Hills, CA: Sage.

Noel, D. L. (1985). A theory of the origin of ethnic stratification. In N. R. Yetman (Ed.), *Majority and minority* (pp. 109–120). Boston: Allyn & Bacon.

Ogbu, J. V. (1981). Origins of human competence: A cultural-ecological perspective. *Child Development,* **52,** 413–429.

Ogbu, J. V. (1985). The consequences of the American caste system. In V. Neisser (Ed.), *The school achievement of minority children: New perspectives* (pp. 19–56). Hillsdale, NJ: Erlbaum.

Ogbu, J. V. (1987). Variability in minority responses to schooling: Nonimmigrants vs. immigrants. In G. Spindler & L. Spindler (Eds.), *Interpretive ethnography of education: At home and abroad* (pp. 255–280). Hillsdale, NJ: Erlbaum.

Olmedo, E. L. (1981). Testing linguistic minorities. *American Psychologist,* **36,** 1018–1085.

Osborne, B. (1985). Research into Native North Americans' cognition: 1973–1982. *Journal of American Indian Education,* **24,** 9–25.

Padilla, E. R., & O'Grady, K. E. (1987). Sexuality among Mexican-Americans: A case of sexual stereotyping. *Journal of Personality and Social Psychology,* **52,** 5–10.

Pan Asian Parent Education Project (1982). *Pan Asian child-rearing practices: Philipino, Japanese, Korean, Samoan, Vietnamese.* San Diego: Union of Pan Asian Communities.

Penalosa, F. (1980). *Chicano sociolinguistics.* Rowley, MA: Newbury House.

Peters, M. F. (1988). Parenting in black families with young children: A historical perspective. In H. P. McAdoo (Ed.), *Black families* (2d ed., pp. 228–241). Beverly Hills, CA: Sage.

Peterson, R. O., & Yamamoto, B. Y. (Eds.). (1980). *Understanding the Pan Asian client: Book II.* San Diego: Union of Pan Asian Communities.

Phinney, J. S., & Rotheram, M. J. (Eds.). (1987). *Children's ethnic socialization: Pluralism and development.* Beverly Hills, CA: Sage.

Powell, G. J., Morales, A., Romero, A., & Yamamoto, J. (Eds.). (1983). *The psychosocial development of minority group children.* New York: Brunner/Mazel.

Ramirez, J. D. (1986). Comparing structural English immersion and bilingual education: First year results of a national study. *American Journal of Education,* **95,** 122–148.

Ramirez, M. (1983). *Psychology of the Americas.* Elmsford, NY: Pergamon.

Ramirez, M., & Castaneda, A. (1974). *Cultural democracy, bicognitive development, and education.* New York: Academic Press.

Red Horse, J. (1983). Indian family values and experiences. In G. J. Powell, A. Morales, A. Romero, & J. Yamamoto (Eds.), *The psychosocial development of minority group children* (pp. 258–272). New York: Brunner/Mazel.

Reed, J. (1982). Black Americans in the 1980s. *Population Bulletin,* **37,** 1–37.

Report on minorities in higher education (1988). Hearing before the Committee on Education and Labor, House of Representatives, One-Hundredth Congress, Serial No. 100-192. Washington, DC: Government Printing Office.

Reuschenberg, E. J., & Buriel, R. (1988). *The effects of acculturation on relationship patterns and system variables within families of Mexican descent.* Unpublished manuscript, the Claremont Graduate School, Claremont, CA.

Rogoff, B. (1982). Integrating context and cognitive development. In M. E. Lamb & A. L. Brown (Eds.), *Advances in developmental psychology* (Vol. **2,** pp. 125–170). Hillsdale, NJ: Erlbaum.

Rogoff, B., Gauvain, M., & Ellis, S. (1984). Development viewed in its context. In M. H. Bornstein & M. E. Lamb (Eds.), *Developmental psychology: An advanced textbook.* Hillsdale, NJ: Erlbaum.

Ryan, R. A. (1981). Strengths of the American Indian family: State of the art. In F. Hoffman (Ed.), *The American Indian family: Strengths and stresses.* American Indian Social Research and Development Associates, Inc., P.O. Box 381, Isleta, NM 87022.

Sabogal, F., Marin, G., Otero-Sabogal, R., Marin, B., & Perez-Stable, E. J. (1987). Hispanic familism and acculturation: What changes and what doesn't? *Hispanic Journal of Behavioral Sciences,* **9,** 397–412.

Sampson, E. E. (1985). The decentralization of identity. *American Psychologist,* **40,** 1203–1211.

Sampson, E. E. (1988). The debate on individualism. *American Psychologists,* **43,** 15–22.

Schneider, D. M. (1968). *American kinship: A cultural account.* Englewood Cliffs, NJ: Prentice-Hall.

Schneider, D. M. (1980). *American kinship: A cultural account* (2d ed.). Englewood Cliffs, NJ: Prentice-Hall.

Scott-Jones, D. (1987). Mother-as-teacher in the families of high- and low-achieving, low-income black first graders. *Journal of Negro Education,* **56,** 21–34.

Seifert, K. L., & Hoffnung, R. J. (1987). *Child and*

adolescent development. Boston: Houghton Mifflin.

Serafica, F. C. (in press). Counseling Asian-American parents: A cultural-developmental framework. In F. C. Serafica et al. (Eds.), *Mental health of ethnic minorities.* New York: Praeger.

Shon, S. P., & Ja, D. Y. (1983). Asian families. In M. McGoldrick, J. K. Pearce, & J. Giordano (Eds.), *Ethnicity and family therapy.* New York: Guilford.

Sigel, M. (1985). A study of maternal beliefs and values within the context of an intervention program. In I. E. Sigel (Ed.), *Parental belief systems* (pp. 271–286). Hillsdale, NJ: Erlbaum.

Sims, S. A. (1978). Effects of modeling processes and resources on sharing among black children. *Psychological Reports, 43,* 463–473.

Sims, S. A. (1979). Sharing in black children: The impact of reference group appeals and other environmental factors. In A. W. Boykin, A. J. Franklin, & J. F. Yates (Eds.), *Research direction of black psychologists* (pp. 146–162). New York: Russell Sage.

Slaughter, D. T., & Epps, E. G. (1987). Home environment and academic achievement of black American children and youth: An overview. *Journal of Negro Education, 56,* 3–20.

Snipp, C. M., & Sandefur, G. O. (1988). Earnings of American Indians and Alaskan Natives: The effects of residence and migration. *Social Forces, 66,* 994–1008.

Soldo, B., & Lauriat, P. (1976). Living arrangements among the elderly in the United States: A log-linear approach. *Journal of Comparative Family Studies, 7,* 351–366.

Spence, J. T. (1985). Achievement American style: The rewards and costs of individualism. *American Psychologist, 40,* 1285–1295.

Spindler, G., & Spindler, L. (1987). *Interpretive ethnography of education.* Hillsdale, NJ: Erlbaum.

Stack, C. (1981). Sex roles and survival strategies in an urban black community. In F. C. Steady (Ed.), *The black woman cross-culturally* (pp. 349–367). Cambridge, MA: Schinkman.

Steward, M., & Steward, D. (1973). The observation of Anglo-Mexican and Chinese-American mothers teaching their young sons. *Child Development, 44,* 329–337.

Sudarkasa, N. (1988). Interpreting the African heritage in Afro-American family organization. In H. P. McAdoo (Ed.), *Black families* (2d ed., pp. 27–43). Beverly Hills, CA: Sage.

Sue, D., & Sue, S. (1987). Cultural factors in the clinical assessment of Asian Americans. *Journal of Consulting and Clinical Psychology, 55,* 479–487.

Suzuki, B. H. (1980). The Asian American family. In M. D. Fanti & R. Cardenas (Eds.), *Parenting in a multicultural society* (pp. 76–101). New York: Longman.

Sweet, J. A. (1977, October). *Further indicators of family structure and process for racial and ethnic minorities.* Paper presented at the Conference on the Demography of Racial and Ethnic Groups, Austin, TX.

Szopocznik, J., & Kurtines, W. (1980). Acculturation, biculturalism, and adjustment among Cuban Americans. In A. M. Padilla (Ed.), *Acculturation: Theory, models and some new findings* (pp. 139–161). Boulder, CO: Westview.

Taylor, R. J. (1988). Structural determinants of religious participation among black Americans. *Review of Religious Research, 2,* 114–125.

Taylor, R. J., Thornton, M. C., & Chatters, L. M. (1988). Black Americans' perceptions of the sociohistorical role of the church. *Journal of Black Studies, 18,* 123–138.

Thornton, M. C., & Taylor, R. J. (1988). Black Americans' perceptions of black Africans. *Ethnic and Racial Studies, 11,* 140–150.

Tseng, W. (1973). The concept of personality in Confucian thought. *Psychiatry, 50,* 76–86.

U.S. Bureau of the Census (1989). *Household and family characteristics: March, 1988* (Current Population Report, Series P-20, No. 437). Washington, DC: Government Printing Office.

U.S. Department of Commerce Series, Bureau of the Census (1988). *We, the Asian and Pacific Islander; We, the Black Americans; We, the first American;* and *We, Nosotros.* Washington, DC: Government Printing Office.

Vygotsky, L. S. (1978). *Mind in society.* Cambridge, MA: Harvard University Press.

Wagner, S. T. (1981). The historical background of bilingualism and biculturalism in the United States. In M. Ridge (Ed.), *The new bilingualism* (pp. 29–52). New Brunswick, NJ: Transaction Books.

Willig, A. (1985). A meta-analysis of selected studies on the effectiveness of bilingual education. *Review of Educational Research, 55,* 269–317.

Wilson, M. N. (1986). The black extended family: An analytical review. *Developmental Psychology, 22,* 246–258.

Wilson, M. N. (1989). Child development in the context of the black extended family. *American Psychologist, 44,* 380–385.

Wolfson, N., & Manes, J. (Eds.). (1985). *Language of inequality.* New York: Mouton.

Yetman, N. R. (Ed.). (1985). *Majority and minority.* Boston: Allyn & Bacon.

Zigler, E. F., Lamb, M. E., & Child, I. L. (1982). *Socialization and personality development.* New York: Oxford University Press.

15 Cultural Differences in the Meaning of Adolescent Pregnancy

Martha M. Dore and Ana O. Dumois

ABSTRACT: *Based on research performed in a program for pregnant and parenting teenagers, the authors examine the cultural differences in the self-descriptions of black and Hispanic adolescents. Although the family plays an important role in both black and Hispanic cultures, family functioning, role definitions, and expectations for individual members are different. The practice implications of these cultural differences are discussed.*

APPRECIATION AND UNDERSTANDING of cultural difference is an essential component of sound practice. The literature increasingly points to the various ways in which members of different ethnic and cultural groups attribute meaning to their daily lives. Beginning with Zborowski's (1969) classic study of ethnic difference in responses to illness and hospitalization, *People in Pain*, social scientists have confirmed the observations of generations of social work practitioners: accurate assessment of the person–problem–situation configuration must be undergirded by awareness of the cultural ecology within which this configuration is embedded.

Despite the profession's theoretical subscription to the importance of understanding cultural difference, little empirical support exists for clinically derived observations of ethnic and cultural difference in client responses to the problems they face. Research on the problems and conditions of clients of social work agencies often fails to distinguish the cultural variations in clients' attitudes or behaviors, or when such differences are noted, fails to draw implications for practice from them.

This article presents research findings on cultural differences in the responses of adolescent mothers to the events of teen pregnancy and parenthood. It examines the self-descriptions of a group of black and Puerto Rican young mothers, relates these descriptions to cultural differences between these two groups, and draws implications for practice from them. As will be demonstrated, these two groups of adolescent mothers are strikingly different; the differences between them must be considered and addressed in developing programs to serve teen parents.

Cultural Differences in Adolescent Pregnancy

Although the literature on adolescent pregnancy is extensive and growing, the preponderance of research to date explores either causes of teen pregnancy, focusing on adolescent sexual activity and contraception, or outcomes, in terms of consequences for mother and child. Although race or ethnicity is usually an identified demographic variable in such studies, only a small portion of these studies explore the meaning of racial differences with respect to implications for inter-

Martha M. Dore is Assistant Professor, School of Social Work, University of Pennsylvania, Philadelphia, Pennsylvania, and Ana O. Dumois is Chief Executive Officer, Community Family Planning Council, New York, New York.

vention. Indeed, differences that appear along racial or ethnic lines are usually ascribed to socioeconomic factors (Moore, Simms, & Betsey, 1986). More attention has been paid to differences attributed to age of adolescent mothers than to ethnic difference, with research findings often distinguishing between young adolescence (fifteen years and younger), midadolescence (sixteen to seventeen years), and older adolescence (eighteen to nineteen years) (Zitner & Miller, 1980).

Of all research on teenage pregnancy, prevalence studies most often address racial differences when analyzing causes of early childbearing. A number of studies analyzing data from the Current Population Survey have compared early childbearing among black, Hispanic, and white women (O'Connell & Rogers, 1984). Available data include fertility rates, births to unmarried women, and marriage rates for these groups. O'Connell and Rodgers (1984) analyzed data from this survey on out-of-wedlock childbearing by race, family income, and mother's education level. They found that racial differences remained equivalent when income and education level were controlled. A second analysis of these data found identifiable racial differences in the tendency to marry before the child's birth (O'Connell & Moore, 1980).

Racial and ethnic differences in onset of sexual activity in adolescence, exclusive of socioeconomic status, have also been identified (Bauman & Udry, 1981). Studies of contraceptive use among teenagers have found racial differences both in method and frequency of use, although these findings may reflect differential access to contraceptives rather than attitudes (Zelnick & Kanter, 1980). Finally, racial and ethnic differences in attitudes toward resolution of unplanned pregnancy are well-documented, particularly with respect to abortion and adoption (Henshaw & O'Reilly, 1983). Evidence suggests that blacks hesitate to consider adoption as a viable alternative because they have traditionally been denied access to adoption resources. However, evidence also suggests that one strength of black families is that they are less rigidly bound than are white families and can more easily accommodate a new and unanticipated member (Hill, 1972).

Although the research cited above provides evidence that identifiable racial and ethnic differences relate to likelihood of teen pregnancy and influence its resolution, fewer research studies identify such differences in outcomes. As Brooks-Gunn and Furstenberg (1986) note, one reason for this lack is that the vast majority of studies on outcomes of teen pregnancy focus on young black parents and their children, particularly those living in low-income, urban communities. Those few studies that do attempt to compare outcomes across racial or ethnic lines frequently compare blacks with whites and little attention is focused on the Hispanic population. Usually, however, outcome comparisons are between adolescent mothers of unidentified racial or ethnic origin and older mothers.

Cultural Differences in Family Life

A second body of literature informing the present study describes ethnic or cultural differences in family life. This literature is particularly useful for researchers and practitioners in the area of adolescent pregnancy and parenthood in that it enhances sensitivity to the meanings teenagers may attribute to these two events in their lives (Nobles, 1978). For example, Stack's (1974) seminal study of supportive and nurturing family relationships that go beyond traditional blood ties in one poor black community provides a theoretical framework for understanding the responses of black adolescents to pregnancy outside marriage. Informal adoption was shown to be a common community practice, reflecting the cultural value of the inherent worth of each child no matter what the birth circumstances. Stack's study and others also demonstrate that many black fathers remain intrinsically connected to their children, either directly or indirectly through the kinship network, whatever their legal relationship to the mothers (Stack, 1974).

Research on black families has described the high value that blacks place on educational achievement for both women and men, regardless of the socioeconomic level of the family. In fact, most studies of educational aspiration have found that young black women have higher educational goals than do their white peers (Moore, Simms, & Betsey, 1986). Education and hard work are valued as vehicles for future economic security, despite the often overwhelming obstacles introduced by racism and socioeconomic class differences.

Reciprocal obligation among family members has also been identified as a strong value in black families (McAdoo, 1978). Those individuals who receive help are considered bound by their obligation to give assistance to others in need. As Hines and Boyd-Franklin (1982) point out, although reciprocal obligation can serve a very positive function, it may also prevent family members from moving away from the family, effectively binding them in a stagnant system.

Like black families, the Hispanic family is an extended family system that includes not only blood relatives but also godparents and informally adopted children (Mizio, 1974). Godparents not only function as substitute parents for the children but also as a support system for the parents. These relationships are formalized through the ritual of infant baptism and carry binding obligations for "economic assistance, encouragement, and even personal correction" (Garcia-Preto, 1982, p. 172).

Unlike black families, in which role flexibility is the norm, family roles are clearly defined in the Hispanic family (Ghali, 1982). The husband is the head of the household with responsibility for protecting and providing for the family unit. The wife is responsible for caring for the home, carrying out household tasks, and childrearing functions. The wife is responsible for managing the expressive needs of family members and for maintaining the family system. The role of mother has high social value in Hispanic culture. A good mother centers her life on her family, sacrificing her own needs for those of others. Submissiveness, passivity, and deference to those in authority are characteristics traditionally valued in Hispanic women (Ghali, 1982).

"Child-keeping" or the informal fostering of children within the kinship system is similar in both black and Hispanic families (Stack, 1974). Like Northern urban black families who may send errant teenagers to relatives in the South, Puerto Rican families often send children to relatives on the island, or back to the mainland, according to their developmental needs. This ease in sharing parenting among extended family members offers additional sources of support to single-parent families. According to one authority on Hispanic culture, young women who become pregnant before marriage are seldom ostracized anymore (Ortiz & Vazquez, 1987). The pregnant teenager is usually assured of a home for herself and her child.

Although the literature on adolescent pregnancy and parenthood is substantial and the literature on cultural variations in family life is growing, cultural differences in the meaning of pregnancy and parenthood in adolescence have seldom been explored. The research presented here addresses this deficit by comparing and contrasting the self-descriptions of black and Hispanic teen mothers in relation to their cultural contexts.

The TASA Project

In response to state legislation mandating scattered-site demonstration projects designed to address the perceived social problem of adolescent pregnancy and parenthood, the Community Family Planning Council of New York City (CFPC), a voluntary, not-for-profit health care agency, developed such a program through their Women's Clinic in the South Bronx. The project, titled Teens Aiming for Self-Improvement (TASA), was designed to provide intensive case-management services to pregnant and parenting teenagers as well as to youngsters perceived to be at risk of early pregnancy. The program included extensive outreach and case finding, mutual client–worker participation in needs assessment and goal setting, and the establishment of an individualized service plan. Case management services included facilitating linkages between clients and community agencies; advocating on clients' behalf in acquiring needed community services and resources; on-site provision of individual, family, and group counseling; and health and family planning services utilizing the Women's Clinic staff.

Clients were recruited for the TASA project in several ways. Because only youth younger than eighteen were eligible according to the state's guidelines, informational letters were sent to all AFDC recipients seventeen years of age and younger in the program's catchment area. About one-third of TASA clients were recruited in this way. Another important source of referrals was CFPC's South Bronx Women's Clinic, a portion of whose space was occupied by TASA. Women's Clinic staff were quick to identify as potential TASA clients any parenting adolescents who came into the clinic for pregnancy testing or birth control counseling. As a result, an additional third of all TASA clients were referred by the Women's Clinic. Finally, once the program was operational and referral inquiries were made to other community resources, those agencies, in turn, began to refer potential clients to TASA. Local hospitals and school personnel became especially important referral sources. Clients of TASA also referred other clients as they benefited from the program's services. The remaining third of the program participants were recruited from these sources. During the first twelve months of operation 138 persons applied to the TASA program; 134 completed at least an initial interview.

Program Participants

Most TASA clients (see Table 1) were between the ages of fifteen and seventeen years. Ten clients were younger than fifteen, the youngest an at-risk eleven-year-old. All but six clients were young women. Those six were sexually active young men who sought counseling regarding contraception and their responsibilities as partners and fathers. Forty-four young women were pregnant at the time of application to the TASA program; four others were awaiting medical confirmation of pregnancy. Five of those who were pregnant were already parenting one child.

Of the eighty female applicants who were not pregnant at the time they applied for TASA services, fifty-nine already had one child and one had two children. Pregnancy or parenting status was not indicated for eight clients. Therefore, of the 128 young women who received TASA services during the program's first year, all but twelve were either pregnant (34 percent), parenting (48 percent), or both (4 percent) at the time of application.

The racial and ethnic composition of the program's client population reflected the South Bronx neighborhood in which the TASA project was located. The South Bronx is an economically deprived area with a predominately black and Hispanic population. Hispanics are primarily of Puerto Rican origin. During its first twelve months of operation, 68 percent of TASA clients were Hispanic and 32 percent were black. No white clients were served. A significant proportion of Hispanic clients, about ten to twelve at any given time, and a somewhat larger number of their adult family members, spoke no English.

Only one client in the TASA program during the first year was legally married; this client had two children. Another client considered herself married through a common-law relationship, whereas twelve others lived with a male partner, either alone or with his family. The overwhelming majority of TASA program participants lived with parents or other family members (77 percent). Only five young mothers lived alone with their children; a few others lived with friends. Three TASA clients were literally homeless at the time of application, and one lived in an agency-run group home.

About half of TASA clients lived in relatively small households of two to four persons; nearly 20 percent lived in households of six or more people. Housing was a critical issue for many TASA clients. Even those who lived with relatives often did so only because no alternatives were available. Living arrangements tended to be precarious and crisis-prone, with clients constantly threatened with expulsion. Many clients moved constantly from one relative's home to another, making ongoing contact very difficult for case managers. Fluidity in living arrangements also had negative implications for connecting clients with community services in that some education, vocational training, and health-care programs served only specific catchment areas. A change in domicile often meant a loss in program eligibility.

The households of TASA clients, like those of a growing majority of low-income families, were headed primarily by women. For those clients who resided with family members, only approximately 20 percent lived in households with a male parent—either father or stepfather. On the other hand, 62 percent resided in households headed by mothers only. Grandmothers were present in 10 percent of families. In black families, the grandmother tended to be the only adult present in the household, whereas Hispanic families were more often multigenerational, with the parent generation present as well.

Of the forty-three TASA clients who were pregnant and not parenting, more than half were still enrolled in school at the time of intake. Eleven (26 percent) had dropped out of school, two had already graduated from high school, and four others had passed a high school equivalency examination. Of the sixty-five applicants who were already mothers at intake, 37 percent were still in school, 62 percent had dropped out, and none had graduated from high school or passed an equivalency examination. Of the "at-risk" clients who were neither pregnant nor parenting at the time of intake, 30 percent had dropped out of school and 70 percent were still attending. The educational status of TASA applicants clearly supports previous research findings on the negative effects of early parenthood on the educational careers of adolescents.

Method

As part of an ongoing research and evaluation effort designed to substantiate the TASA project's effectiveness in meeting its state-man-

TABLE 1. Demographic profile of TASA participants (N = 134).

Variable	%	Variable	%
Age		*Living arrangements*	
11-14	8.1	Married, lives with spouse	1.6
15	22.8	Unmarried, lives with spouse	1.6
16	30.9	Unmarried, lives with partner's family	7.8
17	32.5	Unmarried, lives with own family	77.3
18-20	7.3	Lives alone with child	3.9
		Lives with friend	4.7
Sex		Lives in group home	.8
Female	95.5	Homeless	2.3
Male	4.5		
		Educational status (at intake)	
Race/ethnicity		Pregnant, not parent	35.8
Black	29.1	in school	58.5
Hispanic	70.9	dropped out	26.8
White	0.0	high school grad	4.9
		GED	9.8
Religion		Parent	54.2
Catholic	66.7	in school	34.4
Protestant	27.5	dropped out	65.6
Muslim	1.5	high school grad	0.0
Jewish	0.0	GED	0.0
None	4.3	At risk	10.0
		in school	70.0
Pregnancy/parent status		dropped out	30.0
Pregnant, not parent	35.8	high school grad	0.0
Pregnant, parent	4.2	GED	0.0
Not pregnant, parent	50.0		
		Sources of income	
Trimester of pregnancy at intake (N = 48)		AFDC recipient or application pending	64.2
First Trimester	56.3	Not AFDC recipient, supported by:	36.8
Second Trimester	27.1	parents	48.7
Third Trimester	12.5	partner	17.9
Undetermined	4.2	other relatives	20.5
		friends	5.1
Relationship to child's father (N = 108)		self-supporting	7.7
Live together	14.3		
Have relationship, do not live together	45.9		
Have no contact	36.7		
Undetermined	3.1		

dated goals, program participants were administered a seventy-four-item self-report questionnaire, designated as the Self-Image Inventory, adapted from Offer and associates' work on adolescent self-esteem (Offer, Ostrov, & Howard, 1981).[1] Respondents were required to rate each item on a scale of 1 to 6 as it applied to them. A rating of 1 indicated that a statement "describes me very well," whereas a rating of 6 indicated that a statement "does not describe me at all."

In analyzing clients' responses, data from the seventy-four items can be arrayed in groups of from six to eight questions, representing ten subscales embedded in the questionnaire. These subscales reflect specific areas of psychosocial functioning that have been found through clinical and empirical studies to be components of the overall self-image of the average teenager (Offer, Ostrov, & Howard, 1984). These ten areas include impulse control, emotional tone, body image, social relationships, moral development,

---

1. The original Offer Self-Image Questionnaire contains 130 items. A pretest of this instrument with twenty TASA clients found it to be too lengthy for this client population. Consequently, the instrument was shortened by proportionally reducing the number of items in each subscale as well as omitting one subscale entirely.

attitudes about sex, family relationships, sense of mastery of the external world, vocational and educational goals, and psychopathology.

It was originally intended that the Self-Image Inventory be administered to all clients during the initial interview. Although this could be done with some applications, others were too anxious or in too great a crisis to make administration possible at that point. Indeed, project administrators were concerned that the self-report data would be colored by the crisis event. For some clients, then, the instrument was administered after the initial contact, when the crisis peak had passed. Differences in timing of test administration are a potential source of bias. However, t tests revealed no significant differences in response direction between those who were administered the Self-Image Inventory at first agency contact and those who received it in a subsequent contact.

Cultural Variations in Client Self-Descriptions

Analysis of data from the Self-Image Inventory revealed a number of significant differences between black and Hispanic TASA clients and suggested implications for service provision. These differences will first be discussed in relation to the previously described research on cultural differences in black and Puerto Rican families. Practice implications will then be drawn.

Perhaps the most striking difference between self-description scores for black and Hispanic teens on the Self-Image Inventory was found on those subscales that are reflective of what Offer and associates call the psychological self (Offer, Ostrov, & Howard, 1981). These include subscales describing impulse control, emotional tone, and body image. In each of these areas, Hispanic TASA participants evidenced more positive adjustment than did black clients. This result was particularly evident with regard to items reflecting emotional tone. Black respondents consistently described themselves as being highly sensitive to the opinions and judgments of others. They said they often felt their friends were better than they were and that people just did not like them. They were more frequently afraid that someone was going to make fun of them than were Hispanic adolescents. Nearly 90 percent agreed that "my feelings are easily hurt."

Sixty percent of black TASA clients indicated that the statement "I often feel sad" described them at least fairly well as opposed to 33 percent of Hispanic clients. A similar percentage saw life as an "endless series of problems with no answers." These teenagers "feel tense most of the time" (55 percent) and find it "hard to make decisions" (80 percent).

Black clients on the whole appeared almost hypersensitive to the needs and demands of others. Whether this is the result of living in a racist environment that demands continual monitoring or whether it is a function of growing up in households in which they took on premature parental responsibility for meeting the needs of others, the psychological effect on these young women appears almost paralyzing. They see life as an ongoing string of problems with little likelihood of satisfactory resolution and find it very hard to make meaningful decisions. Understandably, they often feel sad and confused.

Interestingly, despite the more open acceptance of female sensuality in black culture noted by some researchers and the repressive attitudes toward the sexuality of women in Hispanic culture noted by others, Hispanic respondents to the Self-Image Inventory reported higher levels of satisfaction with their physical appearance (Butts, 1981). They more frequently expressed feeling strong and healthy. They also indicated that the statement "I am happy with the way my body looks" described them at least to some extent more often than did black respondents. Black teenagers more frequently found it "hard to know how to handle sex" and reported that "thinking or talking about sex embarrasses me."

According to Medina (1987), in Hispanic culture little girls are socialized early to their docile and submissive role; they are also adorned with earrings, bracelets, and exaggeratedly feminine outfits. Although sexuality is repressed, physical attractiveness is emphasized, which may result in a self-concept of attractiveness that carries young Hispanic women through the developmental threats to their body image that customarily occur during adolescence and pregnancy.

Although black respondents indicated significantly less confidence in their ability to handle their sexuality and higher levels of psychological distress, they simultaneously demonstrated much more confidence in their social interactions with others than did Hispanic teens. Blacks generally saw themselves as effective learners, had high educational and career aspirations, and perceived themselves as potential leaders with something important to offer others.

All of the young black women in the TASA program agreed that the statement "If I put my mind to it, I can learn almost anything" described them very well. Nearly one-third of Hispanic respondents gave more qualified responses to that statement. Blacks also overwhelmingly indicated agreement with the statement "I am a very good student in school." Again, Hispanics gave much more qualified responses when indicating the degree to which that statement described them. Finally, 22 percent of Hispanics reported that the statement "School and studying mean very little to me" described them to some degree as opposed to only 8 percent of black TASA participants.

Impulse control was another area in which Hispanic respondents differed from blacks. Nearly half of the Hispanics responded in a direction indicating positive identification with the statement "At times I have fits of crying or laughing that I can't seem to control." Less than one third of black clients responded in a positive direction to this statement. On the Offer Self-Image Questionnaire, from which the Self-Image Inventory was adapted, a positive response to this question was viewed as indicating lack of impulse control. In Hispanic cultures, however, exaggerated emotionality is an accepted way of handling feelings of anxiety generated by situations of overwhelming stress (Garcia-Preto, 1982). This finding highlights the importance of cultural awareness in interpreting the meaning of such client self-reports.

Black clients indicated a highly developed moral sense as measured by the subscale on morals and development. They did not agree with a statement indicating it was more important to protect themselves than to tell the truth, nor were they in agreement that "as long as I get what I want, I don't worry too much how my actions will affect others." Hispanic clients were more frequently in agreement with both statements.

Finally, a distressingly high proportion of both black and Hispanic clients reported that the statement "I usually feel I am a bother at home" described them to some degree. Generally, however, the responses of Hispanic teenagers reflected much closer family ties and stronger feelings of family support than did those of blacks. For example, only 22 percent of black clients agreed with the statement "When I have a family it will be very similar to my own," as opposed to 40 percent of Hispanics. Fifty percent of Hispanics agreed with the statement "The adults I live with understand me" in contrast with 26 percent of black clients. Hispanic teenagers also found it easier to go to parents or other adults with questions about sex than did black youth, again reflecting more supportive relationships with significant adults in their lives.

On the other hand, Hispanic clients were more reticent than were blacks to share their problems with others, an important finding with implications for developing a counseling relationship. Sixty-eight percent of Hispanic respondents, in contrast with only 17 percent of black respondents, felt that "telling other people your problems is just asking for trouble." The high response to this item may reflect both the Hispanic tradition of relying exclusively on family in times of trouble and a tendency among Hispanics to express stress through somatic complaints rather than talking about one's difficulties. A visit to a physician is culturally acceptable; a visit to a psychiatrist or other mental health professional is not (Ghali, 1977).

Discussion

The following presents a sampling of TASA clients' stories. All are different in their circumstances, yet all have the common theme of economic deprivation and social isolation.

> E, a fifteen-year-old Puerto Rican girl, was referred to the TASA project by the Women's Clinic after a pregnancy test revealed that she was almost three months pregnant. She came to her intake appointment accompanied by her seventeen-year-old boyfriend, R. During the interview, E and R revealed that this was E's second pregnancy by R, the first having been terminated at the insistence of E's furious parents. The young couple insisted they were going to keep and raise their coming child, despite the fact that R had dropped out of high school in the tenth grade and had worked only sporadically since. He planned to enlist in the Navy as soon as he turned eighteen, explaining that he, E, and the baby could easily live on his military pay. The immediate problem was telling E's parents, who had other dreams for their eldest daughter. E had always been a very good student in school. Her family, immigrants who had struggled to eke out a marginal living managing a decaying apartment building in the South Bronx, had hoped that E might use her quick mind and extraordinary beauty to find a different way of life. To them, R, whose mother enthusiastically encouraged his relationship with E and eagerly welcomed the idea of a

grandchild, represented the old life, a dead-end future for their bright young daughter.

T, a seventeen-year-old black girl, was directed to TASA by the eligibility worker at the income maintenance center where she had gone seeking help with housing and food. Five months pregnant, T had left the apartment where she was living with several other people after she refused to help sell crack on the street in payment of her portion of the rent. Her grandmother, who had raised T after her mother's death when T was three, had died a year previously. T and her brother had been placed in foster homes in Brooklyn, but T, feeling abandoned and unwanted, had run away back to the South Bronx neighborhood that reminded her of her grandmother. There, without family, reliant on the generosity of acquaintances, T turned to prostitution and selling crack to survive.

L, a fourteen-year-old Puerto Rican girl, had come to New York from Puerto Rico two years before to live with her mother, M, who had been deserted by her husband shortly after emigrating to the Bronx in the early 1970s. She had sent all but the oldest of her five children back to the island to be raised by family while she tried to pick up the pieces of her life. When L, who had not lived with her mother since she was a baby, approached adolescence, her now-elderly godparents felt they could no longer care for her and sent her to her mother on the mainland. L, who spoke very little English, was miserable and frightened in the South Bronx. The junior high school in her neighborhood was a large gray fortress, cold and forboding. All the students rushed about in the halls, scarcely pausing long enough to answer her timid requests for directions. Only J, the man who lived next door to her mother, seemed interested and concerned about her. L began skipping school to spend the day with the unemployed J, whose wife worked as a sewing machine operator to support the family, which included an infant daughter. By the time L's mother found out that L was spending her days with J instead of in school, her daughter was three months pregnant with J's child.

As illustrated by the stories, most young women who came to TASA seeking help had not intentionally become pregnant. A few, like E, had strong, intact families who hoped for better things for their daughters. Many more, like T and L, were alone and isolated, with few social or personal supports. Even those who lived with their mothers, like L, or with other family members often felt unable to turn to family for understanding or guidance in times of need. These young women were extraordinarily vulnerable, sometimes to the lure of the streets, more often to the promise of belonging held out by some fleeting relationship. Pregnancy was not something to be planned or prevented; it just happened.

Integrating Research with Practice

Although isolation and lack of psychological supports characterized to some degree most of the clients of the TASA project, the cultural differences identified above were important factors in designing service delivery. The reluctance of Hispanic clients to trust others with knowledge of their problems suggested that the case manager had to pay special attention to relationship development in the mix of services offered. Outreach was a crucial component of the TASA program, as was the availability of Spanish-speaking staff. The more clearly defined family roles of the Hispanic participants also made family involvement necessary in case planning. The teenager's mother frequently accompanied her daughter to counseling sessions; her participation was welcomed rather than discouraged (as is frequently the case).

For young black women, encouraging participation of the baby's father in childrearing became an important program focus, whether or not the couple continued to have a romantic relationship. As the literature shows, black fathers are often willing and eager to play an ongoing role with their children. Young fathers sometimes require extra support in helping them understand and learn this role.

Despite the black participants' ease in sharing their problems with others, other obstacles hinder relationship building with a helping professional. A problem for black TASA clients was their inexperience with caring relationships that emphasized their own needs above those of others. Thus, although they were able to express readily their problems and feelings, they didn't anticipate warm, caring attention and support. When this was forthcoming, they would often become anxious and attempt to distance themselves from the relationship. Case managers learned to be more structured and direct in their initial contacts with black clients, waiting until these young women were more comfortable with the relationship before focusing on the feeling level.

Because Hispanic clients, on the other hand, had had experience with positive, attentive relationships within their families, they were able to tolerate a helping, affirming relationship after the initial barriers were crossed. With Hispanic clients, initial contacts were more oriented toward eliciting feelings while simultaneously recognizing the client's difficulty in sharing these feelings with someone outside the family system.

The black culture's strong emphasis on the importance of education for women lent support to black teenage mothers' desires to resume or continue their schooling. The young black women who participated in the TASA project viewed their roles as mothers not as ends in themselves, but as one aspect of their lives. As the findings of this study and others demonstrate, Hispanic teenage mothers have less cultural support for career achievement. The role of mother is valued by the culture as an end in itself. After young Hispanic women have achieved motherhood and experienced the approval it brings, it is more difficult for them to consider additional goals. Encouraging resumption or continuation of education or job training for Hispanic adolescent mothers requires extensive work with the family as a whole, particularly in obtaining the approval of the young woman's father if he is in the family home. It also requires a great deal of support for the teenager herself in that she often must face the obstacle of lack of proficiency in English as well as grudging permission, but lack of real support at home, for her efforts.

As has been demonstrated by the research discussed here, important cultural dimensions surround the issues of adolescent pregnancy and parenthood. Although the family plays an important role in both black and Hispanic cultures, how the family functions, its role definitions, and its expections of individual members are different and have differing implications for working with clients from these two groups. Expectations regarding childrearing roles and education for women are very different as well. Awareness and understanding of such differences are crucial in addressing the needs of pregnant and parenting teens.

REFERENCES

Bauman, K. E., & Udry, J. R. (1981). Subjective expected utility and adolescent sexual behavior. *Adolescence*, 16, 527–535.

Brooks-Gunn, J., & Furstenberg, Jr., F. F. (1986). The children of adolescent mothers: Physical, academic and psychological outcomes. *Developmental Review*, 6, 224–251.

Brown, S. V. (1983). The commitment and concerns of black adolescent parents. *Social Work Research and Abstracts*, 19, 27–34.

Butts, J. D. (1981). Adolescent sexuality and teenage pregnancy from a black perspective. In T. Ooms (Ed.), *Teenage pregnancy in a family context*. Philadelphia: Temple University Press.

Garcia-Preto, N. (1982). Puerto Rican families. In M. McGoldrick, J. K. Pearce, & J. Giordano (Eds.), *Ethnicity and family therapy*. New York: Guilford Press.

Ghali, S. B. (1977). Cultural sensitivity and the Puerto Rican client. *Social Casework*, 58, 459–468.

Ghali, S. B. (1982). Understanding Puerto Rican traditions. *Social Work*, 27, 98–102.

Henshaw, S. K., & O'Reilly, K. (1983). Characteristics of abortion patients in the United States, 1979 and 1980. *Family Planning Perspectives*, 15, 5–16.

Hill, R. (1972). *The strengths of black families*. New York: Emerson Hall.

Hines, P. M., & Boyd-Franklin, N. (1982). Black families. In M. McGoldrick, J. K. Pearce, and J. Giordano (Eds.), *Ethnicity and family therapy*. New York: Guilford Press.

McAdoo, H. P. (1978). Factors related to stability in upwardly mobile black families. *Journal of Marriage and the Family*, 40, 761–776.

Medina, C. (1987). Latino culture and sex education. *SIECUS Report*, 15, 1–4.

Mizio, E. (1974). Impact of external systems on the Puerto Rican family. *Social Casework*, 55, 76–83.

Moore, K. A., Simms, M. C., & Betsey, C. L. (1986). *Choice and circumstance: Racial differences in adolescent sexuality and fertility*. New Brunswick, N.J.: Transaction Books.

Nobles, W. W. (1978). Toward an empirical and theoretical framework for defining black families. *Journal of Marriage and the Family*, 40, 687.

O'Connell, M., & Moore, M. J. (1980). The legitimacy status of first births of U.S. women aged 15–24, 1939–1978. *Family Planning Perspectives*, 12, 16–25.

O'Connell, M., & Rogers, C. C. (1984). Out-of-wedlock births, premarital pregnancies, and their effect on family formation and dissolution. *Family Planning Perspectives*, 16, 157–162.

Offer, D., Ostrov, E., & Howard, K. I. (1981). *The adolescent: A psychological self-portrait*. New York: Basic Books.

Offer, D., Ostrov, E., & Howard, K. I. (1984). (Eds.). *Patterns of adolescent self-image*. San Francisco: Jossey-Bass.

Ortiz, C., & Vazquez, E. (1987). Adolescent pregnancy: Effects of family support, education, and religion on the decision to carry or terminate among Puerto Rican teenagers. *Adolescence*, 22, 897–917.

Stack, C. B. (1974). *All our kin: Strategies for survival in a black community*. New York: Harper and Row.

Zborowski, M. (1969). *People in pain*. San Francisco: Jossey-Bass.

Zelnick, M., & Kanter, J. F. (1980). Sexual activity, contraceptive use and pregnancy among metropolitan-area teenagers: 1971–1979. *Family Planning Perspectives*, 12, 230–237.

Zitner, R., & Miller, S. H. (1980). *Our youngest parents: A study of the use of support services by adolescent mothers*. New York: Child Welfare League of America.

16 The Intergenerational Flow of Income: Family Structure and the Status of Black Americans

Frances K. Goldscheider and Calvin Goldscheider
Brown University and the RAND Corporation

This study examines how income and family structure affect black-white differences in intergenerational financial flows, focusing on the two-way flow between parents and children in the years immediately after high school and how these flows in turn influence educational expectations. Based on data from the High School and Beyond survey, the findings indicate that black young adults receive less and contribute more income to their families at this critical juncture of the life course. These differences reflect not only differential resources but also differences in family structure, particularly in the proportion with only one parent or with a very young parent. Parental financial contributions to their children's educational expenses had a very strong effect on the children's educational expectations, eliminating the direct effects of income on the amount of schooling young people expect. The authors discuss the implications of these findings for the study of parent-child relationships and the effects of these relationships on more general stratification processes.

A flow of resources from parents to children in young adulthood, it has been argued, is a characteristic of modern societies (Caldwell, 1982). Unlike parents in the past or in less developed countries, mothers and fathers in contemporary American society normally support their children monetarily for long periods of time until they become financially independent. They do not commonly expect to receive financial contributions from children, except perhaps at a much later stage of their life cycle. This economic flow from parents to children has become central in the stratification system, since education is a key ingredient of intergenerational social mobility and most American children require substantial parental subsidies in order to continue their education beyond high school (Matras, 1990, chaps. 7 and 13). Further, children who work and contribute to family support are likely to be at an educational disadvantage, since their earnings are not being saved for their future schooling needs and their time is taken from study. So education and social mobility are likely to be linked by the flows of income between generations—from parent to child and from child to parent.

What factors influence the direction and volume of income flows between parents and children? Exploratory research has suggested that ethnicity and family income strongly influence intergenerational financial flows (F. Goldscheider, 1989). It is also likely that the structure of the parental family will influence parental contributions to children. The ratio of children to adults could limit a family's ability to invest in a given child and a parent might invest less in a nonresident child or stepchild. Older parents may have a

---

Population Studies and Training Center, Brown University, Box 1916, Providence, RI 02912.

greater need to divert their income from investments in children to prepare for retirement or disability; children with very young parents attain low levels of education (Mare and Tzeng, 1987), perhaps reflecting differential parental investments. Therefore, the nature of the family economy may condition the direction of income flows between parents and children and thus provide a link in the relationship between family structure and social mobility.

The black population in the United States is characterized by lower income and higher fertility than the white population, which could be expected to limit parental financial investments in children and to lead to educational deficits in the younger generation. However, these trends have been converging in the recent period, giving rise to the expectation that their educational patterns would converge as well. Yet over the last generation there has been a dramatic change in family structure among blacks, with the proportions of children living in female-headed families rising past 60%. Indeed, there has been a sharp decline in the enrollment of black children in post-high-school education compared with the trend for whites (Hauser, 1987).

To what extent are black-white differentials in status linked to differences in the pattern of intergenerational financial flows? Specifically, how are differences in the educational expectations of black and white children linked to differences in the financial investments of their parents? How much of the black-white difference in intergenerational financial flows can be attributed to income, and are there family factors influencing the extent of parental investment? Are there residual "structural" or "cultural" aspects of black patterns that need to be invoked to account for these differences?

To address these questions, we focus our analysis on the factors determining parental financial contributions to students in the period immediately after high school and, in turn, the consequences of such contributions for the educational expectations of these students. We then investigate the determinants of childrens' financial contributions to parents among those children no longer in school and the consequences of these flows for the educational expectations of these young adults.

DATA AND MEASURES

High School and Beyond

We use data from the High School and Beyond survey (seniors in the high school class of 1980). This survey (HSB) is a nationally representative panel study of seniors in American high schools and is uniquely suited to our study, since both parents and children reported information about their own incomes, expenses, and financial contributions to each other. The data set includes background profiles of parents and children, including economic activities, income, and family formation and structure, as well as the educational expectations of the young adults. It provides extensive data from the young adults as well as detailed financial information from parents that students could not be expected to answer as accurately (Rosenthal, Myers, Milne, Ellman, and Ginsberg 1983). The parents surveyed included in most cases either the mother or the father. In all, the data allow us to examine some major issues in the intergenerational income flows among whites and blacks in the United States.

HSB has certain limitations. As a sample of high school seniors, it provides no information about actual educational attainment, thus limiting the analysis to a consideration of educational expectations. Having only seniors further truncates an analysis of differences in educational attainment, since it excludes previous high school dropouts.[1] Hence, an important segment of the educational distribution is missing. It is unlikely that this omission will seriously bias our results, since the factors accounting for educational progress are similar at each of the stages of educational attainment. The odds of attending high school (given ninth grade graduation), of high school graduation (given high school attendance), and of college attendance (given high school graduation) respond to variation by race and socioeconomic status in similar ways (Mare and Winship, 1987).

There is an additional structural problem in this data set, since the young adults were surveyed while they were all in school, in the spring of 1980, but the parents were not contacted until the following fall. Although this does not affect our ability to model the determinants of parent-child financial flows, it poses a problem for the analysis of educational expectations, since we are using financial flows in the first year after high school to predict educational expectations measured six months earlier. There should be relatively little immediate change in educational expectations among those continuing in school after high school (almost none of whom had expected only 12 years of education). However, among those who discover that their parents' contributions are not sufficient to keep them in school, this temporal problem is much greater, since young adults probably adjust their expectations sharply downward. For reasons that we discuss below, we must analyze parent-child financial flows separately for those who continued in school and those who did not. Therefore, this process cannot be examined. Despite these limitations, we can use these data to estimate financial exchanges between parents and young adults. This data set provides a unique opportunity to examine the issue of intergenerational financial flows at this segment of the life course, which is a critical one both for the transition to adulthood for young people and for our understanding of this key element of the stratification system.

Measures of Intergenerational Financial Flows

Our analysis of financial flows from parents to children and from children to parents focuses separately on two subpopulations, students and nonstudents, as a result of constraints imposed by the structure of the data set. Our "student" population includes all young adults reported by their parent to be enrolled in school, full- or part-time, immediately after high school. For this group, our dependent variable was the parent's dollar contribution to the child's tuition and living expenses for 1980-81, the academic year after high school graduation, as reported by the parents. The reported values were both strongly skewed and truncated by the forced choices parents had to use on the questionnaire (which were 0-$100, $100-199, $200-599, $600-1,199, $1,200-1,999, and > $2,000). We recoded these categories to the midpoint for all but the upper category and used $3,000 as an approximate midpoint for the highest category, since a large proportion of students' parents marked the uppermost category (22%) and graphic inspection suggested this as a reasonable approximation of this group. We took the natural logarithm, both because these categories are imprecise and because this transformation led to a more random pattern of residuals. The means of the key variables we constructed and the operationalizations of financial flows between parents and children are presented in Table 1 separately for black, Hispanic, and white students and nonstudents.

Nonstudents were young adults reported by parents as not enrolled in school. For this population, we used a question that asked parents to estimate the dollar amount that the child was expected to contribute to the parental household during 1980-81.[2] It was also necessary to transform this measure of young adults' contributions to the parental household. In this case, the transformation that produced the least distortion required that we take a square root.

Measuring Educational Expectations

The total educational level students expected was

TABLE 1. VARIABLE MEANS FOR BLACK, HISPANIC, AND OTHER STUDENTS AND NONSTUDENTS

	Students			Nonstudents		
Variables	Other	Black	Hispanic	Other	Black	Hispanic
Contribution						
To child	$1,477	$1,087	$919	—	—	—
To parents	—	—	—	$372	$431	$850
Family income (thousands)	$35.2	$19.7	$26.9	$23.8	$12.5	$24.1
Young adult income	$816	$491	$215	$1,329	$745	$240
Mother's education	12.9	13.2	11.6	12.0	12.2	10.8
Parental dependents	2.7	3.0	3.3	2.4	3.2	3.4
Mother-headed family	.12	.36	.16	.12	.40	.11
Stepparent family	.06	.07	.04	.08	.08	.07
Head age < 40	.08	.20	.06	.12	.19	.10
Percentage black in school	—	56.3	—	—	61.3	—
Male	.43	.33	.32	.49	.48	.41
n	1,346	181	111	823	128	69

Note: Values are untransformed and unweighted.

assessed as of their senior year in high school. It was measured by the number of *additional* years of education these young adults expected. We took the natural logarithm, again because the strongly skewed data required it. Although responses allowed the separation of vocational from academic programs, we ignored these differences and combined vocational with nonvocational programs, on the basis of the number of years involved.

Measures of Income and Parental Education

Mother's education: This measure is the educational level reported by the mother, if she were the parent respondent, and of the respondent's spouse, where the father or stepfather answered the parental questionnaire. In all other cases, mother's education was obtained from the child's report. We used mother's education rather than father's education because father's education was not available in the 20% of the cases where there was no father or only a male guardian. As a result, about one quarter had missing data for fathers. We were able to fill a small portion of the missing information on mother's education with data on father's education. We felt that the bias introduced by this method would be least. For the others, we used regression, as described below.[3]

Family income: This variable was constructed from questions asked of the parent about his or her own wage and self-employment income, and the same two categories for the spouse, if any.

Young adult income: There was no specific question on children's earnings among the questions asked of parents in the fall after their child's senior year. A substantial question sequence was included in which parents were asked to estimate how much the child was contributing to schooling and living expenses from summer earnings and work during the academic year. Although the sequence appeared to focus on current students, it was clear that parents responded to it more generally, whether the child was currently a student or a nonstudent, and provided estimates of the child's earnings during the stated periods. More were missing among nonstudents than among students, but the differences were small.

Nearly all the income variables carried a high proportion of missing values: 9% for family income and 26% for a child's post-high-school income. Given the relatively small size of the sample, which was further reduced by the subdivision into students and nonstudents, we wanted to fill in missing values on these variables to the extent justifiable. We followed a regression approach, in which we predicted an expected value for the missing variable by using other variables in the data set.[4]

Measures of Family Type

Measures tapping three dimensions of family type were constructed for this analysis. The first dimension is size, or more specifically, the number of persons dependent on the parents' income, which was also logged in the multivariate analysis. The second dimension was the age of the head of the family. We used the father's age, if he was present, or else the mother's age, and distinguished those with heads at the extremes—those not yet aged 40 and those aged 60 or older.

The third dimension indicates whether the respondent's family currently (1) was female-headed, (2) included a stepparent, or (3) was some other type. These variables are based on students' responses to questions asked about the presence or absence in the household of mother, father, male guardian, or female guardian, as well as other potential household members. Family types were defined as follows:

1. Mother-headed family: A family in which no father or male guardian was present (or where information on these variables was missing) and the student's household included a mother or female guardian.
2. Stepparent family: A family that included a parent of one sex and a guardian of the other.
3. Other family: All other families. Most of these "intact families" (93%) were characterized by seniors as having both a mother and a father (but not a male or female guardian) present.[5]

Racial and Ethnic Variables

We delineated racial and ethnic groups on the basis of young adults' responses to questions about race and national origin. Young adults were asked a very detailed sequence of questions; missing replies were filled in from the parents' information. Blacks were categorized on the basis of the race question and Hispanics were identified with a question on origins. We also included a measure that indicated the perceived racial composition of the school during first, sixth, and ninth grades among young blacks, since studies have shown that extent of segregation is likely to have an impact on the educational process (Crain and Mahard, 1986).

ANALYSIS

The Determinants of Financial Flows from Parent to Child

To examine the determinants of parent-to-child financial flows, we have used multiple regression (ordinary least squares). We predict the logarithm of the dollar amount of educational contributions made by parents, first only by race, and then including the variables likely to be important influences.

The data in Table 2 focus on the student subpopulation and show that black students receive significantly less financial support for educational expenses from parents than white students (col. I). Column II adds income, mother's education, and the family structural variables to the model. These data show that the black-white difference in parental contributions to their children's educational expenses is halved (and is no longer significantly different from zero) when important differences between the two populations are controlled. As expected, family income is significantly and positively related to the amount of money parents contribute. In contrast, the income of children is negatively related to the parents' contribution toward the educational expenses of children, as children appear to substitute for deficits in their parent's contribution. The educational level of mothers has an additional significant impact on the contribution of parents to the educational expenses of children. These patterns characterize the contributions of parents toward the educational expenses of their sons as well as their daughters.

Two additional results emerge from this regression: the importance of current family structure and the age of the parent. There is no significant effect of the number of parents' dependents on parental contributions in this sample, but adult family structure has a strong effect. Mother-headed families and stepparent families contribute significantly less to the educational expenses of children, net of the effects of family income. The age of the parents also has a strong effect. Parents less than age 40 contribute significantly less than the reference category of parents aged 40 to 60 to the educational expenses of their child, net of income and family structure. Data not presented in the table showed that the parents over age 60 also contribute less than parents aged 40–60, but this reflected family income factors. The long-term effects of early parenthood on the contributions of parents to the educational expenses of children is significant for both black and white students.

There is no significant effect of the percentage

TABLE 2. DETERMINANTS OF PARENTAL CONTRIBUTIONS AND STUDENTS' EUCATIONAL EXPECTATIONS

Variables	Parental Contributions			Educational Expectations
	I	II	III	IV
Parental contribution	—	—	—	.049*
Black	−.392*	−.219	−1.362*	.067
Family income	—	.194*	.195*	−.003
Young adult income	—	−.094*	−.121*	−.010
Mother's education	—	.127*	.129*	.066*
Parental dependents	—	−.162	−.072	.031
Mother-headed family	—	−.214*	−.216*	.010
Stepparent family	—	−.240*	−.245+	.029
Head age < 40	—	−.442*	−.425*	−.039
Head age > 60	—	−.141	−.137	.038
Percentage black in school	—	.001	.002	.001
Hispanic	—	−.429*	−.440*	−.074+
Male	—	.007	.015	.100+
Black • young adult income	—	—	.204*	—
Intercept	6.689	5.166	5.306	1.052
Adjusted R^2	.007	.136	.140	.101
n of cases	1,527	1,512	1,512	1,512

+$p \leq .10$. *$p \leq .05$.

black on parental contributions among those in school. Even where black children are most intensely segregated, no difference in parental contributions to educational expenses between blacks and whites appears. This suggests that the black-white difference is a consequence of structural differences between the groups on dimensions measured in our analysis. School segregation may indicate either extreme residential concentration, with a concomitant enhancement of normative community distinctiveness, or politically motivated segregation of the schools, resulting in reduced access for blacks to school resources and programs in more segregated systems. These results suggest that neither factor has much impact on parental contributions to postsecondary education.

In contrast, there is a significant residual Hispanic difference that is not solely accounted for by the variables measured here. These may be attributed to unmeasured structural dimensions (e.g., wealth and immigrant status) or they might tap factors associated with Hispanic culture relating to generational family obligations and the expected direction of financial flows.

We also examined these relationships separately for blacks and whites. The results discussed above regarding the effects on parental educational contributions of family income, family structure, and parental age are similar for both blacks and whites. Even though there are fewer than 200 cases of black students in this sample, since blacks were not oversampled, the effects of family income and parental age were each significant, and the coefficient for mother-headed families was similar for blacks and whites (cf. Mare and Winship, 1987).

However, an important difference emerged in the effect of young adults' income on the magnitude of their parents' contribution to their educational expenses (col. III). It is only among young nonblack adults that their own income substitutes for family income in its effects on parental contribution toward educational expenses; this is not the case among blacks. For whites and Hispanics, the more parents contribute, the less their children pay toward their college expenses. Among blacks, in contrast, there appears to be no income substitution and some indication that parents and children are more likely to be co-contributors toward the child's educational expense. The more black children contribute to their own expenses, the more parents contribute to them.

None of the other coefficients change in any important way between Equations II and III except for the overall black coefficient, which becomes significantly negative. This indicates that for young adults with no income, black parents contribute much less than comparable white parents. However, since the effect of young adult income differs for the two groups, the magnitude of the contributions of black parents increases as their child's income rises, while white parents decrease their contributions as their child's income rises. Thus, these effects eventually cross over, so that black parents actually contribute more than comparable white parents if their children earn more than $700 (which is substantially more than average for black students).

We examined predicted differences in parental contributions to the educational expenses of their child between blacks and whites due to differential family income, family structure, and parental age. This analysis shows that among otherwise comparable young adults, whites can expect 10% more from their parents than blacks as a result of their lower likelihood of living in a mother-headed family, 30% more as the result of mean differences in family income, and 10% more because of their parents' later entry into parenthood.[6] These factors emerge, therefore, as important in reducing black children's access to parental contributions toward their educational expenses.

The Consequences of Differential Flows for Educational Expectations

How does this variation by race in parental contributions to the educational expenses of their child affect the student's educational expectations? Our aim is not to account fully for variation in educational expectations or for black-white differences. We include as controls the main socioeconomic variables found by others to be important—in particular, family income and education. We also include the family structural variables used in the analysis thus far to see how much their effect on educational expectations is mediated through variation in parental contributions. However, we do not include the large array of social-psychological measures that have frequently been found to be important in studies of the formation of educational expectations. While having significant effects, these have not been shown to influence black-white differences consistently (Allen, 1980).

The question that we ask here is, Does the contribution of parents toward their child's educational expenses in the first year after high school have an impact on their children's educational expectations? The regression (col. IV in Table 2) examines this question and shows that the extent of parental contribution is one of the most important effects in the model. Its effects are almost as strong as mother's education (based on standardized regression coefficients, not shown). Neither income (whether of parents or of the children themselves) nor family structure has independent effects, once the volume of parental contributions is controlled. Male postsecondary students have higher educational expectations than comparable females (although they are less likely than young women to have continued their formal education immediately after completing high school). Hispanics expect to attain lower levels of education than do non-Hispanic whites.

However, there are no other significant effects in this model. Unlike earlier studies (e.g., Kerckhoff and Campbell, 1977), the present research does not indicate that blacks have higher educational expectations than whites, other things being equal. Hence, parental financial contributions are a key factor in lowering the educational expectations of blacks. In contrast, Hispanics have lower educational expectations than do non-Hispanic whites after differences in parental financial contributions are controlled, even among those reaching the end of the senior year in high school. Effects of income, head's age, and family structure seem only to be linked to whether parents contribute to their child's educational expenses but not directly to their children's educational expectations.

Contributions of Children to Parents

Given the importance of parental financing for their children's attainment of higher education in the broad context of a resource-flows argument, we have focused our analysis primarily on the contributions of parents to children. However, we also examined variations in the contributions of children (restricted to nonstudents) to their parental household. In turn, we examined whether the extent of these child-to-parent flows influenced the educational expectations of these young adults, many of whom considered themselves to be dropping out only temporarily. It seemed likely that the patterns associated with parent-to-child financial flows might reappear in the analysis of these "negative" flows, since they also reduce the funds available to young people for their further education. The data in Table 3 show, however, that this is not the case.

Blacks in general contribute significantly more to their parental family economy (col. I). This is not simply the result of income or family structural variables, since even in the full regression (col. II), black-white differences remain significant and, in fact, strengthen. This finding characterizes Hispanics, as well. In addition, the major effects are for the income of children and their parents. The more these young adults earn, the more they contribute to their parents' household expenses; the more income the parents have, the less their children contribute. Once these income effects are controlled, the effects of parental family structure are not significant. The indicator for mother-headed family as well as that for young family head significantly increases the children's contribution when the other is omitted from the model. However, because of the high collinearity between early childbearing in the parental generation with later female-headedness, these effects

TABLE 3. DETERMINANTS OF NONSTUDENTS' CONTRIBUTIONS TO PARENTS AND EDUCATIONAL EXPECTATIONS

Variables	Contributions I	Contributions II	Expectations III
Young adult contribution	—	—	.000
Black	3.946*	10.729*	.072
Family income	—	-1.209*	.044*
Young adult income	—	2.453*	-.022
Mother's education	—	.126	.042*
Parental dependents	—	1.616*	.070*
Mother-headed family	—	1.962	.068
Stepparent family	—	.955	.038
Head age < 40	—	1.945	-.053
Head age > 60	—	.095	.086
Percentage black in school	—	-.093	.003
Hispanic	—	6.308*	.236*
Male	—	2.362*	.051
Intercept	12.070	4.378	.239
Adjusted R^2	.005	.077	.047
n of cases	1,037	1,023	1,022

*$p \leq .05$.

cannot be separated in the reduced sample of nonstudents.

Two other factors seem to increase children's financial contributions to their parents. Sons contribute significantly more than daughters, and children whose families have a larger number of dependents, other things being equal, contribute more to their parents. This suggests that older children who are not in school try to help out financially to meet some of the needs of their siblings. However, the differences in all cases are extraordinarily small, at least as measured in these data: other things equal, black children were reported to contribute about $115 more than non-Hispanic white children during 1980–81, while Hispanic children were contributing about $40 more than other whites. Sons were contributing about $6 more than daughters.

In col. III, the data show that variation in the extent of nonstudents' contributions to their parental families has no influence on the amount of education they expect, should they return to school. The major effects are through family income and mother's education. When these influences are controlled, those in larger families (as measured by parental dependents) actually expect slightly more education than others, which suggests that they may have interrupted their education temporarily to help out the family but expect to return to school. A similar pattern characterizes Hispanics.

Discussion

The data we have examined have allowed for the first time a systematic investigation of the determinants of financial flows between parents and children. We have shown with these data that black parents invest less than white parents in the educational expenses of their children beyond high school. However, this lower level of investment solely reflects the much lower family income of blacks and the slightly lower educational attainment of black mothers, together with the higher proportion of black young adults who are growing up in female-headed households and whose parents are very young when their children are growing up. It is these structural factors in combination that account for black-white differences in the contributions of parents to their children's educational expenses.

These findings take on particular significance in the context of our analysis of educational expectations, since we found that it is through parental contributions to children's education that the family's economic standing influences the educational expectations of young adults. Education is not the only, or perhaps even the major, link in the chain that has blocked the intergenerational mobility of blacks; their opportunity to translate their education into income in the racially segregated occupational structure has been severely restricted as well (Stolzenberg, 1975). However, the level of concern over the recent downturn in black's likelihood of college entrance relative to whites testifies to the continuing important of education in the stratification process.

An important dimension of these findings is the sharply lowered amount of parental educational financing that results from the parents' own early parenthood as well as from their current marital status. It is not clear what factors are accounting for these results. Although family income was controlled, it is likely that savings are lower in these families. Early marriage has been shown to reduce wealth accumulation (Freedman and Coombs, 1966), as does bearing children early in marriage (Smith and Ward, 1980); their combination may be particularly problematic, resulting in considerable asset deficits for those who become parents at an early eage. It is also possible that very young parents have made lower cumulative investments in their children over the children's lifetimes, which leads to lower academic achievement (human capital); in turn, parents are less likely to be willing to invest in children with lower grades.

These factors are also likely to characterize mother-only families. Their extreme poverty makes saving difficult, and it may be that the lack of supervision found in many single-parent families results in lower grades as well (McLanahan and Booth, 1989). Children in such families often also have reduced access to the resources of at least one set of grandparents. To the extent that grandparents' contributions to these expenses are treated as part of the "family contribution," such children are at a further disadvantage.

Turning to our results of reverse flows of resources (child-to-parent), we found their average level to be extremely small, although black and, to a lesser extent, Hispanic young adults contribute more than whites to the family economy when they are no longer students. This is an interesting phenomenon, since it reflects continuing traditional family obligations carried on not only by young Hispanics but also by young blacks; it deserves closer study.

We are keenly aware of the limitations of these data, and of the measures of financial flows that we were able to construct, for a full and satisfactory explanation of intergenerational financial flows. The college period is a complex one financially, given the ad hoc and changing policies of governments and the complex roles of both educational and financial institutions. Our analysis has only begun to explore this complexity. Nevertheless, HSB is a unique body of data that have been supplied by both parents and young adults at a critical stage of the family cycle and of the transition to adulthood and independence. These data provide a valuable opportunity to gain insight so that more comprehensive and systematic research can more fully assess the role of parental financial investments in the educational aspirations and attainments of young adults. In particular, these data direct our attention to the inclusion of the generational perspective in the analysis of the status of disadvantaged ethnic and racial groups in American society.

Studies of black status and, more generally, of the educational attainment process of disadvantaged racial and ethnic groups need to incorporate parental financial investments into their broader and more comprehensive models. The generational emphasis may help focus attention on the changing dynamics of economic factors in the family context, linking parents and children to the decision-making process about education as it unfolds. Such a focus may help to explain further the continuing distinctiveness and disadvantages of blacks and other minorities in America, beyond, but in conjunction with, income and family structure.

Notes

The research reported here is part of a project on New Patterns in the Transition to Adulthood supported by NICHD Grant R-01-HD23339-01 to the RAND Corporation, subcontract No. 63220 to Brown University. The authors acknowledge the help of Rebecca Clark, Elizabeth Cooksey, and Joan W. Keesey in organizing the data; Ross M. Stolzenberg and Katherine McCelland provided constructive comments. An earlier version of this article was presented at the 1988 annual meeting of the Population Association of America, New Orleans.

1. There are data taken from a panel of high school sophomores, which is appropriate for studying the family dynamics of high school dropouts. However, only the senior panel provides reliable data for studies focusing on the parental role among the majority who complete high school, since most of the questions about events and plans after high school were poorly answered by tenth graders and their parents, and the parents were not surveyed again. (For further information, see Jones, Sebring, Crawford, Spencer, and Butz, 1986.)

2. We had planned originally to use this variable for the total population, but inspection of the data made it apparent that parents were including the student's contribution to schooling expenses in their responses. This meant that in order to pool the two populations of students and nonstudents, total schooling expenses would have to be included as a control, and it is not clear how the results could be interpreted.

3. For full details on the precise specifications, consult the authors.

4. In filling in missing incomes for the young adults, we treated the two populations separately and used variables different from those in the substantive analysis. These variables were selected to reflect the different sociodemographic characteristics of students and nonstudents. For full details on the precise specifications, consult the authors.

5. The data on others in the household were not always clear. For example, there were some cases with both a male "guardian" and a female "guardian." We wanted to make the mother-headed and stepfamilies as precise as possible. Hence, the fringe cases, which were too small and diverse to treat separately, were folded in with the great majority who reported that they lived with their mother and father.

6. These differences should not be added together to estimate some total racial difference, however, since each of these differences is correlated with the others.

References

Allen, Walter. 1980. "Preludes to achievement: Race, sex, and student achievement orientations." Sociological Quarterly 21: 65-79.

Caldwell, John. 1982. Theories of Fertility Change. New York: Academic Press.

Crain, Robert, and R. Mahard. 1986. "School racial composition and black education." Sociology of Education 81: 86-88.

Freedman, Ronald, and Lolagene Coombs. 1966. "Childspacing and family economic position." American Sociological Review 31: 631-648.

Goldscheider, Frances. 1989. "Children and the household economy." In F. Goldscheider and C. Goldscheider (eds.), Ethnicity and the New Family Economy: Living Arrangements and Intergenerational Financial Flows. Boulder, CO: Westview Press.

Hauser, Robert. 1987. "College entry among black high school graduates: Family income does not explain the decline." CDE Working Paper 87-19, Center for Demography and Ecology, University of Wisconsin, Madison.

Jones, Calvin, P. Sebring, J. Crawford, B. Spencer, and M. Butz. 1986. High School and Beyond: 1980 Senior Cohort, Second Follow-up (1984): Data File Users Manual. Washington, DC: National Center for Education Statistics.

Kerckhoff, Alan, and R. Campbell. 1977. "Black-white differences in the educational attainment process." Sociology of Education 50: 15-27.

Mare, Robert, and M. Tzeng. 1987. "Fathers' ages and the social stratification of sons." CDE Working Paper 87-36, Center for Demography and Ecology, University of Wisconsin, Madison.

Mare, Robert, and C. Winship. 1987. "Ethnic and racial patterns of educational attainment and school enrollment." CDE Working Paper 87-31, Center for Demography and Ecology, University of Wisconsin, Madison.

Matras, Judah. 1990. Dependency, Obligations, and Entitlements. Englewood Cliffs, NJ: Prentice-Hall.

McLanahan, Sara, and K. Booth. 1989. "Mother-Only Families: Problems, Prospects, and Politics." Journal of Marriage and the Family 51: 557-580.

Rosenthal, Al, David E. Myers, Ann M. Milne, Fran M. Ellman, and Alan Ginsberg. 1983. "Failure of student-parent cross-validation in the High School and Beyond Survey." Proceedings of the Social Statistics Section, American Statistical Association meeting, Toronto, Canada.

Smith, James, and Michael Ward. 1980. "Asset accumulation and family size." Demography 17: 243-260.

Stolzenberg, Ross. 1975. "Education, occupation, and wage differences between white and black men." American Journal of Sociology 81: 299-323.

17 Activities, Family Relationships, and Feelings about Aging in a Multicultural Elderly Sample

Mary B. Harris, Ph.D., Cynthia Begay, M.S.W., and Polly Page, M.A.
University of New Mexico

ABSTRACT

This study looked at ethnic and gender differences in activities, family relationships, and feelings about aging in 128 American Indian, Anglo, and Hispanic adults over sixty. Reading, visiting, and watching television were the most popular activities for all subjects, with a number of sex and ethnic differences appearing. Most subjects reported improved relationships with their families on various dimensions after turning sixty. A number of advantages and disadvantages of aging were mentioned. Few ethnic or gender differences were found on these latter variables.

Although it will happen to most of us, the experience of growing old does not affect everyone in the same manner. Theoretically, physical factors such as changes in the body caused by genetic predispositions, illness, and lifestyle should interact with environmental and social factors in determining the phenomenological experience of aging. Research has shown that environmental variables like housing, transportation, and urban versus rural status and personal variables like health, economic factors, social activity, and family support have major impacts on how satisfied elderly people feel with their lives [1-6]. The present study looked at two major social variables—ethnicity and gender—to see whether or not they would be related to various aspects of life for an elderly sample. Both gender and ethnicity can have direct and indirect effects on the physical changes individuals experience with aging as well as on the social support systems available to them. Among the variables studied were activities, relationships with families, and attitudes toward being old, as expressed in responses to questions about the best and worst things about growing old. A number of authors have suggested that there is a need for more research on elderly Hispanics and American Indians [7-11]. Since relatively little research has been done on elderly people in the Southwest, particularly the Indian populations [12-13], it was hoped that this study would add to the general body of knowledge about the life and feelings of elderly people and identify differences in their life styles and feelings that were related to ethnicity and gender.

ACTIVITIES

According to a number of writers, elderly people engage in a great variety of activities, including paid work, housework and cooking, volunteer work, artistic endeavors, attending church, visiting, traveling, gardening, and a number of other pastimes [13-17]. Although Harel did find that whites had higher activity levels than blacks, there is relatively little information to allow one to make predictions about ethnic differences in the activities which occupy elderly people [18]. However, general knowledge about the various cultures in the present study allows a few predictions to be made.

Because Southwestern American Indians are traditionally a rural people who have subsisted partially by farming, it was expected that they would be more likely to farm than Hispanics and Anglos [13]. Similarly, New Mexico Indians are well known for their traditional arts and crafts [13]; therefore, Indians were expected to engage in arts and crafts activities more than Anglos and Hispanics.

Expectations about working for pay are much less clear. Because the income level of elderly Anglo-Americans may be higher than that of Hispanics or American Indians [12], one might expect that financial need would force a greater number of elderly minority group members to work for pay; on the other hand, if more Anglos are self-employed or professional workers, they might be more likely to voluntarily continue to work, rather than to retire.

Although no other predictions of ethnic differences in activities were made, some gender differences were expected. It was predicted that women would be more likely than men to engage in the traditional female sex-typed activities of housework, cooking, and childcare [17, 19]; men, on the other hand, were expected to be more likely to work for pay and to engage in hunting and farming in order to support themselves.

RELATIONSHIP WITH FAMILY

A number of authors have suggested that family ties remain positive between elderly people and their children [7, 20-25], although not all families are loving and supportive, and feelings of closeness may dissipate under the strain of caregiving [19, 26, 27]. Nevertheless, the consistency of the reports led us to predict that feelings of closeness and enjoyment would increase or stay the same and that arguments would decrease or stay the same for study participants after they turned sixty. Because dependency on one's family could either decrease (due to fewer financial responsibilities) or increase (due to impaired mobility and health), no predictions about overall changes in dependency were made. Nor were predictions made about changes in time spent with one's family, as this is dependent upon living conditions, including geographical distance from family members [28].

Gender differences in changes in family relationships were not predicted, but the literature suggesting the importance of the extended family for Indians [10, 12, 13, 22] and Hispanics [7, 21, 29-32] led us to predict that Anglos would be the least likely of the three ethnic groups to show positive changes in family relationships.

ADVANTAGES AND DISADVANTAGES OF AGING

A number of research studies have suggested that negative attitudes toward aging are widespread [33-35] but not universal [34, 36]. Among the reasons given for the low status of the elderly are physical and mental deterioration, changes in appearance, loss of wealth, decline in skills, and loss of children and a family support system [35]. Deteriorating health status may be a particularly important contributor to low levels of life satisfaction [37], and it has been suggested that a feeling "of meaninglessness and disengagement" is common in older adults [38, 39]. On the other hand, contact with friends and neighbors [5, 40, 41], family life [6, 41], a positive mood and a feeling of zest [10, 41], respect from others [11, 31, 42], and an adequate income [41, 43] may be associated with greater life satisfaction and enjoyment of old age. By asking participants to indicate what they considered to be the best and the worst things about growing old, we hoped to elicit and identify some of the major advantages and disadvantages of aging from the individual's point of view, as well as to see whether or not there would be ethnic or gender differences in the perceived advantages and disadvantages of aging.

METHOD

Participants

Participants for the study were 128 adults, 66 percent of whom were female, whose ages ranged from sixty to ninety-two years with a mean of seventy years, $Mdn = 69$. They were surveyed in a variety of locations in central New Mexico, including two American Indian gatherings or Pow-Wows (20%), two shopping centers or stores (10%), an Elderhostel program (6%), and six senior citizen centers (64%), two of which were located in a large city and four at Indian pueblos. Forty-five percent of the participants were Anglo-Americans, 35 percent were American Indians, and 16 percent were Hispanics. The remainder were from mixed or other ethnic backgrounds.

Equal percentages of the participants were currently married (42%) and widowed (42%); 13 percent were divorced and 3 percent had never married. The great majority (92%) were parents, with a mean of 3.3 children. Their educational levels ranged from first grade through advanced degrees, with the median and modal responses being completion of high school. The Anglo subjects ($M = 13.7$) had significantly more years of schooling than the Indians $(M = 10.5)$ or Hispanics ($M = 10.21$), $F(2,117) = 13.24$, $p < .001$.

Procedure

Participants at the Pow-Wows, shopping centers, and the Elderhostel program were approached individually by one of six graduate students in educations, including the two junior authors, and asked whether or not they would be willing to complete a questionnaire dealing with feelings about growing older. They were assured that the instrument was anonymous and were given the option of filling it out as a questionnaire or being asked the questions in an interview. The procedure was the same at the senior citizen centers except that the two junior authors, who were sometimes assisted by the center staff, collected the data. Most of the participants at the centers preferred to be interviewed rather than fill out the questionnaire themselves.

Instrument

The questionnaire consisted of four pages; the first asked for demographic information, and the next two assessed attitudes toward aging which are reported elsewhere and will not be further discussed in the present article [44]. The fourth page of the questionnaire consisted of three sections. In the first, participants were to indicate whether or not they spent time at each of seventeen listed activities; in addition, space was provided for listing others (see Table 1). In the second section, participants were asked about changes in their relationships with their families since turning sixty. They were to indicate increases, decreases, or no change in terms of time spent with them, closeness, dependency, arguing, and enjoying being together. The third section consisted of two open-ended questions which asked participants to indicate, respectively, the three best things and the three worst things about growing older.

RESULTS

Activities

Table 1 presents the percentages by ethnicity and sex of participants who spent time in each of the listed activities. As can be seen from the table, reading, visiting with friends, and watching television were the most popular activities; farming, hunting, and child care were the least common. Specific arts and crafts activities mentioned by the subjects included sewing, quilting, knitting, crocheting, jewelry-making, photography, painting, and ceramics. Other activities mentioned include educational experiences, clubs, singing, dancing, playing bridge, specific sports, research, lecturing, treasure hunting, and basketball cheerleading.

Sex — As can be seen in Table 1, significant sex differences were found on a number of variables. Chi square tests of independence revealed that women were significantly more likely than men to report doing arts and crafts, cooking, housework, thinking, reading, and going to church.

Ethnicity — Chi square tests also revealed a number of significant differences between the three ethnic groups, some of which were significant for females and/or males considered separately, as well as for both sexes combined. Five of these activities showed a pattern of Indians reporting significantly greater involvement than Anglos and Hispanics combined. The chi square values for males and females combined are reported in Table 1.

The ethnic difference in child care was significant for both males, χ^2 (2, $N = 38$) = 6.96, $p < .05$, and females, χ^2 (2, $N = 76$) = 7.85, $p < .05$, reflecting the fact that 50 percent of the Indians but only 14 percent of the Anglos and 32 percent of the Hispanics reported caring for children, χ^2 (1, $N = 114$) = 14.62, $p < .001$. The overall ethnic difference in farming was also significant for both males, χ^2 (2, $N = 38$) = 8.96, $p < .05$, and females, χ^2 (2, $N = 77$), $p < .05$, indicating a much greater participation by Indians (25%) than by Anglos (2%) or Hispanics (5%), χ^2 (1, $N = 115$) = 13.33, $p < .001$.

Indians (82%) were also more likely than Anglos (50%) and Hispanics (68%) to report attending church, χ^2 (1, $N = 115$) = 8.66, $p < .01$, but this ethnic difference was not significant for males, only for females, χ^2 (2, $N = 77$) = 7.14, $p < .05$. Similarly the greater tendency for Indians (68%) than Anglos (35%) or Hispanics (42%) to report doing volunteer work, χ^2 (1, $N = 115$) = 10.84, $p < .001$, reflects an ethnic difference significant for females, χ^2 (2, $N = 77$) = 6.06, $p < .05$, but not for males. On the other hand, the greater tendency for Indians (48%) than Anglos (19%) and Hispanics (16%) to work to support themselves, χ^2 (1, $N = 115$) = 11.29, $p < .001$, represents a significant ethnic difference for males, χ^2 (2, $N = 38$) = 8.95, $p < .01$, but not for females.

The overall ethnic difference in sitting around was significant for females, χ^2 (2, $N = 77$) = 6.72, $p < .05$, but not males and seemed to reflect a tendency

Table 1. Percentage of Males and Females Within Each Ethnic Group Engaging in Each Activity

Overall Percentage	Activity	Indian male	Indian female	Anglo male	Anglo female	Hispanic male	Hispanic female	Ethnicity Chi Square[a]	Sex Chi Square[b]
79%	Reading	50%	81%	61%	88%	92%	86%	1.69	5.35*
78%	Friends	75%	89%	61%	79%	75%	71%	2.75	2.77
77%	TV	75%	78%	72%	77%	92%	71%	0.68	0.11
74%	Traveling	75%	64%	72%	80%	75%	43%	1.97	0.39
68%	Thinking	25%	89%	39%	80%	58%	43%	3.95	14.95***
67%	Housework	25%	83%	39%	74%	58%	86%	1.37	16.86***
65%	Church	63%	86%	33%	59%	75%	57%	10.74**	4.73*
62%	Cooking	38%	81%	33%	71%	42%	71%	3.27	18.84***
60%	Exercising	63%	70%	56%	59%	67%	43%	1.25	0.27
54%	Crafts	38%	72%	22%	68%	8%	57%	8.43*	25.63***
53%	Gardening	88%	53%	22%	62%	58%	29%	1.37	0.22
50%	Volunteer	63%	70%	22%	41%	42%	43%	11.37**	0.04
42%	Sitting	38%	61%	17%	32%	50%	29%	8.83*	1.09
30%	Working to support myself	75%	42%	22%	18%	17%	14%	11.37**	0.04
29%	Child care	50%	50%	6%	18%	33%	29%	14.62***	1.87
13%	Hunting	38%	14%	17%	6%	17%	0%	1.67	3.77
12%	Farming	50%	20%	6%	0%	8%	0%	13.49**	1.08
29%	Other	38%	18%	50%	30%	8%	29%	4.32	1.41

[a] χ^2 (2, N = 115), collapsed across sex
[b] χ^2 (1, N = 121), collapsed across ethnicity
* $p < .05$
** $p < .01$
*** $p < .001$

Table 2. Changes in Family Relationships for People over Sixty

	More	No Change	Less
Time spent with family	47%	10%	43%
Closeness to family	73%	12%	15%
Dependence on family	32%	9%	59%
Amount of arguing with family	10%	14%	76%
Enjoyment of family	83%	10%	7%

for Indians (57%) and Hispanics (42%) to report sitting around more than Anglos (27%), χ^2 (1, N = 115) = 7.62, $p < .01$.

Finally, although the ethnic differences in the activities of thinking and gardening were not significant for males and females combined, there was a significant ethnic difference in thinking for the female subjects, χ^2 (2, N = 77) = 7.96, $p < .05$, and in gardening for the male subjects, χ^2 (2, N = 38) = 10.31, $p < .01$. The findings for thinking were apparently due to the fact that Indian (89%) and Anglo (79%) women were more likely to report spending time thinking than Hispanic women (43%), χ^2 (1, N = 77) = 6.95, $p < .01$. On the other hand, Anglo men (22%) were less likely to spend time gardening than Indian (88%) or Hispanic (58%) men, χ^2 (1, N = 38) = 8.67, $p < .01$.

Relationship with Family

The percentages of all participants giving each response to the questions about changes in family relationships for people over sixty are presented in Table 2. As can be seen from the table, most participants felt closer to their families and enjoyed being with them more since turning sixty. They also argued with them less and felt less dependent on them.

A series of 3 × 2 chi square tests of independence relating responses on these five questions to sex revealed only one significant effect: Whereas 44 percent of the men spent more time, 22 percent spent the same amount of time, and 34 percent spent less time with their families after turning sixty, the corresponding figures for women were 46 percent, 5 percent, and 49 percent, χ^2 (2, N = 108) = 7.16, $p < .05$. Collapsing across cells, it appeared that as they grew older men were significantly more likely than women to continue spending the same amount of time with their families, χ^2 (1, N = 108) = 6.79, $p < .01$.

Chi square tests of independence relating ethnicity to the question about family relationships, both for all participants and for males and females considered separately, revealed no ethnic differences in perceived time spent together, dependency, arguments, or enjoyment. However, there were significant

Table 3. Percentages Reporting Changes in Closeness to Family

	Indian	Anglo	Hispanic	Total
Closer	79%	75%	56%	73%
No Change	2%	11%	38%	12%
Less Close	19%	14%	6%	15%
n	42	44	16	102

differences on the issue of how close people felt to their families, both for all participants, χ^2 (4, N = 102) = 14.31, $p < .01$, and for only males χ^2 (4, N = 29) = 10.87, $p < .05$. The findings for all participants are shown in Table 3. Collapsing across cells, a 2 × 2 chi square test revealed that Indians and Anglos were more likely than Hispanics to report a change in closeness to their family in either direction, χ^2 (1, N = 102) = 12.11, $p < .001$.

Advantages of Aging

When asked to list the three best things about growing old, 105 (82%) participants listed a total of 186 advantages of aging. Response rates varied from 67 percent of the Hispanic males and females and mixed ethnicity males and females to 100 percent of the Anglo males, excluding the two participants who responded "nothing." The responses were classified into thirteen categories, listed in Table 4. As can be seen from the table, the most frequently mentioned advantage was that of increased freedom, free time, and independence. Other commonly mentioned advantages concerned family relationships, reduced stress and increased relaxation, not having to work, increased self-acceptance and valuing of one's personal qualities, and the opportunity to engage in various specific activities, such as fishing.

Chi square tests revealed only one significant sex difference: Women (29%) were more likely than men (15%) to indicate increased freedom as an advantage, χ^2 (1, N = 105) = 5.83, $p < .05$. Only women listed freedom from pregnancy or child care as an advantage, but the numbers were too small for significance tests. None of the ethnic differences in advantages listed was statistically significant.

Disadvantages of Aging

In response to the question about the three worst things about growing old, 100 participants (78%) listed a total of 196 disadvantages. Response rates ranged from 67 percent of the Hispanic males and mixed ethnicity males and females to 89 percent of the Hispanic females, excluding the eight participants who responded "nothing." The responses were classified into fourteen categories,

Table 4. Best Things About Growing Old

	Females				Males			Total	
	Indian	Anglo	Hispanic	Mixed	Indian	Anglo	Hispanic	Mixed	N	%
n	28	32	6	2	5	21	8	3	105	
Advantages:										
Freedom	14	21	0	0	0	7	2	1	45	24%
Family	5	3	2	1	2	5	0	1	19	10%
Less Stress	6	5	1	0	0	3	2	1	18	10%
Not Working	3	3	2	0	1	4	1	1	17	9%
Self, personal	0	6	0	0	4	3	1	0	14	8%
Activities	8	0	0	0	0	0	1	4	13	7%
Travel	3	4	1	1	0	1	1	1	12	6%
Economic	2	3	0	0	2	5	0	0	12	6%
Respect, knowledge	3	1	0	0	0	4	0	1	9	5%
Social life	5	0	0	0	0	3	1	0	9	5%
Life, health	3	2	0	0	0	1	1	0	7	4%
No pregnancy, child care	0	5	1	0	0	0	0	0	6	3%
Fun	2	1	2	0	0	0	0	0	5	3%
TOTAL	54	56	9	2	9	36	10	10	186	100%

Table 5. Worst Things About Growing Old

	Females				Males			Total	
n	Indian 30	Anglo 29	Hispanic 8	Mixed 2	Indian 5	Anglo 16	Hispanic 8	Mixed 2	N 100	%
Disadvantages:										
Health, physical	27	18	5	2	1	11	4	0	68	35%
Limitations	12	9	3	0	2	3	1	1	31	16%
Isolation	9	7	1	1	2	3	0	1	24	12%
Self, personal	4	4	2	0	0	5	0	0	16	8%
Dependency	8	5	0	0	1	0	0	0	14	7%
Memory Loss	3	5	0	0	0	2	0	0	10	5%
Economic	2	4	1	0	0	0	0	0	7	4%
No Future	1	3	0	0	0	2	1	0	7	4%
Appearance	0	3	1	0	0	1	0	0	5	3%
Ageism	0	3	0	0	0	0	2	0	5	3%
Family	1	1	1	0	0	0	0	1	4	2%
Death	1	0	0	0	1	1	0	0	3	2%
Worries	0	0	0	0	1	0	1	0	2	1%
TOTAL	68	62	14	3	8	28	9	4	196	

listed in Table 5. As can be seen from the table, the most frequently mentioned disadvantage was poor health or physical problems, followed by limitations on activities; feeling lonely, isolated, or not cared for; personal traits like being tired, angry, or impatient; and concerns about being dependent. There were no significant sex or ethnic differences in the proportions of answers falling into the different categories.

DISCUSSION

The findings of this study suggest that there are both differences and similarities among people of different ethnic groups and gender in their reactions to growing older. The differences appeared primarily in the activities in which participants participated. In general, the sex differences were in accord with the sex role stereotypes that women are more likely to do housework and cooking, go to church, think or read, and be involved with arts and crafts. However, men were not significantly more likely than women to hunt, farm, or work to support themselves, although the differences were in that direction. American Indians were the most likely of the three ethnic groups to engage in farming, probably reflecting their rural cultural traditions, and in child care, consistent with the tradition of an extended family [10, 13, 17]. Economic factors might account for their greater likelihood to work to support themselves, as American Indians are one of the poorest minority groups in the United States [12].

The fact that most participants reported improved relationships with their families since turning sixty is consistent with other research and theory on the importance of family ties for elderly persons [7, 20-25]. As predicted, most participants felt closer to their families, enjoyed being with them more, and argued with them less; they also felt less dependent on them but showed no consistent pattern of change in time spent together since turning sixty.

Participants also reported a number of good points and bad points about growing older, with no consistent sex or ethnic differences found except that women were more likely than men to mention the most commonly named advantage: increased freedom and free time. Other good points listed included relationships with families, increased relaxation and/or reduced stress, not working, increased self-acceptance and self-respect, and the opportunity to engage in specific activities. Consistent with other research and theory on life satisfaction [37], poor health and physical problems were seen as a major disadvantage of growing old, as were limitations on activities, feelings of loneliness and isolation, personal characteristics, and concerns about dependency. Somewhat surprisingly, only 4 percent of the participants mentioned economic factors as a disadvantage of growing older, whereas 6 percent mentioned them as an advantage. Similarly, memory loss, frequently discussed in textbooks on aging, was mentioned as a problem by only 5 percent of the subjects [45].

Methodological Issues

The present study was similar to most other research on attitudes of elderly persons, in that the majority of respondents were women [39, 46]. As it was not possible to achieve equal representation of participants from all ethnic groups, the findings for Hispanics are based on a smaller number and therefore should be regarded with caution. Moreover, all participants were volunteers and thus may not be representative of all adults in the populations studied.

Although participants did not appear to have trouble understanding the instrument, it is conceivable that they failed to report their activities accurately. As with all self-report data uncorroborated by outside evidence, there is always the possibility that the responses were invalid. However, because the participants were anonymous volunteers and the findings were consistent with previous theory and research, this possibility seems relatively unlikely. Accepting the data at face value, one can conclude that people over sixty engage in a variety of activities which are influenced to some extent by gender and cultural background. In general, family relationships are seen as improved, and a number of advantages as well as disadvantages of aging are perceived. These findings help extend the research on attitudes and activities of elderly persons to two groups rarely studied: Southwestern Indians and Hispanics.

ACKNOWLEDGMENTS

Thanks are due to Ruy Krebs, Peter Harter, Howard Wolfgramm, Robert Budnick, and especially to the staffs of the senior citizen centers for their assistance in gathering the data. This research was supported by the University of New Mexico College of Education and the Department of Educational Foundations.

REFERENCES

1. C. M. Barresi, K. F. Ferraro, and L. L. Hobey, Environmental Satisfaction, Sociability and Well-being Among Urban Elderly, *International Journal of Aging and Human Development, 18*:4, pp. 277-293, 1983-84.
2. A. P. Fengler, Y. C. Little, and N. L. Danigelis, Correlates of Dimensions of Happiness in Urban and Nonurban Settings, *International Journal of Aging and Human Development, 16*:1, pp. 53-65, 1983.
3. P. L. Brennan and L. D. Steinberg, Is Remininscence Adaptive? Relations Among Social Activity Level, Reminiscence, and Morale, *International Journal of Aging and Human Development, 18*:2, pp. 99-110, 1983-84.
4. G. C. Fillenbaum, L. K. George, and E. B. Palmore, Determinants and Consequences of Retirement Among Men of Different Races and Economic Levels, *Journal of Gerontology, 40*:1, pp. 85-94, 1985.
5. M. A. Okun, W. A. Stock, M. J. Haring, and R. A. Witter, The Social Activity/Subjective Well-being Relation: A Quantitative Synthesis, *Research on Aging, 6*:1, pp. 45-65, March 1984.

6. R. Toseland and J. Rasch, Correlates of Life Satisfaction: An Aid Analysis, *International Journal of Aging and Human Development, 10*:2, pp. 203-211, 1979-80.
7. B. E. Aquirre and A. Bigelow, The Aged in Hispanic Groups: A Review, *International Journal of Aging and Human Development, 17*:3, pp. 177-201, 1983.
8. D. E. Gelfand, Ethnicity, Aging and Mental Health, *International Journal of Aging and Human Development, 10*:3, pp. 289-297, 1979-80.
9. C. S. Holzberg, Ethnicity and Aging: Anthropological Perspectives on More Than Just the Minority Elderly, *The Gerontologist, 22*:3, pp. 249-257, 1982.
10. F. L. Johnson, E. Cook, M. J. Foxall, E. Kelleher, E. Kentopp, and E. A. Mannlein, Life Satisfaction of the Elderly American Indian, *White Cloud Journal, 3*:3, pp. 3-13, 1984.
11. S. M. Manson and A. M. Pambrun, Social and Psychological Status of the American Indian Elderly: Past Research, Current Advocacy, and Future Inquiry, *White Cloud Journal, 1*:3, pp. 18-25, 1982.
12. National Indian Council on Aging, *May the Circle be Unbroken: A New Decade. Final Report on the Third National Indian Conference on Aging.* National Indian Council on Aging, Albuquerque, 1980.
13. C. J. Rogers and T. E. Gallion, Characteristics of Elderly Pueblo Indians in New Mexico, *The Gerontologist, 18*, pp. 484-487, 1978.
14. K. S. Berger, *The Developing Person Through the Life Span*, Worth Publishers, Inc., New York, 1983.
15. E. T. Dressel, *To Be "Old" or Not to Be "Old": Exploring Lifestyle Variations and Their Implications for Age Identity*, unpublished doctoral dissertation, University of New Mexico, Albuquerque, 1986.
16. W. M. Usui, T. J. Keil, and K. R. Durig, Socioeconomic Comparisons and Life Satisfaction of Elderly Adults, *Journal of Gerontology, 40*:1, pp. 110-114, 1985.
17. G. C. Williams, Warriors No More: A Study of the American Indian Elderly, in *Aging in Culture and Society*, C. L. Fry (ed.), Praeger Publishers, New York, 1980.
18. Z. Harel, Nutrition Site Service Users: Does Racial Background Make a Difference? *The Gerontologist, 25*:3, pp. 286-291, 1985.
19. C. N. Nydegger, Family Ties of the Aged in Cross-cultural Perspective, *The Gerontologist, 23*:1, pp. 26-31, 1983.
20. E. M. Brody, P. T. Johnson, and M. Fulcomer, What Should Adult Children do for Elderly Parents? Opinions and Preferences of Three Generations of Women, *Journal of Gerontology, 39*:6, pp. 736-746, 1984.
21. K. Markides, J. S. Boldt, and L. Ray, Sources of Helping and Inter-generational Solidarity: A Three-generations Study of Mexican Americans, *Journal of Gerontology, 41*:4, pp. 506-511, 1986.
22. S. H. Murdock and D. Schwartz, Family Structure and the Use of Agency Services: An Examination of Patterns Among Elderly Native Americans, *The Gerontologist, 18*:5, pp. 475-481, 1978.

23. B. Neugarten and E. Hall, Acting One's Age: New Rules for Old, *Psychology Today, 13*, pp. 66-80, April 1980.
24. B. L. Neugarten and R. J. Havighurst, Aging and the Future, in *Social Policy, Social Ethics, and the Aging Society*, B. L. Neugarten and R. J. Havighurst (eds.), National Science Foundation, Washington, D.C., 1977.
25. E. Olbrich and U. Lehr, Social Roles and Contacts in Old Age: Consistency and Patterns of Change, *Contributions to Human Development, 3*, pp. 113-126, 1976.
26. M. H. Cantor, Strain Among Caregivers: A Study of Experience in the United States, *The Gerontologist, 23*:6, pp. 597-604, 1983.
27. W. H. Jarrett, Caregiving Within Kinship Systems: Is Affection Really Necessary? *The Gerontologist, 25*: 1, pp. 5-10, 1985.
28. M. S. Moss, S. Z. Moss, and E. L. Moles, The Quality of Relationships Between Elderly Parents and Their Out-of-town Children, *The Gerontologist, 25*:2, pp. 135-140, 1985.
29. J. J. Dowd and Y. L. Bengston, Aging in Minority Populations: An Examination of the Double Jeopardy Hypothesis, *Journal of Gerontology, 33*:3, pp. 427-436, 1978.
30. J. Griffith and S. Villavicencio, Relationship Among Acculturation, Sociodemographic Characteristics and Social Support in Mexican American Adults, *Hispanic Journal of Behavioral Sciences, 7*: 1, pp. 75-92, 1985.
31. D. Maldonado, Jr., The Chicano Aged, *Social Work, 20*, pp. 213-216, 1975.
32. R. C. Manuel and M. L. Berk, A Look at Similarities and Differences in Older Minority Populations, *Aging, 339*, pp. 21-29, May/June 1983.
33. W. A. Achenbaum, The Obolescence of Old Age, In *Old Age in the New Land: The American Experience Since 1790*, The Johns Hopkins University Press, Baltimore, 1978.
34. G. D. Jensen and F. B. Oakley, Ageism Across Cultures and in Perspective of Sociobiologic and Psychodynamic Theories, *International Journal of Aging and Human Development, 15*:1, pp. 17-26, 1982-83.
35. E. K. Maxwell and R. J. Maxwell, Contempt for the Elderly: A Cross-cultural Analysis, *Current Anthropology, 21*:4, pp. 569-570, 1980.
36. D. G. McTavish, Perceptions of Old People: A Review of Research Methodologists and Findings, *The Gerontologist, 11*, pp. 90-102, 1971.
37. R. E. Barfield and J. N. Morgan, Trends in Satisfaction with Retirement. *The Gerontologist, 18*:1, pp. 19-23, 1978.
38. J. P. Alston and C. J. Dudley, Age, Occupation, and Life Satisfaction, *The Gerontologist, 13*:1, pp. 58-61, 1973.
39. S. K. Baum and R. Boxley, Age Identification in the Elderly, *The Gerontologist, 23*:5, pp. 532-537, 1983.
40. P. A. Baur and M. A. Okun, Stability of Life Satisfaction in Late Life, *The Gerontologist, 23*:3, pp. 261-265, 1983.
41. W. Leonard, Successful Aging: An Elaboration of Social and Pyschological Factors, *International Journal of Aging and Human Development, 14*:3, pp. 223-232, 1981-82.
42. E. Bastida, Reconstructing the Social World at 60: Older Cubans in the United States, *The Gerontologist, 24*:5, pp. 465-470, 1984.

43. U. Lehr and E. Olbrich, Ecological Correlates of Adjustment to Aging, *Contributions to Human Development, 3*, pp. 81-92, 1976.
44. M. B. Harris, P. Page, and C. Begay, Attitudes Toward Aging in a Southwestern Sample, *Psychological Reports, 62*, pp. 735-746, 1988.
45. H. L. Bee, *The Journal of Adulthood*, Macmillan Publishing Company, New York, 1986.

Direct reprint requests to:

Mary B. Harris, Ph.D.
Department of Psychology
University of Georgia
Athens, GA 30602

Chapter 4   Prevention and Intervention: Problems Reframed as Challenges

> A health director... reported that a small mouse, which presumably had been watching television, attacked a little girl and her full grown cat... both mouse and cat survived, and the incident is recorded here as a reminder that things seem to be changing. The mice of the world are no longer doing what the cats say (Reston 1957).

If we have successfully examined society through the eyes of minority families, we have begun to understand why the political process, bureaucracy, and social service systems may not function well for families of varied cultures. Such systems were designed to serve the majority of citizens and have done so quite well in the past. However, inherent assumptions about people in these systems may be inappropriate for various racial/ethnic minority populations. The Establishment has expected minorities to understand and adapt without listening to what minorities had to say or making sure each other was understood. Even multicultural education, as ordinarily practiced, tends to merely insert minorities into the dominant cultural frame of reference (Aoki, Werner, Dahlie, and Connors, 1984). Hopefully, we are learning to listen. Those who dare can hear that, indeed, things "seem to be changing" even more rapidly today than in Reston's 1957 scenario. In fact, a tumultuous change is exploding in our midst. Lest society in its false security of "business as usual" ignores the grave implications of such change, family scientists must lead the way in reframing the resulting problems as challenges. In so doing, the delicate balance between prevention and intervention programs and practices must be reassessed. In Chapter 4, the articles begin to identify for us some patterns of communication and behavior which must become more empathic if we are to reach formerly isolated multicultural pockets of our people. Recognition of differences, that they count and that they are valued, help in the effective delivery of social services.

Issues inherent in counseling with persons who represent distinct ethnic minority families are reframed as challenges by London and Devore. The impact of ethnicity on the daily life of Asian-American, Black, and Native American clients is reviewed. A schematic model of five "layers of understanding" is offered as a framework for practitioners who work with minority families.

Investigating the differences in interactional qualities of family competence and style of Black, Mexican-American, and White families, Hampson et al. failed to substantiate previous research reporting global differences. However, intriguing subscale differences did result in varying patterns of family competence and style. Black families were less likely to be verbally explicit, but more likely to exhibit warm feelings, to discourage offspring dependency, and to exhibit wider variation from the nuclear family model, including extended kin or nonrelated individuals. In contrast, Mexican-American families emphasized emotional bonding between family members, controlling aggressive impulses, and fostering dependency needs.

In a study of children's school-based competence, Patterson et al. compare the strength of four demographic predictors: income level, gender, ethnicity, and household composition in the domains of conduct, peer relations, and academic achievement. Low income and gender were the strongest overall predictors of children's competence across the various domains. The fact that ethnicity as a predictor of achievement test scores was linked to children living in low-income homes highlights the uneven distribution of economic resources among Black and White children in the United States.

Morrow warns that those who identify and serve gifted, talented, and handicapped Southeast Asian students must proceed with caution and base their practices on actual knowledge of cultural differences. Selected values of Southeast Asians and Americans are compared in a usable chart format to assist practitioners in their work with Cambodian, Laotian, and Vietnamese exceptional children. Implications for practitioners can be generalized to other populations of Asian students.

In the concluding article of Chapter 4, Staples offers a superior overview of the history and characteristics of four ethnic/racial groups: Asians, Blacks, Latinos (Hispanics), and Native Americans. The reader will gain insight into reasons for the paucity of literature on the family dynamics of these minority groups, as well as an awareness of the many factors impacting cultural diversity. Important, timely resources for professors and practitioners include lists of books, articles, bibliographies, periodicals, and organizations.

18 Layers of Understanding: Counseling Ethnic Minority Families

Harlan London and Wynetta Devore[*]

Considering the fact that America contains large numbers of families who see themselves as members of ethnic groups and for whom ethnic culture still has important behavioral consequences, it seems appropriate to address the issue of counseling with persons who represent distinct ethnic minority families. This article reviews several issues relating to families who are of Native American, black, or Asian American background, with implications for practitioners in the counseling profession. A schematic model to enhance understanding for counseling ethnic minority families is provided with suggested skills and techniques.

Practitioners in various disciplines must become sensitive to the uniqueness of ethnic minority families if they are to respond in ways that are helpful to clients. One cannot hold to the belief that current practices in mental health are adequate and appropriate for use with the many ethnic minority groups in this country. Nor can the practitioner forget that ethnicity is applicable to all individuals and families and is not limited to those who are identified as minority (Sue et al., 1982). The focus here is on particular groups of families who are at risk in our society due to their national origins and socioeconomic status. The primary aim is to provide a viable framework for practitioners to use as they seek to improve the human condition of minority families.

It is believed that such an effort is timely and needed for the following reasons: (a) the considerable complexity related to the status and conditions associated with minority family life in America, (b) minority families must negotiate and socialize their children to become self-sufficient, competent adults within the ambiguities of a cultural heritage that espouses a democratic equality for all citizens and a caste-like status for minority citizens (Peters, 1981), and (c) demands that result from having to cope within the American social context are multifaceted and inherently contradictory (Boykin & Toms, 1985).

To address some of these concerns, a schematic model is used to display the "Layers of Understanding" for practitioners working with ethnic minority families (Devore & Schlesinger, 1987). In the model (see Table 1) the two initial layers of understanding (a basic knowledge of human behavior and professional values) are introduced as basic requirements for all practitioners. In addition to these two layers, practitioners who work with ethnic minority families are expected to acquire the three additional layers of understanding. Together, the five layers offer the practitioner a practice orientation that recognizes the significance of human growth and development over the life cycle as well as those life experiences related to ethnicity.

A Basic Knowledge of Human Behavior

The competent practitioner should have a basic knowledge of human behavior with particular emphasis upon the developmental cycles of individuals and families. McGoldrick (1982) suggests that ethnicity interacts with individual development and the process of the family life cycle at every stage of development. This basic knowledge becomes the foundation upon which more specific knowledge and information about the experiences of ethnic minority families is built.

It is expected that all families, despite status or national origin, perform a variety of instrumental and expressive tasks such as the provision of food, clothing, shelter, and health as instrumental assignments; and nurture, love, and care as expressive tasks.

Billingsley's (1968) early work provides a discussion that may be generalized to other ethnic minority families. He suggests that most important among the instrumental functions is the expectation that families will be able to remain a stable unit and sustain themselves economically through their own efforts.

Such is not the experience for approximately 50% of ethnic minority families of color who often find themselves with only one parent (U.S. Bureau of Census, 1986). Many of these families need to look to public assistance agencies for financial support. This support provides minimal instrumental needs such as food, clothing, shelter, and medical care.

Table 1.
A Schematic Model Displaying the Layers of Understanding Required of Practitioners Working with Ethnic Minority Families

Basic skills required of all practitioners	Additional layers of understanding required of practitioners who work with ethnic minority families
1. A basic knowledge of human behavior	3. Self-awareness, knowledge of one's own ethnicity and its influence on practice
2. Professional values	4. Understanding the impact of ethnicity on the daily life of clients
	5. Modification and adaptation of skills in response to working with ethnic minority families

[*]Harlan London is an Associate Professor of Family Studies in the College for Human Development, Syracuse University, Syracuse, NY 13244-1250. Wynetta Devore is a Professor in the School of Social Work, Syracuse University, Syracuse, NY 13244-6350.

Key Words: Asian, black, ethnic families, minority counseling, Native American.

From Harlan London and Wynetta Devore, "Layers of Understanding: Counseling Ethnic Minority Families," *Family Relations*, Vol. 37: 310-314, 1988. Copyright © 1988 by National Council on Family Relations, 3989 Central Avenue Northeast, Suite 550, Minneapolis, MN 55421. Reprinted by permission.

The fulfillment of these needs does not begin to address the affective or expressive function so necessary to positive family development. Several components of the expressive function are the tasks of: monitoring and fostering the relationship among family members, preparing and serving meals which is more than the provision of nutrition to the family, and child care which is more than feeding and clothing and providing shelter for children (Huber & Spitze, 1983).

These tasks are attended to throughout the life cycle of the family and require that the family change continually. At the same time, the family must interact with external forces—other people, groups, and institutions. These external forces do not necessarily contribute in positive ways. For example, they may respond to minority families in behaviors which reveal institutional racism (Knowles & Pruitt, 1969).

Development within minority families has an added level of complexity. As ethnic minority children go through the various stages of the life cycle, they must deal with the normal tasks of development *as well as those related to ethnicity.* Logan (1981), in a discussion of development in black children, calls for a concern for variables of race and race awareness as chief determinates of intellect and personal style of children. In addition, Logan suggests an acceptance of black child studies into the education of practitioners and an acceptance of the color black as a symbol of pride, worth, and power.

Although attention is directed to the development of black children, a similar perspective is appropriate as one considers the development of children in other ethnic minority groups. Logan asks for a willingness to reconceptualize one's scientific frame of reference regarding human growth and development, addressing the process through which it occurs (i.e., physical maturation and life experiences). This allows for a practice orientation that recognizes the significance of ethnic dispositions throughout the life cycle of ethnic minority individuals and families.

Professional Values

Practitioners bring to the encounter with ethnic minorities their own set of values that have been developed over a lifetime. Indications of one's values may be found in his/her beliefs, goals, attitudes, ethics, morals, feelings, thoughts, interests, and aspirations (Schulman, 1982). These values influence responses to ethnic minority families. One example of this can be detected in how much the practitioner operates within a traditional American mainstream value such as self-reliance. The practitioner's belief in self-reliance may hamper work with a Native American family, while acceptance of goals set by Asian parents for their children may contribute to greater participation in the helping process.

Professional organizations develop codes of ethics that reinforce the values upheld by the group. These codes serve as guidelines for professional behavior, but at another level they represent the imposition of a set of values that the practitioners may think "ought" to be followed in relation to client populations. Table 2 shows a composite code representing several professional organizations.

It is obvious that some of these codes are more salient to dealing with ethnic minority families than others, but taken as a whole, they provide a useful guide for practitioners' behavior in dealing with all client populations. Presumably, they are safeguards protecting both client and practitioner. Currently, the ethnic minority family is particularly protected as codes demand behavior that does not discriminate in relation to race or financial status. Clients expect responses that recognize their uniqueness without allowing these responses to present barriers to responsible practice.

Self Awareness, Knowledge of One's Own Ethnicity and Its Influence on Practice

Practitioners should have a knowledge of themselves which enables them to be aware of and to take responsibility for their own emotions and attitudes. Awareness is an essential area of knowledge. The disciplined and aware self is one of the practitioner's major tools for practice

Table 2.
Composite Code of Ethics and Professional Organizations who Adhere to the Code

Composite Code of Ethics	AAMFT[a]	COMHC[b]	AMA[c]	ANA[d]	APA[e]	NASW[f]
1. They shall accept as their first goal the performance of competent service.	x	x	x	x	x	x
2. They shall accept as their primary obligation the protection of the client's dignity and welfare.	x	x	x	x	x	x
3. They shall preserve the confidentiality and privacy of the information acquired concerning the client.	x	x	x	x	x	x
4. They shall not discriminate because of race, religion, age, sex, health, or national origin.	x	x		x	x	x
5. They shall try to persuade the client to report to the appropriate authorities when the client's behavior tends to be destructive to him/herself or others.	x	x		x		
6. They shall use every resource available, including referral, to provide the best possible service for the client.	x	x	x	x	x	x
7. They shall safeguard the client from violations of human dignity and from physical and psychological harm.	x	x	x	x	x	x
8. They shall accept responsibility to the institution in which they are employed.	x	x	x	x	x	x
9. They shall participate in activities that contribute to the ongoing development of their professional knowledge and skill.	x	x	x	x	x	x
10. They shall be committed to increase the public's understanding of the needs and potentials of their clients.	x	x	x	x	x	x

Note. Adapted from Schulman, E.D. (1982). *Intervention in human services: A guide to skills and knowledge.* St. Louis: The C. V. Mosby Company.
[a]American Association for Marriage and Family Therapy; [b]Certified Clinical Mental Health Counselors; [c]American Medical Association; [d]American Nurses Association; [e]American Psychological Association; [f]National Association of Social Workers.

(Devore & Schlesinger, 1987). The questions to be answered are, "Who am I?" "Who am I in relation to my feelings about myself and others?" and in these instances discussed here, "Who am I in the ethnic sense?" This question may be followed by: "What does that mean to me?" and "How does it shape my perceptions of persons who are my clients?" (Devore & Schlesinger, 1987).

In a position paper describing the competent counselor, Sue and Associates (1982) stated that the well-functioning practitioner is one who has moved from being culturally unaware to being aware and sensitive to his/her own cultural heritage and to valuing and respecting differences. Practitioners are reminded of the need for self-awareness and sensitivity to one's own ethnicity particularly in relation to the effect they may have on practice. Helping practitioners are reminded of the need for self-awareness and sensitivity to one's own ethnicity, particularly in relation to the effect it may have on practice.

The Impact of Ethnicity on the Daily Life of Clients

Each day American families must cope with the many forces that impinge on their lives. The impact of these external and internal forces will be modified by the ethnic values and characteristics of each family group. In the following pages our emphasis will be on the lives of Native American, black, and Asian families. Through this examination of family life, material is provided that should lead to a greater understanding of minority families and a more effective and sensitive response in the helping process.

Native American families. An examination of the value systems of various Native Americans will reveal universal themes within tribal specific expectations. While the Sioux value generosity in sharing with other members of the tribe, the Chippewa view this as "institutional giveaway." The Hopi call for strength, self-control, intelligence, and wisdom (Dillard, 1983), and the Plains Indians look to the purification rituals, the annual tribal Sun Dance, and the individual spiritual retreat to support their value of spiritual realization of the individual and the group (Brown, 1981). Dillard (1983) presents a general value system for Native American nations with the understanding that the system held by any tribe may not be adhered to by all of its members. Common among all tribal groups are: tribal loyalty, respect for elders, reticence, humility, avoidance of personal glory and gain, giving and sharing with as many as three generations of relatives, an abiding love for their land, and the attributions of human characteristics.

The Native American family serves as the repository of such values and guides behavior through all of the stages of the life cycle. The family system, often misunderstood by practitioners, may consist of three generations in a single household representing a variation on the nuclear model, sometimes referred to as a "stem family." Family composition may also be extended, consisting of several households, extending even to the clan. This extensive active kinship system provides a child with resources of parents, siblings, aunts, uncles, cousins, and grandparents (Red Horse, 1980). Such relationships appear to be blurred to the outsider, yet the system serves to protect children and to provide them with an assurance of love.

The practices which follow serve to illustrate the value placed on children among Native American families. Children are regarded as important to the family, and Native American adults seldom strike a child. Families engage only in those social activities where children are included. Talking loudly, while correcting a child, is greatly disapproved. Competition is considered acceptable as long as the object is not to get the best of or to hurt someone. Children are taught that the land is lent to them and is not for private exploitation (Burgess, 1980). The importance of ownership of private property is not an entrenched value as it is with families with Northeastern European background. The practitioner must understand the Native American family within this context, as counseling and services are provided.

Native American traditions are not difficult to carry out on the reservation, but as families move into cities, life changes. At present, more Native Americans reside in cities than on the reservations and are separated from their traditional helping networks. In this non-Native American society, Native American family life and child-rearing mechanisms are at risk (Cross, 1986).

Government policy has also served to diminish the impact of the extended family. There has been a clear effort to detribalize and assimilate Native American populations. Byler (1977) has written of "The Destruction of Native American Families," explaining how federal policy has served to break up the extended family and the clan structure. As a result of these efforts, the loss of normal controls and protections has contributed to pathological response patterns on the part of the young. Cross (1986) speaks of health problems related to alcohol abuse such as fetal alcohol syndrome and a high percentage of alcohol-related deaths. Also, young adults have a high suicide rate, and many young children are left without protection.

These are the families for whom services by practitioners are needed. The practitioner must understand Native American family life in the present within the context of traditional values and child-rearing practices that have been besieged by federal policy and life in urban areas.

Black American families. A major source of information about black families has been provided by dramatic illustrations of pathology and deficiencies found in these families. In the work of Frazier (1939) and the influential government-sponsored Moynihan report (1965), disorganization and dysfunction were emphasized. Black mothers were said to be responsible for the breakdown and pathology found in black families. Much of this deficit perspective has infiltrated the academic and helping professions over the past 2 decades. Fortunately, many practitioners are beginning to recognize the cultural variations, functionality, and validity of black family lifestyles. Many now realize that, like other ethnic or racial minorities, black families cannot be seen as a homogeneous group (Allen, 1978). Yet, despite their diversity, there are common experiences in discrimination and prejudice. A sense of unity and support has served as a buffer against many of these experiences.

Martin and Martin (1985) examined the helping tradition, an essential element in the black family, tracing its historical roots back to Africa and slavery in America. While the helping tradition remains, they suggest that it diminishes as the family confronts urban environments. When this tradition is intact, it reinforces a kin-structured network of relationships that provide economic and moral supports in daily living (Hall & King, 1982).

The practitioner must bear in mind the strong sense of collective consciousness regarding identity and kinship embedded in black family values. Adaptable family roles would be included as well as high achievement and strong work incentives. Prominent in any listing of values would be religion. The church remains constant, providing a base for the spirituality that is a dominant force in the black family and community.

Again, like Native American families, not all black families hold these values. Interaction and assimilation in mainstream society often call for individual achievement and competition rather than kinship ties and strong group affiliation. Ethnic group membership is not exempt from stress upon the individual regardless of minority group status. Values held dearly by grandparents diminish over the generations.

Variations are also found in the structure of black families. Included in these structures are: nuclear families, extended families, and augmented families. Families may comprise husband and wife, single parent (mother or father), child, and other relatives or nonrelatives (Furstenberg, Hershberg, & Modell, 1975; Billingsley, 1968). These families and the networks that they form serve as loan agencies, emergency food sources, nursing homes, transportation agents, models, and morale boosters (Hall & King, 1982).

The single-parent family headed by women has increased in number and commands considerable attention. Reports (Rainwater, 1966; Schulz, 1969) describe families in disarray. Yet there is evidence that some such families are able to fulfill the universal functions assigned to all American families. There is almost universal agreement that many black family units of mothers and children are strengthened by the support networks of family and friends. Despite burdened, stressful, and restricted lives, many black mothers have shown the ability to provide healthy psychological, physical, and social growth environments for their children (McAdoo, 1983). The children gained a sense of individual, family, and racial identity. Values stressing education and religion, racial pride, and family unity found in the larger black community were found in these families as well. A variety of coping skills, crucial to survival in an urban setting were learned.

Foster (1974) and Kochman (1977) pointed out that many youngsters have developed survival skills and a mental toughness through sustained contact with a social environment which would be devastating to children from other groups. Many black urban youngsters have to know how to deal effectively with pimps, corner grocers, bill collectors, and policeman. Many of these same youngsters are clever in "ribbin' and jivin' " with school personnel, welfare workers, juvenile authorities, and practitioners. The term ribbin' or ribbing is used to describe the verbal game of taunting, denigrating, or making fun of someone (e.g., people, their clothing, or parts of their body), whereas, jivin' or jiving refers to verbal coping and survival techniques which black urban persons use to manipulate or persuade others. For example, "shuckin' and jivin' " often requires an ability to control and conceal one's true emotions. Youngsters realize early in life that they exist in an often hostile and complicated world, and verbal and physically aggressive games are only ways to deal with their pain and struggle. It must be emphasized that gamesmanship and verbal attacks are survival and coping techniques. These almost ritualized games are attempts to cope with and survive the severe economic constraints present in the urban environment.

The sensitive practitioner needs to understand the above-mentioned communication pattern. However, the practitioner should be aware that the name given a verbal contest in one city may be different in another location. Also, there may be some difference between the way the verbal contest is played on the street corner as compared with how it is played in school. For the practitioner the important issue is not the proper designation of verbal games among black youth, but that the practitioner begins to understand these verbal games exist and recognizes them. These skills and adaptations to urban life are used by many blacks. The skillful practitioner must be able to move through and beneath this level of verbal exchange and respond appropriately to the affect of black individuals and families. Some suggested skills and techniques relative to the achievement of this goal are provided for the practitioner in the final section of this article.

Asian-American families. For the purposes of this discussion, Chinese, Japanese, and Vietnamese families are considered to be Asian families. The spectrum is larger including such groups as the Koreans, Filipinos, Pacific Islanders, East Indians, and Indochinese. The focus here on Vietnamese families examines briefly the more recent immigrant experience.

Asian family cultural values can be explained as desirable ideals founded upon the precepts of Confucianism. Traditional cultural values are related to the concepts of humanism, which is based on the belief that virtuous behavior is inherent in all people, and order and hierarchy relative to placing the proper emphasis on relationships between parent and child. Self-discipline is also emphasized and requires that a person should learn to control emotions in order to think logically. As an integral part of Asian cultural values, collectivity is emphasized. This concept places an emphasis on kinship ties and mutual dependence where children are required to pay homage and give unquestioning obedience to their parents. The elderly learned scholars and older sages are revered for their knowledge and wisdom. An individual is obliged not to bring dishonor or shame to the family (Suzuki, 1980).

As the family is influenced by mainstream society, many families will no longer be able to maintain traditional values. There is evidence that filial piety is waning as the elderly, who can command respect, choose to remain in the city when their children move to the suburbs. This separation removes supports that have been an integral part of cultural traditions. Parents can no longer expect complete obedience, as families become more democratic and move away from the partriarchal system of the past. Contemporary Asian-American families still appear to hold the values associated with ethical behavior, respect for authority, and modesty and politeness (Suzuki, 1980).

Modification and Adaptation of Skills in Response to Working with Ethnic Minority Families

This layer of understanding calls for adaptation and modification techniques in response to dispositions of ethnic minority families. Practitioners must be aware of prevailing group inclinations in relation to such issues as privacy, using formally organized helping institutions, self-disclosure, discussion of intimate matters with persons outside the family, and the context in which help is or should be offered (Devore & Schlesinger, 1987).

In presenting a framework for ethnic minority practice, Lum (1986) offers a familiar process that includes contact, problem definition, assessment, intervention, and termination. At the same time, he presents some practice issues related to minority clients.

The initial contact phase includes issues about communication barriers, family and personal background, and ethnic community. Problems relative to identification present issues of disclosure, information, and understanding. Assessment requires consideration of social-environmental impacts as well as psycho-individual reactions. Practitioner and client issues are joined at the point of intervention as they select goals and plan strategies. Termination presents several questions that must be addressed: (a) Was an effort made to connect people to the positive elements of support in the ethnic minority community? and (b) did gaining a sense of self related to "ethnic selfhood" provide motivation for coping efforts?

The techniques for practice with ethnic minority families are familiar to practitioners as Lum has suggested, but the process must be influenced by knowledge of the families' experiences in America in addition to understanding the presenting problems they bring to the helping process.

Three important skills have been presented among the characteristics of culturally sensitive helping practitioners (Sue & Associates, 1982). (a) The ability to generate a wide variety of verbal and nonverbal responses is very important. The wider the repertoire of responses, the greater the chances are for understanding the presenting problem. (b) Another skill requires the ability to send and receive verbal and nonverbal messages "appropriately." Some ethnic groups have a high regard for subtlety and indirectness of communication while others prize directness and confrontation. The practitioner must understand the communication style of an ethnic in order to respond appropriately. (c) The practitioner must be able to exercise appropriate institutional intervention skills on behalf of the client system. This requires a perspective that views many problems and barriers to client success as part of the institutional systems.

Summary

No matter which model for intervention a practitioner may choose, there is a need to consider the layers of understanding: (a) adherence to a set of personal and professional practice values that affirm the qualities of uniqueness, (b) an understanding of development of individuals and families as they mature across the life cycle, in the context of their own ethnic groups, (c) insights into one's own ethnicity and an understanding of how this may affect professional practice, (d) a sensitivity to the experiences of ethnic minority families in America, and (e) the modification and adaptation of familiar techniques in response to the ethnic minority family. These elements can go a long way toward producing the kinds of outcomes which will prove most beneficial to society as well as to the families themselves.

REFERENCES

Allen, W. (1978). The search for applicable theories of black family life. *Journal of Marriage and the Family*, **40**, 117-129.

Billingsley, A. (1968). *Black families in White America*. Englewood Cliffs, NJ: Prentice Hall.

Boykin, A. W., & Toms, F. D. (1985). Black child socialization. In H. P. McAdoo (Ed.), *Black children: Social, educational, and parental environments* (pp. 33-51). Beverly Hills, CA: Sage Publications, Inc.

Brown, J. E. (1981). The persistence of essential values among North American Plains Indians. In R. H. Dana (Ed.), *Human services for cultural minorities* (pp. 5-13). Baltimore: University Park Press.

Burgess, B. M. (1980). Parenting in the Native American community. In M. D. Fantini & R. Cardenas (Eds.), *Parenting in a multicultural society* (pp. 63-73). New York: Longman.

Byler, W. (1977). The destruction of American Indian families. In S. Unger (Ed.), *The destruction of American Indian families*. (pp 1-11). New York: Association of American Indian Affairs.

Cross, T. L. (1986). Drawing on cultural tradition in Indian child welfare practice. *Social Casework*, **37**, 283-298.

Devore, W., & Schlesinger, E. G. (1987). *Ethnic sensitive social work practice* (2nd ed.). Columbus: Merrill Publishing Company.

Dillard, J. M. (1983). *Multicultural counseling*. Chicago: Nelson-Hall.

Foster, H. L. (1974). *Ribbin', jivin', and playin' the dozens*. Cambridge, MA: Ballinger Publishing Company.

Frazier, E. F. (1939). *The Negro family in the United States*. Chicago: The University of Chicago Press.

Furstenberg, F. F., Jr., Hershberg, T., & Modell, J. (1975). The origins of the female-headed black family: The impact of the urban experience. *Journal of Interdisciplinary History*, **6**, 211-233.

Hall, E. H., & King, G. C. (1982). Working with the strengths of black families. *Child Welfare*, **LXI**, 536-544.

Huber, J., & Spitze, G. (1983). *Sex stratification: Children, housework and jobs*. New York: Academic Press.

Knowles, L. L., & Pruitt, K. (1969). *Institutional racism in America*. Englewood Cliffs, NJ: Prentice-Hall.

Kochman, T. (1977). *Rappin' and stylin' out: Communication in urban black America*. Urbana, IL: University of Illinois Press.

Logan, S. L. (1981). Race, identity, and black children: A developmental perspective. *Social Casework*, **62**, 47-56.

Lum, D. (1986). *Social work practice and people of color: A process-stage approach*. Monterey, CA: Brooks/Cole Publishing Company.

Martin, J. M., & Martin, E. P. (1985). *The helping tradition in the black family and community*. Silver Springs, MD: National Association of Social Work.

McAdoo, H. P. (1983). Societal stress: The black family. In H. I. McCubbin & C. R. Figley (Eds.), *Stress and the family: Vol 1. Coping with normative transition* (pp. 178-187). New York: Brunner Mazel.

McGoldrick, M. (1982). Ethnicity and family therapy: An overview. In M. McGoldrick, J. Pearce, & J. Giordano (Eds.), *Ethnicity and family therapy* (pp. 3-30). New York: The Guilford Press.

Moynihan, D. P. (1965). *The Negro family: The case for national action*. Washington, DC: U.S. Department of Labor.

Peters, M. F. (1978). Notes from the guest editor. *Journal of Marriage and the Family*, **40**, 655-658.

Rainwater, L. (1966). Crucible of identity: The Negro lower-class family. *Daedalus*, **95**, 172-216.

Red Horse, J. G. (1980). Family structure and value orientation in American Indians. *Social Casework*, **61**, 462-467.

Schulman, E. D. (1982). *Intervention in human services: A guide to skills and knowledge*. St. Louis: The C. V. Mosby Company.

Schulz, D. (1969). *Coming up black*. Englewood Cliffs, NJ: Prentice-Hall.

Sue, D. W., Bernier, J. E., Durran, A., Feinberg, L., Pederson, P., Smith, E. J., & Vasquez, E. (1982). Cross-cultural counseling competencies. *The Counseling Psychologist*, **10**, 49-51.

Suzuki, B. H. (1980). The Asian-American family. In M. D. Fantani & R. Cardenas (Eds.), *Parenting in a multicultural society* (pp. 74-102). New York: Longman.

U.S. Bureau of Census. (1986). *Money, income and poverty status of families and persons in the United States: 1985*, (Current Population Reports, Series P-60, No. 154, Table 15, p. 21). Washington, DC: U.S. Government Printing Office.

19 Cross-Ethnic Family Differences: Interactional Assessment of White, Black, and Mexican-American Families

Robert B. Hampson
Southern Methodist University

Yosaf Hulgus
Southwest Family Institute, Dallas, TX

W. Robert Beavers
University of Texas, Health Science Center, Dallas, TX

Previous sociological and psychological research has reported differences in patterns of interaction between ethnic groupings of families; much of this literature has been confounded by methodological shortcomings and social class differences between the ethnic groups. This study utilized observational ratings of family interactions using the Beavers Interactional Scales, comparing interactional qualities of 89 White, 79 Black, and 18 Mexican-American families. Importantly, no significant global Competence or Style differences were found between groups, but differences in theoretically important component qualities of Competence and Style generally supported previous literature and clinical reports. Implications for therapists dealing with families of different ethnic groups are also addressed.

Though there have been repeated publications and empirical studies that point out the infinite variety and lack of stereotypy in families of various ethnic groups (Falicov, 1982; Staples & Mirande, 1980; Willie, 1974), there have been at least equally persistent efforts to study significant generalizable contrasts between ethnic groups, especially Whites, Blacks, and Hispanic/Mexican-American families (Allen, 1978; Mindel & Haberstein, 1976; Staples, 1971).

In an earlier article, Henggeler and Tavormina (1980) evaluated scores of such studies and pointed out the major sources of confusion and false assumptions that mar such work. Nonobservational studies utilizing interviews suffer from reporting errors due to the ethnic make-up of interviewers, if different from subjects. Observational studies suffer from similar problems; in addition, the interpretation of behavior may be skewed in pathological ways if the observer does not understand the ethnic group being observed. Further, demographic factors, especially social class differences, can be confounded with ethnic differences.

In addition, methodological problems marred many of the studies. The differences, if any, are frequently subtle, and the wide variety found in ethnic family groups challenges any one specific methodology.

Robert B. Hampson, PhD, is Associate Professor of Psychology, Southern Methodist University, Dallas, TX 75275-0442.

W. Robert Beavers, MD, is Clinical Professor of Psychiatry, University of Texas Health Science Center, Dallas, TX.

Yosaf Hulgus, PhD, is Research Coordinator, Southwest Family Institute, 12532 Nuestra Drive, Dallas, TX 75230.

Black Families

Acknowledging difficulties in methodology, sampling, and frame of reference in studying families of different ethnic backgrounds, some consistent family patterns surfaced in the literature. In studies of nonclinical Black families, there are consistent themes of strong kinship bonds and extended family ties (Hines & Boyd-Franklin, 1982): "... relatives expect and accept reliance on one another in times of need and often live in close proximity. Various people interchange roles, jobs, and family functions" (p. 90). Hence, there is a high degree of role flexibility and adaptability as the situation dictates; this boundary flexibility may look more like chaos to the outside observer accustomed to more predictable patterns of a nuclear household. The nuclear family takes on predominance for the middle-class Blacks (Willie, 1985) who may experience isolation from their extended families (Pinderhughes, 1982).

The church is a major source of socialization and prestige/status for the Black family, having strong roots in tribal customs, the oppression of slavery, and the later civil rights movement. Hence, ministers and parishioners are more often sought in times of need than are mental health professionals (Hines & Boyd-Franklin, 1982). Even when a Black family turns to those professionals, it is usually for child-related academic or behavior problems; there is an aversion to air "dirty laundry" to "outsiders." Hence, it is not surprising to find many studies citing less overt and extensive verbal communication (Henggeler & Tavormina, 1980) and less extensive marital communication (Aldous, 1969; Blood & Wolfe, 1978) in comparison with White families: "Blacks who appear mute in the therapy room may talk endlessly on their home turf" (Hines & Boyd-Franklin, 1982).

More recent writings by Black authors acknowledge the tendency of Black family members (often fathers) in conflict to internalize their feelings, since overt expression is perceived as potentially harmful to relationships (Pinderhughes, 1982). Hence, marital conflict is usually handled by distancing (Hines & Boyd-Franklin, 1982); anxiety is internalized (somaticized) or becomes the trigger for aggression. Hence, therapy can be useful in terms of encouraging assertive and empowering (rather than assaultive) behavior in family members (Pinderhughes, 1982).

The nuclear Black family has evolved earlier than many Anglo families into a more egalitarian power structure, given the historically earlier tendency of Black mothers to enter the workforce; Pinderhughes (1982) suggests that this trend is partly responsible for the undermining of perceived male power in nuclear families. Still, Black males demand and receive recognition as heads of their households, and take pride in providing for the family (Hines & Boyd-Franklin, 1982). In lower-class families, however, there are higher father-absence rates in families with dependent children (40.6% for Blacks as opposed to 12.4% for Whites) (U.S. Census Bureau, 1983). However, this same study also points to the marital stability of the vast majority (70.9%) of first-married Black males, indicating many of the "father-absent" homes stem from never-married single mothers rather than post-marital desertion. These latter families are typically described as matriarchal or "matricentric" systems, yet represent a minority of Black families; the two-parent Black family has been relatively neglected in systemic observational research. One study that examined interactional qualities of two-parent Black families (Lewis & Looney, 1983) found, "... the most competent working-class Black families are much more like than different from the most competent middle- and upper-middle-class white families..."(p. 100).

Mexican-American (Hispanic) Families

Just as with Black families, researchers emphasize the variety and plurality of Mexican-American families, rather than stereotyping (Falicov, 1982). However, generalizations regarding working-class Mexican-American families indicate that the kinship network is extremely important and affiliation and cooperation are stressed while overt confrontation and competition are discouraged. Concomitantly, there is a focus on relationships as more important than task or role performance (Eshleman, 1985).

A high degree of cohesion and heirarchical organization is normal for this group of families. Patterns of interaction are characterized by generational interdependence and loyalty to the family of origin, with high levels of affective resonance, interpersonal involvement, and internal (family) control (Falicov, 1982). Respeto (or respect) is a significant concept, implying a relationship involving a "highly emotionalized dependence and dutifulness, within a fairly authoritative framework" (Diaz-Guerrero, 1975, p. 140). The family protects its individual members, and demands loyalty in return; hence, autonomy is less important than dignidad (dignity). The marital subsystem is often characterized by the ideal of *muy hombre* (manliness) for the husband and *marianismo* (undercover power and centrality of the dutiful and self-sacrificing mother/wife). This rather centripetal pattern is associated with moderately large nuclear families and rather stable intact parental systems (84.0% of first-married males remaining married) (U.S. Census Bureau, 1983).

Family Assessment Methodology

Prior to our earlier research group's family interaction studies, reported in 1976 (Lewis, Beavers, Gossett & Phillips, 1976), no interaction patterns consistently differentiated disturbed from normal families (Jacob, 1975). It is not surprising that any differences among normal or nonlabeled families, which differ only ethnically, would be difficult to substantiate. Bagarozzi (1980) reviewed the subject and made a plea for a systemic interactional approach to the study of ethnic family variations. He considered this approach to be the most likely tool to investigate these more subtle differences.

Since our methodology over the years has been interactional, systems based, and has, in addition, effectively distinguished between nonlabeled and clinical family groups (Jacob, 1975), it seemed appropriate to examine our data regarding possible consistent variability between ethnic groups in a sample of 186 nonlabeled families who possessed a developmentally disabled child, using uniform, school-defined criteria. Our purpose in studying these families was to better understand their coping methods with the stress presented in the family system by developmental disability in an offspring (Beavers, Hampson, Hulgus & Beavers, 1986; Hampson, Hulgus, Beavers, & Beavers, 1988).

METHOD

Subjects

A total of 186 families were observed and rated on interactional qualities of family competence and family style, central to the Beavers Systems Model of family assessment. Each family was observed and interviewed as part of a larger study of family adaption to having a developmentally disabled child. Each family in this study had one child assessed by the school district as functioning at or below two standard deviations below the age-normal mean on academic and intellectual measures. The families were recruited through the division of Special Education of the Dallas (Texas) Independent School District. To begin the recruitment process, a social worker from the school district's special education division called families with developmentally disabled children; if tentative consent was granted by the family, the social worker visited the home to offer more information. Interviews (at which the social worker was also present) were scheduled at the neighborhood school attended by the Special Education Student, to standardize setting and reduce reactivity across families. The school personnel also greeted the families, so the families encountered familiar school personnel.

In several preceding studies of these families, we have studied overall levels of competence and style; the findings indicate that overall, these families are not significantly different from nonclinical control families without handicapped children (Hampson, Hulgus, Beavers, & Beavers, 1988). As a general rule, single-parent families fared less well than two-parent or multi-generational families, but the presence of the disabled child per se was not associated with overall system dysfunction.

The present sample consisted of 89 White, 79 Black, and 18 Mexican-American families. Table 1 presents the family composition demographics of the sample. The most striking difference across ethnic groups is the percentage of single-parent families: 11% of White, 33% of Black, and 0% of Mexican-American families were single-parent families.

These families were generally lower middle-class and blue-collar in occupational and educational status (73.5%), while 21.7% of the sample held professional-technical or managerial occupations. In order to study the associations between social class (educational and occupational indices) and family ratings across and between ethnic groups, a subset of the larger sample was used. This subset of 129 families consisted of 44 White, 67 Black and 18 Mexican-American families with developmentally disabled children in the preschool and elementary school years. This group was more balanced in representation of the ethnic groups, had more definitive occupational and educational information about the parents, and was a more homogeneous group in terms of age of children and occupational status. (The other subsample of 45 White, 12 Black, and 0 Mexican-American families was a subsequent cross-age sample with less definitive demographic information.) Consequently, the former subset of 129 families was used for the comparisons of ethnicity by social-class.

Family Interviews

Structured 45-minute interviews were conducted with all families. These interviews, videotaped for later analysis, consisted of two phases. In the first phase, families were asked about the composition of the family and about supports available to the family; they were also asked how the presence of a handicapped child had affected their family, what they thought they had done well and what they might like to change, and what advice they might have for other families in similar circumstances. In the second phase, there was an unstructured family play period of approximately 10 minutes, during which family members were offered toys or drawing materials to use together.

All interviews were videotaped in their entirety, and ratings were based upon pairs of trained raters observing and rating tapes independently. The ratings were based on 10-minute segments from the middle portion of each interview, to provide raters consistent family interaction-discussion protocols. Observers in this study were two White

Table 1
Sample Composition for Observational Family Ratings

	Ethnic Group		
	White	Black	Mexican-American
Nuclear Family	59	23	15
Multi-generational	3	18	1
Single parent	10	26	0
Foster/Adoptive	3	1	1
Blended (Step)	14	10	1
Other	0	1	0
Total	89	79	18

female social workers, each with at least 6 years of professional experience in working with families of diverse ethnic groupings.

Instruments

The following observational rating scales from the Beavers Systems Model were used: 1. The Beavers Interactional Competence Scale (Beavers, 1981; Lewis et al., 1976) is a 13-item structured observational rating scale. Ratings are completed by trained observers' evaluations of family interaction for a minimum of a 10-minute period. These evaluations result in a rating for the family on global Competence and on 12 subscales. The scale evolved from general systems theory and studies of well-functioning vs. dysfunctional families.

The Competence Scale, previously titled the Beavers-Timberlawn Scale (Lewis et al., 1976), provides anchored rating points on subscales and the global health/competence scale; the former scales are rated from 1 (healthiest) to 5 (dysfunctional), while the global health scale is rated from 1 (optimal functioning) to 10 (severely dysfunctional). The subscales of the Competence Scale represent critical elements of family functioning central to the Beavers Systems Model (Beavers, 1981). These include (with current interrater reliabilities for each subscale in parentheses):

I. *Structure of the Family*
   Overt Power: chaotic to egalitarian (.83)
   Parental Coalition: parent-child to strong parental (.85)
   Closeness: indistinct boundaries to close, distinct boundaries (.72)
II. *Mythology:* reality perception of family: incongruent to congruent (.86)
III. *Goal-Directed Negotiation:* efficient to inefficient problem-solving (.73)
IV. *Autonomy*
   Clarity of Expression: directness of expression of thoughts and feelings (.82)
   Responsibility: voicing of responsibility for personal actions (.86)
   Permeability: open vs. unreceptive to statements of others (.86)
V. *Family Affect*
   Range of feelings: broad range to limits and controls on certain emotions (.84)
   Mood and Tone: open and optimistic to cynical and pessimistic (.79)
   Unresolvable conflict: chronic underlying conflict vs. ability to resolve conflict (.77)
   Empathy: empathic vs. inappropriate responses to affect and nonverbal cues (.88)
VI. *Global Health/Pathology* (.85)
   Average of Subscales (.94)

The observational rating is completed by trained clinical raters, who reach at least 90% overall interrater reliability in training, and who maintain a minimum of 85% reliability throughout the studies. The scale also shows a high degree of internal consistency (Cronbach's *Alpha* = .94).

The validity of the Competence Scale has been demonstrated in a number of clinical and empirical demonstrations. The original Timberlawn study (Lewis et al., 1976) found that the Competence Scale successfully discriminated families with hospitalized adolescents from nonclinical families, with significant differences on the Global Health scale and 11 subscales. The Competence Scale also shows a high degree of construct validity with self-report versions of the Beavers Systems Model (the Self-Report Family Inventory), R = .62 (canonical Correlation).

2. The Beavers Interactional Style Scale, previously titled the Centripetal/Centrifugal Style Scale (Kelsey-Smith & Beavers, 1981) is an observational rating scale designed to measure a family's systemic interactional and emotional stylistic patterns. Based on systems theory regarding extreme differences in binding (CP) and expelling (CF) pat-

terns and affective styles (conflicts subdued, anger threatening [CP]; versus open conflicts and hostility [CF]) in disturbed families, this style dimension represents elements of enmeshment and disengagement at its extreme points. The scale ranges from highly centripetal (most satisfaction sought inside the family) to extemely centrifugal (most satisfaction sought outside the family).

The 9-item Style Scale is comprised of 8 subscales and a global style rating, each based on a 1 (CP) to 5 (CF) scale. These scales, with current inter-rater reliabilities in parentheses are:

1. Dependency Needs: encouragement vs. discouragement (.73)
2. Style of Adult Conflict: open vs. covert/hidden (.64)
3. Proximity: Physical closeness vs. distancing (.83)
4. Social Presentation: overly concerned vs. unconcerned about impression (.64)
5. Verbal Expression of Closeness: high vs. no emphasis of family closeness (.72)
6. Aggressive/Assertive Behaviors: discouraging vs. soliciting/encouragement of aggression (.67)
7. Expression of Feelings: positive (warm) vs. negative (angry) feelings expressed easily (.83)
8. Internal Scapegoating: always vs. never one member scapegoated (.61)
9. Global CP/CF rating (.75)
   Average of Subscales (.79)

These interrater reliabilities represent exact-point agreement between pairs of trained raters. The internal consistency of the Style scale is .91 (Cronbach's *Alpha*).

Validation research on the Style Scale is currently in progress. Pilot data indicate that significant differences in self-reported family style were found across goupings of psychiatric patients at similar levels of family competence (Hampson, Beavers, & Hulgus, 1988).

RESULTS

Ethnic Comparisons

When the pattern of competence and style ratings were analyzed on the basis of ethnic classification, no significant differences were found on global ratings on either dimension in these nonclinical families. Across groups, then, no significant differences in ratings of global Competence or global Style existed between White, Black, and Mexican-American families. Had such differences existed, the "culture fairness" of these rating scales would come under question. However, there are some intriguing differences between ethnic groups on certain competence and stylistic subscales. These differences provide a glimpse of variations in some subtle ways that the families in these different ethnic groups express their family competence.

On competence subscales (Table 2), there were no significant differences between ethnic groups regarding family structure, though there was a trend for Mexican-American families to be rated as showing more dominant power exchanges than White or Black families (Overt Power, $p<.10$). On the mythology subscale, regarding how the family's concept of itself is congruent with the outside raters, the Mexican-American families were rated as significantly more congruent than were White or Black families. Black families, in contrast, were rated as significantly less able to express or state feelings and thoughts directly and clearly (clarity of expression), less apt to respond openly and receptively to efforts of family members to interrupt or make personal statements (Permeability), and to show a more consistent, less varied range of feelings in their various interactional exchanges. In the overall pattern of competence ratings, the Mexican-American families in the sample tended toward consistently higher pat-

Table 2
Means of Observed Family Competence by Ethnic Group

Beavers Interactional Competence Scale	White (N = 89)	Black (N = 79)	Mexican-American (N = 18)
Overt Power	4.09	3.81	3.32
Parental Coalition	4.14	3.76	3.80
Closeness	3.98	3.59	3.81
Mythology	2.04	2.29	1.75*
Goal-Directed Negotiation	2.15	2.45	1.88
Clarity of Expression	2.12	2.80*	2.25
Responsibility	2.01	2.27	1.63
Permeability	2.26*	2.91*	2.63
Range of Feelings	2.65	3.29*	2.75
Mood and Tone	2.06	2.42	2.13
Unresolved Conflict	4.07	3.94	4.44
Empathy	2.35	2.88	2.81
Global Competence	4.07	4.91	4.13

[a]Lower scores = greater competence; all others, higher scores = greater competence. [b]Based on 10-point scaling; all other subscales based on 5-point ratings.
*$p<.05$.

terns of ratings, White families tended toward middle positions, and Black families tended toward consistently less competent ratings, though these differences were mostly nonsignificant. This pattern is obviously influenced by the differential weighting of nuclear vs. single-parent families in the ethnic groups. However, when only non-single parent families were compared (two-parent nuclear, multi-generational, blended), highly similar patterns of family ratings occurred (Table 3). Black families were rated as significantly lower than White or Mexican-American families on Clarity of Expression, less permeable to others' thoughts and feelings than White families, and showing a less varied range of feelings than Mexican-American families. Mexican-American

Table 3
Means of Observed Family Competence by Ethnic Group
(No Single-Parent Families)

Beavers Interactional Style Scale	White (N = 79)	Black (N = 53)	Mexican-American (N = 18)
Overt Power	4.24	3.90	3.31
Parental Coalition	4.18	3.74	3.80
Closeness	3.79	3.63	3.81
Mythology	1.89	2.39	1.75
Goal-Directed Negotiation[a]	2.07	2.41	1.88
Clarity of Expression[a]	2.21	2.81	2.25
Responsibility[a]	1.96	2.27	1.63
Permeability[a]	2.31*	2.89*	2.63
Range of Feelings[a]	2.89	3.33	2.75
Mood and Tone[a]	2.24	2.40	2.13
Unresolved Conflict	4.07	3.69	4.44
Empathy[a]	2.63	2.93	2.81
Global Competence[a,b]	4.39	4.84	4.13

[a]Lower scores = greater competence; all others, higher scores = greater competence. [b]Based on 10-point scaling; all other subscales based on 5-point ratings.
*$p<.05$.

families showed a greater range of feelings expressed overtly, and a more congruent sense of family concept than White or Black families. Again, no significant differences were found on global family competence between ethnic groups, but, rather, in the subtle differences between elements of competence.

On ratings of family style, (Table 4) no significant differences were found on global ratings of centripetal/centrifugal style across ethnic groups; the Mexican-American subsample showed more consistent ratings toward the inner-directed centripetal style, although most subscale differences were nonsignificant. Mexican-Americans were rated as being more attuned to and encouraging of dependency needs in their children than both other groups, while Black families were significantly more discouraging of such behaviors than both other groups. Hispanic families were also rated as significantly more likely to describe themselves as close-knit (verbal expression of closeness), and significantly more discouraging of aggressive, defiant, or disruptive behavior from members (assertive/aggressive qualities).

Black families were rated as significantly different from the other groups in the relative ease with which positive, rather than negative, feelings are expressed. White families tended toward the middle on most of the stylistic ratings. Hence, while no significant differences were found on the global rating of family style, subtle differences exist in the way the families present themselves in group interaction.

When comparisons were made between ethnic groups using only non-single-parent families (Table 5), fewer and less significant differences in family Style ratings were

Table 4
Means of Observed Family Style by Ethnic Group

Beavers Interactional Style Scale	White ($N=89$)	Black ($N=79$)	Mexican-American ($N=18$)
Dependency Needs	2.99*	2.62*	4.00*
Adult Conflict	3.00	2.70	2.56
Proxemics	2.79	2.61	3.13
Social Presentation[a]	2.60	2.40	3.00
Verbal Expression of Closeness[a]	2.39	2.07	3.00*
Assertive/Aggressive Qualities[a]	2.70	2.83	1.71*
Positive/Negative Feeling[a]	2.68	2.47*	2.75
Internal Scapegoating[a]	3.06	2.58	2.88
Global Style[a]	2.87	2.81	2.50

[a]Lower numeric values = more Centripetal; all others, lower = more Centrifugal.
*$p<.05$.

Table 5
Means of Observed Family Style by Ethnic Group (No Single Parents)

Beavers Interactional Style Scale	White ($N=79$)	Black ($N=53$)	Mexican-American ($N=18$)
Dependency Needs	2.85	2.32	4.00
Adult Conflict	3.19	2.98	2.56
Proxemics	2.83	2.58	3.13
Social Presentation[a]	2.57	2.40	3.00
Verbal Expression of Closeness[a]	2.33	1.90	3.00
Assertive/Aggressive Qualities[a]	2.59	2.72	1.71
Positive/Negative Feeling[a]	2.85	2.46	2.75
Internal Scapegoating[a]	2.86	2.60	2.88
Global Style[a]	2.75	2.90	2.50

[a]Lower numeric values = more Centripetal; all others, lower = more Centrifugal.

noted. As with the larger sample, there were no significant differences in overall family Style. On only 2 subscales was there a nonsignificant trend ($p < .10$), which revealed a tendency for Mexican-American families to describe themselves as close-knit (Verbal Expression of Closeness) and as more discouraging of assertive or aggressive qualities in members, both in comparison to Black families.

Social Class Comparisons

Since social class has been acknowledged as a major confound in studies of ethnic groupings of families, a series of correlational and between-groups analyses were conducted on a subset of 129 families (as described in the Subjects section). The breakdown of the ethnic groups by type of occupation is presented in Table 6. Even though the overall income levels across the ethnic groups were not significant, there were still proportionally more professional-level White families than Mexican-American families; Black families' occupational classifications generally fell between these other groups. Also, there were disproportionately fewer Mexican-American men in "managerial" and office clerical positions ($X^2(10) = 27.07; p < .05$).

Consequently, the associations between occupations (income) status and family ratings were computed both across and between the three ethnic groups. Table 7 presents the correlations between occupational rating and observational family ratings for those rated subscales which showed significant between-group ethnic differences in Tables 2 and 4. First, it is noteworthy that for White families there was a consistent pattern for higher social class to be associated with ratings of higher competence, while the pattern for Black and Mexican-Americans was dramatically less consistently related to occupational status. On only two subscales, and, importantly, *not* global competence ratings, were there significant correlations between occupational class and family competence ratings. Both Black families and Mexican-American families showed significant, though modest, occupational class correlations with rated permeability, (the degree to which they responded to make personal clarifications and self-referencing statements); hence, this difference between ethnic groups rated on Table 2 may reflect more social class than ethnic difference. Likewise, Black families showed a significant correlation between occupation and range of feelings; hence, the finding that Black families were rated as showing a more truncated range of feelings may reflect more social class than ethnicity differences.

In terms of family style ratings, none of the individual style subscales showed any significant correlations with occupational status for Black or Mexican-American families, while only one (verbal expression of closeness) was so for White families.

Table 6
Breakdown of Sample by Ethnicity and Occupation

	White Father	White Mother	Black Father	Black Mother	Mexican-American Father	Mexican-American Mother
Professional	7	4	4	3	0	0
Managerial/Clerical	7	8	10	13	0	1
Craft	6	0	3	1	7	3
Mechanical/Domestic Service	12	3	8	25	4	6
Laborer	5	1	7	7	5	0
Homemaker	—	26	—	16	—	9
Unemployed	1	2	8	2	0	0
	38	44	40	67	17 (one missing)	18

Note. For fathers $X^2(10) = 27.07$ $p<.05$. For mothers $X^2(12) = 24.52$ $p<.05$.

Table 7
Pearson Correlations Between Occupational Status of Principal
Breadwinners and Interactional Ratings

Interactional Ratings Subscale	White (N = 44)	Black (N = 67)	Mexican-American (N = 18)	Overall (N = 129)
Competence:				
Mythology	.49*	.22	−.26	.31
Clarity of Expression	.62*	.19	.24	.35
Permeability	.45*	.36*	.42*	.38*
Range of Feelings	.49*	.42*	.00	.39*
GLOBAL	.53*	.20	.16	.31*
Style:				
Dependency Needs	−.19	.15	.13	.03
Verbal Express. Closeness	.45**	.15	−.24	.22**
Assertive/Aggressive Qualities	.17	.08	.20	.01
Positive/Negative Feelings	.02	−.20	−.17	−.15
GLOBAL	.42**	.62**	.55*	.44**

*$p<.05$ (Higher occupational status scored as more competent). **$p<.05$ (Higher occupational status scored as more centripetal).

Hence, the significant differences noted between ethnic groups appear to be more related to ethnic variations in the manifestations of centripetal and centrifugal tendencies in these families. In contrast, global ratings of family style, based on summary impressions of subscale-based binding vs. expelling patterns in families, were highly correlated with occupational status for all three ethnic groups (there were no significant differences on this global rating between groups). Hence, overall ratings of centripetality vs. centrifugality are highly related to occupational status, while the significant differences between ethnic groups on specific (subscale) stylistic qualities appear to be related more to between-ethnic group differences than to socioeconomic levels.

DISCUSSION

These findings are consistent with and supportive of the hypothesis that any differences found between ethnic groups are likely to be differences in style of structure or interaction rather than differences in competence or health. Since the competence ratings were not significantly different between groups, intergroup variations would suggest that implications of differential pathology, or threat of pathology, are not warranted. This position is compatible with one of the alternatives for interpreting ethnic family differences suggested by Henggeler and Tavormina: not deficits or methodological shortcomings perhaps, but "socio-cultural differences in behaving, without any necessary implications of psychopathology" (Henggeler & Tavormina, 1980, p. 212, 1980).

Black Families

Black families expressed significantly fewer feelings and thoughts in a verbally direct and clear fashion in this interview context, but they were significantly higher in sanctioning the expression of positive over negative feelings. They were less apt to respond well to efforts of family members to interrupt or make personal statements and they showed a less varied range of feelings while performing the requested family task. Further, the Black families were rated as more discouraging of the expression of dependency needs by children.

Perhaps the significant differences found between subscales can assume greater importance when placed in context with previous supported studies of ethnic family differences. From several sociological studies, three distinct patterns of Black family patterns have emerged: (a) the matriarchal, (b) the egalitarian two-parent, and (c) the patriarchal affluent pattern. There are apt to be a variety of distant kin or unrelated individuals included in a nuclear or single-parent family. These variables do not represent pathology but adaptive mechanisms, and Eshleman states that none of the patterns is a family "falling apart" but, on the contrary, a family capable of successful adaptation (Eshleman, 1985).

Blood and Wolfe (1978) and Aldous (1969) found that lower class Black wives and husbands reported significantly less marital communication than a comparable White sample. Bee, Van Egeren, Streissguth, Nyman & Leckie, (1969) found that there was less mother/child dyadic interaction than that found in White controls. Henggeler and Tavormina (1980), however, concluded that many of these differences could be a product of variables not directly related to race, such as social class or the experimental setting.

These studies, combined with the data presented here, suggest a pattern of healthy Black families being less verbally explicit, generally warm in feeling tone, yet discouraging dependency in offspring. They are more apt to have variations from the nuclear family model, frequently including other extended kin, or nonrelated individuals, especially in the single parent families.

Mexican-American Families

The Mexican-American families described themselves more nearly as our observers perceived them than did the other two groups. They were the most comfortable in allowing the expression of dependency needs. They described themselves as close more frequently than the other family groups and they clearly discouraged aggressive or disruptive behavior of children more energetically and more consistently than did the other families.

Just as in Black families, family researchers emphasize the variety and plurality of Hispanic and Mexican families (Falicov, 1982). However, there are some common themes in literature regarding the working class Mexican-American family whose forebears migrated to the United States from Mexico. The kinship network is extremely important, and affiliation and cooperation are stressed, while more competitive and aggressive qualities are discouraged. There appears to be a focus on relationship rather than tasks (Eshleman, 1985).

These sociological observations are consistent with the interactional group differences noted. Capable Mexican-American families emphasize emotional bonding between family members, control aggressive impulses, and foster the seeking and obtaining of dependency needs.

These interactional observations are supportive of ethnic family descriptions already developed from other research methods. In our sample, the most likely confounding variable was that of social class, since we could not control for this variable completely in selecting subjects. The data regarding social class differences as determined by occupations between and within family groups indicate that there are no differences in family competence levels in the Black and Hispanic samples, but there is a positive correlation of social class and competence in the White sample. This may be due to the greater variation in range of occupational status in the White sample. It may also be that the minority groups have more limited access to a range of "healthier" neighborhoods, despite variation in occupational status in individual families.

Since most of the rated subscales did not show significant influence of social class, and since the data is compatible with observations reported in papers utilizing nonsystemic means of study, we believe most of the obtained differences stem from ethnic syslistic differences in developing and maintaining a family. These differences are potentially useful for the therapist dealing with families of various ethnic backgrounds. Specifically, therapists working with Black families may be frustrated in attempts to foster higher levels of verbal expression initially or to promote verbal overtures regarding dependency needs of their children. However, our research indicates that lower levels of these qualities exist in competent Black families in the interview room; the adage "if it's not broken, don't try to fix it" can well apply to these circumstances.

Similarly, in working with Mexican-American families, therapists must attend to subtle variations in the expression of family competence. Since many of these families show a more centripetal style, including control of aggressive and angry feelings (especially in the presence of an "outsider"), expressing closeness and harmony, and encouraging dependency needs of offspring, therapists may be frustrated in attempts to enter such families initially. In addition, fostering clarity in potential conflict situations and encouraging family members to "break away" from the nucleus may often be difficult and even counterproductive.

These data encourage the view that for families of all ethnic backgrounds, subtle ethnic and social class differences exist, and imposing one's own ethnically influenced standards regarding clarity of expression, autonomy, egalitarianism, and even sex-role standards may limit therapeutic efficacy. Appreciation of a variety of manifestations of family competence and style are necessary for effective intervention, rather than relying on a single concept of family health and family therapy.

REFERENCES

Aldous, J. (1969). Wives' employment status and lower-class men as husband-fathers: Support for Moynihan thesis. *Journal of Marriage and the Family, 31*, 469–476.

Allen, W. R. (1978). The search for applicable theories of Black family life. *Journal of Marriage and the Family, 40*, 117–129.

Bagarozzi, D. A. (1980). Family therapy and the Black middle-class: A neglected area of study. *Journal of Marital and Family Therapy, 6*, 159–166.

Beavers, J., Hampson, R. B., Hulgus, Y. F. & Beavers, W. R. (1986). Coping in families with a retarded child. *Family Process, 25*, 365–378.

Beavers, W. R. (1981). A systems model of family for family therapists. *Journal of Marital and Family Therapy, 7*, 299–307.

Beavers, W. R., Hampson, R. B. & Hulgus, Y. F. (1985). Commentary: The Beavers systems approach to family assessment. *Family Process, 24*, 398–405.

Bee, H. L., Van Egeren, L. F., Streissguth, A. P., Nyman, B. A. & Leckie, M. S. (1969). Social class differences in maternal teaching strategies and speech patterns. *Developmental Psychology, 2*, 726–734.

Blood, R. O., Jr. & Wolfe, D. M. (1978). Negro-White differences in blue-collar marriages in a northern metropolis. In R. Staples (Ed.), *The Black family: Essays and studies*. Belmont, CA: Wadsworth Publishing Co., Inc. (171–178).

Diaz-Guerrero, R. (1975). *Psychology of the Mexican: Cultural and personality*. Austin, TX: University of Texas Press.

Eshleman, J. R. (1985). *The family* (4th ed.). Boston: Allyn & Bacon.

Falicov, C. J. (1982). Mexican families. In M. McGoldrick, J. K. Pearce & J. Giordano, (Eds.), *Ethnicity and family therapy*, New York: Guilford (134–163).

Hampson, R. B., Beavers, W. R. & Hulgus, Y. F. (1988). Commentary: Comparing the Beavers and Circumplex Models of family functioning. *Family Process, 27*, 85–92.

Hampson, R. B., Hulgus, Y. F., Beavers, W. R. & Beavers, J. S. (1988). The assessment of competence in families with a retarded child. *Journal of Family Psychology, 2*, 32–53.

Henggeler, S. W. & Tavormina, J. B. (1980). Social class and race differences in family interaction: Pathological, normative, or confounding methodological factors? *Journal of Genetic Psychology, 137*, 211–222.

Hines, P. M. & Boyd-Franklin, N. (1982). Black families, In M. McGoldrick, J. K. Pearce & J. Giordano, *Ethnicity and family therapy*. New York: Guilford.

Jacob, T. (1975). Family interaction in disturbed and normal families: A methodological and substantive review. *Psychological Bulletin, 82*, 33–65.

Kelsey-Smith, M. & Beavers, W. R. (1981). Family assessment: Centripetal and centrifugal family systems. *American Journal of Family Therapy, 9*, 3–12.

Lewis, J. M., Beavers, W. R., Gossett, J. T. & Phillips, V. A. (1976). *No single thread: Psychological health in family systems*. New York: Brunner/Mazel.

Lewis, J. M. & Looney, J. G. (1983). *The long struggle: Well functioning working-class Black families*. New York: Brunner-Mazel.

Levine, E. S. & Padilla, A. M. (1980) *Crossing cultures in therapy*. Belmont, CA: Wadsworth.

Mindel, C. & Haberstein, R. (Eds.). (1976). *Ethnic families in America*. New York: Elsevier.

Pinderhughes, E. (1982). Afro-American families and the victim system. In M. McGoldrick, J. K. Pearce & J. Giordano, *Ethnicity and family therapy*. New York: Guilford.

Staples, R. (1971). Toward a sociology of the Black family: A theoretical and methodological assessment. *Journal of Marriage and the Family, 33*, 119–138.

Staples, R. & Mirande, A. (1980). Racial and cultural variations among American families: A decennial review of the literature on minority families. *Journal of Marriage and the Family, 42*, 886–903.

U.S. Bureau of Census. (1983). *Current population reports, Household and family characteristics: March 1982* (Series P-20, No. 381). Washington, DC: U.S. Government Printing Office.

Willie, C. V. (1974). The Black family and social class. *American Journal of Orthopsychiatry, 44*, 50–60.

Willie, C. V. (1985). *Black and White families: A study in complementarity*. Bayside, NY: General Hall, Inc.

NOTE

[1]This article was accepted during the tenure of the previous editor.

20 Income Level, Gender, Ethnicity, and Household Composition as Predictors of Children's School-Based Competence

Charlotte J. Patterson, Janis B. Kupersmidt, and Nancy A. Vaden
University of Virginia

PATTERSON, CHARLOTTE J.; KUPERSMIDT, JANIS B.; and VADEN, NANCY A. *Income Level, Gender, Ethnicity, and Household Composition as Predictors of Children's School-Based Competence.* CHILD DEVELOPMENT, 1990, **61**, 485–494. In the United States, being black, male, or growing up in a low-income and/or single-parent household have all been identified as risk factors for maladjustment during childhood. Interpretation of these findings is, however, often difficult because of the well-known associations among these variables. In the present study, we compared predictions of 3 different forms of children's competence from each of these 4 variables. In a sample of 868 black and white elementary school children from 2-parent and mother-headed 1-parent homes, we studied 3 aspects of school-based competence: conduct, peer relations, and academic achievement. Results showed that although the independent variables accounted for different amounts of variance in each domain of competence, income level and gender were better overall predictors of children's competence in conduct and peer relations than were ethnicity or household composition. Income level and ethnicity were better overall predictors of academic achievement than were gender or household composition, although each of the 4 variables made a significant contribution. Overall, income level and gender were thus the strongest predictors of children's competence. Black children were, however, more likely than white children to live in low-income homes. Our results thus highlighted some correlates of the unequal distribution of economic resources among black and white children growing up in the United States today.

Competence among children may be assessed in schools, neighborhoods, churches, and/or other community settings (Bronfenbrenner, 1979; Bronfenbrenner, Moen, & Garbarino, 1984). Especially for children who are members of minority groups, effective functioning in some settings such as their homes and neighborhoods may require different skills than effective functioning in other settings, such as their schools (Holliday, 1985; Ogbu, 1981, 1985). In the present study, we focus on predictors of children's school-based competence.

We view competence as the achievement by appropriate means of successful outcomes in particular domains. In the current study, we focus attention on three especially important domains of children's competence at school: peer relations, behavior or conduct, and academic achievement. Because children's competence in each of these domains has been linked to probability of subsequent school dropout, delinquency, and psychopathology (Parker & Asher, 1987; Rutter & Garmezy, 1983), there is reason to believe that each is an important domain of children's competence.

Poverty, gender, ethnicity, and household composition have all been associated with various indices of school-based competence among American children. Being male, of minority ethnic status, and growing up in low-income, single-parent homes have all been identified as heightening the risk of disturbances in peer relations (Coie, Dodge, & Kupersmidt, in press; Hallinan, 1981; Patterson, Vaden, & Kupersmidt, 1989). Each of these factors has also been associated with higher incidence of behavior problems and psychological disorders (Rutter & Garmezy, 1983) and, except for gender, with lower academic achievement in school (Alexander &

This work was supported in part by a grant from the W. Alton Jones Foundation. We wish to thank Pamela Griesler for technical assistance, William P. Gardner for statistical advice, Vincent Cibbarelli and the staff and students of the Charlottesville Public Schools for their cooperation, and our anonymous reviewers for their helpful suggestions. Janis B. Kupersmidt is now at the Department of Psychology, University of North Carolina at Chapel Hill. Requests for reprints should be sent to Charlotte J. Patterson, Department of Psychology, Gilmer Hall, University of Virginia, Charlottesville, VA 22903.

Entwisle, 1988; Bronfenbrenner et al., 1984; Entwisle & Hayduk, 1982; Neisser, 1986).

One of the difficulties in interpretation of such associations is the well-known fact that for American children, poverty, ethnicity, and the likelihood of growing up in single-parent homes are themselves interrelated (Edelman, 1985, 1987; Glick, 1988; Laosa, 1988; Slaughter, 1988). Of children under 18 years of age in the United States today, about one in five lives in a home that is below the federally defined poverty line; of black children, however, almost half live in poverty. Similarly, female-headed households are disproportionately represented among the poor; almost half of female-headed families are below the poverty line. In 1982, over 70% of black, female-headed households in this country were poor (Edelman, 1985). Black children are also more likely than white children to grow up in female-headed homes; for example, about half of all black children are born to single mothers (Laosa, 1988). In short, black children in this country are more likely than white children to grow up in low-income, mother-headed, single-parent homes (Edelman, 1985, 1987; Glick, 1988; Laosa, 1988; Slaughter, 1988; Wilson & Tolson, 1988).

Univariate analyses assessing the predictive value of any one of these variables are thus very likely to be confounded by the effects of the other variables as well. For example, the association of minority ethnic group membership and sociometric status in the study of children's peer relations (Hallinan, 1981) could in some cases be attributable at least in part to the effects of growing up in low-income and/or single-parent homes. Likewise, the greater incidence of behavior problems among children living in single-parent homes (Rutter & Garmezy, 1983) could result at least in part from the fact that many mother-headed single-parent families have low incomes (Emery, 1988). To assess the predictive value of these variables relative to one another, a multivariate approach is clearly needed.

In addition to the influence of family income, ethnicity, and household composition, another important predictor of at least some aspects of childhood competence is gender. Sex differences in behavior problems have been widely reported, with boys exhibiting more behavior problems during the childhood years (Rutter & Garmezy, 1983). Boys are also more likely than girls to show serious disturbances of peer relations during childhood (Coie, Dodge, & Coppotelli, 1982; Hartup, 1983). In addition, boys appear to suffer more adverse effects of economic deprivation and single-parent rearing than do girls (Elder, 1979; Hetherington, Camara, & Featherman, 1981).

Concern has recently been voiced about development among black males in particular. Noting low school achievement and high behavior problems shown by black male children and youth, Hare and Castenell (1985) have argued that black boys should be seen as an at-risk group. It is not yet clear, however, to what extent the difficulties of black boys may be associated with economic hardship rather than, or in addition to, ethnicity as such. Spencer, Dobbs, and Phillips (1988) recently reported that poverty had more deleterious effects for black boys than it did for black girls. Because there were no white children in their sample, however, the possible influence of ethnicity could not be assessed. Research is needed to disentangle the contributions of gender, ethnicity, income, and household composition (Hofferth, 1985).

The present study was conducted to evaluate income level, gender, ethnicity, and household composition as predictors of children's competence at school. We used data from a large community sample of elementary school children that included significant numbers of black and white children growing up in both one- and two-parent homes that were or were not described by teachers as having low incomes. We studied three different indices of competence: peer relations, assessed via sociometric nominations; conduct, assessed via teacher ratings of classroom behavior; and academic achievement, assessed via scores on standardized achievement tests. In this way, we sought to explore the relations of the four independent variables to different aspects of school-based competence among elementary school children.

Method

Subjects.—The subjects were 868 children in grades 2 through 4, enrolled in the six public elementary schools of a small Southern city. The sample is described in greater detail below.

Materials.—Teacher ratings of classroom behavior were collected using a reduced version of the Classroom Adjustment Rating Scales (CARS—Lorion, Cowen, & Caldwell, 1975). The CARS was developed as an instrument for assessing school behavior problems of elementary school aged children. We administered subscales for Acting Out and for

Shy Anxious behavior. Teachers rated the severity of each child's behavior problems on 5-point scales (1 = not a problem, 5 = a serious problem).

Factor analysis of responses failed to replicate the factor structure reported by Lorion et al. (1975), and hence further factor-analytic work was undertaken. Reduced versions of each of the two scales proved to have more satisfactory psychometric properties (i.e., all items loading above .50 on their own and below .40 on the other subscale), and these were used in the present study.

The five items on the reduced Acting Out subscale were (1) overly aggressive to peers, (2) constantly seeks attention, (3) disruptive in class, (4) fidgety, hyperactive, can't stay in seat, (5) talks out of turn, disturbs others. The four items on the reduced Shy Anxious subscale were (1) shy, timid, (2) anxious, (3) depressed, and (4) lacks self-confidence. A total Behavior Problems score was obtained by summing each child's scores on the two reduced subscales, and it was used in all further analyses as the measure of children's conduct at school (range of scores was from 9 to 41).

Family income (coded dichotomously as "low" versus "not low") was assessed as part of a teacher checklist of family background variables. Teachers were asked to indicate those children who came from families characterized by economic difficulty, which was defined as whether or not the family received public assistance (i.e., the child had free or reduced price lunches at school and/or the child's family lived in subsidized housing). Children who were identified in this way were coded as living in low-income homes. No further information about family incomes was available to us, and so all others were simply coded as "not low income."

Procedure.—Group sociometric testing was conducted in each classroom by an adult experimenter and one or two aides according to the procedures adopted by Coie et al. (1982). Children were presented with an alphabetized list of peers in their grade (for third and fourth graders) or in their class (for second graders) and were asked to nominate three children whom they liked most and three whom they liked least.

While the sociometric testing was conducted in his or her classroom, each teacher was individually interviewed in a separate room. The interviewer read each item aloud and recorded the teacher's responses. Teachers were provided with class rosters to aid their memories, and were asked to report the answers which, in their experience, were most appropriate for each child.

Information about each child's gender, ethnicity, and household composition was collected from school records. Ethnicity was coded as white, black, or other; since there were too few children in the other category ($n = 30$) to allow statistical analyses in the present framework, they were dropped from these analyses. Household composition was coded as living with both parents, with mother only, or other; again, since there were too few children in the other category ($n = 35$), they were dropped from the sample for these analyses. All analyses were conducted using the remaining sample of 868 children.

SRA achievement tests had been administered to all children the month before we conducted the classroom assessments and teacher interviews. We used each child's composite (reading/math/language) national percentile score, also collected from school records, as an index of academic achievement. The scores covered the full range, from the first to the ninety-ninth percentile.

Coding of the sociometric nomination data was accomplished using the criteria and procedures developed by Coie and his colleagues (1982). Standardized liked-most and liked-least scores were computed to derive values for a child's social preference among peers (the difference between standardized liked-most and standardized liked-least nominations). These were then restandardized to yield the social preference scores used here (see Coie et al., 1982).

Reliability of teacher reports.—Because each child had only one classroom teacher, interrater reliability of teacher ratings of behavior problems could not be assessed. The fact that siblings share the same home environment did, however, suggest a method for assessing the reliability of teacher reports about low income homes. Sibling pairs were identified in the sample by locating pairs of children who shared the same last name, same parent name, and same home address in the school records. Teacher reports of low income were then compared for the two siblings. Since none of the sibling pairs were in the same classroom, these two reports were always provided by two different teachers.

There were 73 sibling pairs for whom teacher checklist information about low family income was available; of these 61, or 84%,

TABLE 1

NUMBERS OF CHILDREN IN THE SAMPLE AS A FUNCTION OF INCOME LEVEL, GENDER, ETHNICITY, AND HOUSEHOLD COMPOSITION

| | LOW INCOME |||| NOT LOW INCOME |||| |
| | 2 Parent || 1 Parent || 2 Parent || 1 Parent || |
	Black	White	Black	White	Black	White	Black	White	TOTALS
Girls	25	17	82	41	35	174	31	46	451
Boys	14	25	90	31	32	165	31	29	417
Totals	39	42	172	72	67	339	62	75	868

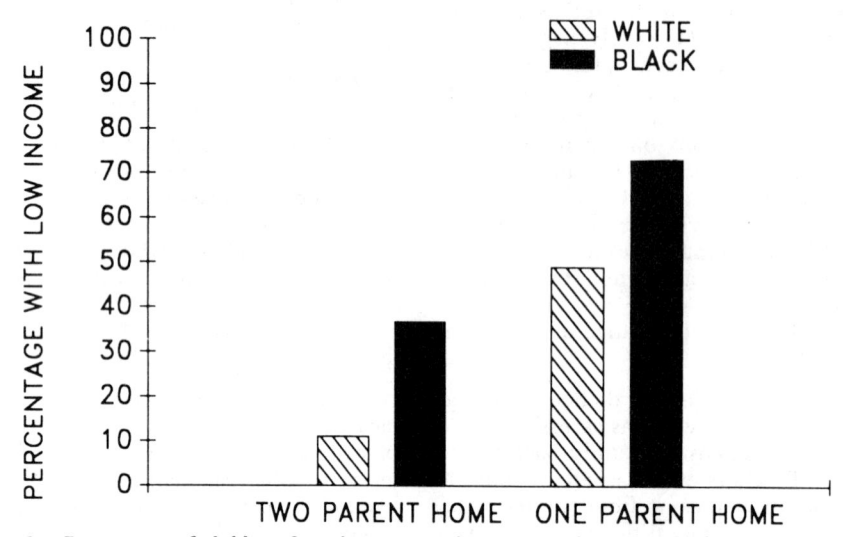

FIG. 1.—Percentage of children from low-income homes as a function of ethnicity and household composition.

had the same score (kappa = .67). Thus, the teacher reports about family income showed satisfactory reliability.

Results

Sample characteristics and intercorrelations among variables.—The numbers of children in the sample in each category of income level, gender, ethnicity, and household composition are shown in Table 1. Although the distribution of children was uneven across categories, there were sufficient numbers of children in each of the major categories to allow analysis (see Table 1).

As expected on the basis of national figures, household composition, income level, and ethnicity were strongly related in this sample. For example, children from single-parent homes were three times as likely as those from two-parent homes, and black children were twice as likely as white children, to come from low-income homes. In addition, black children were twice as likely as white children to live with only one parent. The net result of these trends is shown in Figure 1, which shows that the probability of low income in this sample ranged from 11% for white children growing up in two-parent homes to 73.5% for black children growing up in one-parent homes.

The intercorrelations of all variables are shown in Table 2. As expected, both the independent and the dependent variables were intercorrelated to some degree. The relatively high correlations among ethnicity, household composition, and income level were, of course, consistent with the frequencies of children in each category presented above. Consistent with earlier findings (Green, Forehand, Beck, & Vosk, 1980), correlations among the three measures of competence were significant (see Table 2), accounting on average for about 10% of the variance. Thus,

TABLE 2
INTERCORRELATIONS OF VARIABLES

Variables	1	2	3	4	5	6
1. Income level		.414***	.462***	−.147***	.183***	.391***
2. Ethnicity	.402***		.333***	−.050	.046	.340***
3. Household composition	.513***	.479***		−.101*	.129**	.257***
4. Conduct	−.298***	−.240***	−.279***		−.276***	−.325***
5. Peer relations	.220***	.039	.153***	−.328***		.241***
6. Achievement	.409***	.411***	.356***	−.416***	.238***	

NOTE.—Low income, black, male, and one parent were coded as 0; not low income, white, female, and two-parent homes were coded as 1. The measure of conduct was the total number of behavior problems; of peer relations, it was standardized social preference scores; and of achievement, it was national percentile scores for composite reading/math/language achievement (see text). Correlations for girls are shown above and those for boys below the diagonal.

* $p < .05$.
** $p < .01$.
*** $p < .001$.

although there was a significant tendency for children who were highly competent in one domain to be competent in others, there was also considerable variability.

Prediction of child competence in three domains.—Taking into account the intercorrelations among independent variables, our major questions focused on the relative contributions of each of the four predictor variables to prediction of child competence. To examine this issue, a series of simultaneous (standard) regression analyses were conducted, using income level, gender, ethnicity, household composition, and their interactions as independent variables. In these analyses, the dependent measure for peer relations was each child's standardized social preference score; for conduct, it was total score for teacher-rated behavior problems; and for academic achievement, it was the national percentile score for composite reading/math/language achievement. Significant results of the regression analyses are summarized in Table 3.

Overall, the predictors accounted for 20% of the variance in scores for conduct. As can be seen in Table 3, there were four main effects, which revealed that, as expected, boys, those from low-income families, those from one-parent homes, and black children were rated as having more behavior problems at school.

These main effects were, however, qualified by significant interactions. The income × gender interaction resulted from the fact that, although the basic findings were similar and statistically significant for both sexes, income level was more strongly related to conduct scores for boys than for girls (standardized regression coefficients = −.19 and −.11, respectively, both p's < .05). Boys from low-income families showed more behavior problems (mean = 18.7) than boys from other families (mean = 14.3); the same effect was also present, though smaller in size, for girls (means = 12.9 and 11.7, for low-income versus other families, respectively).

Examination of the ethnicity × household composition interaction revealed that household composition had a significant effect on conduct for white children (standard regression coefficient = −.19, $p < .001$); white children from one-parent homes had more behavior problems (mean = 14.7) than white children from two-parent homes (mean = 12.7). For black children, there were no differences in conduct as a function of household composition (standard regression coefficient = −.01, N.S.; means = 15.6 and 14.1 for black children from one- and from two-parent homes, respectively).

The two-way ethnicity × household composition interaction was, however, itself qualified by a three-way interaction involving ethnicity, household composition, and income level. The three-way interaction revealed that income level was significantly related to behavior problems in three of the four ethnicity × household composition subgroups. Children from low-income families were rated as showing more behavior problems than children from other (i.e., middle-income) families in white one-parent (means = 16.2 and 13.2), black one-parent (means = 16.2 and 14.2), and black two-parent (means = 15.5 and 13.4) homes (standardized regression coefficients = −.22, −.12, and −.24, respectively; all p's < .05). Only among white children from two-parent homes did income level fail to predict behavior problems at a

TABLE 3

SUMMARY OF SIMULTANEOUS MULTIPLE REGRESSION ANALYSES FOR PREDICTION OF CHILD COMPETENCE IN CONDUCT, PEER RELATIONS, AND ACADEMIC ACHIEVEMENT

PREDICTOR VARIABLES	DOMAIN OF COMPETENCE		
	Conduct	Peer Relations	Academic Achievement
Gender (G)	−2.42***	.14***	4.60***
Income (I)	−1.03***	.19***	7.78***
Household (H)	−.62**	.07	2.30*
Ethnicity (E)	−.55*	−.06	7.21***
G × I	.56*	−.04	.22
G × H	.22	.00	−.22
G × E	.42	.03	−.35
I × E	.21	.05	1.22
I × H	.15	.02	.59
E × H	.56*	.04	1.78
G × I × H	.34	−.06	−.24
G × I × E	−.14	−.06	−.09
G × H × E	.25	.05	.42
I × H × E	.48*	−.04	−1.61
G × I × H × E	−.02	.00	−1.74
Overall R^2	.20	.07	.25

NOTE.—Because standardized regression coefficients are constrained by the dichotomous nature of the predictor variables, only unstandardized regression coefficients are shown here.

* $p < .05$.
** $p < .01$.
*** $p < .001$.

significant level, and even in this case, the results were in the same direction (means = 13.4 and 12.6 for children from low-income and middle-income homes, respectively; standardized regression coefficient = −.03, N.S.). Compared to other variables we studied, then, these results underline the relative generality of family income level as a predictor of children's conduct at school.

Overall, the predictors accounted for 7% of the variance in peer relations. Income level was the best predictor, followed by gender; there were no significant interactions. Boys and children from low-income homes were less well liked by their peers at school than were other children.

Overall, the predictors accounted for 25% of the variance in academic achievement. The best predictors were income level and ethnicity, followed by gender and household composition. Children from low-income homes, black children, boys, and those from single-parent homes scored lower on tests of achievement.

In summary, although the independent variables accounted for different amounts of variance in each domain of competence, income level and gender emerged as the best overall predictors. Gender was the strongest predictor of competence in conduct, and income level was the strongest predictor of competence in achievement and in peer relations. As in previous research, ethnicity was a strong predictor of academic achievement test scores in this sample. For conduct and for peer relations, however, results of the regression analyses showed that ethnicity was overshadowed by other predictors of children's competence at school.

Discussion

There were four major findings. First, income level and gender were better overall predictors of children's conduct and peer relations than were ethnicity or household composition. Boys and children from low-income homes were less likely than other children to be competent across domains. Second, income level and ethnicity were the best predictors of academic achievement; blacks and those from low-income homes received lower scores. Third, prediction was better for some domains of competence than others. The predictors accounted for more of the variance in measures of children's conduct and academic achievement than they did in measures of peer relations. Finally, and consistent with national figures, there were strong associations among all of the predictor variables except gender; black children were more likely than white children to live in low-income and/or single-parent homes. Thus, although income and gender were the strongest overall predictors of competence at school, some domains of competence were predicted better than others, and black children were more likely than white children to live in low-income homes.

These results can be seen as generally consistent with what Edelman (1987) has called the "social class view" of black families. From this standpoint, poverty is the most important variable accounting for observed differences in functioning between black and white children. This perspective suggests both that discrimination and economic inequities suffered by blacks result in their increased likelihood of living in poverty, and that problems engendered by economic stress have a negative impact on child competence at school. If their families were provided with equal economic circumstances and compensation for past inequities, black children would be expected from this viewpoint to perform as well at school as white children (Edelman, 1987).

From the standpoint of the social class view, a number of possible pathways from economic stress to low child competence might be suggested (see Rubin, LeMare, & Lollis, in press). As we have reported elsewhere, there was a significant association in this sample between family background and the likelihood that children had recently experienced stressful life events (Patterson et al., 1989). The direct effects of such stressors on children might include lowered mood, reduced attention span, and/or emotional distress. Effects of stress on parents might also have adverse consequences for children through reduced parental involvement in their schooling (Stevenson & Baker, 1987) and/or reduced parental monitoring and attention (Patterson, 1986). Investigation of such possibilities is an important task for future research.

Although consistent with different versions of the social class view just described, our results by no means establish the causal patterns suggested by this hypothesis. Many other explanatory frameworks would be equally consistent with the present data. For example, some (e.g., Scarr, 1981) have entertained the possibility that differences in genetic endowments might account for variations in both family income and child competence. Others (Ogbu, 1981, 1985) have emphasized the degree to which black children in poverty grow up in a cultural environment that devalues academic achievement and other types of school-related success. The present study was not designed to evaluate these alternative explanations of ethnic group differences.

As a matter of fact, an interesting aspect of our results is the rather limited extent to which ethnic differences in competence emerged at all. Although ethnicity was an important predictor of academic achievement test scores, it contributed only modestly to prediction of conduct or peer relations. Particularly for conduct and for peer relations, ethnicity was overshadowed by income and gender as predictors of competence.

Although income contributed significantly to prediction of achievement and peer relations for both sexes, it contributed more to prediction of behavior problems for boys than for girls. Boys from low-income homes were rated as showing more behavior problems than boys from other homes, and this was true both for blacks and for whites. Although a greater proportion of black than white children in our sample suffered economic disadvantage, it was apparently low income rather than ethnicity that was most strongly associated with behavior problems among boys. These results suggest that concerns about black boys such as those expressed by Hare and Castenell (1985) should probably be extended to economic as well as ethnic issues.

As a predictor of behavior problems at school, however, income was a more important predictor for black than for white children of both sexes. Regardless of whether they lived with one parent or with two, black children from low-income families had more behavior problems than other black children. Among white children from one-parent families, those with low incomes also showed more behavior problems. Among white children from two-parent homes, however, there was no significant correlation between income level and behavior problems. In addition to its main effects on achievement and peer relations, then, family income was thus also a significant predictor of children's conduct in three of four race × household composition subgroups.

Although low income and gender were generally stronger predictors than ethnicity or household composition in this study, much of the variance in child competence remained unexplained. For instance, no combination of the predictors accounted for as much as a third of the variance in any domain of child competence. In addition to revealing the importance of the demographic variables relative to one another, then, our results also provide estimates of the absolute size of their associations with child competence. As these estimates make clear, many other variables must be considered before a complete understanding of children's school-based competence will emerge.

In this research, we sampled three domains of children's school-based competence. We did not study other forms of competence relevant in school, such as skill in music, art, or athletics; nor did we examine aspects of child competence primarily associated with activities in nonschool settings such as homes, churches, or neighborhoods. Given the heterogeneity of children's levels of competence across three school-based domains, it seems likely that even greater variability will become apparent as competence in other domains is also examined.

The sex differences in competence that we observed are consistent with those reported in the literature (Rutter & Garmezy, 1983) for children at this age. Gender contributed most to prediction in the area of conduct, but it was also a significant predictor for achievement and for peer relations. In each case, girls showed greater competence. Although boys show more adjustment problems than girls during childhood, the trend apparently reverses in adolescence (Rutter & Garmezy, 1983). In future work, it will be interesting to compare gender effects in early adolescence.

From a methodological standpoint, concerns might be raised about the reliability of school records that we used to assess household composition. Although household composition was probably quite stable from month to month for most families represented in this sample, it may be that, for some families, it was more volatile. To the extent that any recent changes in household composition were not reflected in the official school records, their impact would not be evident in the cross-sectional data we have presented here. Concerns about this issue could be addressed by longitudinal research that takes such changes in household composition over time into account. In the context of the present study, however, the contributions of changes in household composition over time cannot be evaluated.

Another interpretive issue relates to the partial nonindependence of data sources employed in the present study. Although information about children's competence in the academic and peer domains was obtained independently of teacher reports about income level, this was not the case for our assessments of children's behavior problems. For this reason, the possibility of negative teacher bias with respect to the conduct of low-income children cannot be ruled out, nor can the possibility that some teachers may regard low income as a factor in children's behavior problems at school. As a result, some caution should be exercised when considering conclusions about the relations of income level and behavior problems, based on our current data. In future work, it would be preferable to obtain information from entirely independent sources.

In summary, this study was conducted to compare the strength of four demographic predictors of children's school-based competence in three domains. Results showed that, although ethnicity was a strong predictor of achievement test scores, low income and gender were stronger overall predictors of children's competence across domains than ethnicity or household composition. The likelihood of children living in a low-income home was, however, itself strongly linked to ethnicity and to household composition; black children were more likely to live in single-parent and/or low-income homes. Our results thus highlighted some correlates of the unequal distribution of economic resources among black and white children growing up in the United States today.

References

Alexander, K. L., & Entwisle, D. R. (1988). Achievement in the first two years of school: Patterns and processes. *Monographs of the Society for Research in Child Development*, 53(2, Serial No. 218).

Bronfenbrenner, U. (1979). *The ecology of human development: Experiments by nature and design*. Cambridge, MA: Harvard University Press.

Bronfenbrenner, U., Moen, P., & Garbarino, J. (1984). Child, family, and community. In R. D. Parke (Ed.), *Review of child development research: Vol. 7. The family* (pp. 283–328). Chicago: University of Chicago Press.

Coie, J. D., Dodge, K. A., & Coppotelli, R. (1982). Dimensions and types of social status: A cross age perspective. *Developmental Psychology*, 18, 557–570.

Coie, J. D., Dodge, K. A., & Kupersmidt, J. B. (in press). Peer group behavior and social status. In S. R. Asher & J. D. Coie (Eds.), *Peer rejection in childhood*. New York: Cambridge University Press.

Edelman, M. W. (1985). The sea is so wide and my boat is so small: Problems facing black children today. In H. P. McAdoo & J. L. McAdoo (Eds.), *Black children: Social, educational, and parental environments* (pp. 72–82). Beverly Hills, CA: Sage.

Edelman, M. W. (1987). *Families in peril: An agenda for social change*. Cambridge, MA: Harvard University Press.

Elder, G. H. (1979). Historical change in life patterns and personality. In P. B. Baltes & O. G. Brim, Jr. (Eds.), *Life span development and behavior* (Vol. 2, pp. 117–159). New York: Academic Press.

Emery, R. E. (1988). *Marriage, divorce, and children's adjustment*. Beverly Hills, CA: Sage.

Entwisle, D. R., & Hayduk, L. A. (1982). *Early schooling*. Baltimore: Johns Hopkins University Press.

Glick, P. C. (1988). Demographic pictures of black families. In H. P. McAdoo (Ed.), *Black families* (pp. 111–132). Beverly Hills, CA: Sage.

Green, K. D., Forehand, R., Beck, S. J., & Vosk, B. (1980). An assessment of the relationship among measures of children's social competence and children's academic achievement. *Child Development*, 51, 1149–1156.

Hallinan, M. T. (1981). Recent advances in sociometry. In S. R. Asher & J. M. Gottman (Eds.), *The development of children's friendships* (pp. 91–115). New York: Cambridge University Press.

Hare, B. R., & Castenell, L. A., Jr. (1985). No place to run, no place to hide: Comparative status and future prospects of black boys. In M. B. Spencer, G. K. Brookins, & W. R. Allen (Eds.), *Beginnings: The social and affective development of black children* (pp. 201–214). Hillsdale, NJ: Erlbaum.

Hartup, W. W. (1983). The peer system. In E. M. Hetherington (Ed.), P. H. Mussen (Series Ed.), *Handbook of child psychology: Vol. 4. Socialization, personality, and social development* (pp. 103–196). New York: Wiley.

Hetherington, E. M., Camara, K. A., & Featherman, D. L. (1981). Achievement and intellectual functioning in one-parent households. In J. Spence (Ed.), *Assessing achievement* (pp. 205–284). San Francisco: W. H. Freeman.

Hofferth, S. L. (1985). Children's life course: Family structure and living arrangements in cohort perspective. In G. H. Elder (Ed.), *Life course dynamics: Trajectories and transitions* (pp. 75–112). Ithaca, NY: Cornell University Press.

Holliday, B. G. (1985). Towards a model of teacher-child transactional processes affecting black children's academic achievement. In M. B. Spencer, G. K. Brookins, & W. R. Allen (Eds.), *Beginnings: The social and affective development of black children* (pp. 117–130). Hillsdale, NJ: Erlbaum.

Laosa, L. M. (1988). Ethnicity and single parenting in the United States. In E. M. Hetherington & J. D. Arasteh (Eds.), *Impact of divorce, single parenting, and stepparenting on children* (pp. 23–49). Hillsdale, NJ: Erlbaum.

Lorion, R. P., Cowen, E. L., & Caldwell, R. A. (1975). Normative and parametric analyses of school adjustment. *American Journal of Community Psychology*, 3, 291–301.

Neisser, U. (Ed.). (1986). *The school achievement of minority children: New perspectives*. Hillsdale, NJ: Erlbaum.

Ogbu, J. U. (1981). Origins of human competence: A cultural-ecological perspective. *Child Development*, 52, 413–429.

Ogbu, J. U. (1985). A cultural ecology of competence among inner-city blacks. In M. B. Spencer, G. K. Brookins, & W. R. Allen (Eds.), *Beginnings: The social and affective development of black children* (pp. 775–911). Hillsdale, NJ: Erlbaum.

Parker, J., & Asher, S. R. (1987). Peer acceptance and later personal adjustment: Are low accepted children "at risk"? *Psychological Bulletin*, 102, 357–389.

Patterson, C. J., Vaden, N., & Kupersmidt, J. B. (1989). *Family background, recent life events, and peer rejection during childhood*. Unpublished manuscript, Department of Psychology, University of Virginia.

Patterson, G. R. (1986). Performance models for antisocial boys. *American Psychologist*, 41, 431–444.

Rubin, K. H., LeMare, L., & Lollis, S. (in press). Social withdrawal in childhood: Developmental pathways to peer rejection. In S. R. Asher & J. D. Coie (Eds.), *Peer rejection in childhood*. New York: Cambridge University Press.

Rutter, M., & Garmezy, N. (1983). Developmental psychopathology. In E. M. Hetherington (Ed.), P. H. Mussen (Series Ed.), *Handbook of child psychology: Vol. 4. Socialization, personality, and social development* (pp. 775–911). New York: Wiley.

Scarr, S. (1981). *Race, social class, and individual differences in IQ*. Hillsdale, NJ: Erlbaum.

Slaughter, D. T. (Ed.). (1988). *Black children and

poverty: A developmental perspective. New Directions for Child Development, No. 42. San Francisco: Jossey-Bass.

Spencer, M. B., Dobbs, B., & Phillips, D. (1988). African American adolescents: Adaptational processes and socioeconomic diversity in behavioral outcomes. *Journal of Adolescence,* **11,** 117–137.

Stevenson, D. L., & Baker, D. P. (1987). The family-school relation and the child's school performance. *Child Development,* **58,** 1348–1357.

Wilson, M. N., & Tolson, T. F. J. (1988). Single parenting in the context of three-generational black families. In E. M. Hetherington & J. D. Arasteh (Eds.), *Impact of divorce, single parenting, and stepparenting on children* (pp. 215–241). Hillsdale, NJ: Erlbaum.

21 Cultural Differences—Be Aware!

Robert D. Morrow

The vast differences in various cultures require that teachers, when conferencing with Southeast Asian parents, approach the subject of exceptionality with insight and caution.

When I recently took my faculty leave from the University of the Pacific, my focus was on the impact of special education on Southeast Asians, including Vietnamese, Cambodian, and Laotian. I intended to study learning styles, learning modalities, and ways of assessing the ever-growing numbers of Southeast Asian refugees in our school system.

As I read about and discussed the topic with colleagues, I found I was in for a rude awakening! Southeast Asian cultural attitudes toward "singling out" any individual in their society as being "different" in any way (gifted, talented, or handicapped) are literally worlds apart from expectations prevalent in the United States—i.e., meeting the needs of all individuals in our society.

Indeed, the struggle to achieve the goal of providing education for all handicapped individuals in the U.S., ages 3-21, was a difficult one. It took dozens of court cases, years of parental pressure, and the dedication of forward-thinking educators and legislators to gain passage of PL94-142, which guarantees the educational civil rights of handicapped individuals. Parents and educators alike hailed this new law as special education's "finest hour."

Today, screening, diagnosing, and placing handicapped students in the least restrictive environment are routine. IEP meetings, individualized goals, one-on-one help for handicapped students abound in our school systems.

But, when identifying and serving handicapped Southeast Asian students, let me offer some advice: *proceed with caution!*

Child-Rearing Practices Differ

United States. In the U.S. we begin early to groom our children to become independent. We stress early weaning, dressing and feeding oneself at the preschool level, thinking for yourself, being your "own person," and becoming self-sufficient children and adults.

Almost as soon as an American child is born, he sleeps by himself, often in his own bedroom. Toys and other possessions are identified as "mine" or "yours." American parents foster self-reliance, assertiveness, speaking one's mind, and looking out for "number one."

Southeast Asians. With the Southeast Asians, the opposite is true.

Southeast Asian children are taught from an early age to view their role within the family and society in terms of relationships and obligations. Each family member must develop a sense of moral obligation and primary loyalty to the family. Cultural values dictate that only those behaviors that maintain and enhance the family name and home are considered valuable.

Thus, there is a strict code of conduct expected of all Southeast Asian family members. In contrast to the American emphasis on egocentric, independent behavior, the Southeast Asian child is trained to think of the family first and must learn to subjugate his own personal desires and concerns. Parents, in an attempt to control their child's behavior, appeal to the child's sense of obligation to others (Chan 1986).

If this sense of obligation is betrayed, the consequences are severe. Such forms of punishment as locking the child outside the house, isolating the child from the family social life, shaming the child, scolding or guilt induction that results in a "loss of face" are commonplace in Southeast Asian households.

From Robert D. Morrow, "Cultural Differences—Be Aware!" *Academic Therapy*, Vol. 23: 143-149, 1987. Copyright © 1987 by PRO-ED, Inc. Reprinted by permission.

"Pride and Shame" Principle

Chan (1986) indicates that the "pride and shame" principle has a tremendous impact on Southeast Asian family members. This principle states that all individual behavior reflects, either positively or negatively, on the entire family. On the one hand, highly-valued individual academic and/or occupational achievements promote family pride. But, on the other hand, negatively-valued behavior (e.g., disobedience, disrespect, shirking responsibilities) results in a collective family shame.

Included in the category "negative-valued behavior" are such handicapping conditions as severe emotional disturbance, mental retardation, and physical or sensory disabilities. These are viewed by Southeast Asians with considerable stigma (Chan 1986). Such stigma is related to Southeast Asian beliefs in what causes handicaps.

One of the more common explanations for a handicap is that the condition represents a punishment for sins or moral transgressions committed by the child's parents or his ancestors. Another cause, as perceived by Southeast Asians, is the assumption that the handicapped person is possessed by demons, ghosts, or evil spirits. For example, the mother of a child with a cleft palate believed that the handicap was related to her having seen horror films and pictures of evil gods during the early stages of her pregnancy. Another mother of an autistic child insisted that her temper outbursts during her pregnancy caused the child's disorder (Chan-sew 1980).

Still another belief held by Southeast Asians to explain handicapping conditions is an imbalance in the mind-body relationships and the principle that overall health is maintained when the forces of "Yin" and "Yang" are balanced and in harmony. If an imbalance occurs, according to many Southeast Asians, illness results. This imbalance may be an unbalanced diet, including drinking inadequate amounts of beef bone soup during pregnancy, eating veal or lamb (which is believed to cause epilepsy), eating bananas or watermelon. Excessive iron intake is believed by some to result in a fetus with hard bones, thus contributing to a potentially difficult labor and delivery (Chan 1986).

According to Lim-Yee (1983), the classic grief-cycle phases such as denial and guilt are directly affected by cultural values and beliefs. This, then, challenges the assumption that parents of handicapped children, regardless of the culture, proceed through an ordered sequence of discrete "stages of adjustment" and ultimately attain a final stage of acceptance.

For most Southeast Asians, life is presumed to be unalterable and unpredictable, requiring a resignation to external conditions and events over which they have little or no control. Accepting this fate, human suffering is part of the natural order. Maintaining inner strength, persevering without complaint and emotional strength under all circumstances is considered by Southeast Asians as an expression of dignity (Chan 1986).

Most importantly, each of these traditional views of the cause of handicaps creates overwhelming family shame, embarrassment, and stigma. A child's handicap forces the parents to cope with the impact their child's disability has on fulfilling academic and/or occupational achievements, the primary source of giving the family a "good name."

Working With Parents

Based on the views held by Southeast Asian parents about handicapped individuals and the underlying causes of a handicap, it is essential that special education teachers, at a minimum, do the following:

1. *Learn Cultural Differences.* Develop an understanding of those Southeast Asian cultural values that differ from our own. Many behaviors that we value and take for granted (e.g., openness, independence, directness) are not valued by Southeast Asians. (See Table 1 on next two pages for a detailed breakdown of selected contrasting behaviors.)

2. *Recognize the Family's "Face Saving" Needs.* As mentioned, many Southeast Asian parents of a handicapped child experience intense shame, guilt, and anxiety. Be cautious and don't discuss the problem too quickly (see Table 1) as Southeast Asians typically "talk around" the subject, especially one that evokes such feelings of guilt. Rather, spend time establishing personal rapport and allow a discussion that may be only indirectly related or completely unrelated to the problem. Gradually bring in your concern about their child. Proceed slowly.

3. *Develop a Sense of Trust.* Southeast Asians revere education (especially the Vietnamese) and rarely question educators' decisions. Be certain your diagnosis and placement of their child is professionally accomplished. Southeast Asians view their children as "gifts from heaven." Maintain this trust as you have tremendous power over both the parents and child.

TABLE 1
*A Comparison of American and Southeast Cultures (Selected Values)

	AMERICAN	VIETNAMESE	CAMBODIAN	LAOTIAN
1.	Realistic philosophy of life.	Geared more to spiritualism.	Same as Vietnamese.	Same as Vietnamese.
2.	Individual rights are most important.	Family, not the individual, is the basis of society.	Same as Vietnamese.	Same as Vietnamese.
3.	Americans make plans for the future.	Live on day-to-day basis (due to recent wars).	Same as Vietnamese.	Same as Vietnamese.
4.	Teachers do not get automatic respect from others.	Traditionally, teachers are more respected than parents.	Parents are more respected than teachers.	Parents are more respected than teachers.
5.	Young children have much independence.	Children must obey and respect their parents and do not have much independence.	Same as Vietnamese.	Same as Vietnamese.
6.	The family relationship is not always close.	Family relationship is very close.	Same as Vietnamese.	Same as Vietnamese.
7.	Children sleep in their own bedrooms.	Children often sleep with their parents.	Children often sleep with their parents (up to 10 years old).	Same as Vietnamese.
8.	Americans make eye contact in all situations.	While talking, Vietnamese should not look steadily at respected person's eyes.	Same as Vietnamese.	Same as Vietnamese.
9.	Americans can greet any one in the family first.	Greets the head of a family or an older person first.	Same as Vietnamese.	Same as Vietnamese.
10.	Punctuality is important.	Time is not part of their way of life.	Punctuality is important to city-dwellers, not to rural people.	Same as Vietnamese.
11.	Time is valuable.	Time is "elastic"; it can be stretched or contracted.	Same as Vietnamese.	Same as Vietnamese.
12.	Most of the population is Christian.	About 90% of the population practice ancestor worship or Buddhism.	96% of the population follow Buddhism, 2% are Christian, 2% are Moslem.	Same as Vietnamese.
13.	Man attempts to dominate nature.	Man is supposed to live in harmony with nature.	Same as Vietnamese.	Same as Vietnamese.
14.	Sons and daughters are valued equally.	Sons are valued more than daughters.	Same as Vietnamese.	Same as Vietnamese.
15.	Talking directly about the main subject is preferable.	Talk around a subject before coming to the point.	Same as Vietnamese.	Same as Vietnamese.
16.	A smile usually means happiness.	A smile can mean anything, happiness or sorrow, agreement or disagreement, understanding or not, etc.	Same as Vietnamese.	Same as Vietnamese.

*Adopted from the following materials: (Reproduced with permission)
1. *Vietnamese Themes,* The Regional Cross-Cultural Training and Regional Center. Title VII. Office of Bilingual Education, City of New York.
2. *Social/Cultural Custom*: Similarities and Differences Between Vietnamese-Cambodian-H'Mong-Lao, Team Associates, 1625 Eye Street, N.W., Washington, D.C. 20006.

References

Chan, S. 1986. Parents of exceptional Asian children. In M.K. Kitano and P.C. Chinn (Eds.), *Exceptional Asian and Youth*. Washington, D.C.: ERIC Exceptional Child Education Report, pp. 36–53.

Chan-sew, S. 1980. Issues and concerns in the provision of services to Asians with developmental disabilities. Paper presented at the First Annual Conference of the Committee on Asians with Developmental Disabilities, Berkeley, CA.

Leung, B. 1986. Psychoeducational assessment of Asian students. In M.K. Kitano and P.C. Chinn (Eds.), *Exceptional Asian and Youth*. Washington, D.C.: ERIC Exceptional Child Education Report, pp. 29–35.

Lim-Yee, N. 1983. Parental reactions to a special needs child: Cultural differences and Chinese families. Paper presented at the Annual Convention of the Western Psychological Association, San Francisco, CA.

Robert D. Morrow, EdD, is an associate professor in the Department of Special Education, School of Education, University of the Pacific, Stockton, CA 95211.

22 The Emerging Majority: Resources for Nonwhite Families in the United States

Robert Staples*

The nonwhite family as a concern of family life educators has enjoyed a renaissance in the last twenty years, partly as a result of this nation's increasing awareness of the growing number of nonwhite citizens in the United States. In addition to the above factor the augmentation of trade and cultural contacts with nonwhite nations has led to the need for objective studies of nonwhite peoples, including their family life. This article briefly reviews the history and characteristics of four nonwhite groups: American Indians, Asians, Black Americans and Latinos. The important books, articles, periodicals, and organizations are described and listed, with an emphasis on those most relevant to the family educator and practitioner.

In attempting to locate and describe resources for understanding racial and ethnic "minority" families it is necessary to begin by defining and classifying the groups to be included in that category. The term minority would appear to be a misnomer since it generally applies only to groups physically distinctive from the Euro-American majority in the United States. Black Americans, for instance, are not regarded as a "minority" solely due to their numbers but are differentiated from white ethnic groups based on physical traits such as skin color and hair texture. No serious student of race and ethnicity would suggest that the status of blacks can be legitimately compared to that of white American ethnic groups (e.g., Jews, Italians, Irish) (Mindel & Habenstein, 1988). Yet, a larger number of Black Americans can identify their ancestry to Africa than any white group can identify their ancestry with a single country except Germans (Hacker, 1983). Obviously, the concept of "minority" is based on much broader phenomenon than the relative size in the population. Ethnicity, for example, refers to a national identity and distinctive culture and language whereas minority status connotes a history of discrimination, social stratification, and phenotypic characteristics (Wilkinson & King, 1987).

The last 50 years have witnessed such changes in international migration, booming fertility rates, and volatile economic systems that would bring into question the use of national borders to define a group as a minority. The geopolitical changes of the last century have resulted in the decline of population in the largely white nations from 30% of the world's population to 15% in 1985. Thus, the groups that North America defines as minorities constitute about 85% of the world's population and the number is rising. In almost every predominantly white nation, Marxist, socialist, and capitalist, the downturn in fertility rates has resulted in zero population growth while 90% of population growth has occurred in nonwhite societies (Carlson, 1986). Of greater significance, with significant policy implications, is the fact that immigration patterns and fertility rates will irreducibly alter the racial composition of the largely white nations. Demographic projections are that the 10 most populous countries in the year 2100 will have a majority of nonwhite population, including the Soviet Union and the United States. By the year 2080, if current immigration and birthrate trends hold up, slightly less than half of all Americans will be non-Hispanic whites.

Variations within Racial Minorities

For classificatory purposes, the minority groups included in our discussion are American Indians, Black Americans, Asian-Americans and Latinos. While most of the groups and

---

*Robert Staples is Professor of Sociology, Department of Social and Behavioral Sciences, School of Nursing, N631-Box 0612, University of California, San Francisco, CA 94143.

Key Words: *ethnic, family, minority.*

From Robert Staples, "The Emerging Majority: Resources for Nonwhite Families in the United States," *Family Relations*, Vol. 37: 348-354, 1988. Copyright © 1988 by National Council on Family Relations, 3989 Central Avenue Northeast, Suite 550, Minneapolis, MN 55421. Reprinted by permission.

subgroups will deviate from the phenotypic norm and have a shared history of racial discrimination by the Euro-American majority, many individuals in those groups will share none of the above characteristics. Some Latinos, for instance, have the same phenotypical traits as the Euro-American majority and, depending on their country of origin, will have been members of the upper classes in those societies. The discrimination they still face will be based on their cultural difference and not their socioeconomic status or physical traits. Conversely, Japanese-Americans have one of the highest educational and economic attainments in the United States. Although one of the most acculturated groups in North America, they still have to confront current attitudes and practices of racial discrimination based on their physical differences. Black Americans and American Indians represent a special case since the first had involuntary entry into and the second were indigenous to this white settler nation. While having the longest tenure of all the racial "minorities," they are disproportionately subjected to poverty status and institutions insensitive or hostile to their aspirations.

Class differences exist in all the racial "minority" groups and are said to be more of a fundamental barrier than race to structural integration into American society. Yet the basic problem is that the Euro-American majority sees the minority groups as monolithic, independent of the minority groups' socioeconomic status. Much attention has been paid to the Black American family, not as a unique cultural institution but as the focus of social problems such as welfare dependency, teenage pregnancy, illegitimacy, and female-headed households. Yet a third of all black families earn $25,000 to $50,000 and are not the concern of any public policy (Landry, 1987). It is obvious that there are economic, not racial or cultural, factors behind those social problems. However, Black Americans of all social classes find themselves identified with the lowest members of their group while Euro-Americans are identified with the highest achieving members of their group (Wade, 1987).

Contemporary Literature on Minority Families

Given the importance of the four major groups in the future of American life, it is surprising to find there is very little literature on the family dynamics of these groups. There is not one textbook on the family lifestyle of any of the four groups. The Black American is the only group that has a substantial body of literature devoted to it and those works tend to be clustered in the area of gender roles, fertility, and the extended family (Mindel & Habenstein, 1988; Staples & Mirande, 1980). Although a majority of blacks are not married and living with a spouse, few works on Black Americans deal with male/female relationships, marriage, and divorce or sexuality (Staples, 1981, 1986). Moreover, the literature on black families is slanted toward poorer, lower income blacks and virtually ignores the 40% that is middle class and involved in stable families (Johnson, 1981).

While there is a substantial body of literature on black families, albeit limited to certain areas, the other "minority" families suffer from a paucity of research on their family system. Several factors account for the scarcity of family literature on American Indians, Asians, and Latinos. Whereas Black Americans are visible and represented in most regions of the United States, the other groups are concentrated on the Pacific Coast and in the Southwest. Because most research of a sociological nature, until recently, came out of universities located along the Eastern seaboard and in the Midwest, groups not located in some proximity to those research centers were largely ignored. The other nonwhite groups did not have a cadre of trained social scientists in their own community who could study their family system from an insider's perspective. Very few American Indian or Latino scholars were developed by mainstream universities until recent years, and the few that existed often preferred to engage in universalistic research. Although Asian Americans were more likely to have research skills, they were concentrated in the physical and natural sciences.

Concomitant with the above-mentioned factors is the recent arrival of some of the racial minorities. Although Black Americans and American Indians go back to the origin of this country as a white settler nation, other groups such as Central Americans, Cubans, Koreans, and the Indo-Chinese are recent arrivals and concentrated in only a few areas of the United States. However, a major reason for the exclusion of many racial minorities from the family literature has been the ethnocentrism of Euro-Americans that assumes the inherent inferiority of any group that deviated from the Anglo-Saxon ideal. When minority families were studied, it was as an exotic group or one whose flawed family structure poorly prepared its members for achievement in the larger society. Or, the focus was on problem areas such as teenage pregnancy, single-parent households, female dominance, and out-of-wedlock births (Staples & Mirande, 1980).

Who Are the "Minority" Families?

No universal or precise definition of what constitutes a minority group exists. As we have already observed, the individuals in some minority groups possess none of the traits that define them as a minority, such as dark skin, poverty status, and cultural differences. For our purposes, a minority group is a composite construct reflecting unique and historically specific experiences (e.g., cultural practices, inequality, discrimination) (Wilkinson & King, 1987). Because persons and populations deviating from the dominant physical norms are perceived and treated categorically, we have selected groups whose phenotypic characteristics generally define them as nonwhite. However, the inclusion of Latinos has to be clarified. The United States Census Bureau classifies them into two groups: Hispanic-Black and Hispanic-White. If we use the racial definitions of Latin nations, individuals with a dominance of Caucasian physical traits are often allowed the "privilege" of a white classification. By the standards of the United States Bureau of the Census and numerous state legal statutes, the only way to become white is to have almost exclusively white ancestry, the history of miscegenation in Latin America since 1502 would exclude most Latinos from the category defined as "Caucasian" (U.S. Bureau of Census, 1987a).

Asian-American and Pacific Islander Families

These groups have their origin in the area known as the Far East and the South Pacific region. The six largest Asian groups are Asian Indian, Chinese, Filipino, Japanese, Korean, and Vietnamese. The three largest Pacific Islander groups are Guamanian, Hawaiian, and Samoan. Almost 60% of Asians and Pacific Islanders were born in foreign countries compared to only 6% for other American residents. Among Asians, the percent varied from 94% for Cambodians and Laotians to 28% for the Japanese. For Pacific Islanders, the ranges were from 75%

for Tongans to 2% for Hawaiians. More than 33% of Asians and Pacific Islanders aged 25 and over were college graduates vis-a-vis 16% for the nation. In 1979 median family income for Asian and Pacific Islander families was $22,700 in contrast to the national median of $19,900 (U.S. Bureau of Census, 1988a).

Because Asians are often depicted as a relatively prosperous segment of the population, with educational and income levels higher than any other nonwhite group and frequently higher than some whites, they are perceived as the "model minority," and an example to other nonwhite groups of what hard work and discipline can accomplish. What this positive stereotype ignores is that most of the affluent Asians only arrived in the United States after 1965 when the quota on nonwhite immigration was lifted. Thus, they are the products of a selective immigration that favored the more educated and affluent members of Asian society. The long-term Asian residents are the descendents of the original Asians imported to the American mainland to work on the railroad and agricultural plantations. Those Asians were subjected to exclusionary immigration laws and barriers to property ownership, and the Japanese-Americans were confined in concentration camps during World War II (Takaki, 1983). Not only is their high median income achieved by a higher percentage of two-worker families (63% to 54% in 1980 for all American families) but they receive a lower income for their educational level than their white counterparts (U.S. Bureau of Census, 1988a).

As for their family life, it appears more "stable" than the nation as a whole, partly because their marital stability is a function of their higher educational and income level, a relationship that holds for most racial groups in the United States. About 84% of Asian and Pacific Islander families were married couples in 1980 compared with 83% for the national population. Among Asians, the Asian Indians and Pakistanis had the highest proportion at almost 90% and Vietnamese the lowest at 73%. Tongans and Hawaiians had the highest and lowest proportions among Pacific Islanders at 95% and 73% (U.S. Bureau of Census, 1988a). The fertility rate of foreign born Asian women was 105 births per 1,000 American born women. Again, the selective nature of immigration distorts the data on family stability of Asians. Among long-term Asian residents, the fertility and divorce rate is similar to that of comparable groups in the same socioeconomic status (U.S. Bureau of Census, 1988b).

North American Indian Families

Certainly, there can be no question about American Indians' status as a minority, although different standards may be applied to their racial identity. As the original settlers of the American continent, they are known to most Americans, but few Americans have had personal contact with them and even fewer Americans have much of an understanding of the group known as American Indians. It is impossible to give a succinct description of this diverse population, which is comprised of 161 different linguistic groups. American Indians number about 1.5 million people and largely inhabit the Western part of the United States (U.S. Bureau of Census, 1984). Among the many falsehoods about American Indians is the conventional wisdom that they are a dying breed. While their official numbers are less than first encountered by European settlers 400 years ago, there are more than 15 million Americans who claim some Indian ancestry (Hacker, 1983). Had this country applied the same racial standards to Indians that were imposed on Black Americans, those 15 million Americans would today be categorized as Indians. Instead, they became members of the non-Indian parent's race (mostly Caucasian) (U.S. Bureau of Census, 1983).

A review of the family literature on American Indians brings up several problems. Foremost among them is that there is no such thing as an American Indian family. There are only tribes and family systems, which vary from tribe to tribe. Although there have been numerous attempts to impose the Western model of the nuclear, monogamous family on them, diverse family forms are still extant among the 280 different tribal units. They will range from polygamy to monogamy, matrilineality to patrilineality (Price, 1988; McAddo, 1978). What literature exists on them can generally be found in social work, anthropological, and mental health journals. They can be found in that genre of journal because of the focus on the American Indians as cultural and sociological deviants. However, it is clear that North American Indians have not wanted nor acquiesed to acculturation and assimilation into mainstream society. Instead of being viewed as a culturally different but well-functioning society, they have largely received societal opprobrium for their resistance to the norms and models of American society (Unger, 1977).

Black Americans

As a group that appears more monolithic than the other racial minorities, Black Americans are the subject of numerous research studies and empirical generalizations. In comparison to the other minorities, except American Indians, it is a group that is poorer and ranks lower in social acceptance. Still it is a group of immense differentiation in terms of socioeconomic status, color gradations, cultural values, country of origin, and regional values. Many, for instance, are foreign born and are relative newcomers to the United States. We do not have precise numbers of the blacks who are first and second generation Americans because the Bureau of the Census lumped all foreign people of African ancestry together until recently. Yet they are estimated to number in the millions and will have a culture different from that of native blacks (Wilson, 1987). This racial minority is increasingly organized along social class lines. An estimated 37% of Black American families are said to have middle-class incomes and lifestyles (Landry, 1987), while 31% had incomes below the poverty level (U.S. Bureau of Census, 1987b). Cultural values and lifestyles may vary by region, and differences are particularly sharp between Southern born and Northern urban blacks.

The family structure of blacks has received a great deal of attention in the popular and scholarly press. However, the subject of this attention has been the urban black underclass and its deteriorating family structure. More than 70% of poor black families were headed by women in 1986, a condition preceded by an out-of-wedlock birth rate of 57%. Almost 30% of black babies are born to women under the age of twenty and 89% of them are illegitimate (U.S. Bureau of Census, 1987b). Rather than reflecting some unique cultural value of the black underclass, those statistical data mirror the high unemployment rates of black males. Among blacks with an income under $10,000 a year, 69.3% were single parents who had children living with them. Only 6.5% of black children lived with a parent whose income was between $20,000 to $30,000 a year. As income rises, so do the births in wedlock and men who are married and living with their spouse (U.S. Bureau of Census, 1987b).

Latino Families

Not only are Latinos a diverse group, their composition and characteristics are constantly changing. Latino women, on average, have their first children at an earlier age and have more children than their non-Latino counterparts. Between the childbearing years (18-44), Latino women averaged 1.7 children compared with 1.3 for non-Latino women. About 40% of Latino women aged 18-24 had children vis-a-vis 28% of their non-Latino peers. More than a third of the children born to immigrant women in 1986 were the offspring of Mexican born women (U.S. Bureau of Census, 1988b). In addition to high fertility rates, the Latino population is rapidly growing through immigration. Numbering 18.8 million persons in 1987, a 30% increase over 1980 figures, the greatest emigration came from Central and South America. The Mexican total increased to 11.8 million, a 22% increase, Puerto Ricans grew by 11% to 2.3 million and the number of Cubans was up by 7% to 1 million (U.S. Bureau of Census, 1987a).

The emigration of Latinos has been fueled by a number of sociocultural forces, including the proximity of the United States, poor economic conditions in their homeland, repressive governments, and warlike conditions in many Latin nations. The last two forces have sent both the poor and the bourgeoisie of Central America nations fleeing to the comparative "security" of the United States. Because the number of poor Latinos is far greater than the middle class, it is understandable that most of the emigrants will be poor and uneducated. In 1986 one quarter of Latino families had incomes below the poverty level compared with 10% non-Latino families. About one half of those poor Latino families could be accounted for by the fact that they were maintained by women with no husband present. Because 200,000 more Latino families were living in poverty in 1986 than in 1981, there was a corresponding drop from 74% in 1982 to 71% in 1987 in the proportion of Latino married couple families (U.S. Burea of Census, 1987b).

Poverty is not evenly spread among the various Latino groups. The median income of the darker-skinned Puerto Ricans was $12,271 in 1985 compared to $19,184 for Chicanos, and $19,785 for Central and South Americans. Most affluent of all were the fair-skinned and middle-class Cubans with a median income of $22,587, close to the national median of $26,433. Consequently, more than 40% of Puerto Rican families are headed by single women while most Chicano and Cuban children grow up in two-parent families (U.S. Bureau of Census, 1987a).

Resources

Books on Minority Families

- Ho, M. K. (1987). *Family Therapy with Ethnic Minorities*. Beverly Hills: Sage Publications, 288 pages.

The most up-to-date examination of the theory, models, and techniques relevant to ethnic minority family functioning and therapy. Distinctive cultural values of each ethnic group are explored as well as a theory-based "how-to" (i.e., specific guidelines and suggestions on culturally significant family therapy strategies and skills).

- Hutter, M. (1988). *The Changing Family: Comparative Perspectives*. New York: MacMillan, 606 pages.

This book is designed to aid in the understanding of contemporary family structures and processes in a world of change. Those changes, the author believes, can best be comprehended by comparing the similarities and diversities of families in the United States and other societies. While much of the book is devoted to family systems in developing nations, such as African and Indian countries, entire sections are dedicated to black, Japanese, and Chicano families in the United States. The author's text is supplemented and enhanced by the inclusion of short articles from newspapers. While primarily aimed at the introductory student in family courses, it can be of use to the family practitioner with its focus on topical issues such as the feminization of poverty, AIDS, abortion, and family violence.

- McGoldrick, M., Pearce, J. K., & Giordano, J. (Eds.). (1982). *Ethnicity and Family Therapy*. New York: Guilford Press, 600 pages.

One of the few books on a variety of "minority" families for the family practitioner. As a guide to practicing family therapists and other general readers interested in different cultures, the material presented will prove to be endlessly fascinating and eminently useful. For a different perspective on America's vibrant subcultures, this book represents a good beginning in breaking through the barriers toward honest dealing with American minority families. For once, ethnicity as an important variable in psychological evaluation and practice is highlighted. It is recommended reading for all psychotherapists and human services providers who wish to gain a greater understanding of the immense cultural variability of the American family and its relevance to treatment practices.

This book is based on the premise that just as individual behavior can not be separated from the family context, the behavior of families only makes sense in the larger context of ethnicity—a major form of group identity that orders the social and belief patterns of individuals. The book draws cultural profiles relating to different clinical strategies based on the clinician and the patient's perceptions of reality that is conditioned by subcultural values. More than 25 different ethnic groups are discussed by 25 authors, most of them members of the ethnic group under discussion. Among those ethnic groups are such rarely studied ones as West Indians, Iranian, and Vietnamese. Each chapter has an historical overview, specific cultural traits, value structure, family characteristics, and clinical considerations.

- Mindel, C. H., & Habenstein, R. W. (Eds.). (1988). *Ethnic Families in America: Patterns and Variations* (3rd ed.). New York: Elsevier, 432 pages.

This is one of the most popular and well done of the anthologies on "minority" families. Now in its third edition, it contains 17 chapters on different ethnic families, including 7 chapters on families of color. Unlike the McGoldrick book, the audience for this book seems to be upper division college students. Most of the authors are members of the ethnic group about whom they write. The orientation of the book is evident in the fact that the editors and most of the authors are sociologists. At the time this book was first written (in 1971) it was a fairly revolutionary idea to examine ethnic family strengths as well as weaknesses, besides allowing native members of the group to write about their family system. Each author was asked to follow a common outline so that a certain consistency would exist and that the book would be seen as an integrated whole rather than a collection of readings.

Of interest to the family educator will be the chapters on Chinese, Arab, Puerto Rican, Indian, Black, Chicano and Japanese families. The editors write an excellent introductory chapter distinguishing between ethnic and minority groups, and the differences between ethnic groups based on early or recent arrival. Because they have the least savory group life histories, blacks, American Indians and Latinos are categorized as "Historically Subjugated But Volatile Ethnic Minorities." Most of the chapters are organized into sections on historical background and demographic characteristics of the modern ethnic family such as employment, income, and education. Social structure, social class lifestyles, the aged, and change and adaptation are brought up in the last third of each chapter. Each author tries to distinguish between characteristics or changes in the ethnic family that are ethnic-cultural and traits that are due to social class and social mobility trends, and how those two forces have interacted with each other. Finally, each author addresses the impact of various liberation movements on the family and how acculturation has changed the way the elderly and women are treated.

• Queen, S. A., Habenstein, R. W., & Quadagno, J. S. (1985). *The Family in Various Cultures* (5th ed.). New York: Harper and Row, 401 pages.

This book has been a classic text since 1952 and is renowned for its well-rounded cross-cultural presentation and unique historical anthropological perspective that features the diverse ways the family has structured itself from the beginning of Homo sapiens. All the chapters were written by the three authors and only three involve our minority families—Black Americans, Chicanos, and American Indians. Two other chapters have family life in China and India as their focus. While this book is only partly addressing the minority families of our concern, it does serve to illuminate the various forms the family can take in different societies. As true of the Mindel and Habenstein book, its perspective is sociological and aimed at the undergraduate student in marriage and the family classes. The book begins with a descriptive analysis of five rather unique family types that existed at some time in history, from the polyandrous Toda family in India to the minimum family of the midcentury kibbutz. Subsequently, ancient, classical, and European backgrounds of the Western family are examined before analyzing the development of the family in North America. In addition to discussing the modern American family and its ethnic variations, major and minor profiles of the Canadian family end the book.

Articles

• McAdoo, H. (1978). Minority families. In J. Stevens & M. Matthews (Eds.), *Mother/Child, Father/Child Relationships* (pp. 177–195). Washington, DC: National Association of Young Children.

A review of the literature on children, their development, and problems in American Indian, Afro-American, Chinese-American, and Spanish-speaking American families. As a person with the instincts of a social worker and the intellectual skills of a psychologist, McAdoo weaves a tapestry of cultural motifs in the family literature with the ultimate end of applying it to the use of family practitioners. Each minority family is described in terms of its historical background and contemporary structure. Then, there is a lengthy review and discussion of the role of education for minority children and the differential outcome of the educational process for Chinese-Americans (largely successful in the American school system) and its usefulness for American Indian and Latino children (mostly unsuccessful). The final section deals with the implications for parent education of minority family research.

• Staples, R., & Mirande, A. (1980). Racial and cultural variations among American families: A decennial review of the literature on minority families. *Journal of Marriage and the Family,* **42,** 887–903.

A black and a Chicano sociologist review and assess the literature on Asian, American Indian, Black American, and Chicano families between the years 1970 and 1980. The level of writing and sophistication of the theoretical formulations discussed makes this article appropriate for graduate students and family scholars. For the limited time frame, it is one of the most comprehensive reviews of the minority family literature available. The authors look at how the family literature on minorities has changed over the decade. They consider and discuss the salient themes and controversies for each minority. Their article concludes with the call for more and better conducted research on minority families that will give a balanced representation of the strengths and weaknesses of minority families.

Bibliographies

There are numerous bibliographies on minority families, especially the black family. The ones most relevant to family practitioners that have an orientation toward applied sciences have been selected.

• Allen, W., English, R. A., & Hall, J. A. (1986). *Black American Families: A Classified, Selectively Annotated Bibliography.* Westport, CT: Greenwood Press.

• Center for Research on Women (1984). *Selected Bibliography of Social Science Readings on Women of Color in the United States.* Memphis, TN: Memphis State University.

• Davis, L. (1986). *The Black Family in the United States: A Revised Updated, Selectively Annotated Bibliography.* Westport, CT: Greenwood Press.

• Engram, E. (1982). *Science, Myth, Reality: The Black Family in One-Half Century of Research.* Westport, CT: Greenwood Press.

• Green, R. (1983). *Native-American Women: A Bibliography.* Bloomington, IN: University of Indiana Press.

• Howard, C. S. (1980). *A Resource Guide on Black Families in America.* Washington, D.C.: Institute for Urban Affairs and Research, Howard University.

• Kelso, D. R., & Attneave, C. L. (1981). *Bibliography of North American Indian Mental Health.* Westport, CT: Greenwood Press.

• National Urban League (1977). *A Selected Annotated Bibliography on Black Families: Prepared for Human Service Practitioners.* New York: National Urban League.

• Nelson, M. F., & Walton, M. F. (1982). *Ohoyo Ikhana: A Bibliography of American Indian/Alaska Native Curriculum Materials.* Wichita Falls, TX: Ohoyo Resource Center.

• Norell, I. P. (1976). *Literature of the Filipino American in the United States: A Selective and Annotated Bibliography.* Saratoga, CA: R and E Research Publishers.

• Padilla, A. M., Olmedo, E. L., Lopez, S., & Perez, R. (1978). *Hispanic Mental Health Bibliography II* (Monograph No. 6). Los Angeles: University of California, Spanish Speaking Mental Health Research Center.

• White Cloud Center (1980). *Bibliography on American Indian/Alaskan Native Families and Traditional Child Rearing.* Portland, OR: White Cloud Center.

• Women's Health and Healing Project (1986). *Minority Women, Health and Healing: A Selected Bibliography and Resource Guide.* San Francisco: University of California, Department of Social and Behavioral Sciences.

- Wong, J. LO. (1981). *A Selected Bibliography on the Asians in America.* Saratoga, CA: R and E Research Publishers.
- Young, G. S., & Sims-Wood, J. (1984). *The Psychology and Mental Health of Afro-American Women.* Temple Hills, MD: Afro-Resources, Inc.

Periodicals

Hundreds of magazines and journals, mostly black, contain articles on black and other minority families. Because the family is such an important institution to minority groups, it will be discussed in any periodical controlled by them. Moreover, a number of minority scholars will publish in popular venues because they do not subscribe to the rigid dichotomy between lay and academic audiences. Even academic journals designed to be an intellectual forum will have a balance between articles based on empirical research and those regarded as review or polemical works. Since some of there periodicals have limited distribution and short life spans, some of the stable ones that are known to a national audience have been selected.

- *Black Family.* This magazine is published quarterly by its parent company, Welcome Neighbor Service. Its primary purpose is to provide a forum for the concerns of black family life: food, clothing, shelter, recreation, education, travel, religion, and health. It appears to be a black version of *The Ladies Home Journal* and is devoted to presenting a positive, mostly middle-class view of the black family. A number of the articles are written by doctorally trained black scholars.
- *The Black Scholar.* Published on a bimonthly basis by The Black World Foundation, this intellectual organ of black scholarship has been on the cutting edge of black thought for the past two decades. It would best be characterized as interdisciplinary in nature and centered around Afro-American political movements. A number of special issues have been devoted to the theme of black sex roles, children, feminism, and the black family. During its 20-year history, the leading black scholars in the diaspora have been published in its pages.
- *Ebony.* This popular periodical with the largest mass circulation of any black magazine is published by the Johnson Publishing company. Published on a monthly basis, almost every issue contains some article related to the black family, mostly written by members of its staff. Each year it publishes a special issue with one theme and frequently those issues will have numerous articles on the black family written by some of the leading black scholars in the field. A general interest magazine, it was originally modeled after *Life Magazine.*
- *Essence.* A monthly magazine owned by Essence Communications, Incorporated, it is largely aimed at black female readers and carries a number of articles on food, fashions, and celebrity profiles. Most issues will contain articles on black female empowerment or male/female relationships. Occasionally an entire issue is devoted to the theme of black male/female relationships. Some of the leading black female, and some male, scholars have written for or been interviewed by this magazine.
- *Hispanic Journal of Behavioral Sciences.* Published as a quarterly journal, it is directed by Editor Amado Padillo from the Spanish Speaking Mental Health Research Center at the University of California, Los Angeles. Devoted to the publication of theory and research on Latinos, it is a major venue for the works of leading Latino scholars in the United States.
- *Journal of American Indian Education.* Published three times a year by Arizona State University, it addresses the educational concerns and issues in the American Indian community. Articles are rather academic in nature and many of the authors are non-Indians.
- *Journal of Black Studies.* Published as a quarterly journal by Sage Publications and edited by Malefi Asante of the Department of Afro-American Studies at Temple University, it presents a variety of scholarly works on the black condition from both a theoretical and empirical perspective.
- *Sage. A Scholarly Journal on Black Women.* A relatively new scholarly journal on black women, it began publication in 1984 on a biannual basis. Owned and directed by the Sage Women's Educational Press, it devotes each issue to various intellectual aspects of black women's lives. As typical of other black journals, it provides a balance between the humanities and social sciences, the empirical and literature review article. Writers are generally based in universities or research centers. Among the special themes so far have been black women writers, mothers and daughters, black women's health and black women's education.
- *Western Journal of Black Studies.* Owned by Washington State University and edited by Talmadge Anderson, it is published four times a year and is probably the most academic of all the black journals. Organized into three separate themes each issue, a number of articles would fit into the family rubric. Almost all of the authors are associated with the academy and the articles are balanced between empirical studies and theoretical formulations.

Organizations

There are hundreds of organizations serving minority families throughout the United States, many of them local in character. The organizations listed below represent only a fraction of the universe of family-oriented agencies and organizations. This is a selective list of research organizations (those engaged in family research) and associations (those providing some form of service to minority families).

- *American Indian Social Research and Development Associates, Inc.,* P.O. Box 381, Isleta, NM 87022.

Serves as an advocate for American Indian issues, conducts research relevant to the Indian condition, sponsors conferences on research issues, and publishes papers and monographs.

- *Center for Research on Women.* Clement Hall—Room 339, Memphis State University, Memphis, TN 38152.

A multiracial institute that focuses on the study of race, culture, gender, and occasionally class, it sponsors a variety of activities related to nonwhite and white women. Based in a Southern university, the cohesive and racially diverse team of scholars publishes a tri-yearly newsletter and provides a clearinghouse of social science research (including history) on women of color and Southern women that has been published in the last 10 years or is in progress. In addition it generates research, publishes papers and monographs, and offers summer institutes and workshops.

- *COSSMHO—The National Coalition of Hispanic Mental Health and Human Services Organizations,* 1015-15th Northwest, Suite 402, Washington, DC 20005.

COSSMHO publishes monographs and holds a national conference on Hispanic issues every 2 years. A diverse group, it is dedicated to furthering the provision of mental health services to all Spanish surnamed groups and individuals.

- *Institute for the Black Family,* University of Pittsburgh, Pittsburgh, PA 15238.

An interdisciplinary center whose mission is to enhance the viability of the black family. Those objectives include (a) the development of conceptual frameworks, intervention and analytic models; (b) developing a mechanism for utilizing the results of policy analysis; (c) participating in evaluation research; (d) creation of instructional materials; and (e) providing learning opportunities for scholars interested in the black family.

- *National Institute for Women of Color,* 1712 "N" Street N.W., Washington, DC 20036.

A nonprofit organization created to enhance the strengths of diversity and to promote educational and economic equity for women of color. It publishes bibliographies and sponsors a national conference each year.

- *Ohoya Resource Center,* 2301 Midwestern Parkway, Suite 214, Wichita Falls, TX 76308.

A national communication and network system among American Indian women, it provides a number of publications, services, and products for and about American Indians. It also sponsors annual regional conferences.

- *Spanish Family Guidance Center,* University of Miami School of Medicine, 747 Ponce de Leon Blvd., Suite 303, Coral Gables, FL 33134.

A group that promotes research and serves the Latino community. Founded in 1972 it offers a variety of services to Latino families and provides a bibliography and publications catalogue.

- *The Institute for the Advanced Study of Black Family Life and Culture, Inc.,* P.O. Box 24739, Oakland, CA 94607.

A community based nonprofit research, educational, and training corporation committed to the reunification of the black family and the revitalization of the black family, it is the only independent "think tank" in the United States devoted to the growth and development of black family life and culture. Its programmatic activities include basic research, seminars, conferences, and publications.

REFERENCES

Carlson, A. (1986, May 14). Collapse of Birthrates in Industrial Democracies. *San Francisco Chronicle*, A, p. 4.
Hacker, A. (1983). *U/S: A statistical profile of the American people.* New York: Viking.
Johnson, L. B. (1981). Perspectives on Black family empirical research: 1965-1978. In H. McAdoo (Ed.), *Black Families* (pp. 87-102). Beverly Hills, CA: Sage Publications.
Landry, B. (1987). *The new black middle class.* Berkeley: University of California Press.
McAdoo, H. (1978). Minority families. In J. Stevens & M. Mathews (Eds.), *Mother/child, father/child relationships* (pp. 177-195). Washington, DC: National Association of Young Children.
Mindel, C., & Habenstein, R. (1988). *Ethnic families in America* (3rd ed.). New York: Elsevier.
Price, J. A. (1988). North American Indian families. In C. Mindel & R. Habenstein (Eds.), *Ethnic families in America* (pp. 245-268). New York: Elsevier.
Staples, R., & Mirande, A. (1980). Racial and cultural variations among American families: A decennial review of the literature on minority families. *Journal of Marriage and the Family,* 42, 887-903.
Staples, R. (1981). *The world of black singles.* Westport, CT: Greenwood Press.
Staples, R. (Ed.). (1986). *The black family: Essays and studies.* Belmont, CA: Wadsworth.
Takaki, R. (1983). *Pau hana: Plantation life and labor in Hawaii 1835-1920.* Honolulu: University of Hawaii.
Unger, S. (Ed.). (1977). *The destruction of American Indian families.* New York: Association on American Indian Affairs.
U.S. Bureau of Census (1983). *Ancestry of the Population by States: 1980* (PC80-S1-10). Washington, DC: U.S. Government Printing Office.
U.S. Bureau of Census (1984). *American Indian areas and Alaska native villages 1980* (PC80-S1-13). Washington, DC: U.S. Government Printing Office.
U.S. Bureau of Census (1987a). *The Hispanic Population in the United States: March 1986 and 1987* (Series P-20, No. 416). Washington, DC: U.S. Government Printing Office.
U.S. Bureau of Census (1987b). *Money income and poverty status of families and persons in the United States: 1986* (Series P-60, No. 157). Washington, DC: U.S. Government Printing Office.
U.S. Bureau of Census (1988a). *Asian and Pacific Islander population in the United States: 1980* (PC80-2-1E). Washington, DC: U.S. Government Printing Office.
U.S. Bureau of Census (1988b). *Fertility of American Women: June 1986* (Series P-20, No. 421). Washington, DC: U.S. Government Printing Office.
Wade, J. E. (1987). Race and raceness: A theoretical perspective of the Black American experience. *Western Journal of Black Studies,* 11, 31-38.
Wilkinson, D. Y., & King, G. (1987). Conceptual and methodological issues in the use of race as a variable: Policy implications. *The Milbank Quarterly,* 65, 56-70.
Wilson, C. G. (1987). The dilemma of Afro-Latinos. *Panama Chronicle,* 3, 18-20.

References

Aoki, T., Werner, W., Dahlie, J., and Connors, B. 1984. Who's culture? Who's heritage? Ethnicity within Canadian social studies curricula. In *Cultural diversity and Canadian education,* eds. J. Mallea and J. C. Young, 265–89. Ottawa: Oxford University Press.

Boyd, R. L. 1989. Minority status and childlessness. *Sociological Inquiry* 59: 331–42.

Carby, H. V. 1980. *Multicultural fictions* (Race Series, S.P. No. 58). Birmingham, England: University of Birmingham, Centre for Contemporary Cultural Studies.

Carroll, L. 1946. *Through the looking glass and what Alice found there.* New York: Random House.

Chiang, S. 1990. The last link. *The Salad Bowl* 15: 30–32.

Dilworth-Anderson, P., and McAdoo, H. P. 1988. The study of ethnic minority families: Implications for practitioners and policymakers. *Family Relations* 37: 265–67.

Dore, M. M., and Dumois, A. O. 1990. Cultural differences in the meaning of adolescent pregnancy. *Families in Society: The Journal of Contemporary Human Services* 71(2): 93–101.

Goldscheider, F. K., and Goldscheider, C. 1991. The intergenerational flow of income: Family structure and the status of Black Americans. *Journal of Marriage and the Family* 53: 499–508.

Hampson, R. B., Beavers, W. R., and Hulgus, Y. 1990. Cross-ethnic family differences: Interactional assessment of White, Black, and Mexican-American families. *Journal of Marital and Family Therapy* 16: 307–19.

Harris, M. B., Begay, C., and Page, P. 1989. Activities, family relationships, and feelings about aging in a multicultural elderly sample. *International Journal of Aging & Human Development* 29(2): 103–17.

Harrison, A. O., Wilson, M. N., Pine, C. J., Chan, S. Q., and Buriel, R. 1990. Family ecologies of ethnic minority children. *Child Development* 61: 347–62.

Locke, D. C. 1986. Cross-cultural counseling issues. In *Foundations of mental health counseling,* eds. A. J. Palmo and W. J. Winkel, 119–37. Springfield, IL: C. C. Thomas.

London, H., and Devore, W. 1988. Layers of understanding: Counseling ethnic minority families. *Family Relations* 37: 310–14.

Mead, M., and Heyman, K. 1965. *Family.* New York: Macmillan.

Morrow, R. D. 1987. Cultural differences—be aware! *Academic Therapy* 23: 143–49.

Njeri, I. (5 February 1991). The American melting pot has lent itself to diversity. *Austin American-Statesman* D1, D4.

O'Brien, S. 1991. Tribal governments. *National Forum: The Phi Kappa Phi Journal* 71(2): 18–20.

O'Hare, W. P., Pollard, K. M., Mann, T. L., and Kent, M. M. 1991. African Americans in the 1990s. *Population Bulletin* 46(1): 1–38.

Olneck, M. R. 1990. The recurring dream: Symbolism and ideology in intercultural and multicultural education. *American Journal of Education* 98: 147–74.

Patterson, C. J., Kupersmidt, J. B., and Vaden, N. A. 1990. Income level, gender, ethnicity, and household composition as predictors of children's school-based competence. *Child Development* 61: 485–94.

Reston, J. (7 July 1957). The world seen from a higher place. *The New York Times,* 6E.

Shakespeare, W. 1924. *As you like it.* In *The complete works of William Shakespeare,* ed. W. J. Craig, 249–78. New York: Oxford University Press.

Staples, R. 1988. The emerging majority: Resources for nonwhite families in the United States. *Family Relations* 37: 348–54.

Steichen, E. 1955. *The family of man.* New York: The Museum of Modern Art.

Stephan, C. W., and Stephan, W. G. 1989. After intermarriage: Ethnic identity among mixed-heritage Japanese-Americans and Hispanics. *Journal of Marriage and the Family* 51: 507–19.

Taylor, R. J., Chatters, L. M., Tucker, M. B., and Lewis, E. 1990. Developments in research on black families: A decade review. *Journal of Marriage and the Family* 52: 993–1014.

Thao, T. C. 1986. Hmong customs on marriage, divorce, and the rights of married women. In *The Hmong World,* eds. B. Johns and D. Staecker, 74–99. New Haven: Yale Center for International & Area Studies.

Timberlake, C. A., and Carpenter, W. D. 1990. Sexuality attitudes of Black adults. *Family Relations* 39: 87–91.

Vega, W. A. 1990. Hispanic families in the 1980s: A decade of research. *Journal of Marriage and the Family* 52: 1015–24.

Vega, W. A., Patterson, T., Sallis, J., Nader, P., Atkins, C., and Abramson, I. 1986. Cohesion and adaptability in Mexican-American and Anglo families. *Journal of Marriage and Family* 48: 857–67.

Wong, F. F. 1991. Diversity and community: Right objectives and wrong arguments. *Change* 23(4): 48–54.

Yee, B. W. K. 1990. Gender and family issues in minority groups *Generations: Gender & Aging* 14(3): 39–42.